Rivalry in Eurasia

RIVALRY IN EURASIA

RUSSIA, THE UNITED STATES, AND
THE WAR ON TERROR

Minton F. Goldman

L.C.C.C. LIBRARY

PRAEGER SECURITY INTERNATIONAL
An Imprint of ABC-CLIO, LLC

A B C ☙ C L I O

Santa Barbara, California • Denver, Colorado • Oxford, England

Library of Congress Cataloging-in-Publication Data

Goldman, Minton F.
    Rivalry in Eurasia : Russia, the United States, and the war on terror / Minton F. Goldman.
      p. cm.
    Includes bibliographical references and index.
    ISBN 978-0-275-97752-8 (hard copy : alk. paper) — ISBN 978-0-275-97753-5
    (paperback : alk. paper) — ISBN 978-0-313-38153-9 (ebook)
    1. Asia, Central—Foreign relations—1991– 2. War on Terrorism, 2001– 3. Asia, Central—
Foreign relations—Russia (Federation) 4. Russia (Federation)—Foreign relations—Asia,
Central. 5. Asia, Central—Foreign relations—United States. 6. United States—Foreign
relations—Asia, Central. 7. Russia (Federation)—Foreign relations—United States. 8. United
States—Foreign relations—Russia (Federation) 9. Russia (Federation)—Foreign relations. I.
Title.
DK859.57.G65   2009
958'.043—dc22   2009018927

13 12 11 10 9   1 2 3 4 5

This book is also available on the World Wide Web as an eBook.
Visit www.abc-clio.com for details.

ABC-CLIO, LLC
130 Cremona Drive, P.O. Box 1911
Santa Barbara, California 93116-1911

This book is printed on acid-free paper ∞

Manufactured in the United States of America

To Maureen for all her valuable help and encouragement

Contents

Chapter 1—Introduction   1

Chapter 2—Kazakhstan   33

Chapter 3—Turkmenistan   61

Chapter 4—Tajikistan   87

Chapter 5—Uzbekistan   117

Chapter 6—Kyrgyzstan   153

Chapter 7—Conclusion   189

Notes   201

Bibliography   231

Index   251

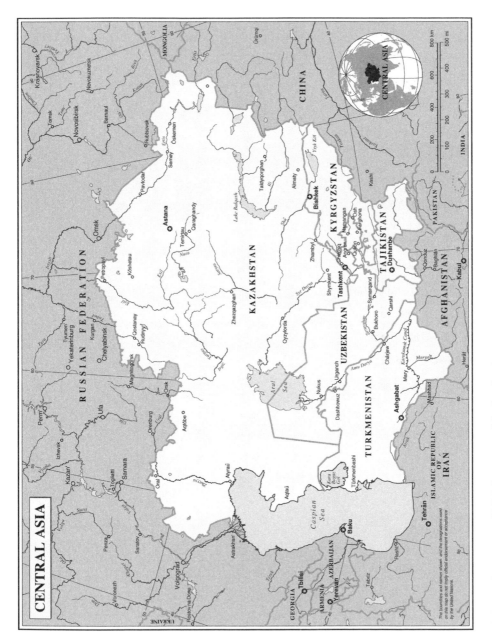

Central Asia (Courtesy of UN Cartographic Section)

1

Introduction

Russia's interests in the central Asian republics, notably Tajikistan, Kazakhstan, Uzbekistan, Turkmenistan, and Kyrgyzstan, are complex and compelling and as basic as protecting Russia's security and global power.[1] Post–Soviet Russia's first president Boris Yeltsin and his successor Vladimir Putin both assigned top priority to expanding Russia's influence in these ex-Soviet states. From the beginning, this Russian foreign policy strategy was carefully monitored by the United States, although before the September 11, 2001 (9/11) terrorist attack, U.S. national security interests had been cautious, careful, and modest with the Clinton administration more or less acknowledging Russia's paramountcy in the region.

After the 9/11 attack, however, U.S. President George W. Bush sharply escalated U.S. involvement in central Asia. Initially, Russian President Vladimir Putin accepted the new U.S. focus on central Asia given the region's proximity to Afghanistan where al Qaeda terrorists responsible for the 9/11 United States were headquartered. But he grew increasingly wary of the steady U.S. influence-building in the five ex-Soviet central Asian republics independent of the Kremlin since the end of 1991 and susceptible to the new U.S. approaches to them as a counterweight in their relations with Russia. In the opening years of the new century, it was possible to speak of a new Russian-American rivalry for influence in ex-Soviet Asia reminiscent of the relations between the United States and the former Soviet Union in the cold war era.

POST-9/11 CONSIDERATIONS

The post-9/11 tragedy explains the strong escalation of the U.S. involvement in central Asia in the early years of the new century. The United States needed to strengthen ties with the ex-Soviet central Asian republics so that they could help the United States with the war on terrorism declared by President George W. Bush in late 2001. Some of these republics bordered on Afghanistan (Turkmenistan, Uzbekistan, and Tajikistan) or were proximate to it (Kazakhstan and Kyrgyzstan). The United States wanted to develop military capabilities in the central Asian republics to battle the Taliban and al Qaeda in Afghanistan. As part of that strategic goal, the United States wanted pro-Western leadership in the ex-Soviet region and to that end the Bush administration pushed for democratization. The administration did so despite—and, also because of—the fact that five of the ex-Soviet central Asian republics had authoritarian governments backed by the Kremlin, which saw democratization as a threat to its goal of subordinating them to Russia.

Further complicating U.S. efforts to strengthen ties to the central Asian republics after 9/11 was the U.S.-Russian relationship. The United States found itself competing with Russia for military bases in the central Asian countries and also access to the region's vast resources of oil and natural gas. As the United States moved to have a role in the production and distribution of these resources, the Kremlin resisted. Russia wanted not only a commanding role in the development of these energy resources, it also wanted to block U.S. initiatives in cooperation with the central Asian leaders, all of whom had had close ties to Russia throughout their history. So both Russia and the United States found themselves in conflict even as they shared a goal in the region of keeping out radical Islam and defeating terrorism.[2]

RUSSIA AND CENTRAL ASIA UNDER BORIS YELTSIN, 1992–1999

For several years after the collapse of the Soviet Union, the newly independent Russian state, known as the Russian Federation, showed only minimal interest in expanding Russian influence in the territory once part of the Soviet Union. The Russian Federation's first foreign minister Andrei Kozyrev preferred to focus his country's foreign policy on strengthening relations with the West, in particular the United States, which had enormous resources that could help the new Russian state democratize and prosper. Kozyrev viewed good relations with the United States and other Western countries as essential to building an international environment of security and stability critical for Russia's successful post-Soviet, post-Communist transformation.[3]

But, Kozyrev's disregard of the importance of the central Asian republics to Russian interests was controversial with opponents such as General

Alexandr Labed and Vladimir Zhirinovsky, leader of the small but influential Liberal Democrats in the Russian parliament, who complained of a sell-out of Russian interests in the ex-Soviet space frequently referred to by Russians as the "Near Abroad." These ultranationalists expressed a strong Russian proprietary claim to control of the region and called for Russian dominance of the Commonwealth of Independent States (CIS), an organization set up in December 1991 by the three Slavic republics of the former Soviet Union (Russia, Ukraine, and Belarus) to further Russian interests in the Near Abroad. They wanted to bring all ex-Soviet republics, including those in central Asia, into the CIS.[4]

In the 1990s, Russian nationalistic politicians advocating an expansion of Russian influence in the ex-Soviet spaces were convinced that this region, especially central Asia, was a natural, logical, and arguably inevitable area of Russian influence-building. In their view, this region also showed more promise for Russia than cultivating the West which they believed asked for too much in the way of Russian acceptance of Western international policies in places like the Middle East, the Balkans, and central Europe. Politicians with these views steadily increased their influence over Russian government in the mid and late 1990s.

A new period of Russian policy in central Asia began in January 1996 when Yevgeni Primakov replaced Andrei Kozyrev as Foreign Minister. Primakov was a specialist in Arab-Islamic affairs, had a background in Soviet and Russian foreign intelligence work, and was a former director of IMEMO, a prestigious Soviet foreign policy "think tank." Primakov favored Russian influence-building in central Asia while also maintaining good working relations with the West. He also did not want Russia to do too much to conciliate Western countries in places like the Balkans where Russian and Western interests in the 1990s were frequently at odds.

Overall, during the 1990s, despite Yeltsin's pro-West orientation and his conviction that Russia should refrain from undertaking costly policies of influence-building in central Asia and elsewhere in the Near Abroad, there was a gradual shift in Russian policy toward the former Soviet republics in central Asia and the Caucasus. This was largely in consequence of Russia's evident loss during these years of influence in central and Eastern Europe and a fear that if Russia remained neutral or inert, foreign states would fill the vacuum in central Asia to the detriment of Russia, especially its territorial security. In fact, the central Asian republics were already showing an interest in diversifying their foreign policy to develop ties with outside states, especially in the West.

Determinants of Influence-Building in Central Asia

In the early 1990s, arguments for Russian influence-building in the ex-Soviet central Asian republics were persuasive, especially the argument that the potential for success of Russian efforts in a region so geographically close to Russia and one which traditionally had been susceptible to Russian influence.[5] But, with its own economy struggling, Russia faced major hurdles as it developed a policy for involvement in ex-Soviet central Asia. The area was marked by economic underdevelopment and pervasive poverty, and political instability as the central Asian leaders opened their societies to political pluralism while trying to maintain their authoritarian and secular governments. They tried to cope with the spread of militant and extremist Islamic parties inspired partly by strong nationalist and implicitly anti-Russian sentiment that provoked sociocultural tensions and civil conflict. Finally, all the countries in the region confronted in one way or another the Taliban ascendancy in Afghanistan. By the late 1990s, the Taliban regime in Afghanistan had become a serious threat to the stability and security of central Asian governments and Russia felt obliged to step in and help them preserve the secular status quo.

Economic Underdevelopment

The newly independent central Asian republics were manifestly weak as nation-states. Even after 75 years of intensive economic growth and development under Communist rule from 1917 to 1991, the central Asian region was underdeveloped and poverty-stricken, with its agricultural base in decline. The new central Asian states did not have money for seeds, fertilizers, pesticides, and spare parts for tractors. Indeed, the agricultural system was quasi-feudal. State farms inherited from the Communist era were run by directors who were accountable to upper-level administrators in a hierarchical system based on the centralized economic organization of the Communists. As in other such command economies, the planting for crops was planned top-down by the authorities instead of bottom-up by farmers. Production levels were low and labor was inefficient. Workers were poorly paid as compared, say, with workers in Russia and were literally bound to the land because of severe restrictions on their movement. Though some privatization of land had taken place with the collapse of Communist rule, the governments of the central Asian republics were skeptical of the free market economy in agriculture and allowed only a very limited amount of private farming.

Political Instability

In the newly independent central Asian republics of the former Soviet Union, political parties, parliaments, and courts existed but their freedom to act independently remained severely limited because their presidents insisted on absolute loyalty. Mostly, holdovers from the Soviet era, when they were in control of the local republic-level branches of national branches of the Soviet Communist Party, the presidents were and remain anti-reformist and autocratic. This neo-Communist political behavior has ensured a degree of apparent stability but there was and remains a strong undercurrent of opposition. Local populations have resent the persistence of dictatorship and poverty, and when it comes to radical Islamic thought, religious repression. These economic, political, and sociocultural conditions have made the societies of the central Asian republics susceptible to extremist beliefs of Islamic fundamentalism, whose influence has been growing throughout the region.[6]

The central Asian governments in the aftermath of their achievement of independence in 1991 were and have remained authoritarian dictatorships with only the trappings of parliamentary democracy. The monolithic political environment in the central Asian republics made them look very much like they were in the Soviet/Communist era before 1991. Political opposition groups, which flourished in the immediate aftermath of Communist collapse, were quickly subjected to harsh restrictions that made growth of an effective opposition and the evolution of political pluralism almost impossible. The only way opposition groups could attract attention and try to have an impact on national policymaking was through antigovernment demonstrations and these were promptly, decisively, and retributively suppressed.

Many opposition groups in the region have looked increasingly to religion as a means of mobilizing popular sympathy and support against the central Asian dictators. All over the region militant Islamic fundamentalism has gained followers. Sensitive to any political instability and determined to stop the spread of Islamic fundamentalism, the Kremlin has supported the conservative secular regime of the presidential dictators, all of whom were friendly to Russia and willing to tolerate Russian influence in their countries.

Societal Conflicts and Civil War

The Kremlin realized that conflict in central Asia could spread into Russia and became convinced that such conflicts were the most serious threat to Russia's own stability and security. The most dangerous conflicts involved the expression of aggressive nationalism with a strong undercurrent of anti-Russian feelings and religious extremism spreading throughout ex-Soviet central Asia. Conflicts over the spread of Islamic fundamentalism were identified as the worst kind of threat to Russia because they might eventually spread into the multiethnic heartland of Russia. In Chechnya and other areas in the Caucasus region, these conflicts generated disintegrative tendencies in an already conflict-ridden Russian society.[7]

Strategic Concerns

Under President Yeltsin, the increased Russian focus on central Asia was in part a response to strategic setbacks elsewhere. With NATO planning to expand its membership to include countries in central Europe once allied with Russia, notably Poland, Hungary, and the Czech Republic, Yeltsin saw a decline in Russian power. Although membership of these countries was a long way off in the future and although NATO went out of its way to strengthen friendly and cooperative relations with Russia in the May 1997 "Founding Act" that provided for regular consultations between NATO and Russia, the Yeltsin Kremlin was concerned and sought a strategic counterbalance in the form of a strengthening of Russian economic, political, and military links to the central Asian republics and other countries once part of the Soviet Union.

Another strategic setback for Russia that strengthened its incentives in the 1990s to expand influence in the central Asian republics was the diplomatic setback to Russian diplomacy in the Balkans. Despite its strong backing of the Serbian government in the 1990s, in its confrontation with the West over the political future of Bosnia-Herzegovina, the Kremlin was obliged to accept and cooperate in the implementation of the Dayton agreement, which blocked the Bosnian Serb ambition for a Serb-dominated Bosnian state. Russia suffered another setback in the Balkans when the West brought an end to the Milosevic government's military effort to restore its authority in Kosovo and installed a UN administration of the province.

The Russian Minority Communities

Still another major determinant of Russian influence-building ambitions in central Asia had to do with the Russian-speaking minorities throughout the region. (In the mid-1990s, about 40% of the Kazakh population was of Russian ancestry and almost 20% of the Kyrgyz population was Russian with Tajikistan having the smallest percentage of Russians in its population.) In the Soviet era, Russian minorities had been fairly well treated. But, with independence, there was a near explosion of local nationalism and a downgrading of the status of the Russian minorities. For example, in Tajikistan, the Russian language no longer was of much interest to young Tajiks, who preferred to master English, which apparently provided more opportunity for self-advancement in the economic sphere than Russian. Gradually this shift of interest in central Asia from Russian to English affirmed the steady decline of Russian influence.

Frequent explosions of nationalism in the central Asian republics also were driven by their heightened sensitivity to their unique cultural identity, which the Russian-dominated Soviet government in Moscow had tried to undermine in the process of developing a new "Soviet" identity based on the shared commitment to building socialism. After independence in 1991, some central Asian leaders, especially President Nursultan Nazarbayev of Kazakhstan, did try to preserve a sense of community among Kazakhstan's Russian residents by insuring them of good jobs and access to the centers of power. He did this to placate Russia, especially those Russian politicians concerned about the well-being of Russian-speaking Kazakh citizens. But, even his policies gradually became more nationalistic with anti-Russian overtones.

To the Kremlin's dismay, all the central Asian leaders found themselves challenged by indigenous, Islamist-based political groups who wanted the Russians out of their influential and well-paying jobs in the country's bureaucracy. The ethnic majorities believed they should have these preferred jobs even if they did not have the same level of training and expertise as the Russians. The central Asian political leaders tried to resist such prejudice, knowing that any indignity suffered by Russian-speaking residents could provoke Russia and seriously strain relations.

Russian minority communities in central Asia reacted with fear and distrust to the nationalism around them, so much so that some emigrated back to Russia, a troubling development for the Yeltsin government, which could not afford to take them back. The Russian economy throughout the 1990s was in a near shambles as Yeltsin accelerated the transition from state control of the country's economic life to a more free market economy, which had caused unemployment. Russians returning to the motherland from the central Asian republics seeking work just exacerbated the situation. Not only were there no jobs for them but their return caused some resentment among Russians who resented their competition for the scarce jobs that were available.

A strong cadre of Russian nationalists pushed the Kremlin to "protect" Russian-speaking communities in the central Asian republics. Among them were President Yeltsin's Vice President in the early 1990s Alexander Rutskoi, as well as Russian Communist Party Chief Gennady Zyuganov, and the Liberal Democratic Party leader and ultranationalist Vladimir Zhirinovsky and General Alexandr Labed. Each was ultranationalist in his own way. By the mid-1990s, each had become very influential members of the new post–Soviet Russian leadership elite. The post–Soviet Russian military leadership joined this "Eurasian Camp" in the early 1990s, urging Moscow to rejuvenate its influence in the region. President Yeltsin and then President Vladimir Putin could not ignore this political reality, which subsequently exerted a substantial influence over Russian foreign policy in the central Asian republics.[8]

Despite the priority he assigned to maintaining good Russian relations with the West, Foreign Minister Kozyrev himself shared the concern of the nationalists about the future well-being of Russian residents outside of Russia. He reportedly said in September 1993 that Russia had a right to intervene militarily in the ex-Soviet space to protect the interests of Russian minorities and he rejected the argument to the effect that what happened to Russians abroad was a local matter.[9]

The Islamist Threat from Afghanistan

A critical determinant of Russian influence-building in central Asia under Yeltsin was a threat to Russian security posed by Islamic militancy and pervasive drug trafficking.[10] With the Taliban ascendancy in Afghanistan in the mid-1990s, the Kremlin felt a heightened threat to Russian security and stability and to that of much of central Asia as well as the Caucasus region. The Taliban were as much anti-Russian as anti-American, and when they took control of Kabul in 1996, they became a kind of "second front" in the expansion of an Islamic fundamentalism that was uncompromising and belligerent.

Most threatened of the central Asian states at this time was Tajikistan; but, so also were Russian and other central Asian leaders who became alarmed at the prospect of an eastward expansion of radical Islamic fundamentalism to which they were vulnerable because of the region's pervasive poverty and deep-seated popular hostility to Russia. Central Asian leaders met to discuss the threat in Almaty, Kazakhstan in October 1996; but they reached no agreement and it became clear that there was no agreement on how to defend the region. While Russia and Uzbekistan favored a military kind of response to the Taliban, Kyrgyzstan and Kazakhstan demurred, unwilling to become involved in internal Afghan politics. Turkmenistan had its own response to the Taliban, proclaiming its neutrality which the United Nations endorsed.[11]

In the mid and late 1990s, even in Russia itself, there were differences of opinion over what to do about the Taliban which, according to the Russian media, surely were expanding their influence in the central Asian republics. General Labed warned about the vulnerability of southern Russia to Taliban expansionism, saying that with the Taliban's successful takeover of Afghanistan, the way would be open to Bukhara and the Russian city of Orenburg. He favored backing the anti-Taliban forces. By contrast, Foreign Minister Yevgeni Primakov was inclined to proceed with caution and restraint, preferring neutrality for Russia. Primakov's position had the support of Russian military commanders stationed on the Afghan-Tajik frontier. They insisted there was no immediate danger of a spillover of the Taliban into other parts of central Asia and concluded that it was not necessary to increase the number of Russian forces deployed along the Tajik-Afghan boundary.[12]

The Yeltsin leadership could not remain aloof as the Taliban consolidated their power in Afghanistan given their radical Islamic fundamentalist orientation and the possibility of their appeal to Muslim groups in the neighboring central Asian states. Accordingly, late in Yeltsin's presidency, the Kremlin gave clandestine aid to the anti-Taliban forces in Afghanistan, notably to those of General Abdurrashid Dostum and other anti-Taliban leaders such as Burhanuddin Rabbani and Ahmed Shah Massoud. In addition, the Kremlin cooperated with Uzbek efforts to arm these anti-Taliban fighters, especially General Dostum. But, despite such efforts, the Afghan situation deteriorated from the Russian vantage point. By 1996, the Taliban in effect had obtained control of the northern part of the country formerly held by Dostum's forces.[13]

Turkmenistan and Uzbekistan Oppose Russian Harshness toward the Taliban

Leaders in both Turkmenistan and Uzbekistan did not share Russian hostility to the Taliban movement in Afghanistan and, indeed, suspected that the Kremlin was trying to use its ascendancy to justify drawing the countries of the region closer to Russia ostensibly to resist the spread of Islamic fundamentalist ideology. Turkmenistan President Sepamurad Niyazov was quite direct in rejecting the Russian view of an imminent threat of Islamic fundamentalism to his government and that of his neighbors.[14]

Uzbekistan also had misgivings about the Russian view of a threat from Afghanistan and withdrew from the Russian-led Collective Security Treaty Organization (CSTO) in April 1999. Though the Taliban success intimidated the Uzbek leadership, Uzbek President Islam Karimov refrained from speaking of a "Taliban threat," taking the position that the Taliban control of most (about 80%) of Afghanistan was a domestic issue for the Afghans into which outsiders should not intrude. The new Uzbek position on Afghanistan was to support a negotiated settlement of the war between the Taliban and the remaining territory still free of Taliban control in the northern reaches of Afghanistan.[15]

Kazakhstan as well was suspicious of Russian policy toward Afghanistan in the late 1990s, sharing the view of Turkmenistan and Uzbekistan that Russian policy toward the Taliban was part of a larger influence-building strategy in central Asia to promote Russian dominance.[16]

Russian-American Cooperation against the Taliban?

By 1999, as leadership in the Kremlin was about to change from Yeltsin to Putin, Russia was virtually isolated in believing that the Taliban takeover of Afghanistan had dangerous implications for the security of central Asia and southern Russia, especially Chechnya where little progress had been made in restoring Russian authority. Indeed, with the successful Taliban incursions into the north of Afghanistan in 2000, the Kremlin had to decide how much further it could go in supporting Ahmed Shah Massoud, whose forces suffered serious military setbacks in the Spring of 2000. By that time, the Kremlin apparently had decided to refrain from any major effort to rescue Massoud and assure his survival along with that of the Northern Alliance of anti-Taliban tribes.

When Putin became acting president of the Russian Federation at the end of 1999, the central Asian republics preferred to deal with the Taliban by diplomacy and politics rather than rely on Russian military force. Turkmenistan continued normal diplomatic relations with the Taliban. The Uzbekistan leadership left no doubt about its aversion to a military confrontation with Kabul. Kazakhstan was never profoundly troubled by the Taliban. In October 2000,

Tajikistan announced that it did not consider the Taliban regime in Kabul a threat to its national security.[17]

But the Putin government saw the Taliban ascendancy in more ominous terms. The Kremlin linked the Taliban regime in Afghanistan directly to international terrorism. In the Russian view, Afghanistan under the Taliban was a haven for Islamic terrorists operating throughout central Asia. In response, the Kremlin decided to pursue a military approach to restraining the Taliban by continuing the delivery of weapons to Northern Alliance commanders, including Massoud. Tajikistan was covertly helpful in this Russian policy by allowing the Kremlin to use its airspace to get supplies to Massoud, even as it worked to avoid a direct confrontation with the Taliban.[18]

Russian pressure on the Taliban eventually involved the United States, which shared Moscow's opposition to the Taliban takeover of Afghanistan. In 1999, Russia and the United States participated in multilateral talks on the Taliban situation called the "6 plus 2" talks. The "2" referred to Russia and the United States, while the "6" referred to six countries that bordered Afghanistan and were vulnerable to Taliban subversion abroad, namely Iran, China, Pakistan, Tajikistan, Turkmenistan, and Uzbekistan. The "6 plus 2" talks were intended to develop a plan to bring the warring parties in Afghanistan to a peace table. This effort turned out to be futile with dangerous consequences for at least some of Afghanistan's contiguous neighbors in central Asia, who earned the enmity of the Taliban-friendly Islamic fundamentalists. The failure of the "6 plus 2" talks also strengthened incentives of both Moscow and Washington to take it upon themselves to try to resolve the civil war in Afghanistan. For example, at the end of 2000, they supported a joint proposal on UN sanctions against Afghanistan.[19]

An underlying assumption of Russian-American cooperation in countering the Islamic threat to the security of central Asia was that if it did occur—and there was much evidence before, never mind after 9/11, to indicate there was such a threat—coping with it would require the strategic cooperation of several countries. For example, with the Kremlin's approval, in April 2000, the outgoing Clinton administration responded to increased central Asian concern about the terrorist issue by sending FBI Director Louis Freeh to Tashkent to discuss how to fight crime and terrorism. Also, the FBI opened a field office in Almaty, Kazakhstan, to monitor developments throughout the region. Freeh's visit was quickly followed up by a visit of Secretary of State Madeline Albright who met with the presidents of Kazakhstan, Uzbekistan, and Kyrgyzstan to discuss regional security.[20]

This Russian-American anti-Taliban-inspired cooperation was buttressed somewhat by a December 2000 UN Security Council resolution calling for limited sanctions against Afghanistan if the Taliban regime failed to extradite Osama bin Laden. The sanctions included a ban on air traffic to and from Afghanistan and an arms embargo. The resolution seemed to punctuate the willingness of the Russians and Americans, whatever their differences elsewhere in the world, to cooperate against militant Islamic expansionism into central Asia. For the moment, Russian cooperation with the United States seemed to offset the refusal of the central Asian republics to take a strong, military-based stand against the Taliban regime.[21]

Indeed, both sides now had substantial incentives to contain the spread of militant Islamic fundamentalism into central Asia and agreed on a means, including economic aid and military diplomacy involving deployment of military power in some Eurasian republics. In the view of Vladimir Rzauvayev, the General Director of the Center for Economic and Political Research, Russian cooperation with the United States in central Asia was essential. Rzauvayev argued that the Kremlin must encourage cooperation between the CIS and the West, notably the European Union (EU) and the United States—such cooperation will benefit Russia's influence-building in Eurasia, especially in central Asia.[22]

Though this Russian-American give-and-take had little impact on developments in Afghanistan, it seemed, along with other developments, a prelude to the strengthening of Russian-American cooperation. But, the Kremlin found the Bush administration far less interested than the Clinton administration in working through the United Nations, a tactic Moscow preferred as an alternative to getting directly involved in the Afghan civil war.[23]

Constraints on Russian Influence-Building under Yeltsin

Throughout the 1990s, the Yeltsin Kremlin faced obstacles to and constraints on its influence-building policies in the Near Abroad, especially in central Asia, notably the suspicion and fear of local leaders. This fear reflected the local nationalism in the central Asian republics that had a strong undercurrent of anti-Russian sentiment born of exploitation by Russia, not only in the Soviet/Communist era but also under the Russian czars in the eighteenth and nineteenth centuries. A tendency toward independence of Moscow in the post-Soviet era was also a drag on the Kremlin's efforts to expand Russian influence in the area.

Central Asian Nationalism

Central Asian leaders in the 1990s, hypersensitive to their newly won sovereignty and independence of Moscow, worried that the Kremlin wanted to restore the kind of complete control it had over the region in the Soviet era. For evidence they could point to radical Russian nationalists who did little to conceal their regret over the breakup of the Soviet Union. Moreover, local nationalist movements opposed the continuing presence of Soviet influence in many sectors of national life. Some ex-Soviet republics in central Asia, notably Turkmenistan, occasionally resisted the Kremlin's overbearing efforts to keep them close and loyal to Russia. Although there was a deep-seated predilection to remain on close terms with the Kremlin for sentimental as well as political, economic, and strategic grounds, they sought to protect their autonomy. In 1992, Turkmenistan refused to sign a Russian-proffered Collective Security Treaty and scrupulously avoided signing later CIS-sponsored military agreements. It also reduced bilateral military cooperation with Russia. In 1999, Turkmenistan unilaterally terminated a 1992 border cooperation agreement with Russia. By 1999, other central Asian republics as well showed evidence of wanting a diversified foreign policy that preserved but clearly limited Russian ties. It was then in 1993 that Turkmenistan declared itself a "neutral" country, and in 1995, the UN General Assembly recognized Turkmenistan's "neutrality."

Disintegrative Tendencies in the CIS

By the late 1990s, the CIS seemed to be disintegrating. Initiated by Russia, the CIS was originally set up in December 1991 by Russia, Belarus, and Ukraine to foster friendship, cooperation, and integration. It was driven by a concern of the then Russian republic's president, Boris Yeltsin, over the eagerness of almost all of the ex-Soviet republics to go in separate directions in foreign policy making. Anxious about any uncoordinated foreign policy actions by the former Soviet republics and seeing its own security threatened when there was political instability in this region, as there appeared to be with the threat of Islamic extremism, Yeltsin thought the CIS might be the answer. A 1994 report by the Foreign Intelligence Service under the direction of Yevgeni Primakov vindicated his concern. It warned that Muslim states might use Islamic organizations to divide and weaken former Soviet republics with large Muslim populations under secular leaders.[24]

RUSSIAN POLICY IN CENTRAL ASIA UNDER PUTIN, 2000–2008

The terrorist attack on the World Trade Center in New York City on September 11, 2001, heightened and accelerated a heretofore slow, perhaps even sluggish, U.S. interest and influence-building in central Asia. But, any possibility that the shared Russian-American opposition to Islamic-inspired terrorism could result in an entente between them to resist the expansion of al Qaeda quickly disappeared. Although newly elected President Vladimir Putin extended a helping hand, supporting the U.S. desire for military bases in central Asia as part of its effort to destroy al Qaeda's headquarters in Afghanistan and remove the Taliban regime from power, he saw an American military presence in central Asia as a threat to Russia's interests. He was as much partisan as Yeltsin in defense of the view that Russia had special interests in the five central Asian republics that were "distinctive" and "preeminent."[25] The Putin Kremlin, as its predecessor, believed that outside Powers starting with the United States must acknowledge and respect the predominance of Russia's interests in central Asia. The newly installed Bush administration hardly had shared this Russian view, though it was inclined to recognize Russia's special interests in ex-Soviet central Asia.[26]

So, while the Kremlin after 9/11 was concerned about resisting the spread of radical Islamic influence into the central Asian republics, they worried also about the strategic implications for Russia of a steady expansion of a U.S. military presence in the region. Indeed, when the Bush administration called the central Asian republics allies or potential allies of the United States in the war against terrorism, the Putin-led Kremlin was deeply troubled by the possibility that the United States would displace Russia in the war on terrorism which the Kremlin was just as eager as Washington to fight and win.

Russia and the United States after 9/11

In the immediate aftermath of 9/11, Putin put aside some of these concerns and offered substantial help to the Americans in the form of intelligence concerning infrastructure and the locations of terrorist camps. The Russians also expressed support when some of the central Asian republics opened airspace to flights with humanitarian cargos to Afghanistan, approving of the opening of airspace of the central Asian republics to the United States and its allies for sending military and other supplies to the anti-Taliban Northern Alliance in Afghanistan.[27] But, the mutual trust needed for a Russian-American partnership simply did not exist. The Russian side soon referred to the interaction of the two countries in central Asia as "negative mutual dependence."[28] The biggest concern of the Putin Kremlin was a fear that the United States inevitably would dominate the war against terrorism in the central Asian backyard.

This Russian concern was evident at a summit meeting in September 2003 between Putin and Bush in Washington. Putin called for a "strategic partnership." He emphasized cooperation between the two countries and spoke of "allies in fighting terrorism." Underlying Putin's pronouncements was a fundamental principle of Russian policy in central Asia in the post-9/11 period to the effect that while the Kremlin was willing to acknowledge U.S. interests in central Asia, Russia was the "operator" of those interests and reserved for itself a leadership position. This in no way meant a Russian effort to "squeeze" the Americans out as an alternative to working with them closely. The Kremlin's thinking in a way was reminiscent of, if not inspired by, a request of Yeltsin in 1993 that the United Nations recognize Russia's responsibility for keeping the peace in the former Soviet space of Eurasia.[29]

Thus, in the weeks and months immediately following 9/11, when several central Asian republics, notably Uzbekistan and Tajikistan, promptly expressed willingness to cooperate with the United States, Putin tried to impose some parameters to limit their freedom to join the U.S. declared war on terrorism. Several high-ranking Russian officials, such as Russian Security Council Secretary Vladimir Rushailo and Chief of the Russian General Staff Anatolyi Kvashin, went to central Asia to impress upon the region's national leaders that they must coordinate with Moscow in their response to the United States in the aftermath of 9/11.[30]

That Russia had no intention of playing second fiddle to the Americans in central Asia found expression in the writing of Anatolyi Chubais, a prominent liberal politician and one of the leaders of the Union of Right Forces. In October 2003, Chubais said that Russia had a "mission" in Eurasia to foster democracy and free enterprise throughout the ex-Soviet space whatever other "mission" the United States set for itself. And Russian Foreign Minister Ivan S. Ivanov held that Russia should be ready, if needed, to interfere in the politics of the Eurasian republics to fulfill this mission.[31] As events developed, Russian interests and ambitions in central Asia were clearly at odds with the United States, leading to competition and confrontation with the United States in each of the five central Asian republics.

Putin's Goals in Central Asia

Putin's grand goal was to restore to a degree the influence the Kremlin had had over the region in the Soviet era. In this strategy he was driven, as Yeltsin had been, by concerns about Russian security seeing the vulnerability of the secular political regimes of the central Asian republics to Islamic extremism. He also felt threatened by the growing American involvement in the region. Also influencing Putin's views about central Asia was his belief that Russia was entitled to dominance in the exploration and exploitation of natural gas and oil reserves in the region. As had Yeltsin, Putin considered Russia the paramount power in central Asia and not only did he expect, he insisted on, the loyalty of the five republics.[32]

Beyond the expanding role of the United States in central Asia, other strategic considerations underlay Putin's ambitions in ex-Soviet central Asia. Close neighbors such as Afghanistan, Iran, and China had ambitions in the area. The Putin government saw its job as managing and containing these interests and leading the central Asian republics in a coordinated policy toward the "outsiders."

Coping with the Islamic Threat

Putin was no less concerned than Yeltsin had been about the Islamic threat. Even before the 9/11 terrorist attack in the United States, Putin had called attention to the terrorist training camps in Afghanistan and the linkages between these camps and well-financed terrorist networks operating in Chechnya. Putin attributed Russia's difficulty in restoring order in Chechnya to Islamic militants and terrorists operating in the Eurasian region and neighboring areas to the south and west of the ex-Soviet zone.[33] When in August 1999 Chechen insurgents invaded Dagestan, Putin called it "an act of terrorism." Shortly thereafter, when the Islamic Movement of Uzbekistan (IMU) invaded the Batken region of Kyrgyzstan from bases in Afghanistan and Tajikistan, taking hostages and attracting world attention, Putin called this action "terrorism," and at his urging, signatories of the Collective Security Treaty denounced the Batken incursion as "international terrorism." In March 2000, with the events in Dagestan and Batken uppermost in his mind, Putin assigned priority to the war against Islamic extremism in central Asia.[34]

But, Putin was not ready to make large military deployments in central Asia given Russia's parlous economic situation. Instead, he called for "collective" action against threats to the security and stability of central Asia, emphasizing the responsibility of the central Asian states themselves to meet their security needs. When it came to using military force, Putin wanted them to act through the CSTO whose signatories agreed in October 2000 to set up a regional self-defense force. Russia would encourage, advise, and assist the central Asian republics to cope with the threat of Islamic expansionism in nonmilitary technical ways.[35]

Making Up for Past Weakness in Eurasia

In the post-9/11 years, concern grew inside the Russian leadership establishment about Russia's perceived "strategic displacement" in the region. Nationalists in the State Duma expressed doubts about the durability of Russia's strategic, political, and economic primacy in its "geopolitical space." Restoring and preserving this primacy in Ukraine, the Caucasus, and central Asia was a popular political issue. Those nationalist politicians who supported Russian influence-building in Eurasia gave Putin political support in the Duma. In addition, the bureaucrats with whom he had surrounded himself shared with Putin not only a background in intelligence and police work but also a commitment to maintaining Russia's primacy in Eurasia and in particular in central Asia.[36]

Energy Development, Trade, and Strategy

Another goal of Putin's policymaking in central Asia was energy development. From the 1990s, some newly independent central Asian republics with huge reserves of oil and natural gas, notably Azerbaijan, Kazakhstan, and Turkmenistan, needed help in extracting these resources, refining them for commercial use and transporting them to markets in the West and China. At the very least, Russia stood to make a lot of money by helping the ex-Soviet republics develop and profit from their oil and natural gas wealth.[37] In addition, it served Russia's strategic interest to have a measure of control over this vast source of oil and natural gas wealth in the region.

The Putin Kremlin was ready and willing to provide both capital and technical expertise to cash-strapped countries such as Kazakhstan and Turkmenistan with huge resources but without the capital needed to mine and export them. Even though the Russian government itself had limited cash, Russian energy companies had the money and expertise to help these countries market their oil and gas. The Kremlin used these wealthy Russian energy-producing concerns, notably Gazprom, to work to develop the vast energy resources of the ex-Soviet Caucasus and central Asian regions.[38]

Putin also extended government control over Russian gas and oil industries and the pipelines they constructed. Because the Kremlin could give access to the pipelines owned by the Russian energy companies, the Russian government had leverage in persuading the central Asian oil-producing states to sign agreements giving Russia through these companies a major, if not primary, role in helping with the exploitation and marketing of oil and gas. For example, a Russian-Kazakhstan oil transit agreement of June 2002 gave Russia a dominant role in the transit of Kazakh oil to markets in the West for a 15-year period. And Gazprom, the giant oil and natural gas carte in which the Russian government had acquired a 50 percent plus interest, had a gas pipeline it offered central Asian energy-producing countries, if Russia were given a long-term role in exploiting their energy resources.[39]

A recent example of the Putin Kremlin's energy policies to gain political leverage for Russia in dealing with the central Asian republics was evident in Kyrgyzstan in the Summer of 2005. According to an article in *Kommersant* daily issue in early September, the Kremlin had developed "a special plan" for expanding Russian influence in Kyrgyzstan by establishing Russian control over the Kyrgyz energy sector through Gazprom, which was to start an exploration of the Kyrgyz natural gas fields. The Kremlin envisaged construction of gas pipelines under the control of Gazprom. In return for acquiescence of Kyrgyzstan to this Russian plan, the Kremlin forgave one-half of a large debt the Kyrgyzstan government owed the late Soviet Union and now owed the post–Soviet Russian Federation. The Kremlin also gave the Kyrgyz leadership reassurance about the well-being of Kyrgyz workers living and employed in Russia who sent a lot of their earnings back to Kyrgyzstan.[40]

Other Economic Ambitions

The central Asian region was for Putin, as it had been for Yeltsin, a vast market for Russian goods and services. Over a long period of time in the Soviet era, Russia had developed these lucrative patterns of trade and the Kremlin certainly wanted to reserve and expand that trade. To this end, the Russians even encouraged the ex-Soviet republics to adopt the ruble as national currency, a step most were reluctant to take for political as well as economic and financial reasons. As Yeltsin, Putin wanted to protect these patterns of trade and discouraged the central Asian republics from developing new economic ties, especially with the United States.[41]

Protective Russian Control of Central Asia

Some have argued that the Putin Kremlin after 2000 sought to transform the central Asian republics into Russian protectorates. Some recent evidence supported this view. In 1992, Russia had interfered directly in the civil war in Tajikistan to prop up the secular governments of Tajik presidents Rahmon Nabiyev and Emomali Rakhmonov. The goal of Russian policy in Tajikistan seemed to be to gain overall control of the country, while leaving local Tajik officials to administer day-to-day domestic affairs, a policy reminiscent of that of the Russian czars in the nineteenth and early twentieth centuries.[42]

While the Russians never got the degree of control they sought, their actions were cautionary to the leaders of the central Asian republics. There was little, if any, likelihood the Kremlin had the resources to engage in such neo-imperialistic behavior in central Asia. Moreover, the central Asian republics in fact had leaders acceptable to Russia. Though they shared a pervasive and popular undercurrent of fear and distrust of Russia, these leaders valued close political, economic, and strategic ties to Moscow. The leaders of post-Soviet central Asia, indeed, looked to Russia to support them in power and protect their political dominance. For them, Russia is the only country on which these leaders can rely for the external security of their country. For the central Asian republics, close economic and military links to Russia, no matter how controversial they may become in local politics, remained, as one writer put it, "indispensable to the region's future."[43]

The central Asian republics were dependent on Russia in some mundane ways as well. Russia supports temporary migrant employment, remittances, and energy subsidies, though such subsidies seemed to be diminishing in 2006 and 2007. Also, Russia has been the primary market for central Asian exports which are much cheaper than, but not competitive with, goods produced in the West. Energy exports are the only area in which some central Asian republics can be independent of Russia since there is an insatiable energy demand; but to date a few central Asian republics have energy sources for export.[44]

These continuing links to Russia limit how far any of the central Asian republics can proceed independently of Russia in strengthening relations with other countries, especially ones the Kremlin views as rivals and competitors. This consideration plays to Russia's advantage, tempting some Russian nationalists to at least hope, if not work for, something in the nature of a revived Moscow-led Soviet-style federation of the republics.

In particular, its military help has made Russia an invaluable and essential ally in the war on terrorism. Moreover, whatever Russia's limits and short-comings have been as a neighbor of the central Asian republics, it is seen as more reliable than the Americans, who have gained a reputation in the region not only for lack of predictability and reliability but also for insisting on caveats and constraints in its aid to them, such as calls for accelerated political democratization. By contrast, though Russia gives quantitatively less aid to central Asian countries, it generally has refrained from insisting that recipients make political changes they do not want.[45]

Limits on Putin's Influence-Building in Central Asia

Balanced against these incentives and advantages of Russian influence-building in the Putin years are limits and constraints. For example, Russia has lacked the military resources needed to dominate the region, despite impressive Russian economic growth in Putin's second administration from 2004 to 2008. Other limits on Russian influence-building under Putin include the hypersensitivity of central Asian leaders to perceived Russian efforts to diminish their sovereignty. And still another critical limit on Russian influence-building was U.S. policy in central Asia before 9/11. The U.S. government vocally supported the five republics' achievement of independence of Moscow in 1991 and made clear to the Kremlin its aversion to any actions by the Kremlin to revive the Soviet Union. After 9/11, the U.S. government's interest and actions in central Asia, in particular recruitment of the republics as allies of the United States in its declared war on terrorism, was a serious obstacle to the expansion of Russian influence in the region. Also, the ambitions of other countries adjacent to the ex-Soviet central Asian region, in particular Iran and China, had the effect of limiting the scope of Russian influence-building.

A Still Weak Russian Military Capability

Throughout the 1990s and in the early years of the new century, the Russian military was not capable of backing up any aggressive Russian influence-building campaigns in central Asia. Tied down in Chechnya, the military's overall weakness was evident as it failed to end the insurgency there. Many reasons explain the weak Russian military inherited by Putin, not least a loss of morale with the collapse and disintegration of the Soviet Union, and the cost-cutting policies of Gorbachev and Yeltsin. During his administration from 2000 to 2004, Putin never devoted the national resources to modernize and strengthen the Russian army, navy, and air forces, which remained almost in a shambles through the end of his second administration in early 2008. The most it seemed able to do was successfully attack in mid-August 2008 the territory of the republic of Georgia, Russia's western neighbor with an extremely weak military establishment that made it vulnerable to the numerically superior Russian forces. There were reports in the Western media about the breakdown of weapons, notably tanks whose engines could not easily be restarted.

Local Resistance to Putin's Influence-Building Policies

Despite Putin's efforts, economic and political, to support the governments of the central Asian republics, there remained a pervasive sensitivity on the part of local leadership elites to Russian interference. Leaders of the central Asian republics, many in power since 1991, were determined, more than ever in the aftermath of 9/11, to protect and preserve their newly gained sovereignty and independence of Moscow. They were on their guard because the Russian military demanded base facilities in the central Asian republics, especially if they had granted the United States such facilities. They also resented not only the continuing Russian military presence that involved air bases and Russian troop deployments on their territory but also a Russian idea that the borders of the central Asian republics are the same as Russia's own borders.[46]

To the Kremlin's dismay, most of the central Asian republics looked to the outside world, in particular their Islamic neighbors and the West, especially the United States, for a counterweight to the overbearing Russians. Some central Asian leaders went farther in dreaming about a vast central Asian Islamic federation linking them with one another and with the Islamic Middle East. With this national self-confidence they welcomed opportunities for friendship with powerful outsiders which in some instances were and remain rivals of Russia for influence in the greater Eurasian region. This has not unexpectedly led to a growing independence of Moscow.[47]

That said, central Asian leaders view Russia as an invaluable and essential ally in the war on terrorism given their still significant economic and military weaknesses.[48] Russia also is seen by today's central Asian leaders as more reliable than the United States under the Bush administration, which had a growing reputation in the region for lack of predictability and reliability. In contrast with the United States which most of the time attached "strings," namely caveats and constraints, to aid it gives, especially in the area of ideology, Russia gave less aid but in giving it refrained from calling for political democratizations for which most central Asian leaders had little sympathy.[49]

Moreover, the central Asian republics have looked to one another for mutual support to the exclusion of Russia. For example, Kazakhstan and Uzbekistan created the intra-regional Central Asian Union in 1994 that excluded Russia and was intended to foster trilateral strategic and other kinds of cooperation to counterbalance the Russian pressures on them.[50] Other collective efforts by the central Asian republics to strengthen ties among themselves, however, have not resulted in much concrete achievement and have been mainly of symbolic significance. Still, the Kremlin has been aware of them, their threat to the future of the CIS, and, ultimately, to Russia's influence-building ambitions.

The mixed sentiments of central Asian leaders toward Russia were evident also in their mixed attitude toward membership in the Russian-led CSTO, founded in 1992 and, so it seemed, modeled somewhat along the same lines as NATO. Kazakhstan and Turkmenistan soon opted out of CSTO, while other central Asian leaders suspected that the Kremlin would exploit perceived threats to the region to gain more power for themselves.[51] For example, central Asian leaders made no secret of their concern that the Kremlin might use peacekeeping initiatives on their territory to prevent an Islamic challenge or counter-narcotic activities to further their own expansionist goals. While Kazakhstan, Kyrgyzstan, and Tajikistan had entered the CSTO primarily to take advantage of a Russian offer to sell military equipment to them at deeply discounted prices, they quickly became wary of granting Russia a role in their defense.

With evident misgivings of the real purpose and intent of the CSTO, the central Asian republics balked when the Russians proposed to transform the organization into a tightly knit highly integrated rapid response force led, of course, by Russia and seen by the Kremlin as a means of fostering a higher level of integration of the military forces of the central Asian and other ex-Soviet republics.[52] Still, in October 2003, the Putin Kremlin's influence-building campaign made a significant stride when Russia acquired a new air base at Kant in Kyrgyzstan, not far from a U.S. air base in Manas.[53]

Ambitions of Outsiders

The Putin government has had to contend with stepped-up actions by other Powers with an interest in central Asia. In the 15 years or more since the central Asian republics became independent, Turkey, Iran, Afghanistan, China, and the United States have become increasingly active in the central Asian region, rivaling and challenging Russia's own influence-building agenda. These outsiders saw in the disintegration of Soviet power in central Asia in late 1991 a once in a lifetime opportunity to further their own ambitious goals in a region closed off to them when it was part of the now defunct Soviet state. In some respects, the interests of these outsiders mirror Russia's interest. With Turkey and Iran, there is a concern with the well-being of the ethnic and religious groups that have a shared heritage with these two states. Outsiders all want to participate in the development of the region's energy resources.

China and Central Asia

China in recent years has become especially interested in the central Asian republics now that they are independent states.[54] China sees the region as a tremendous market for all kinds of inexpensive manufactured goods. The two provinces of China which have the most trade with central Asia are Xinjiang and Sichuan, which plan to increase trade with central Asia 30–50 times the present volume in another decade, making China the dominant foreign investor. Since the early 1990s, China also has invested in the central Asian economic infrastructure, playing a positive and valuable role in facilitating regional economic growth and development, strengthening in still another way the inclination of the ex-Soviet republics to strengthen ties to Beijing.[55]

China also has an increasingly compelling interest in central Asia as a source of energy, focusing especially on the oil and natural gas in Kazakhstan and Turkmenistan. In this calculus, Iran has a role to play in cooperating with China to develop pipelines across the central Asian region. And China is well positioned to work with Iran, in competition, incidentally, with Russia and the United States, because the Sino-Iranian diplomatic slate is tension-free, unlike the situation in Iranian relations with the West, especially the United States.[56]

One area where China may cooperate rather than compete with Russia is in the area of security. In this regard, China is a potential ally of Russia and the United States because for these countries, the biggest threat in the region remains Islamic insurgencies. China, which has a border with Kazakhstan, Kyrgyzstan, and Tajikistan, wants to contain and suppress the ultranationalistic, highly militant, and religious-based movement threatening the secular Asian governments of all five of the ex-Soviet central Asian republics.[57]

Turkey and Central Asia

To the west of the ex-Soviet central Asian region one country with a substantial interest in central Asia is Turkey.[58] Turkish thinking about the region is sociocultural and strategic. There are Turkic minorities in several Eurasian republics, notably Turkmenistan in which Turkey's government has an abiding and strong interest. In addition, good political and economic relations with the Eurasian republics are important for Turkish security by providing Ankara with significant leverage in its dealings with the Kremlin. This goal is reciprocal, especially in light of the interest of the central Asian republics in strengthening ties with Turkey to give them some leverage with Moscow.

Turkey has offered credit and technical assistance to the Turkic-speaking states of central Asia, notably Turkmenistan. It has also expanded trade relations with Uzbekistan and in particular supported, with the blessing of the United States, the construction of a pipeline from Kazakhstan to Western markets. Recently opened, this pipeline, much to the dismay of Russia, allows Kazakhstan to sell oil to the West without Russian involvement. Finally, Turkey obliquely offers a model of development for the central Asian republics that shows how political and economic growth can occur in a secular framework and with a large predominantly Islamic population. By secularizing its development along Turkish lines, at the very least, the central Asian republics could attract the attention of the West and to that extent provide themselves with a modest leverage in dealing with Russia.[59]

There are obstacles to Turkish influence-building in the ex-Soviet central Asian republics which are hypersensitive to any Turkish gestures that suggest a "big brother" relationship with them: they resist any moves toward a "Pan-Turkic" solidarity almost as much as they resisted Putin's drive for Russian hegemony. In addition, Turkey cannot buy its way to influence. It is in no economic shape to field a vast, credible foreign aid program accompanied by an extensive amount of direct foreign investment as the West is, and as Putin's Russia seems increasingly able to do with its new-found wealth in petrodollars.[60]

Nevertheless, Turkey has a role to play that has an impact on Russian-American relations in central Asia; and since 2000, Turkey has carried on a campaign to strengthen political, economic, and military ties to the central Asian republics, with a focus on ex-Soviet Turkic states threatened by militant Islam. Uzbekistan and Kyrgyzstan fit the profile, and Turkey has started to provide weapons for border defense to these countries and signed agreements providing for Turkish training of the armies of each country. Uzbekistan has been especially appreciative of this help given its internal problem with Islamic militants supported by the Taliban on its territory, and its efforts to resist Russian influence-building in the guise of Russian military assistance. The United States also welcomed the new Turkish initiatives and to some extent so has Russia—both countries out of worry about the spread of Taliban influence throughout central Asia.[61]

Turkey is a NATO ally of the United States and ready up to a point to cooperate with the United States in central Asia where they share one significant strategic objective: limiting and constraining the accelerated Russian influence-building in the Putin era. Turkey considers the resurgence of Russian power in central Asia a threat to its security. In addition, as seen in the construction and opening of the Baku-Tbilisi-Ceyhan pipeline in 2006, which carries Caspian oil to Western markets, bypassing Russia, Turkey is a potentially valuable ally in the U.S. rivalry with Russia for power and influence in the central Asian states.[62]

Iran and Central Asia

Iran has substantial economic, sociocultural, and ideological interests in the region. Iran like others in the region wants to participate in the exploration of gas and oil in the part of the Caspian Sea proximate to Turkmenistan and Kazakhstan and has concluded agreements with those countries to cooperate in the transit of these resources to Western markets. In addition, there are small minorities of Persian-speaking Iranians scattered throughout the central Asian republics in which Teheran has a modicum of concern given the heavily secularist orientation of the central Asian republics and their strong opposition to Islamic fundamentalism.[63]

By strengthening political ties with the central Asian states, especially in the post-9/11 years, Iran also intends to lessen its isolation in the region, despite U.S. efforts to keep them out. Moreover, Iran is Muslim and committed to the Shi'ite strain of Islam. It seeks to offer sympathy and support to Shi'ite Muslim populations in other countries in central Asia, an initiative not welcomed by the secular leaders of the central Asian republics and Russia. But, Iran cultivates the region's leaders by offering them oil and gas transit routes for their exports that do not include Russia. For example, on September 23, 2005, Iran's ambassador to Kazakhstan, Ramin Mehman-perast, announced his government's readiness to participate in joint investment projects in Kazakhstan in various areas, including transportation and the oil, gas, and petrochemical industries.[64] Although interested in fostering the spread of its model of government in which religion plays a virtually dominant role, Teheran's position has been that the region is not yet ready for an Islamic fundamentalist ascendancy and to some extent it has kept to that view.[65]

Iran could go much faster in its influence-building in central Asia were it to improve relations with the United States, which has tried to block its expansion eastward, especially Iran's efforts to get involved in the development of oil and natural gas pipelines that would be laid through Iranian territory.[66] Another block to Iranian ambitions in the region is that it lacks the resources to be a major player in the central Asian region. Iranian economic and cultural relations with the central Asian republics may increase, but given these limited resources, Iranian political and military influence-building will remain minimal, and as a consequence, so will its threat to Russian and American interests.[67]

THE UNITED STATES AND CENTRAL ASIA

The most important and most powerful outsider interested in the central Asian republics as far as Russia is concerned is the United States, which has shown increasing interest in the central Asian republics. After 9/11, the United States looked to this region for military bases from which it could move against al Qaeda and the Taliban. But U.S. interests in the region go even deeper and include economic reasons (participation in the expansion of resource-rich economies) and ideological and strategic reasons.

The United States wants to be part of the process as the central Asian republics exploit their vast oil and natural gas wealth, especially in the Caspian basin which is reputed to have more oil reserves than Iraq and Kuwait combined. Also, the United States wants to foster democratic development in these autocratically run countries. Finally, the United States wants to strengthen the central Asia's newly won independence of Moscow and undermine perceived Russian efforts to establish control in the region.

Most important, the United States has sought to prevent the "Afghanization" of central Asia, that is, to prevent the ascendancy to power of radical Islamic fundamentalist regimes in the central Asian republics. It has been clear to both Washington and Moscow that central Asian republics, because of their high level of poverty and the repressiveness of their neo-Communist leaders, are vulnerable to the appeal of radical Islamic parties with programs of religious-inspired change. In particular, their abiding distrust these populations have of Russia and their military weakness have rendered them vulnerable to subversive and potentially destructive forces coming from outside the region, notably Iran and Afghanistan, countries dominated by militant fundamentalists.

While the populations of central Asia might be vulnerable to the kind of militant Islamic thinking and actions the United States opposes, there leaders are potential allies in the war against the Taliban regime and al Qaeda. In the 1990s, for example, Uzbekistan, which has a border in the southeastern part of the country with Afghanistan, was already fighting the Taliban ascendancy by supporting the so-called Northern Alliance of anti-Taliban forces headquartered in the northernmost part of Afghanistan. The United States also supported the Northern Alliance. When the Taliban eventually succeeded in taking control of Afghanistan, Uzbekistan and the other central Asian republics were both alarmed. Uzbekistan became a launching point for anti-Taliban incursions, including air strikes and search and rescue missions, into Afghanistan.

By the end of the 1990s, the U.S. involvement in central Asia heightened in response to efforts of the militant and radicalized IMU to spread Islamic fundamentalism throughout the region, especially in Uzbekistan and neighboring Kyrgyzstan.[68] American interest in the central Asian republics spiked profoundly in the wake of the 9/11 terrorist attack by radical Islamists such as Osama bin Laden and his al Qaeda organization headquartered in and protected by Afghanistan.[69]

U.S. Policy in the Aftermath of 9/11

While the new Bush administration continued past U.S. policy of encouraging democratization, promoting U.S. involvement in the production and marketing of oil, and restraining the Kremlin's efforts to expand Russian political, economic, and military influence in the ex-Soviet central Asian republics, the main focus of U.S. policy after 9/11 was getting central Asian cooperation in the war against terrorism. In October 2001, a first phase of the war on terrorism was the U.S. invasion of Afghanistan to remove the Taliban government from power in Kabul because of its support for and protection of Osama bin Laden. In this effort, the Bush administration considered the support of the central Asian republics in the war essential. Some of these republics bordered Afghanistan and all of them could provide the United States with the kind of military help, like base facilities, needed for the war.

The central Asian republics were willing and some even eager to help the United States to an extent that dismayed the Kremlin which increasingly after 9/11 viewed the United States more as a rival than an ally in the war on terrorism. Uzbekistan Foreign Minister Abdulaziz Kamilov on September 16, 2001, declared that his country was ready to cooperate in any way possible in the war on terrorism, including the possible use of Uzbek territory for strikes on terrorist camps in Afghanistan. Tajikistan's foreign minister spoke equivalently when he expressed interest in cooperating with the United States, though he introduced a significant caveat to the effect that the Tajik government would consult with Moscow before taking any concrete steps.[70]

But, Washington quickly discovered a serious contradiction in its approaches to the five ex-Soviet central Asian republics: the effort to gain their military cooperation was being undercut by the U.S. determination to foster democratization. The central Asian leaders were all for the most part authoritarian, some fostering the appearance of democracy but all maintaining a reality of dictatorship and political repression.[71]

These leaders were far more inclined to the Kremlin, which had no problem with their authoritarian ways. So, even though the central Asian republics have tried to maintain links of all kinds to the United States, the balance of power in the region increasingly has gone to Russia. Indeed, most of the central Asian republics, just as in the Yeltsin years, needed and wanted close ties to Russia in the realization that it was the only country both willing and able to help assure their domestic stability and international security.[72]

Deployment of U.S. Military Power

In the immediate aftermath of 9/11, the Bush administration established a military presence in the central Asian republics to buttress its invasion of Afghanistan. The United States acquired bases in Uzbekistan (Khanabad) and Kyrgyzstan (Manas) and landing rights at bases in Kulyab and other locations in Tajikistan. Kazakhstan concluded agreements for U.S. technical and military assistance but was reluctant to allow a U.S. military base on its territory to avoid provoking the Kremlin.[73]

These military arrangements alarmed Russia and China both of which called for the closure of the bases no sooner had they been opened. In recent years, however, the central Asian republics, in varying degrees, have resisted the pressure. For example, Uzbekistan, which gave Washington a formal notice of eviction from the U.S. base at Khanabad in 2005, still allows some

U.S. military activity there. Tajikistan and Kazakhstan have argued they needed strategic assistance from both Russia and the United States. And, for its part, the United States, with the unexpected escalation of Taliban resistance in Afghanistan since 2005, has insisted on the need to maintain a military presence in central Asia, along with Russia, to protect the region against expansion of Islamic fundamentalism that would weaken the secular governments that both Russia and the U.S. support whatever their flaws.[74]

U.S. Democratization Policy

Since the early 1990s, there has been a very substantial ideological component in U.S. policy toward central Asia, namely the encouragement of democratization. In August 2003, Assistant Secretary of State A. Elizabeth Jones stated the U.S. ideological goal in central Asia, clearly saying that the United States had a vested interest in assuring the independence and democratization of the central Asian countries. Democratic systems would keep them stable and prosperous and were essential to the success of their role as partners of the United States. She added in particular that the United States wanted these countries to respect human rights, join the global economy, and in other ways protect themselves against the expansion of terrorism.[75]

Partly in response to American pressure to step up the pace of democratization, the central Asian dictatorships tried to give the appearance—and only the appearance—of practicing what they viewed as a Western style of parliamentary democracy characterized by a multiplicity of parties competing in regular elections on national and local levels of government. A decade after their independence and the end of Communist rule, there still is no real political pluralism because the government party overshadows all other groups and there is unrelenting political repression of political protest and dissent.

Obstacles to Democratization

The United States faced a dilemma as it encouraged democratization in the region. How could U.S. policymakers cultivate central Asian leaders for strategic reasons while these same leaders violated human rights? But, any public U.S. display of hostility toward autocratic and repressive leaders compromised their political base at home and strengthened the voice of local, frequently Islamic-driven nationalist forces. Also, when the United States did criticize them for rights abuses, the criticism had the effect of souring relations between them and the United States and also of driving these leaders toward Russia.[76]

Driving these countries into the arms of Russia, which all but ignored the antidemocratic policies of central Asian leaders, certainly was not the intent of Washington. Quite the contrary. But, as the United States persistently stated its concern with their human rights violations and other impediments to democratization, the insecure leaders of the region increasingly listened to Russia's campaign to show itself as a "traditional, reliable partner."[77]

Countering Russian Influence-Building

A third large aspect of U.S. policy in central Asia from the early 1990s onward was strengthening the independence and sovereignty of the central Asian republics vis-à-vis Russia. A starting point of this American strategy was the prompt and formal recognition of the existence of the ex-Soviet central Asian republics as independent entities almost immediately after the collapse of the Soviet Union at the end of 1991, giving the newly independent republics a psychological boost and strengthening their innate tendencies to resist escalating pressures of the Kremlin to influence their postindependence development and link them closely to Russia.[78]

In the early and mid-1990s, the Clinton administration encouraged interested republics to strengthen ties with NATO as junior partners of an alliance called "Partnership for Peace" that made them eligible to participate in NATO-sponsored defense initiatives. Although such initiatives toward the central Asian republics were minimal in the 1990s, serving merely as a way to provide them with at least psychological leverage in dealing with Russia, they worked in the sense that the Kremlin was hard put to openly fault the United States.[79]

But a flaw in this policy was an emphasis on security that paid little attention to the conditions that interfered with democratization, notably the pervasive poverty throughout much of central Asia. Indeed, the Clinton administration devoted much less attention and much less money to economic development, the alleviation of health and social problems, and the cultivation of a civil society than it did for defense. For example, though some economic aid went to Kazakhstan and Uzbekistan, it hardly changed policy in a positive way—Uzbekistan's Karimov remained hostile to free market reform and Kazakhstan's Nazarbayev conducted a flawed privatization process. This neglect contradicted the expressed American commitment to helping the central Asian countries develop the conditions needed to make democratization achievable. Moreover, by focusing more on security in the region than on its domestic development, the United States inadvertently strengthened the grip on power of conservative autocrats like Uzbekistan's Karimov, Tajikistan's Rakhmonov, Turkmenistan's neo-Stalinistic Niyazov, and Kazakhstan's Nazarbayev who were strongly pro-Russian, at least in the immediate aftermath of the collapse of the Soviet Union, and uncertain about the future development, and even survival, of their recently emancipated countries.[80]

There was little change of focus during the two Bush administrations between 2001 and 2009. While the United States continued programs of

financial and economic assistance that were clearly earmarked for encouragement of democratization, notably in the form of U.S. money for political organizations inside individual central Asian republics to educate and energize the
societies of these countries in favor of democracy, and while what the United
States offered was always worth more than any Russian assistance to these
countries in this period, U.S. assistance was never enough to make a real impact
on the pace of democratization which, at best, was sluggish everywhere.

The Energy Trade

A final aspect of U.S. policy toward the central Asian countries after
9/11, and of special concern to the Kremlin, has do with the production
and marketing of the region's huge oil and natural gas supplies. The United
States wants to participate, at least as an equal, in the development of
region's energy resources. This policy is a clear challenge to the Kremlin
which wants a Russian monopoly of the central Asian energy trade. But,
the United States wants to diversify its own sources of energy and in particular reduce U.S. dependence on oil from the Middle East.

The problem for the United States in seeking a key role in the central Asian
energy trade was and remains Russian control of pipeline routes for the marketing of the region's energy products. To weaken and eventually break that
monopoly, the Bush administration in the early years of the new century
pressed for construction of pipelines, like the Baku-Tbilisi-Ceyhan route
encouraged by the Clinton administration at the end of the 1990s, financed
by British Petroleum (BP) and other Western oil firms, and opened in 2005.
This pipeline circumvented Russian territory and provided an alternative to
the pipelines built and planned by Russia through its government-controlled
energy cartel known as Gazprom.

More recently, the United States has been eager to have other pipelines
carrying central Asian oil, notably from the enormous Kashagan oil field in
the northern Caspian belonging to Kazakhstan. It is reputed to hold over
10 billion barrels, and the United States wants to exclude Russia from
monopolizing the transit of oil from this field. While oil from Kashagan is
not expected to start flowing for at least five years, the consortium of investors that includes Exxon-Mobil wants to transit the first gushes through the
BTC pipeline. This would require the construction of a second BTC route
pipeline under the Caspian Sea. If the United States has its way, Russia
would again be excluded from the marketing of the new source of Kazakh
oil and the Kremlin is likely to try to block such a development.[81]

RUSSIAN REACTIONS TO U.S. POLICIES, 2000–2008

The Kremlin initially tolerated the new post-9/11 influence-building
campaign, for example, accepting the expanding American military

presence in the central Asian republics as a necessity, despite its threat to Russian interests. Initially for Putin the United States was a putative ally of Russia in its own on terrorism in Chechnya. But, as the United States moved increasing amounts of military materials into central Asia, the Kremlin became worried by this ongoing U.S. political, economic, and military influence.

The "Ivanov Doctrine"

Putin reiterated the claim the Yeltsin leadership often had made of Russia's logical and inevitable predominance in the Near Abroad and in central Asia. In the beginning of October 2003, Russian Defense Minister Sergei Ivanov unveiled with much fanfare an unofficial draft of a new strategic doctrine incorporating Russia's own formulation of unilateralism in Eurasia, a doctrine that seemed inspired by a perceived American expansionism in the ex-Soviet region, especially the central Asian part most affected by the war on terrorism. According to this "Ivanov Doctrine," Russia reserved the right to carry out preemptive strikes anywhere in the world, including the CIS member states, to protect its security as well as theirs from a perceived threat. Ivan pointedly raised the possibility of a Russian intervention to protect a country threatened by political and/or ethnic conflict as well as by dangers to Russia's economic well-being. Much of this doctrine may have been designed mostly to reassure Russia's own cadre of ultranationalists, especially a pursuit of it required a strong military capability that Russia manifestly lacked in the Putin years.[82]

The doctrine, a product of thinking by both Defense Minister Sergei Ivanov and President Putin, had an intrinsic logic that could not be dismissed by Washington or the central Asian leaders themselves. Bottom line: there was no doubt that the Putin Kremlin was quite serious about maintaining and expanding Russian influence in the central Asian republics, more intensively and efficiently than his predecessor, President Boris Yeltsin.[83]

Expanding Military Preparedness

Even before the "Ivanov Doctrine" was in place, Putin had taken concrete steps to strengthen Russia's military capability to support a forward policy in central Asia and elsewhere in the Near Abroad. For example, in May 2000, Putin established a new position for the purpose of coordinating Eurasian policymaking at the highest executive level. He appointed a Special Representative for the Caspian area with the rank of deputy foreign minister. This official worked outside the administrative framework of the Foreign Ministry and reported directly to the president. The immediate objective was to reconcile differences among civilian commercial interests and the geopolitical objectives of the government.[84]

The influence-building agenda advanced on a number of fronts. Putin expanded the work of a group as *Siloviki*, made up of government officials from different administrative offices, including those with background in the security services. These appointees shared President Putin's security background and his view on how to further Russian influence-building, say through increased cooperation with particular central Asian republics, notably Tajikistan, in the area of border control. This group showed its influence, for example, when Federal Security Service chief Nikolai Petrushev became a significant voice in the formation of Russian policy in Eurasia, especially the central Asian republics, even though the official source of decision-making below the presidential level remained Defense Minister Sergei Ivanov, who, incidentally, also had a background in state security as a member of the old Soviet era KGB.[85]

To achieve the military power needed to project Russian influence in the ex-Soviet space, Putin undertook a comprehensive reform of the Russian armed forces' structure and composition, devoting substantial funds to that end with the evident idea of using these forces in central Asia. With these beefed-up military resources, the Kremlin forged a new military alliance modeled after NATO for central Asia known as the Collective Security Treaty Organization (CSTO); increased the country's on-the-ground military presence in Tajikistan and Kyrgyzstan; concluded an agreement with Uzbekistan in 2005, providing for the rapid deployment of Russian troops in Uzbekistan; and initiated arms sales agreements with central Asian republics at subsidized prices often in return for access to Soviet defense plants or installations.[86]

Russian Diplomacy

The Kremlin also used diplomacy in trying to limit and reverse U.S. influence-building in the central Asian region, for example, by pushing in 2001 for the transformation of the Shanghai Cooperation Organization (SCO), formed originally in 1996, to manage cross-border problems and into a military and defense alliance. Including Russia, China, and several central Asian republics, the SCO's goal is to promote security and strategic cooperation in the large region composed of its members. Though officially the Kremlin denied it was doing this with the SCO, it encouraged members to undertake military exercises and to develop defense-related capabilities. Russian Defense Minister Ivanov was the diplomatic "point-man" in this strategy, having advocated at an April 2006 SCO summit meeting of defense ministers of member states the creation of a unified command center.[87]

Russia used the SCO to take China along with the three central Asian members in a strategy designed to undermine and perhaps reverse the U.S. military presence in central Asia. At a SCO summit meeting in Kazakhstan in July 2005, for example, the SCO called upon the United States to remove its military forces from base facilities it was using in the various central Asian republics.[88]

But, sometimes SCO members, in particular China, resisted the Russian drive for closer strategic cooperation, convinced that doing so would be at the expense of their sovereignty and to the strategic advantage of Russia. Kazakhstan also opposed strengthening of the SCO and the United States has encouraged Kazakh President Nursultan Nazarbayev in his policy, providing Kazakhstan with military assistance. Still, with the persistent and expanding American involvement in central Asia, the Kremlin is likely to continue its effort to "beef up" the SCO along NATO lines, especially as it does have the support for this of other republics, notably Uzbekistan and Kyrgyzstan which place a high value on Russian strategic support.[89]

Another aspect of Russian diplomacy in responding to the U.S. challenge in central Asia after 9/11 has been to exploit the discomfort of the central Asian leaders as the U.S. intrusion into their domestic affairs particularly as the United States has supported opposition groups that want more democracy. The Putin Kremlin has been supportive of the region's dictatorial leaders who maintain political stability through severe neo-Communist-style political repression and has had no problem with the prevalent central Asian view that it has been necessary to limit democracy for the sake of resisting the spread of Islamic fundamentalism.

But, some Russian politicians and commentators faulted Putin's seemingly indiscriminate backing of dictatorial central Asian leaders, saying that Putin's support of autocrats would lead to problems in Russia's relations with the West. They also said that backing autocratic leaders because of their willingness to strengthen political, economic, and military links with the Kremlin could backfire and bring about a decline in Russian influence.[90] Konstantin Kosachev, leader of the Russian State Duma's Committee for Foreign Affairs, has argued that Russia should use its influence in the region to encourage democracy and show local governments that the Kremlin does not want to reimpose Soviet-style military and economic dominance on the region. He stated that Russian clout with the domestic political processes in these countries should be used to promote the development of truly democratic states.[91]

Putin early on set diplomatic parameters he wanted the region's leaders to accept in their relations with the United States after 9/11. He set out these limits when he telephoned the central Asian leaders, especially of Tajikistan and Uzbekistan, who seemingly could not wait to draw closer to the United States militarily as well as in other ways in fighting terrorism at the end of 2001, discussing how they should respond to U.S. approaches to them, namely, with caution, restraint, and due concern for the interests of their real ally Russia. Moreover, several high-ranking Russian officials such as Russian Security Council Secretary Vladimir Rushailo and Chief of the Russian General Staff Anatolyi Kvashin went to central Asia to impress upon the region's national leaders that they must coordinate with Moscow in their response to the United States in the aftermath of 9/11.[92]

CONCLUSIONS

As of 9/11, and despite the affirmative response of Russia to the U.S. request for support for the war against al Qaeda in the region, the basis was set for Russian and U.S. conflict in central Asia. While each of the five countries responded to this Russian-U.S. tension in different ways, and while each tried to act to maintain its independence of foreign control and develop its own foreign policy, much of the peace and stability in the region has depended on the skill or lack of it that Russian and U.S. leaders have shown in resolving their differences.

2

Kazakhstan

Full name: Republic of Kazakhstan

- Population: 15.4 million (UN, 2005)
- Capital: Astana
- Largest city: Almaty
- Area: 2.7 million sq. km (1 million sq. miles)
- Ethnic makeup: 53.4% Kazakh; 30% Russian; 3.7% Ukrainian; 2.5% Uzbek; 2.4% German; 1.7% Tatar; 6.3% others (chiefly Azeri, Belarussian, Korean, Kurd, and Uighur)
- Major languages: Kazakh, Russian
- Major religions: Islam, Christianity
- Life expectancy: 58 years (men), 69 years (women) (UN)
- Monetary unit: 1 Kazakh tenge = 100 tiyn
- Main exports: Oil, uranium, ferrous and nonferrous metals, machinery, chemicals, grain, wool, meat, coal
- GNI per capita: US$2,930 (World Bank, 2006)

Good Russian relations with Kazakhstan are essential to the Kremlin's influence-building strategy in ex-Soviet central Asia.[1] Strategically Kazakhstan is important for Russia because it borders Russia, China, the Caspian Sea, and three other central Asian republics, Turkmenistan, Uzbekistan, and Kyrgyzstan, all vulnerable to the subversive influence of militant Islamic

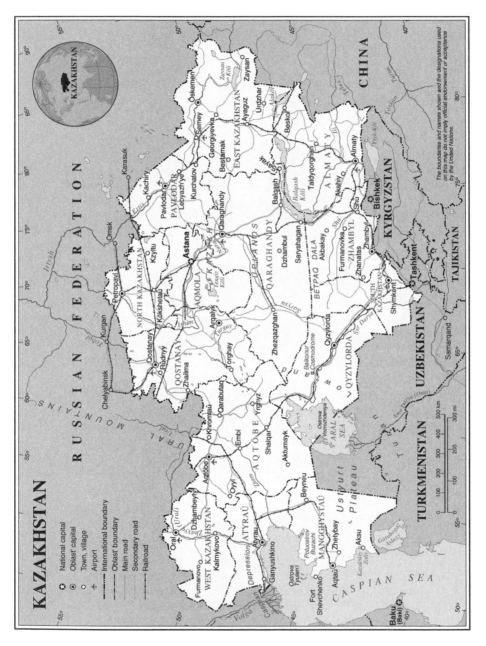

KAZAKHSTAN

- ⊛ National capital
- ⊙ Oblast capital
- ○ Town, village
- ✈ Airport
- ⋯ International boundary
- ⋯ Oblast boundary
- Main road
- Secondary road
- Railroad

Kazakhstan (Courtesy of UN Cartographic Section)

fundamentalism coming from Iran and Afghanistan. Kazakhstan is important to Russia also because of its enormous energy and other natural resources, including gold, silver, chrome, zinc, coal, and iron ore as well as wheat. This enormous economic wealth, especially oil and natural gas, also has attracted the attention of the West, which has sought to participate in its exploitation, especially the oil reserves of the Tengiz fields along the eastern Caspian. Kazakhstan has the largest percentage of Russian residents in ex-Soviet central Asia. Moreover, this minority is deeply involved in the management of the country's economy and political system. In the post-Soviet era, it has also become an object of discrimination by hypernationalist Kazakhs who would like to diminish Russian influence as much as possible so that their country is in no way subservient to Moscow as it had been for much of its recent history.

RUSSIAN-KAZAKH RELATIONS IN THE YELTSIN ERA, 1992–1999[2]

In the early years of the post-Soviet era, the Kremlin attached great importance to the cultivation of Kazakhstan. Russian President Boris Yeltsin and Russian Foreign Minister Andrei Kozyrev kept the management of Russian relations with newly independent Kazakhstan in the forefront of Russia's strategic thinking believing that it was destined to play a major role as a buffer between Russia and the threat of Islamic radicalism emanating from Afghanistan in the aftermath of the collapse of Communist rule there in the early 1990s.[3]

In its policies toward Kazakhstan, Russia could build on its historically deep ties. Kazakhstan President Nursultan Nazarbayev, in power since the 1980s, highly valued Kazakhstan's friendly relationship with Russia, especially the tangible benefits in the economic sphere that his country gained from its closeness to Russia. He showed his loyalty when Kazakhstan became the first of the non-Slavic republics to seek membership in the new Slavic entente of Russia, Belarus, and Ukraine created by Russian President Boris Yeltsin in the Fall of 1991 and called the CIS by its charter members (Russia, Belarus, and Ukraine). Yeltsin, who took the lead in the founding of the CIS, intended it as a successor to—though not a replacement of—the Soviet Union. Initially, Yeltsin did not envisage entry into the CIS of the non-Slavic republics in the Caucasus, Caspian, and central Asian areas of the defunct Soviet state. But, when other ex-Soviet republics starting with Kazakhstan sought membership in the CIS, Yeltsin adopted a broader view of its membership and started dreaming, with the encouragement of Russian nationalists, of a new Russian-dominated reincarnation of the former Soviet Union open to all the republics that had belonged to the 1922 union founded by Lenin.

For his part, Nazarbayev maintained close contact with Russian leaders in the post-Soviet era and kept his country's political fences mended with

Moscow. He went out of his way to promote the well-being of Kazakhstan's Russian minority. To Moscow's satisfaction, Nazarbayev kept Russian as the language of administration in Astana, the new capital of the country, and ensured the equality of Russian with the Kazakh language in the Constitution for the newly independent country. Nazarbayev, at least initially, urged other central Asian republics to join the CIS. He also agreed to include Russia in a major energy deal and merged part of his military with the Russian army.

On the other hand, Nazarbayev was wary of the Kremlin's ambitions to integrate Kazakhstan within the framework of the CIS under Russian leadership and, sensitive to Kazakhstan's newly achieved independence of Moscow, tried to resist this tendency. By the end of the Yeltsin era, Nazarbayev had lost much of the enthusiasm he once had for membership of his country in the CIS and had proposed replacement of it by a less Russian-dominated, more egalitarian institution he called the Euro-Asian Union.[4] While the Russian-Kazakh relationship had much going for it, throughout the 1990s, the Kremlin faced some serious problems difficult to resolve. Of these the two most important involved some Kazakh discrimination against the country's Russian minority growing out of a strong undercurrent of anti-Russian nationalism within Kazakhstan. Also, by the late 1990s, Nazarbayev was charting a foreign policy diversifying Kazakhstan's relations with the outside world at Russia's expense, at least in the Kremlin's view, starting with a willingness to cooperate with major international institutions, especially in the economic sphere where Kazakhstan stood to benefit greatly from links to the International Monetary Fund and the World Bank.[5] The Yeltsin Kremlin saw in a growing Kazakh relationship with the United States serious strategic liabilities for Russia.

Discrimination against the Russian Minority

In the Soviet system before 1991, ethnic Kazakhs long resented the privileged, superior lifestyle of the Russian minority, and when it became independent, Kazakhs, especially the youth, looked to limit the presence and influence of this minority. The Russians constituted a kind of "upper class" in a country where the overwhelming majority of people were and are very poor. Anti-Russian feeling was apparent in a 1989 language law passed by the Kazakh parliament. Although liberal in the sense of assigning Russian a special place in Kazakh society by referring to it as "the language of inter-ethnic communication," which in interpretation, at least, suggested a second-class status, and although Russian could be used everywhere in the country for all purposes, a kind of linguistic discrimination in favor of the Kazakh tongue developed. For example, Russians working for local administrative authorities soon found that promotions and other aspects of professional advancement hinged on familiarity with the Kazakh tongue, with which most Russians had little familiarity. Russians started demanding that their language be elevated from the existing status as "the language of inter-ethnic communication" (a term never really defined by the Kazakh authorities) to the status of a full-fledged second national language.[6]

Nazarbayev could not dismiss, never mind, suppress, this anti-Russian sentiment, an important aspect of indigenous Kazakh nationalism. If he did, he would have risked weakening his political base on which his authority rested. He tried to conciliate Kazakh nationalists by appointing an increasing number of ethnic Kazakhs to positions of power and responsibility. In some cases, he gave priority to ethnic Kazakhs in obtaining government contracts for their private firms. But, in another conciliatory gesture toward the Russian minority, he agreed to a stipulation in the new Kazakh Constitution of January 1993 prohibiting the restriction of anyone's rights or freedoms on the grounds that he or she does not know the state language.[7]

Nevertheless, the Russian leadership in Moscow was sensitive to a perceived downgrading of the status of Russian-speaking Kazakhs. Nationalist politicians in the Russian State Duma, the lower, popularly elected house of the Russian national parliament, complained about Kazakh discrimination against the Russian minority, demanding better all-around treatment by the Kazakh authorities. They called on the Kremlin to defend the rights of all Russians living abroad. In the early 1990s, the Russian media, for its part, cataloged almost on a daily basis the difficulties facing Kazakhstan's Russian minority. Extreme nationalists called on the Kremlin to pay attention to the plight of ethnic Russians "stranded" in the newly independent central Asian republics.[8]

But, the Kremlin was not inclined to pick a fight with one of its most congenial neighbors in the so-called "ex-Soviet space."[9] Though making veiled references to the discontent of Russians living in Kazakhstan, the Kremlin made no formal protest. This restraint paid off. Wary of troubling his relations with Moscow, Nazarbayev took steps to diminish the discontent of Kazakhstan's Russian community, starting with the early dissolution of nationalist parliament elected in March 1994. He postponed elections for a new parliament until the end of 1995, to give Russian residents a chance to organize themselves politically and thereby improve the chances of their candidates. Furthermore, in a new Constitution approved by voters in a 1995 referendum, the status of the Russian language was advanced to "coequality" with the Kazakh tongue. And, in a referendum in 1996, Kazakh voters approved the creation of a new, smaller, weaker bicameral legislature that would weaken the popular and potentially anti-Russian voice in the Kazakh electorate. That said, to the dismay of the Kremlin, Nazarbayev worked to strengthen Kazakh ties to other countries to the East as well as the West to bolster his independence within the Russian-dominated CIS.

Kazakhstan and the United States

Also complicating Kazakhstan's relationship with Russia in the 1990s was Nazarbayev's growing friendship with the United States. Nazarbayev shrewdly exploited the Clinton administration's overall strategy of befriending and supporting ex-Soviet republics as a means of blunting Russian expansionism in the region. Even though Kazakhstan was one of the most loyal of the ex-Soviet republics to Russia, Nazarbayev moved the country slowly but steadily toward a free market, opening the country to foreign investment to a much greater extent than any of his neighbors, including Russia, and most importantly for Washington, agreed to turn over ex-Soviet nuclear weapons to Russia and become "nonnuclear" and an advocate of nuclear nonproliferation.

In these policies, Nazarbayev scored points with Washington. And this was exactly his intention. His policy began to pay off handsomely in early 1994, when U.S. President Bill Clinton agreed to more than triple American aid to Kazakhstan, from $91 million in 1994 to $311 million in 1995.[10]

U.S. Misgivings about Nazarbayev

That said, the Clinton administration made no secret of its displeasure over Nazarbayev's authoritarian bent and his slowness in developing a free market, but it has been unwilling to pressure him to hold to promises of fair elections and a free press. American interest in helping Kazakhstan drill and market its enormous oil reserves in the 1990s was more important for the Clinton administration than ideological concerns about Kazakh political and economic conservatism.

Still, the administration remained concerned about Nazarbayev's dictatorial leadership and cavalier attitude toward democratization and human rights, in particular his persecution of Prime Minister Akezhan Kazhegeldin. In October 1997, to the dismay of the Clinton administration, Nazarbayev replaced Kazhegeldin in what was seen in Kazakhstan as a "power grab" with Nurlan Balgimbeyev, a technocrat with expertise in the oil industry. He was a close confidant of Nazarbayev.[11]

The removal of Kazhegeldin was explainable also by Nazarbayev's relations with the Yeltsin Kremlin. The Russians were suspicious of Kazhegeldin's liberal reformism, in particular his opening of Kazakhstan to foreign investment, especially U.S. and Chinese investment, as well as the speed with which he was implementing privatization. Just before leaving office he had concluded a $9.5 billion oil deal with China.[12]

That said, Nazarbayev did not retreat in any significant way from his cultivation of the United States that was niggling the Kremlin. Kazakhstan's growing friendship with the United States provided Nazarbayev a measure of psychological as well as political leverage in dealing with the aggressive efforts of the Kremlin to expand Russian influence in the ex-Soviet space, especially in central Asia. His willingness to conciliate Washington was seen in the flap he had with Washington over the sale in 1999 of 40 Russian-built jets to North Korea. The Clinton administration pressured the Kazakh government to cancel the deal, implying that the sale could seriously compromise Kazakh-American relations. There was also a thinly veiled threat of U.S. sanctions against Kazakhstan. As a measure of the importance Nazarbayev attached to good relations with the United States, he canceled the deal with North Korea. He also called for an investigation in cooperation with U.S. authorities of the circumstances surrounding the sale; and, to discourage further deals of this kind, he transferred supervision of Kazakh arms sales abroad to the prime minister's office.[13]

For its part, the Clinton administration was not inclined to make "a federal case" out of the sale despite opposition to it given the willingness of Nazarbayev to go out of his way to assuage the United States. In addition, the administration was eager to preserve a good working relationship with the Nazarbayev government because of its interest in the transit of Kazakh oil through a Caspian region pipeline to Turkey that circumvented Russia and interfered with the perceived effort of the Kremlin to expand Russian influence over the huge Caspian oil fields. Vice President Al Gore accordingly went to Kazakhstan in December 1999 to reassure Nazarbayev that U.S. concern about the MIG sale was being addressed to its satisfaction.[14]

Nazarbayev, indeed, promptly followed through with an investigation of the decision to sell the MIGs to North Korea. In early January 2000, a Kazakhstan military tribunal opened hearings against two individuals, including a top military official, Army Chief of Staff Bakhitzhan Yertayev, charging them with the illegal sale of the Russian-made fighter planes to North Korea.[15]

Oil and Gas in Kazakh-American Relations

Of special concern to Russia by the late 1990s was an expansion of American interest in helping Kazakhstan exploit and market its vast energy resources off its Caspian shore.[16] In 1998, the State Department estimated the Caspian region's reserves to be about 178 billion barrels or more and a major portion of this wealth is in western Kazakhstan. In addition, Nazarbayev told the Organization for Security and Cooperation in Europe (OSCE) and others that he was determined to make his country one of the world's top five oil producers. For this Nazarbayev needed new routes to Kazakhstan's oil exports to Western markets. When Kazakhstan was a Soviet republic, all oil went through Russia, providing the Kremlin with significant leverage over the Kazakh leadership in the form of power to Russian closure. Nazarbayev found himself in agreement with Washington's policy of seeking new routes for the transit of central Asian oil westward that circumvented Russia, depriving the Kremlin of leverage it was ready to use to back up its influence-building initiatives. When Nazarbayev spoke in these last years of the Yeltsin era of "diversifying transport routes," he was on the same wavelength with the Americans.[17]

To Moscow's dismay, the United States backed construction of a pipeline that would carry Caspian oil of Azerbaijan and Kazakhstan to Western markets and would skirt Russia. This project was called the Baku-Tbilisi-Ceyhan pipeline and had the strong support of the governments in the territories through which the line would pass because it was a welcome means of avoiding dependence on Russian-built pipelines and of depriving the Kremlin of economic leverage that could be used to expand Russian influence. In November 1999, Nazarbayev pledged Kazakh oil for the BTC should new oil reserves be discovered, as they were, for example, around Kashagan on Kazakhstan's northern coast. In March 2001, the United States persuaded Nazarbayev to sign a memorandum of understanding in Astana confirming Kazakhstan's intention to join the BTC. The U.S. officials considered this event a signal achievement for U.S. policy in central Asia, consolidating and strengthening Kazakhstan's links to the West.[18]

The new Putin Kremlin was deeply troubled by the BTC project considering it a diplomatic setback for Russian influence-building in Kazakhstan but refused to denounce it to avoid straining relations with the United States beyond saying that the pipeline was not economically viable. But, the Kremlin also decided to match the BTC project with a new pipeline project of its own that would compete with the BTC for the oil business of Azerbaijan and Kazakhstan and exclude Georgia under the leadership of Mikhail Saakashvili, elected Georgian president in 2003. Saakashvili's leadership, with its strong undertone of anti-Russian sentiment, would become troublesome for the Kremlin given the new Georgian leadership's strong pro-West orientation—he was educated in the United States and spoke English fluently and had dreams of strengthening Georgia's links to Western Europe and the United States.[19]

It was not long, however, before it became clear that Nazarbayev did not want to see himself as a protégé of Washington and contribute to a weakening of ties to Russia. He took some of the wind out of the sails of the new Bush administration regarding the perceived achievements of its policy of influence-building in Kazakhstan. In late 2000, Kazakh officials noted that Kazakhstan favored "multiple oil transit routes, hinting at a route through Iran." Moreover, Nazarbayev refused to back a pipeline project sought by the United States that involved construction of a line underneath the Caspian to carry Kazakh oil from Kashagan to the BTC aware of the opposition to such an extension of the BTC line from both Russia and Iran purportedly on ecological grounds.[20]

Moreover, by 2004, the Nazarbayev leadership seemed to have lost some of the enthusiasm for the BTC line, citing high cost concerns and raising some doubt about a lack of certainty about the pipeline's economic viability. No doubt, Nazarbayev's apparent uncertainty about Kazakh support of the BTC was a reaction to the critical attitude of Moscow and a desire to keep Kazakh fences with Russia in good repair while, of course, keeping on the good side of the United States in the area of oil diplomacy.[21]

Russian Reactions

To some extent, Russia was a beneficiary of American help to Kazakhstan. It contributed to Kazakhstan's economic stability and, to that extent, undercut challenges to Nazarbayev's rule from extremists. And the more developed the Kazakh economy became, the more valuable it was as a partner of Russia in regional economic growth and development. Under Yeltsin these calculations served to keep Russian concerns about Kazakh-American relations at a low-key level.

On the other hand, Russian nationalists with strong anti-American sentiments did not see the situation in this light and sought a stronger Kazakh orientation toward Russia. While Nazarbayev values American friendship, he cannot afford to antagonize Moscow, which alone can protect Kazakhstan from the spread of Islamic fundamentalism from Iran and Afghanistan. Moreover, Moscow had a pretext for intervening in Kazakh internal affairs—to protect the interests of the Russian minority in Kazakhstan. Nazarbayev had skillfully balanced Kazakhstan's relations with Moscow and Washington, extracting the most he can from both. They want his friendship and are willing to pay for it.

PUTIN AND KAZAKHSTAN, 2000–2008

In the early years of the new century, newly elected Russian President Vladimir Putin was determined to conciliate Nazarbayev to assure the friendship and cooperation of Kazakhstan, especially as he focused on its oil reserves in which Russia wanted to become heavily involved. By early 2004, Putin signed agreements with Nazarbayev that linked the two countries closely together in a variety of areas. The two countries agreed that Russia would continue to rent the Baikonur Cosmodrome until the middle of the new century. Another agreement settled 98 percent of the Russian-Kazakhstan border. The two countries also agreed to increase military-technical cooperation and pledged bilateral cooperation in a host of Eurasian multilateral organizations in which both countries had membership; notably the Eurasian Economic Community, the Single Economic Space, the CIS, the CSTO, the SCO, and the Conference on Interaction and Confidence Building Measures in Asia. There also were agreements on energy cooperation. Russia provided the primary pipeline export routes, participated directly in Kazakhstan's oil production, and by 2004, Russian shareholders had bought a large number of shares of the Caspian Pipeline Consortium which had a 900-mile pipeline from Kazakhstan to the Russian Black Sea port of Novorossiysk.[22]

New Russian Difficulties in Dealing with Nazarbayev

Like Yeltsin, Putin had problems with Nazarbayev that complicated relations between Russia and Kazakhstan on the eve of 9/11. Nazarbayev wanted to protect Kazakhstan against dependence on Russian oil transit routes the Kremlin was trying to finesse. The Kazakh leader intended that Kazakhstan use a newly constructed and recently opened oil pipeline from Baku via Tbilisi to Ceyhan that skirted Russia and was supported by the United States, just the kind of behavior the Kremlin wanted to discourage for strategic and commercial reasons. In addition, Kazakhstan joined with China to build an oil pipeline from Atyrau on the Caspian seacoast to Alashankou on the Kazakh frontier with China. Nazarbayev effectively had undercut this particular aspect of Russian influence-building in his country. He was encouraged in this strategy by the United States.[23]

The Putin-led Kremlin's energy trade policy complicated its efforts to protect the interests of the Russian minority in Kazakhstan. The Kremlin could not afford to press Nazarbayev too hard on the minority issue and risk his willingness to share with Russia the production and marketing of Kazakh oil. Russian companies like LUKOIL expected the Kremlin to generate and protect opportunities to do so.

Also, Putin's attempt to "help" Kazakhstan defend its borders against other central Asian republics and the spread of Islamic fundamentalism from Iran and Afghanistan met some Kazakh resistance. Putin offered to "beef up" the Russian military force already deployed in Kazakhstan to supplement and strengthen Kazakhstan's very weak military establishment, but Nazarbayev responded cautiously to what he perceived as an intrusion into Kazakhstan's sovereignty.

Kazakhstan Draws Closer to the United States after 9/11

Nazarbayev created problems for the Russians when he decided to strengthen ties to the United States following the 9/11 tragedy.[24] Like other central Asian leaders, Nazarbayev was eager for U.S. help in the war against Islamic-inspired terrorism that worried him as much as it did the Bush administration. Though a devout Muslim, Nazarbayev is a secularist opposed to the militant and radical Islamist ideas taking hold in his country. He saw the genesis of radical Islamic political groups as a threat to his leadership and authority. The U.S. declaration of war against the terrorism of al Qaeda resonated with Nazarbayev, and while deeply loyal to Russia, he saw a strengthening of Kazakhstan's relations with the United States in its best interests. Ironically, on the issue of fighting terrorism, he had the support and cooperation of the Kremlin despite its growing concern about American influence-building agenda in ex-Soviet central Asia.[25]

Nazarbayev offered the United States the use of Kazakhstan territory for the refueling of American aircraft going to and from Afghanistan. Then, at the end of March 2003, he took another step to strengthen relations with Washington. Foreign Minister Kassym-Jomart Tokyaev expressed support for the U.S. policy in Iraq, especially the goal of demilitarizing the country in the wake of a long and intense military built by Saddam Hussein, allegedly in the area of nuclear weapons. Tokyaev saw that Iraq's perceived military buildup threatened the security of central Asia, including Kazakhstan. Washington responded approvingly with Secretary of Defense Donald Rumsfeld's visit to Kazakhstan to underline the U.S. concern with security in the Caspian basin.[26] On May 30, 2003, the Kazakh parliament voted to send 25 peacekeeping troops to Iraq to help with de-mining and the restoration of water supplies.[27] In addition, Nazarbayev, having joined the U.S. -sponsored Partnership for Peace in 1997, by 2004 had become more active in the organization.[28] And, on February 23, 2004, Kazakhstan announced its intention of formally joining the U.S.-backed Baku-Tbilisi-Ceyhan (BTC) oil pipeline project which is needed to Kazakh business to become profitable.[29]

For its part, the United States envisaged a "strategic partnership" with Kazakhstan which would be a coequal ally in its war against terrorism. In addition, the United States sought an expansion of trade with Kazakhstan and a role in strengthening its border security. The United States also had certain expectations that ultimately would not be easily fulfilled. The Bush administration wanted the Kazakh government to improve the investment climate compromised by rampant corruption through making it "transparent"; it wanted Nazarbayev to maintain a pace of democratization which meant movement away from his neo-Communist dictatorship of Kazakhstan since its independence in 1991. And in the area of trade expansion, the United States made clear its interest in sharing a role in the mining and marketing of Kazakhstan's enormous reservoir of energy resources, in particular offshore Caspian oil.[30]

U.S. POLICY IN KAZAKHSTAN, 2000–2008

It was not long before the newly elected Bush administration encountered problems with Kazakhstan. These problems had to do with the domestic policies of the Kazakh government, notably Nazarbayev's relentless authoritarianism. Other problems had to do with corruption throughout the Kazakh political system, especially in elections, and Nazarbayev's unrelenting closeness to Russia while he tried to cooperate with the United States.[31]

Nazarbayev's Authoritarian Rule

The Bush administration was deeply troubled by the broad sweep of Nazarbayev's authoritarianism and political repression. The U.S. State Department took note of further harassment of former Prime Minister Kazhegeldin. In September 2001, Kazhegeldin, who by this time had fled Kazakhstan, fearing for his life, was sentenced in absentia to 10 years in prison on charges of abuse of authority and taking bribes. Kazhegeldin's supporters charged that the authorities were out to get him in order to keep him from challenging Nazarbayev's leadership. The State Department seemed to agree, saying that the investigation and punishment of Kazhegeldin "appeared motivated politically."[32]

Furthermore, in 2002, Nazarbayev's repressive behavior seemed to reach something of a climax with a crackdown on the media. Journalists were attacked and beaten, threatened with death, and jailed, while media outlets critical of Nazarbayev's authoritarian leadership and supportive of opposition political groups were special targets. These groups had provoked the ire of the regime because of their interest in investigating state corruption, in particular Nazarbayev's personal control of about $1.4 billion in U.S. aid that had been deposited in a Swiss bank account under his name. While aware of the Kazakh government's financial irregularities in handling U.S. funds, Washington was not inclined to make a big issue of them and risk antagonizing Kazakhstan.[33]

Corruption in the Kazakh Government

That said, in early 2003, the U.S. government did start investigating the practice of "kickbacks" involving payments by U.S. oil interests to Kazakh officials for rights to participate in the mining of Kazakh oil. From the Kazakh vantage point, these deals were justified given the fact that when the United States and other oil enterprises started coming to Kazakhstan in the early 1990s, the Kazakh government was very generous to them and now believed the time had come to make foreigners pay more. Washington strongly disapproved of the perceived Kazakh view that it was "payback time" for the wealthy U.S. oil companies.[34]

But, there certainly were other important aspects of the rampant corruption plaguing Kazakhstan and deeply troubling the United States. Nazarbayev's government was a nepotistic kleptocracy that made U.S. dealings with it difficult inasmuch as the Bush administration had introduced its "National Strategy to Internationalize Efforts against Kleptocracy," which can be roughly defined as a perennial, pervasive public graft. The administration called for the denial of access to the U.S. financial system by corrupt leaders. Bush called for the kind of transparent and accountable government that Kazakhstan under Nazarbayev conspicuously lacked. And, of course, continued cooperation between the United States and Kazakhstan in Afghanistan and Iraq risked being undermined by the administration's public complaints about corruption in central Asian republics.[35]

Electoral Fraud

Widespread irregularities in the September 2004 parliamentary elections also caused tension between Nazarbayev and the United States. Human rights monitors from the OSCE deployed throughout the country complained that the election had been rigged. Government employees told other voters how to vote and threatened some voters with loss of economic privileges such as subsidized housing if they voted the wrong way. This happened despite promises by government officials that the election would be free and fair.[36]

Results of the parliamentary election were what the Nazarbayev regime wanted and had worked for. Nazarbayev's Otan Party won the largest block of seats and controlled the new parliament, continuing its "rubber-stamp" tradition of supporting most of the president's policies. In the succeeding months, the Kazakh parliament passed a battery of laws restricting political freedoms designed to harass and undermine potential sources of criticism of and opposition to the Nazarbayev regime. The Kazakh parliament amended the election law to ban demonstrations between elections and the announcement of results.[37]

The Nazarbayev regime dismissed accusations of antidemocratic behavior, encouraged by Russian silence on this issue that confirmed in still another way the Kremlin's tolerance of Kazakhstan's rough authoritarian rule. In addition, there was a steady growth of Kazakh resentment toward the United States over its irritating and somewhat patronizing insistence that Nazarbayev pay more attention to human rights, press freedom, and the holding of elections free of government interference.[38]

The Manipulated 2005 Presidential Election

George Soros's advice was ignored as Nazarbayev made plans for the upcoming presidential election in December 2005, which he was determined to win and get another seven-year term, his third since Kazakhstan gained independence in 1991. Nazarbayev's chief advantage in the weeks leading up to the election was his popularity throughout Kazakhstan. In this respect, he had a great advantage over the incumbent presidential candidates in recent elections in Georgia in 2003 and Ukraine in 2004 where Shevardnadze and Kuchma, respectively, had become immensely unpopular and, therefore, vulnerable to defeat. In particular, Nazarbayev increased pressure on opposition groups, intimidating them to discourage them from mounting a real challenge to his candidacy. He acted equivalently with the country's media, alerting them, as he had done many times in the past, to the danger of supporting opposition to him and to his reelection. He unabashedly asked Kazakh voters not to read opposition newspapers calling for change, insisting that his government was the best guarantor of national economic well-being.[39]

Nazarbayev was warned by Soros in June 2005 that his authoritarian behavior, in particular the obstacles he has placed in the way of democratization through the enactment of restrictive legislation, was opening the way to the kind of political explosions he was trying to avoid. Soros told Nazarbayev that by oppressing his critics, he was inviting the growth of the kind of political extremism other Eurasian republics had experienced recently and that toppled governments and wrought the kind of political change in Kazakhstan that would lead sooner than later to an end of his rule.[40]

Nazarbayev ignored Soros; but he was sensitive to American criticism. Washington was annoyed and alarmed as it was now as clear as ever before that Nazarbayev in all likelihood would not allow free, open, and competitive elections. Nazarbayev had to disarm American criticisms of him. In August 2005, he sent Foreign Minister Tokyaev to Washington to reassure the Bush administration that, whatever criticism it might have of aspects of his domestic policies, on the international scene, he was in agreement with the U.S. policy in Iraq. Bush administration officials acknowledged approvingly Kazakhstan's strategic importance to the United States. U.S. Secretary of State Condoleeza Rice and Secretary of Defense Donald Rumsfeld both spoke supportively of Nazarbayev as a "reliable strategic partner," suggesting that whatever qualms the Bush leadership had about Nazarbayev's authoritarian behavior, he was still a valuable backer of the United States in its fight against terrorism in the central Asian region.[41]

The United States was dismayed by the 2005 Kazakh presidential election. Nazarbayev won another seven-year term with more than 90 percent of the vote. But, the OSCE said the voting had been rigged to assure Nazarbayev's stunning victory. According to the OSCE, there were cases of multiple voting and ballot box stuffing. The OSCE said further that there was pressure on students to vote for Nazarbayev and that in some places where there were electronic voting machines, votes were cast automatically for the voter in favor of Nazarbayev.[42]

Nazarbayev's Closeness to Russia

Not surprisingly—indeed, predictably—the persistence of American criticisms of the authoritarian character of his leadership and his failure to make the significant progress in democratization he had pledged to the U.S. authorities had annoyed—and may even have some what undermined—Nazarbayev's reputation if not his authority, encouraging him in 2004 and afterward to tilt Kazakhstan toward Russia. Even as he strengthened ties with the United States in the opening years of the new century, Nazarbayev had been careful, if not artful, in avoiding actions that could prejudice the strong, close relations he had with Russia which, he knew, was annoyed by his receptivity to U.S. overtures. Clearly, to Russia's satisfaction, Nazarbayev never wanted to allow his policy toward the United States to be seen as a gesture at Russia's expense or, worse, a sign that his pro-Russian sentiment had diminished.

For its part, Russia helped Nazarbayev make a tilt in its favor by carefully refraining from criticizing the Kazakh government's repressive policies. Indeed, the Kremlin indirectly supported Nazarbayev's authoritarian rule, which the Kremlin considered the norm in CIS countries at the present stage of their political development in the post-Soviet era. In addition, Nazarbayev reportedly preferred dealing with Russia because the Kremlin did not put him down, as it seemed the Americans were willing to do when they spoke critically and even patronizingly of democratization in Kazakhstan. Moreover, Nazarbayev apparently felt he could negotiate with Russia from a position of strength given Kazakhstan's economic stability attributable to its steady economic growth and energy wealth.[43]

The January 2004 Kazakh-Russian Summit

Indeed, the Nazarbayev regime left no doubt with the Kremlin about the importance it attached to good relations with Russia. In January 2004, Putin and Nazarbayev held a summit in the Kazakh capital of Astana with each emphasizing its commitment to bilateral friendship and cooperation. The summit had great symbolic importance even though the Kazakh leadership made no great concessions to the Russians—for example, shying away from a Russian proposal to create a "Common Economic Space" (CES) in Eurasia that would include Kazakhstan, Belarus, and Ukraine. Of special concern was the Russian wish that CES members use the ruble as a medium of exchange. The negative impact of the August 1968 Russian currency crisis made CES members wary.[44]

Nevertheless, the summit did illustrate, and contribute to, a new stage in Kazakh-Russian friendship despite Nazarbayev's continuing, if more cautious, interest in preserving links to the United States. For example, during the summit, Kazakh Foreign Minister Kassym-Jomart Tokyaev characterized Kazakh-Russian relations as a "real strategic partnership." On January 12, after the conclusion of the summit, *Izvestia* noted that "Kazakhstan is the only Common Economic Space country maintaining constructive relations with Russia."[45]

At the January 2004 conference, Tokyaev also showed enthusiasm about developing a joint Kazakh-Russian space program, and other Kazakh officials spoke of improving trade between the two countries. In addition, Nazarbayev strengthened Kazakh-Russian relations in the strategic sphere when defense officials of both sides agreed to cooperate in the planning of troop deployments under the auspices of the Russian-led CSTO.[46]

At the summit, Nazarbayev accommodated Russia in the economic area. Russia had been lobbying aggressively to get Kazakhstan to give some oil transit business to the Russian Baku-Novorossiysk pipeline. Nazarbayev was personally inclined to accommodate Russia—Kazakhstan still had not firmly committed to the BTC pipeline—and cut a deal with Russia to cooperate jointly in developing the Tyub-Karagan and Atash offshore sectors of the Caspian Sea, a project in which the Russian side, that is, LUKOIL, might end up investing several billion dollars.[47]

The momentum of improving Kazakh relations with Russia continued, especially as Kazakh relations with the United States deteriorated over Nazarbayev's increasingly authoritarian style of leadership. Following the January 2004 summit, there were other high-level meetings between Nazarbayev and Putin, one in early April in Novo-Ogasrevo in the Moscow region and others in May. In mid-May, the two leaders agreed to allow visa-free travel between the two countries.[48]

In June 2005, Putin held still another summit with Nazarbayev to discuss an expansion of trade between their countries, especially in the energy sector. Kazakhstan's trade with Russia had been steadily increasing, having reached $7 billion in value by mid-2005 and Nazarbayev observed that the Russian oil company LUKOIL had contributed about $2 billion to Kazakhstan's economy. Putin seemed ready in the Summer and Fall of 2005 to back Nazarbayev's planned bid for still another seven-year presidential term in presidential election tentatively slated for early December.[49]

THE UNITED STATES AND NAZARBAYEV'S PRO-RUSSIAN TILT

The evident pro-Russian tilt of Nazarbayev had a sobering impact on the Bush administration. Bush did not want to compromise the friendship and cooperation of a moderate Muslim leader in central Asia who had allowed NATO aircraft headed for Afghanistan to fly over his country, sent a company of soldiers to Iraq, and controlled vast resources of oil and gas that American companies were helping him to exploit. Indeed, Nazarbayev's strategic importance to the United States increased when it had to cut off relations with Uzbekistan in response to the brutality of its government's crackdown on protestors in Andijon in May 2005. The United States needed a reliable partner in the region and Nazarbayev wanted very much to remain a friend and ally of the United States, especially in its war against terrorism.

A Softening of U.S. Policy

In April 2005, the U.S. Senate congratulated Kazakhstan on the 10th anniversary of Nazarbayev's decision to transfer nuclear weapons deployed in Kazakhstan in the Soviet period to Russia, making the country nuclear-free, in response to demands from both the Kremlin and Washington. After the last nuclear warhead was shipped to Russia in April 1995, Kazakhstan subsequently adhered to the Nuclear Non-Proliferation Treaty.[50]

The Senate's gesture seemed intended to remind Nazarbayev that whatever complaints the United States had made about aspects of his domestic policies, Washington still considered friendship between the two countries of significant strategic importance and expected Kazakh-American cooperation to continue. Richard Lugar, Republican Chairman of the Senate Foreign Relations, in offering the resolution of commemoration to the Senate for its approval underscored the contrast between Kazakhstan and states in Asia such as India, Pakistan, and North Korea which continued to test nuclear weapons.[51]

Furthermore, the United States had been very careful in commenting on Nazarbayev's "landslide" victory of 90 percent of the popular vote in the Kazakh presidential election in December 2005. Criticism of its failure to meet democratic standards, especially in regard to freedom of the media, was restrained with the U.S. Ambassador to Kazakhstan John Ordway commenting on "very positive steps in the electoral process" though he quickly acknowledged that "more work needs to be done for Kazakhstan to come up to the standards that Kazakhstan aspires to and has committed to in its international obligations."[52]

Adam Ereli, deputy spokesman for the U.S. Department of State, commented on the more positive aspects of the OSCE assessments of the 2005 presidential election, saying that there had been improvements and the election reflected the will of the Kazakh voters even if the actual voting was not completely in line with OSCE standards and that there would have to be "investigations of irregularities and prosecution of those suspected of violating electoral law."[53] Nevertheless, Ereli also said that the United States "looks forward to working with . . . the Government of Kazakhstan to strengthen the culture and institutions of democracy."[54] Clearly, the Bush administration, like Nazarbayev himself, wanted to preserve a good working relationship between the United States and Kazakhstan while maintaining the best of ties possible with the Russians.

This U.S. restraint was criticized by the country's political opposition, which was disappointed by the failure of the United States to be more critical and more openly sympathetic to its complaints about Nazarbayev's unfair tactics that helped him win his 90 percent plus majority.[55] Lest there was any doubt about new U.S. priorities in Kazakhstan and other central Asian republics, U.S. Secretary of State Condoleeza Rice observed at this time that "Washington is ready to cooperate even with non-democratic regimes in the struggle against terrorism," implying that the struggle against terrorism *was* more important to the United States than support of democracy.[56]

Throughout 2006 and 2007, the United States proceeded cautiously in its concern about the Kazakhstan government's repressive policies to avoid alienating Nazarbayev. For example, in May 2006, on a brief visit to Kazakhstan, Vice President Dick Cheney acknowledged the importance the United States attached to good relations with Kazakhstan, praising Nazarbayev for the stability of his leadership. Cheney did not lecture the Kazakh regime on its perceived antidemocratic behavior despite strong feelings about it in Washington.[57]

The September 2006 Kazakh-U.S. Summit

U.S.-Kazakh relations received a boost with Nazarbayev's visit to Washington at the end of September 2006. The Kazakh president hoped to solidify relations with the United States and gain its support of his ambition to make Kazakhstan a regional leader. He knew the Americans were, as usual, unhappy with repressive aspects of his leadership, especially his poor human rights record, its manipulation of elections, and its harsh treatment of pro-democracy groups.

Nazarbayev visited Washington also to polish his country's image, tarnished by charges by the United States, as well as other outsiders, of corruption and nepotism that he correctly believed scared off foreign investment. At the moment of his visit, Nazarbayev stood accused of accepting bribes in the 1990s from an American businessman, James Giffen. As he went to Washington, he certainly had no intention of changing his authoritarian style even as Kazakh officials insisted without regard for the facts that Kazakhstan was making progress with a program of democratization that obviously was no more than what one critic called "window dressing."[58]

Nazarbayev counted on the Bush administration to keep a lid on criticism of its repressive behavior at least, because of its need of his cooperation with the U.S.-driven Baku-Tbilisi-Ceyhan oil pipeline. This line bypassed Russia even while the Kazakh government insisted that Kazakhstan valued highly its relationship with Russia and under no circumstances intended, as Senat Kushkumbayev, deputy director of the Kazakhstan Institute for Strategic Studies, put it, that the United States would become "the sole and exclusive partner for our country."[59]

The United States was willing to limit criticism of Nazarbayev's leadership. For example, in a meeting with Kazakh Foreign Minister Tokyaev, Secretary of State in September 2006 Condoleeza Rice carefully avoided reference to the Kazakh government's complaint that two prominent American-funded democracy organizations in Kazakhstan were spying for the United States. The Kazakh government had forced these organizations, the Democratic Institute for International Affairs and the International Republican Institute, led by major U.S. political figures, notably former Secretary of State Madeline Albright and Senator John McCain, and funded by the U.S. government, to suspend operations. Moreover, in response to what Nazarbayev considered the anti-regime purposes and activities of foreign-funded nongovernmental organizations, his government had put through a law very similar to one passed in Russia to restrict the activities of foreign organizations funded by outsiders and used to support political opposition groups.[60]

Complexities of the U.S.-Kazakh Relationship

By early 2007, the Bush administration's handling of Kazakhstan had become extremely complicated, requiring a delicate diplomacy difficult to manage. The administration had to balance the objective of promoting democracy with the need to protect and preserve friendship with a country like Kazakhstan that was making little, if any, progress toward democratization. Yevgeny Zhovtis of the Kazakhstan International Bureau for Human Rights and Rule of Law, a nongovernmental organization that received funds from the U.S. Embassy and the National Endowment for Democracy, put the U.S. dilemma in Kazakhstan and other ex-Soviet central Asian republics bluntly but accurately: "There are four enemies of human rights [in Kazakhstan]: oil, gas, the war on terrorism, and geopolitical considerations."[61]

Complicating U.S. diplomacy with Kazakhstan has been Nazarbayev's popularity despite his ruthless use of coercion to reinforce loyalty to him. According to S. Frederick Starr of the Johns Hopkins University, part of this popularity derives from the fact that Kazakhstan's petrodollars are beginning to trickle down to an emerging middle class, which seems willing to tolerate, at least for the moment, his repressive leadership for the sake of economic benefits it brings to them.[62]

The United States has no alternative other than patience and caution in furthering the cause of democratization in Kazakhstan.[63] There are no opposition leaders or organization capable of challenging his antidemocratic rule should Washington seek to back such forces for the sake of encouraging regime change, as it did in presidential elections held in Georgia in 2003 and Ukraine in 2004. The best the Bush administration seemed able to do is to gently nudge the Nazarbayev regime to go easy on individuals and groups not under government control, and to try to persuade Nazarbayev to let them survive and criticize his rule as long as they did not challenge it, disrupt it, or attack it. For his part, Nazarbayev has been willing to indulge the United States, though only minimally, on the issue of ideology while continuing to act as if he was entitled to U.S. restraint in return for his cooperation with U.S. policy in central Asia, especially his support of the BTC pipeline.[64]

That said, Kazakh relations with the United States remained solid and stable as the Bush-Putin eras were drawing to a close in 2008, at least as strong as Kazakh relations with Russia. By 2008 the United States had become the largest foreign investor in Kazakhstan with a growth of overall trade between the United States and Kazakhstan to a value of $12 billion.

It was clear that Kazakhstan under Nazarbayev remained a firm partner of the United States in the war against terrorism in the greater Caspian/central Asian region despite the maintenance of strong and close strategic links between Kazakhstan and Russia.[65]

Furthermore, during his visit to Astana in May 2006, Vice President Dick Cheney made only an oblique reference to Nazarbayev's still robust authoritarianism in leading his country, being careful not to open any can of political worms that might compromise or undermine the Kazakh-American cooperation. He made a passing reference to the way in which Russia seemed to resist development of strong democracies in many countries of the ex-Soviet space. Hardly anything critical was said about the sluggishness of democratization in Kazakhstan under Nazarbayev's leadership, and Cheney said nothing about the country's rampant corruption that reached up to the highest levels of the political system. Clearly, by this time, the Bush administration had downgraded the ideological aspect of the U.S. policy toward ex-Soviet central Asia, opting for caution and restraint in that area to assure continued cooperation in the areas of strategy and security.[66]

Countervailing Pressures from Russia and the SCO

While the United States worked to strengthen ties with Kazakhstan, especially in the economic and military areas, the Kremlin was in a campaign of its own to weaken the U.S. pitch and lure Kazakhstan closer to Moscow. Moreover, during 2006 and 2007, the SCO asked Nazarbayev to support a call to the United States to end its military presence in central Asia. Indeed, Nazarbayev shared the palpable fear of the Kremlin of the spread of U.S.-encouraged "color revolutions," which referred to U.S. and Western support of pro-democratic and pro-West political opposition candidates in presidential elections. For all his pro-U.S. policies, Nazarbayev shares the concern of Russia and China of the U.S. policy of regime change. And whenever he is criticized for antidemocratic behavior, he tended to accelerate his tilt toward Russia and also China.

Some in the Kazakh ruling elite have even sharper views about the American military presence on central Asian territory. Bolat Sultanov, director of the Kazakhstan Institute for Strategic Studies, which was founded and is controlled by Nazarbayev, has said that a U.S. military presence in central Asia undermines Russian and Chinese security. He has called for the withdrawal of American bases and military personnel from Kazakhstan to place the country in conformity with the views of the SCO and in particular its leading members.[67] Still, Nazarbayev has tried to keep his fences mended with the United States, continuing to value Kazakhstan's links to Washington, even in the military area because of substantial benefits, not least in military training and education to strengthen Kazakhstan's counterterrorism capability.

The May 2007 Turkmenbasy Meeting

Nazarbayev continued to cultivate and accommodate the Kremlin and to preserve a balance of interest in his dealings with Russia and the United States. For example, in May 2007, at Turkmenbasy on Turkmenistan's Caspian coast, Nazarbayev signed a tentative agreement to be formalized in September with Putin and Turkmenistan President Gurbanguly Berdimukhamedov to construct a new gas pipeline to Russia.[68] This agreement, when executed, would be a tremendous plus for Russia and a significant setback for the United States. With such a pipeline running through Russian territory and therefore under its control, Russia would have a much greater influence over the marketing of west central Asia's enormous natural gas reserves. The Kremlin could expand its policy of buying central Asian gas cheap and sell it dear in lucrative Western markets, including the United States which is already buying oil from Russia's LUKOIL. Moreover, by expanding its control over the marketing of central Asian energy resources, Russia increased its ability to influence the domestic and foreign policies of the central Asian republics and also gained leverage with the Western countries that buy this gas and oil.

At the Turkmenbasy meeting, Russia's Minister for Energy Viktor Khristenko demeaned the proposed BTC that would allow Caspian oil headed for Western markets to bypass Russia, observing that this project had big "technological, legal, and environmental risks."[69] But, central Asian leaders, including Nazarbayev, refused to rule out participation in the BTC pipeline or others that might be built and would bypass Russia. Nazarbayev and the other leaders were determined not to burn any bridges to the West, especially the United States, in response to Russian pressure.

That said, the Kazakh leadership did please the Kremlin when it suspended environmental permits for a consortium of foreign energy companies developing the huge Kashagan oil field in the Caspian threatening to slow transit of Kazakh oil to lucrative Western markets. The ostensible reason for the Kazakh action was environmental and monetary. A Kazakh accusation that the consortium drillers were damaging the sea's marine life was not without some justification. But, it was also true that the Kazakh government simply wanted more compensation for its concessions to foreigners developing its energy resources. Moreover, the action also was intended to send a message to the Kremlin that Nazarbayev was far from being in the pocket of Western investors and was ready to imitate Russian actions against the U.S. corporation SHELL in the Sakhalin Islands where the Kremlin wanted SHELL to cede control of oil exploration to Gazprom. Finally, the Kazakh action also seemed to aim at keeping something of a balance between Russia and the West in their commercial relations with Kazakhstan as it continued to welcome Western investment in developing the Kazakh energy sector.[70]

For its part, the United States has continued to encourage Nazarbayev and other central Asian leaders not to look to Russia but to the United States for deals to sell natural gas and oil in Western markets using pipelines that do not cross Russian territory and therefore are not under Russian control. In the case of Kazakhstan, Vice President Dick Cheney on a visit to Astana in August 2006 had lobbied hard with Nazarbayev for his support of new oil and gas transit facilities that bypassed Russia. Cheney was blunt about his objective: he told Nazarbayev that cooperation in the marketing of energy with Russia would only encourage and strengthen the Kremlin's "tools for intimidation and blackmail" in its dealings with the ex-Soviet states.[71]

THE CHINA FACTOR

By 2004, China was already an important factor in the Russian-American rivalry in Kazakhstan, as well as in other ex-Soviet central Asian republics, partly because of Chinese ambitions in the region and partly because Nazarbayev wanted good relations with Beijing, a competitor and rival of both the Russians and the Americans in central Asia and in particular in Kazakhstan. Chinese interest in Kazakhstan is driven by several circumstances, not least eagerness to participate in—and profit from—oil exploration, production, and marketing. Kazakhstan is planning construction of a pipeline eastward to funnel some 73 million barrels (10 tons) of crude oil to the Chinese market.[72] In its oil-driven competition for influence with Russia and the United States, China has not asked embarrassing questions about Nazarbayev's conservative and repressive rule of Kazakhstan. Beijing has no problem practicing a benevolent neutrality on the issue of Nazarbayev's harsh rule because he seems able to maintain his country's internal stability and external security in the face of the expansion of Islamic radicalism.[73]

For its part, Kazakhstan had much to gain from, and therefore has worked for, good relations with China. The Nazarbayev leadership recognizes that China intends to be a regional player, and he wants to exploit this Chinese ambition to the benefit of Kazakhstan in its relations with Moscow and Washington. Indeed, friendly relations with China have automatically strengthened the hand of Kazakhstan in dealing with Russia and the United States as they try to befriend him and tilt his government's policies in their direction. In Nazarbayev's view, China can be just as helpful in fighting terrorism, religious extremism, and drug trafficking and assisting in the marketing of Kazakh energy exports in Asian markets.[74]

There are tensions that Nazarbayev has to manage in Kazakhstan's relations with China. Kazakhstan for some time has tolerated the presence of Uighur separatists who live close to China's Xinjiang province, have been a bone of contention between Kazakhstan and China, and in a Kazakh view provide China with a pretext of seeking control of Kazakh territory where the separatists have a refuge. In particular, the Uighurstan Liberation Organization and the United Revolutionary Front of East Turkestan have caused trouble for China. Beijing has called upon Kazakhstan to do something about this irritant and prevent it from worsening, say by endorsing, as some members of Nazarbayev's government would like the establishment of an independent Uighur nation in the Chinese province of Xinjiang.[75] As of 2008, this issue remains a bone of contention.

Possible implications of a growing friendship between Kazakhstan and China for Moscow and Washington include increased Kazakh independence both in the areas of energy and security. Possibly, Russia and the United States might draw closer in central Asia, diminishing the competitive aspect of their relationship for the sake of countering an expansion of Chinese influence in the region. Or, Moscow and Washington might form a triple entente, including China, to manage development of Kazakhstan and other ex-Soviet central Asian states, say by blocking ambitions of any one of them for regional hegemony that would reinforce their independence vis-à-vis powerful outsiders, never mind strengthening and protecting the secular states from the onslaught of militant Islamic radicals.

THE IRAN FACTOR

After the 9/11 tragedy and the escalation of U.S. interest in central Asia, Kazakhstan's relations with Iran steadily improved though they had been good if not "eventful" since 1992. In part the expansion of ties between the two countries was the result of initiatives by both Astana and Teheran. For Nazarbayev, a good relationship between the two countries was useful in diminishing Kazakhstan's isolation and increasing its leverage with Russia and the United States. Iran was motivated to strengthen ties with Kazakhstan because of its own influence-building agenda in central Asia that seemed logical and inevitable given the commitment of both countries to Islam. Iran in particular shared with Russia the goal of limiting U.S. influence in Kazakhstan and elsewhere in central Asia, especially after 9/11. In addition, Iran had a special interest in the Caspian Sea, demanding a 20 percent share in Caspian natural resources.[76]

But, the major Iranian objective in Kazakhstan after 9/11 was persuasion of Nazarbayev to avoid allowing the United States to establish a military presence in Kazakhstan or anywhere else in central Asia, according to Iranian President Mohammed Khatami who met with Nazarbayev in Kazakhstan in April 2002 to develop a common front against the United States. The prospect of an *entente* between these two Muslim leaders despite their sharp religious differences apparently deeply troubled the Bush administration which promptly sent Secretary of Defense Donald Rumsfeld to Kazakhstan and other central Asian republics to assure they would live up to their pledges and promises of cooperation with the United States in the war against terrorism. Washington dreaded the prospect of a "geographical union" of Iran, Russia, Kazakhstan, and possibly China to oppose post-9/11 U.S. military influence-building in central Asia.[77]

For his part, Nazarbayev was committed to staying on good terms with both the United States and Iran, taking steps to conciliate both. After providing Khatami with a very warm reception in Astana, Nazarbayev raised the possibility of building an oil pipeline from Kazakhstan to Iran through Turkmenistan, spoke of the value of Kazakhstan's grain trade with Iran, and praised an Iranian-Kazakhstan railway that began service in March 2002. At the same time, however, Nazarbayev signed with the United States a Protocol of Commission for Commercial, Technical, and Cultural Cooperation and a declaration of friendly relations. But, the symbolic importance of the Protocol for Kazakh-American relations was diminished somewhat by an evident improvement of Kazakh-Chinese relations, with China looking to Kazakhstan for help in limiting the expansion of Iranian influence in ex-Soviet central Asia. In April 2002, Chinese Premier Jiang Zemin visited Iran and spoke about a revival of "Silk Road Ties" that had to do with an ancient trade route from China across central Asia. While the United States might benefit from a Kazakh-China entente to constrain Iranian influence-building in central Asia, it would not like to see Kazakhstan drawing closer to China which opposed the post-9/11 buildup of U.S. military power in the region to the detriment of China's own influence-building agenda there.[78]

A reaffirmation of Nazarbayev's determination to maintain good ties to Iran despite its escalating conflict with the United States was his visit to Teheran in mid-October 2007 to meet with Ayatollah Khamenei and President Mahmoud Ahmadinejad. Both sides were eager to expand trade, which had exceeded $2 billion in 2006. On the summit agenda was cooperation in the construction of a railway from Kazakhstan to Iran by way of Turkmenistan 800 kilometers in length and of an oil terminal at Neka in northern Iran. Moreover, the trade in Kazakh grain had become so important for Iran that it had built a grain elevator for storage.[79] These strong Kazakh economic ties with Iran precluded the possibility of a disruption in relations between the two countries that would have been of advantage to both the United States and China.

Eventually, however, the severe deterioration in Iranian relations with the United States and other Western countries over Teheran's nuclear policies became a source of concern to Kazakhstan. While Kazakhstan has unequivocally supported Iran's sovereign right to use nuclear technology for peaceful purposes, it has echoed Western calls for a guarantee that Teheran will not use its nuclear technology to build weapons of mass destruction. Indeed, in June 2008, Kazakhstan's Foreign Minister Kassym-Jomart Tokyaev reminded the Iranian leadership of Kazakhstan's elimination of its nuclear weapons arsenal and has opposed use of nuclear technology for military purposes. At the same time, during a visit to Teheran on June 6, 2008, Tokyaev tried to reassure the Iranian government that Kazakhstan was not, as the Iranians seemed to think, negotiating with the United States over the establishment of an American military base on Kazakhstan's territory that could be used for the purpose of launching a Western air strike on Iran. Unconvinced, the Iranian side refused to give a guarantee not to make nuclear weapons.[80]

By mid-2008, Nazarbayev's strategy of preserving a friendship with states in rivalry with one another for the benefit of Kazakh interests had reached a new level of complexity. While Kazakhstan continued to place high value on friendly and cooperative relations with Iran, especially in the area of trade in oil and grain—Kazakhstan was steadily increasing its sale of oil to Iran, despite the latter's own enormous oil reserves—the Kazakh leader could not let this relationship undermine in any way Kazakhstan's growing and equally valuable relationship with the United States. Moreover, there were Chinese interests in the Iranian-American imbroglio for Kazakhstan to consider, in particular China's interest in admitting Iran and Afghanistan into the SCO, a step that Tokyaev strongly opposed, saying that these countries "were not ready for membership."[81]

What Tokyaev really meant was that the United States and Western Europe opposed Iranian membership in the SCO lest it encourages an expansion of Iran influence-building in central Asia, and Kazakhstan did not want to antagonize the United States by supporting an expansion of Iranian influence in Asia. Moreover, there was a growing sense in the West that the SCO, dominated by Russia and China, was becoming increasingly anti-American, making it all the more difficult for the Kazakh leadership to remain on good terms with both Teheran and Washington. In sum, Kazakhstan would like to see a normalization of relations between Iran and the United States because of the frustrating difficulties of remaining friendly with both Teheran and Washington while they seem to be heading inexorably to a military clash—Iran "upped the ante" on prospects of such a clash when it threatened in mid-2008 to close the Strait of Hormuz if it were attacked.[82]

THE GEORGIA FACTOR

The Russian military penetration of Georgia in August 2008 provoked by long-standing Russian grievances against the Saakashvili leadership, especially in regard to its efforts to coerce a return of South Ossetia to full Georgian control, was a clear message to Nazarbayev. The Kremlin did not want Kazakhstan and the other ex-Soviet republics in the Caucasus and Caspian region to draw too closely to the West, especially the United States, and was prepared to use force to block a conspicuous tilt on the part of the countries in this region toward the United States. While Nazarbayev has been far more deferential to and respectful of Russia and has carefully avoided rhetoric and/or actions suggestive of a challenge to its claims to be the paramount Power in the ex-Soviet space, aggressive Russian policy toward Georgia was meant as a signal to him and other central Asian leaders that an excessive closeness to the United States in the name of fighting terrorism in the region was unacceptable and would not be tolerated.[83]

That said, while Nazarbayev did tell Putin that "Georgia had been 'unwise' to send troops into South Ossetia and urged all involved parties to seek diplomatic solutions,"[84] like other central Asian members of the SCO, Nazarbayev, for all his deferentiality to the Kremlin, refused to accommodate its request in mid-August for an endorsement of Russian policy in Georgia. Nazarbayev saw his country's best interests in the East-West international crisis over Georgia served by remaining aloof and denying Russia the kind of backing that could help legitimize the Russian occupation of South Ossetia, the Russian military penetration of Georgian territory as far west as Gori, and the Russian decision to recognize the independence of South Ossetia and Abkhazia. The liabilities for Nazarbayev of supporting Russian policy in Georgia were several, not least the imposition of a strain in Kazakh-U.S. relations which Nazarbayev was determined to keep in good repair. At the same time, Nazarbayev, like other central Asian leaders, were reluctant to give their blessing to a Russian policy that could be used against them should they become unacceptably, in the view of Moscow, independent in ways the Kremlin considered detrimental to Russian strategic interests, notably by allowing the United States a military presence on their territory for an extended period of time.

CONCLUSIONS

On balance, the United States has benefited from its efforts to work with Nazarbayev despite his dictatorial antidemocratic leadership of Kazakhstan. In the first place, his compulsive dictatorship left opposition groups, including Islamists, little room for maneuver, marginalizing their political influence. From the U.S. perspective, this means one less place for terrorists to find a base. The Bush administration also counts Kazakhstan in the American-led entente of nations willing to confront Islamic-inspired terrorism in central Asia. The United States has been willing to risk some of this cooperation in order to promote democratic values in Kazakhstan. Nazarbayev is annoyed by the unrelenting American calls for democratization. Indeed, the heavy U.S. pressure on him had the effect of encouraging him to maintain close ties to the Kremlin and refrain from actions that could provoke it. In effect, the contradictory character of U.S. policy, which offers support but complicates Nazarbayev's inclination to take it by relentlessly criticizing him in ways that could weaken his grip on power, has kept him open to Moscow's influence-building.

In the case of Kazakhstan as in some other central Asian republics, notably Turkmenistan, an important aspect of Russian and American policy had to do with its vast energy resources. Both Russia and the United States want to help Kazakhstan market its oil and natural gas. For the Kremlin, it was a matter of increasing its earnings from the sale of imported Kazakh energy to the West and simultaneously keeping other Powers such as the United States and China from doing the same. For its part, the United States wants to exploit and market Kazakh oil and natural gas for profit and also to limit Russian access and block Russian efforts to use Kazakh energy for political leverage in Kazakhstan and other countries in the region and in the West. In this game, however, Kazakhstan on balance favors Russian interests.

To date, the Russian side seems to have a stronger hand in Kazakhstan than the United States. For this, Putin must be given credit. His influence-building policies toward Kazakhstan have been somewhat more skillful than those of the United States. The Kremlin has taken full advantage of the huge benefit of Russia's proximity to Kazakhstan and has gone to great lengths to keep the relationship strong because it has simply too much to lose if the United States got the upper hand with Nazarbayev who, himself, has doubts about putting too many eggs in the American basket.

One wild card in the Russian-American involvement in post-Soviet Kazakhstan's development is the policy of China, which is, arguably, the hungriest consumer of Kazakh energy. China wants Kazakhstan to become a strategic friend and economic partner. Now that it is independent and free to pursue whatever policies at home and abroad they see as in their best national interest. China has never had such an opportunity to expand its influence in the central Asian region and in particular in the energy-rich Kazakh state as it seems to have in the post-Soviet era, now that the ex-Soviet republics seemed determined to cut their historical umbilical cord with Russia.

It remains to be seen how Russia and the United States react to what already seems to be a three-dimensional rivalry. Should Russia join China in a concerted effort to shut out the United States? Can they do that? Or should China join with the United States in a grand strategy to limit and diminish Russian influence-building in Kazakhstan, especially in the energy sector? The heavy ideological component of U.S. policy would seem to undermine chances of the United States working in the near term with either major power and also with Kazakhstan itself, especially if the crisis in U.S. relations with Iran does not abate. Kazakhstan has good economic and other reasons to want friendly relations with Iran. Nazarbayev does not want to jeopardize by allowing the United States a military advantage on Kazakh territory that could be subversive of Iran's security.

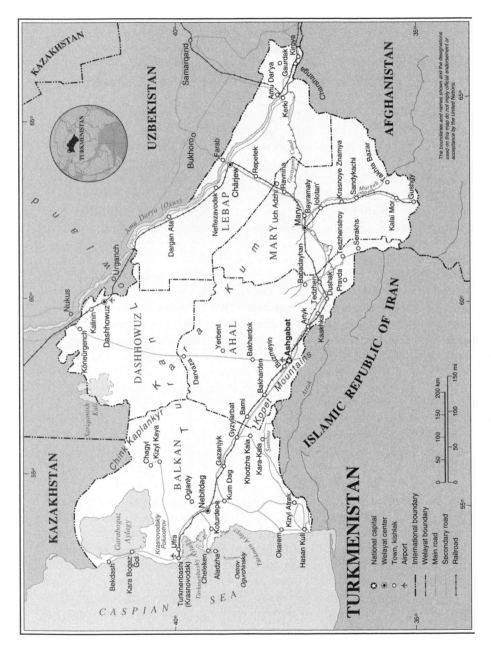

Turkmenistan (Courtesy of UN Cartographic Section)

3

Turkmenistan

- Population: 5 million (UN, 2005)
- Capital: Ashgabat
- Area: 488,100 sq. km (188,456 sq. miles)
- Major languages: Turkmen, Russian
- Major religion: Islam
- Life expectancy: 58 years (men), 67 years (women) (UN)
- Monetary unit: 1 Turkmen manat = 100 tenge
- Main exports: Oil, gas, textiles, raw cotton
- GNI per capita: US$1,340 (World Bank, 2005)

Almost from the beginning of the post-Soviet era, Russia wanted to regain at least some of the influence it had had over Turkmenistan in the Soviet and late czarist eras. Moscow's aggressive instincts toward Turkmenistan in the post-Soviet era derived from several sources, especially its eagerness to exploit the country's vast natural gas and oil reserves. To this end, Russia backed Turkmenistan's late President Sepamurad Niyazov's repressive regime which looked to Russia as a bulwark against the spread of militant Iranian-style Islamic fundamentalism the Kremlin insisted was fueling the war in Chechnya. Turkmenistan also was a buffer against the Taliban in Afghanistan in the mid and late 1990s, and against al Qaeda after 9/11.

Despite close personal ties with the former Soviet bureaucracy and Turkmenistan's historic links to Russia, Niyazov, a nationalist, was hardly ready for Turkmenistan to become a vassal of post–Soviet Russia. Niyazov was fully determined that his country pursue its own separate and independent path in international relations. While he signed agreements with the Kremlin providing for economic and strategic cooperation in which Russia provided help in policing Turkmenistan's borders, Niyazov was careful to keep lines of diplomatic communication open with other countries outside the ex-Soviet space, notably Turkey, Iran, China, and the United States, especially after 9/11. Niyazov welcomed opportunities to broaden these lines of contact for Turkmenistan as a means of obtaining some leverage in dealing with the compulsive and intrusive Kremlin, especially in the Putin era.

Niyazov never contemplated a break with post–Soviet Russia as he pursued a broad foreign policy independent of Moscow. He was always the realist, fully aware of the strategic importance of Turkmenistan's need for Russian friendship in both the domestic and the external dimensions. He realized that Turkmenistan depended for the bulk of its foreign trade, especially the export of its natural gas and oil, its transportation and communications infrastructure, and its national security on Russia. Niyazov also understood how Turkmenistan's relations with other countries could be even more problematical for his country since links with Russia went back a long time and remained extensive and essential for Turkmenistan's security and economic development.

In the immediate post-Soviet era of the early 1990s, Turkmenistan had to start from scratch, so to speak, in developing a system of foreign relations, since prior to 1991, the country had no foreign policy separate from and independent of Moscow. Upon Turkmenistan's independence, Niyazov hired former U.S. Secretary of State Alexander Haig to advise him on foreign policy. Haig was instrumental in helping Niyazov negotiate a treaty with the United States that gave Turkmenistan trade most favored nation treatment.[1]

In the 1990s, in one of his earliest major foreign policy initiatives, Niyazov also tried to protect his country's newly gained sovereignty. He adopted a diplomatic posture he called "positive neutrality," whereby Turkmenistan would seek the recognition of its independence from all countries and agree with other countries to refrain from interference in their internal affairs and to have them act reciprocally toward Turkmenistan which would maintain neutrality in external conflicts.[2]

RUSSIAN-TURKMEN RELATIONS UNDER YELTSIN, 1992–1999

Relations between the two countries remained good throughout the Yeltsin years. Niyazov kept Turkmenistan aligned with Russia on political, economic, and military issues. There was much cooperation between the two countries in these areas.

Military Ties

Niyazov allowed Russia a substantial Russian military influence in his country. Russia maintained a number of military bases. The Russian military presence in Turkmenistan was important not only for Turkmenistan's security vis-à-vis its neighbors, especially Afghanistan after the Taliban seized control of Kabul. It was also of strategic importance for Russia, especially for its influence in the Middle East. In 1992, Niyazov signed a bilateral military accord with Moscow, providing for Russian assistance in the creation of a Turkmen national army, which included detachments of the former Red (Soviet) Army. The Russian side insisted on a joint Russian-Turkmen command of the army and on sole Russian command over air defense and some strategic air force units. While ethnic Turkmen constituted 70 percent of the Turkmenistan military, they made up only 15–20 percent of the officers corps.[3]

Dual Citizenship

In addition to close military ties to Russia, Turkmenistan concluded an agreement on dual citizenship with Russia. At a meeting of the heads of CIS in December 1993, Niyazov symbolically presented Russian President Yeltsin with a new Turkmen passport, declaring him an honorary Turkmen. While other central Asian leaders opposed the principle of dual citizenship, fearing that it would encourage divided loyalties, Niyazov hoped that dual citizenship might help the Russian minority, which is about 4 percent of the population, to remain in the country. Niyazov needed such a symbolic gesture of support for the Russians because Turkmen nationalists were pushing through the parliament a series of measures such as a requirement of Russian residents in Turkmenistan to speak the Turkmen language. The nationalists wanted to keep lucrative and prestigious jobs in the country for ethnic Turkmen. Yeltsin was pleased by this symbolism, appreciating its significance for Russian efforts to enhance the standing of the Russian minorities living in the central Asian states. Despite Niyazov's efforts, however, Russia saw a decline of Russian cultural influence in Turkmenistan that did not bode well for the future well-being of the small Russian minority.[4]

Turkmenistan's Skepticism of the CIS

In the mid and late 1990s, sensitive about his country's newly won sovereignty, Niyazov was ill at ease with Russian efforts to influence and control his government. Niyazov was at all times skeptical of multilateral treaties regulating trade and commerce in the ex-Soviet space, though he was ready to conclude selective bilateral trade and security agreements with one or two individual countries.[5] By the end of the 1990s, Turkmenistan clearly was pursuing independent domestic and foreign policies suited in its view to its national interests.

Energy Resources

In the Yeltsin era, Russia aggressively tried to control Turkmenistan's oil and natural gas pipelines and to some extent succeeded. As of 1996, all of Turkmenistan's natural gas pipelines went north into Russia and other states in the Russian-dominated CIS. But, there was a significant economic downside to Russian purchases of Turkmen natural gas, and Niyazov was determined over the long haul to remedy the situation. Simply put, the problem was that while the Russian energy conglomerate Gazprom made a killing buying Turkmenistan gas cheaply and then selling it dearly in Europe, Niyazov was obliged to sell what was left of Turkmen gas to impoverished neighbors who frequently could not afford to pay their bills.[6] At the end of 1997, Niyazov took a major step to increase Turkmenistan's export revenue by opening a pipeline to Iran that could eventually link up with other pipelines to let gas from the Caspian Sea reach Europe, through Turkey. It was a problematical move, however, annoying not only Russia but also the United States, which wanted any new routes for Caspian gas to avoid Iran.

Russia and Turkmenistan Relations with Iran

Turkmenistan's developing ties with Iran in the Yeltsin years went beyond the pipelines and unsettled the equilibrium of interstate relations within central Asia, though the growing ties were understandable. Turkmenistan shares a border with Iran, and there are significant cultural and tribal connections between Turkmen and Iranians. Moreover, there is a large Turkmen minority of more than 1 million people in northern Iran, a very significant number given the fact that there are only about 4 million Turkmen in Turkmenistan itself. Religious differences exist between Turkmenistan and Iran (Iranians are for the most part Shia Muslims, while the Turkmen are Sunni) though these differences have not provoked conflict. The Kremlin watched with some concern about the development of ties between Turkmenistan and Iran outside the framework of the CIS and independent of Moscow.

RUSSIA AND TURKMENISTAN UNDER PUTIN, 2000–2008

As a consequence of the growing ties beyond Russia and Niyazov's pursuit of some independent policies, the Putin Kremlin experienced problems with Niyazov's leadership that strained relations between the two countries.

One such problem had to do with a growing discrimination by Turkmenistan against the country's small Russian minority. Turkmen political groups had downgraded the Russian cultural presence in Turkmenistan and mostly assured priority in the local job market to Turkmen citizens. Still another problem for Russia was Niyazov's independence in and diversification of Turkmen foreign policy that involved an effort to loosen ties to Moscow while strengthening them with other countries in central Asia and the West, especially the United States. Also, the Kremlin had difficulty getting control over the expanding trade in energy. Putin wanted Russia to control the exploitation and marketing of Turkmenistan's gas and oil resources.

The Russian Minority

One aspect of discrimination against the Russian minority in the Putin era had to do with the Russian language imposed on the Turkmen people when they came under Russian control in the late czarist era. Beginning in the 1990s, the Russian language increasingly gave way to the Turkmen language. As a consequence, Russian officers and other members of the small Russian-speaking community in Turkmenistan questioned whether they should remain there. Indeed, daily life became more difficult for them because during this period Turkmenistan experienced a renewal of interest in Islamic traditions accompanied by the growth of an ethno-culturally based nationalism. Turkmen citizens became increasingly intolerant of the highly visible Russian presence in and management of the country's economic life, which the Niyazov regime tolerated for reasons of political expediency—he did not want to risk antagonizing the Kremlin.[7]

In addition, Russians in Turkmenistan experienced a continuing deterioration in their level of material well-being that has been gradual but steady. Once having held good jobs living better than most ethnic Turkmen citizens right through into the new century, they have since seen a more rapid deterioration of their status. For example, the Niyazov regime closed down Russian language schools and in 2000 decreed that all official business must be conducted in the Turkmen language, which most Russians had never bothered to learn. This cultural discrimination had the effect of marginalizing the ethnic Russian community, eventually making many Russians living permanently in Turkmenistan feel like second-class citizens.[8]

In April 2003, the Niyazov regime terminated dual citizenship. Ethnic Russian citizens of Turkmenistan were given two months to decide which passport they would relinquish. Many in the Russian community felt betrayed by the Kremlin which offered little help to them. They had been encouraged by the Soviet government to come to Turkmenistan to help build the country and assure a substantial Russian influence over its development. Now they were about to be harmed in one way or another as a result of a perceived indifference by the post–Soviet Russian government to protect their interests. If they stayed much longer in Turkmenistan, they would lose the right of free return to Russia. If they chose to keep their Russian passport, they would lose Turkmenistan citizenship. If they did leave Turkmenistan, they would have to sell their property at short notice, taking a substantial loss of value in what they sold, and going back to a country where they knew there would be problems of resettlement.

These problems influenced many Russian-speaking Turkmen citizens to keep their Turkmen passports. They had heard rumors of the difficulty getting a job in the new Russia where life would be much tougher than it presently was in Turkmenistan. Russian officials lobbied hard with Ashgabat to reverse its decision but Niyazov refused to retreat.[9]

In early 2003, Russian Prime Minister Mikhail Kazyonov refused to scrap dual citizenship because doing so would likely be detrimental to Russian-speaking citizens of Turkmenistan who wanted to continue to enjoy citizenship in Russia. The end of dual citizenship for Russians and Turkmen would also make it difficult for Turkmen political refugees living in Russia to escape the Niyazov's wrath for their opposition to him.

Putin was severely criticized by a variety of advocates of dual citizenship starting with the Union of Rightist Forces, a liberal party headed by the democratic reformer Boris Nemtsov.[10]

Furthermore, Putin's position on the issue of the Russian minority in Turkmenistan, according to his critics, seemed indifferent to the prospect of a worsening of conditions for the Turkmeni Russians under Niyazov's dictatorial and implicitly xenophobic dictatorship. To accommodate the growing sensitivity of the members of the DUMA concerned about the well-being of the Russian minority in Turkmenistan as well as in other ex-Soviet republics, Putin declared in June 2003, in support of the beleaguered Russian community of about 100,000 in Turkmenistan, that the Russian government had the duty to defend the rights of its citizens in Turkmenistan.[11]

That said, Putin decided not to make an issue of the Turkmen decision to end dual citizenship in April 2003, despite knowing that he would appear to be abandoning Russian-speaking Turkmen citizens who had looked to Russia for help. To soften the impact of his policy, Putin told a Kremlin news conference in June 2003 that Russia would always defend Russian residents outside the country, including those in Turkmenistan. But, he was very careful to avoid saying exactly what kind of action he would take to defend fellow Russians abroad. He was also very careful to tell Russians in Russia not to become emotional over complaints by Russians living abroad about treatment by host governments like that of Niyazov in Turkmenistan. Acknowledging that, indeed, dual citizenship for Russians living permanently in Turkmenistan was over, he said that Niyazov had assured him that no harm would be done to Russians in Turkmenistan.[12]

In sum, Putin was cautious about the Turkmenistan Russian community leaving them to deal with the Niyazov regime to avoid provoking Niyazov regime, say by complaining about discrimination against the Russian minority. In Putin's view, there were more pressing economic and security issues, and many ethnic Russians have concluded that the Kremlin has sacrificed their cause with the Turkmen regime for the sake of other interests, say in the energy sector—in April 2003, the Kremlin had concluded a lucrative oil deal (for Russia) with Turkmenistan.[13]

Putin and Turkmen Energy

A major problem for the Kremlin in the Putin era and a reason for keeping on the good side of Niyazov was initiatives toward Afghanistan and Pakistan involving construction of a gas pipeline from Turkmenistan westward through these two countries driven by eagerness to assure Turkmen independence of Russia in the energy trade. The Afghan and Pakistani governments were interested in this proposed project. Afghan President Hamid Karzai visited Niyazov in Ashgabat in early 2002. The two leaders concluded several agreements, including an energy cooperation deal. Turkmenistan also pledged to help the Karzai government revive Afghanistan's broken down health care sector. Fruition of these initiatives toward its regional neighbors would diminish further Turkmenistan's traditional isolation and further strengthen its hand in dealing with Russia.[14]

Niyazov's determination to counter Russian efforts to influence management of Turkmenistan's energy resources was evident in his decision at the end of 2004 to shut off temporarily natural gas supplies to Russia and Ukraine. According to Turkmen officials, gas deliveries were suspended for a week because of maintenance problems. But, the cause of the cutoff also was an effort to squeeze more revenue out of Russia, a brazen gesture by Niyazov of independence of the Russians given Turkmenistan's physical vulnerability to them as well as economic and strategic reasons for remaining on good terms with them.[15]

The Kremlin believed there was still another reason for the Turkmen suspension of gas deliveries that had to do with the United States. A hypersensitive Kremlin saw the cutoff, however temporary, as another effort of Niyazov to curry favor with the Bush administration which encouraged the ex-Soviet central Asian republics to assert themselves in dealings with Russia to "stand up" to the Kremlin, so to speak, thereby, at least in the U.S. view, blunting or compromising Russian influence-building efforts in the region.[16]

Turkmenistan's Relations with the United States

Arguably the most serious problem for Russian relations with Turkmenistan during Putin's two presidential terms from 2000 to 2008 was not only Turkmenistan's growing interest in strengthening relations with the United States, a competitor of Russia in ex-Soviet Eurasia. The Kremlin also was taken aback by the Bush administration's aggressive efforts to enlist the cooperation of Turkmenistan and its immediate neighbors in the war against terrorism in Afghanistan.[17]

Turkmenistan Seeks Ties to the United States

After the 9/11 terrorist attack in the United States, Niyazov was quick to capitalize on the situation. He offered support, agreeing in September 2001 to the formation of a permanent UN body in the worldwide fight against terrorism, telling the United States he too was fighting terrorism in Turkmenistan as he suppressed his own political opponents whom he accused of being terrorists. Cooperation with the United States had several advantages for Turkmenistan, not least providing Niyazov with a new and powerful friend that psychologically bolstered him in his dealings with the Kremlin. The cooperation also brought new funds to Turkmenistan. And the successful American expulsion of the Taliban from Kabul was a big plus for Turkmenistan's security and stability and for the survival of Niyazov's secular leadership.[18]

Certainly, a critical determinant of post-9/11 U.S. policy toward Turkmenistan was the country's 446-mile border with Afghanistan and in particular its vulnerability to encroachment by extremist Muslim groups with bases in Afghanistan. Fundamentally, the United States wanted military cooperation with Turkmenistan, and in August 2002, General Tommy Franks, commander of American forces in the central Asian region, met with Niyazov to formalize arrangements for the United States to train and equip Turkmenistan's small military establishment, to play a larger role in border security and policing, areas in which Russia had been helping not only Turkmenistan but other ex-Soviet central Asian republics throughout the 1990s.[19]

The United States also wanted to participate in the exploitation and marketing of Turkmenistan's energy resources so much so that it suggested a rivalry with Russia in this area. Moreover, there was a strong ideological component in the administration's post-9/11 policy toward Turkmenistan: the U.S. encouragement of a rapid and comprehensive political democratization and of the introduction of a free market economy, advocating for sweeping systemic reforms that would bring to an end once and for all vestiges of Communist and Soviet rule before 1991.[20]

The Bush administration was also more than willing to encourage Turkmenistan, along with other countries in the ex-Soviet space, to resist perceived Russian efforts to influence their development. Washington was determined to reserve for itself leadership of the war against international terrorism. This was an extension of Russian efforts to transform the central Asian republics into allies of Russia against terrorism. U.S. policy since the collapse of the Soviet state in the early 1990s had aimed at blocking the reappearance in any shape or form of the old Soviet structure of relations between Russia and the other ex-Soviet republics in which Moscow was predominant.[21]

Limits on U.S.-Turkmen Relations Following 9/11

To Russia's advantage were limits to any tilt by Turkmenistan toward the United States after 9/11. Niyazov wanted a kind of strategic balance between Russian and American influence-building in his country, a policy of "positive neutrality," in place since 1991, and that Niyazov used to stay away from alliances, agreements, and ententes with outsiders that restricted its capacity to pursue an independent course in foreign policy. "Positive neutrality" was the basis of Turkmenistan's rejection of membership in Russian-led organizations of ex-Soviet Eurasian states such as the CIS. It also meant a refusal to allow the deployment of foreign, in particular American, troops on Turkmen territory.[22]

Niyazov's Authoritarianism

An important limit on the scope of the U.S. relationship with Turkmenistan after 9/11 was Niyazov's repressive authoritarianism of which the Bush administration remained highly critical and tried to moderate. As was the case in many other central Asian countries, Washington was faced with the problem of balancing its strategic need to keep on good terms with Niyazov to have his cooperation in the war against terrorism in central Asia with trying to push him in the direction of democratization, which Niyazov saw as subversive of his neo-Stalinist power system.[23]

When, in November 2002, Niyazov survived an assassination attempt, his regime in a typically "Stalinist" fashion implemented a sweeping purge of opposition figures whose only crime was criticizing the government. The regime left no stone unturned in a brutal campaign to punish perceived dissent. In April of 2002, Niyazov went so far as to fire the head of national security, the head of border service, and the defense minister, and in May he removed some functionaries from the Interior Ministry which he considered honeycombed with political opponents of his leadership. There was a spate of Stalinist-like "show trials" with forced confessions reminiscent of the harshest phase of Soviet life under Stalin in the 1930s. While the Kremlin refrained from criticism of Niyazov's excesses, the United States did criticize him but showed a measure of restraint to avoid damaging relations with him.[24]

Indeed, so upset was Washington that in mid-2003, it came very close to imposing trade sanctions on Turkmenistan. It did so because, apart from the harshness of the regime's reactions to the assassination attempt, the United States was frustrated when Niyazov regime restricted the right of

Turkmenistan citizens to emigrate freely from the country. In early August 2003, the Bush administration in effect put the Turkmen government on official notice that it was liable for such trade sanctions if it did not respect the freedom of its citizens to leave from and return to their home country.[25]

Niyazov ultimately ignored U.S. warnings. After initially suspending the requirement for an exit visa for Turkmen citizens going out of the country, he restored it. He effectively ended the right of Turkmen citizens to emigrate or travel, a restriction on personal liberty reminiscent of rules in effect during the Soviet era.

Turkmenistan and the War in Afghanistan

Niyazov also avoided any kind of direct Turkmen military involvement with the Americans, discouraging throughout 2004 any overt American initiatives to finesse a military presence in Turkmenistan. That was just as well since the United States would be courting a public relations disaster if the Pentagon had made concessions to Niyazov in return for permission to have a military base in Turkmenistan, given his extreme authoritarian bent. For his part, Niyazov would have contradicted his past policy of neutrality that required him not to allow the United States in the name of fighting terrorism to deploy military forces in his country. A U.S. deal with Niyazov carried other risks for Washington. In the view of Erika Dailey, director of the Turkmenistan Project, an initiative of the New York-based Open Society Institute which was devoted to promoting civil society in central Asia, Niyazov was unreliable and unpredictable, as well as being erratic in policymaking and also isolationist with an incurable suspicion of foreigners.[26]

RUSSIA COUNTERS U.S. POLICY IN TURKMENISTAN

The Putin Kremlin was and remains very sensitive to Turkmenistan's ties to the United States in the aftermath of 9/11 and is determined either to block or to match U.S. influence-building there. A U.S.-friendly government in Turkmenistan could undermine Russia's goal of dominating the export of Turkmen gas and oil, which the Kremlin wants under its control. Additionally, a stronger U.S. presence in Turkmenistan would get in the way of Russian dominance in the region. For example, as a border state to Iran, Turkmenistan has strong interests in that country, just as the Russians do. A pro-U.S. Turkmenistan in this view could limit Russian options in Iran, a situation the Kremlin would not be willing to tolerate—Iran in effect would be virtually surrounded by states friendly to and linked with the United States giving Washington too much influence in the central Asian region of the ex-Soviet space. Still worse for Russia would be a prospect of NATO expansion into central Asia. A pro-U.S. Turkmenistan was another strategic liability for Russia in its central Asian "backyard."[27]

Putin Strengthens Russian Ties to Turkmenistan

The Kremlin's task of offsetting U.S. influence was not easy: the new relationship between Ashgabat and Washington was too strategically convenient for Turkmenistan to be reversed. In addition, it was difficult for the Kremlin to fault the Bush administration's antiterrorist strategy, since Russia also benefited from it. By itself it had a limited capability to protect the ex-Soviet central Asian republics from the subversive appeal of Islamic fundamentalism, which was almost as much anti-Russian as it was anti-American.

Moreover, for some time, even the Kremlin had been uncomfortable over the Niyazov regime's repressive political rule, almost as if it were embarrassed by this perceived "holdover" from the Stalinist era. Indeed, in its ill-concealed discomfort with Niyazov, the Kremlin had been trying to make a statement about its own post-Communist commitment to a democratic order the Turkmen leader conspicuously shunned. Kremlin motives here were linked to a concern about not only the political safety of Turkmenistan's Russian minority but also Russia's image in the West, especially the United States, with which Putin wanted good relations. For the record, *Izvestia* correspondent Aleksandr Arkhangelski observed that one of the reasons for Russian influence-building in Turkmenistan was to show that Russia favored a "strong law-governed state."[28]

Putin skillfully used an opportunity to strengthen Russian ties with Niyazov during the domestic crisis after the assassination attempt in the Spring of 2002. Putin refrained from making an issue of Niyazov's repressive treatment of the political opposition even as Western countries, especially the United States, were condemning it. Washington demanded that the Turkmen regime show more tolerance of diverse political opinion, and the European Bank for Reconstruction and Development was urging Turkmenistan to move further and faster with free market reforms, as well as with democratization.[29]

Russia for its part was offering the beleaguered Niyazov psychological help and political backing. In another conciliatory gesture toward the Niyazov regime, the Kremlin offered to help the Turkmenistan government's investigation of the roots of the assassination attempt for which, incidentally, Niyazov eventually put some blame on the United States given its persistent criticism of the Turkmen government for its violation of the human rights of its citizens. Indeed, the Turkmen leadership joined the Kremlin in asserting that the assassination effort was an act of terrorism in the fight against international terrorism, somewhat undermining Turkmen view of American complicity.[30] By its silence, the Kremlin implicitly endorsed the Niyazov regime's arrest in November 2002 of the former Turkmen Foreign Minister Boris Shikhumaradov for his alleged role in the assassination plot although there was no strong evidence that he was involved.[31] Furthermore, the Turkmen leadership joined the Kremlin in asserting that the assassination effort was an act of terrorism in the fight against international terrorism, somewhat undermining Turkmen view of American complicity.[32]

On the security front, Vladimir Rushailo, head of the Russian Security Council, during a visit to Ashgabat in early 2003, reiterated Russian co-operation between the two countries in the war against terrorism. Russian and Turkmen diplomats signed a protocol providing for cooperation between the security councils of the two countries to fight terrorism.[33]

These initiatives toward Niyazov had the endorsement of a majority of Russian foreign policy analysts who were in agreement on the necessity of Russia's need to cooperate with and not confront Turkmenistan and other central Asian governments in their flirtation with the United States after 9/11. Putin reportedly hinted at linkage between the newly developing Iraq crisis in the Spring of 2003 and Russia's policy not to raise the issue of "neo-Stalinism" in the governments of central Asian republics. He said that the Russian cooperation with Turkmenistan in the security area will "make our efforts to fight terrorism more systematic and efficient."[34]

The "Payoff" for Russia

Putin's careful cultivation of Niyazov led to a strengthening of ties between Turkmenistan and Russia that had the effect of offsetting U.S. influence. In April 2002, Russia was able to get Niyazov's agreement to extend the Treaty of Friendship and Cooperation signed by the two countries in 1992, basically saying that Russia and Turkmenistan would not allow their territories to be used in ways that damaged the security of the other side. The signatories agreed to cooperate in particular in the war against international terrorism, with both sides agreeing to deny refuge for terrorists. They agreed to exchange of intelligence on terrorist activities and pledged to keep each other informed of any additional steps taken in the fight against terrorism, including participation in antiterrorist agreements, coalitions, and associations.[35]

The agreement was very much a win for Russia and was a linchpin in Russian influence-building in a large area stretching from the Caspian to Afghanistan. Moreover, the Russian-Turkmenistan agreement seemed to make the Turkmen protestations of neutrality academic as far as Russia was concerned because in effect it made Turkmenistan a partner of Russia in the war against terrorism in a far more explicit way than any equivalent arrangements with the United States.[36]

Furthermore, in April 2003, during a summit meeting with Putin in Moscow, in return for Russia's signals of sympathy for his regime in its confrontation with its political opposition, Niyazov signed a 25-year agreement giving Gazprom the right to buy all of Turkmenistan's gas except for commitments under existing agreements with partners such as Ukraine and Iran.

With this agreement, Moscow was working to monopolize the transit of Turkmen gas enhancing its ability to expand its influence ever more deeply into ex-Soviet central Asia. According to an editorial in *Nezavisimaya Gazeta*, "Moscow hopes . . . to restore its weakened geopolitical situation."[37]

While this April 2003 agreement heightened Turkmenistan's dependence on Russian pipelines for transit of its gas exports except in the case of a line directly to Iran, Niyazov had in fact cut a good deal with the Russians regarding the price of Turkmenistan's oil. It was to be $44 per 1,000 cubic meters, the same somewhat elevated price in the Russian view that the Turkmen leader had been insisting on—and the Russians resisting—for several years.[38]

Putin's conciliatory diplomacy with Niyazov was successful in assuring Turkmenistan's friendship with Russia and in no way did it seem to be at the expense of Turkmen ties with the United States. Niyazov appreciated Russian restraint when it came to judging his rule and he resented the American charges of repression. In Niyazov's view, an American presence in his country could well offer Washington an opportunity to work against his leadership and force him out of power.[39] As a consequence of these fears, Niyazov listened to Russia's opposition to an American military base on Turkmenistan territory. The Kremlin did not want an American military base in Turkmenistan because it could use such a base to attack Iran or at the very least contain Iran's activities. According to at least two Russian news organs, one in Turkmenistan, the United States would close the "ring" around Iran if it were in Turkmenistan since it already had bases in other countries bordering Iran.[40]

U.S. RESPONSES TO RUSSIAN POLICY, 2005–2008

Despite, and arguably because of, Russian efforts to constrain U.S. influence-building in Turkmenistan, the Bush administration decided on concrete steps to expand military cooperation with Turkmenistan. On August 23, 2005, General John Abizaid, chief of the U.S. Central Command (CENTCOM), met with Niyazov in Ashgabat to discuss areas of mutual interest of the two countries and regional security issues. Abizaid assured Niyazov that the sole reason for the American military presence in central Asia was stability in Afghanistan and that the United States had no interest in "confronting" other nations in the region. Abizaid reportedly also discussed how an oil pipeline through Afghanistan could facilitate Turkmenistan's export of energy to markets in Pakistan and India.[41] Not coincidentally, Abizaid's visit coincided with a major American setback in Uzbekistan, namely the decision of Uzbek President Islam Karimov to terminate the American military presence in his country in response to Washington's severe criticism of his brutal repression of political dissent in the Andijon region of his country.

U.S. Policy Alarms the Kremlin

Abizaid's dealings with Niyazov in 2005 troubled the Kremlin which was still very much concerned about the prospect of an expansion of existing U.S. military deployments in central Asia in the Summer of 2005, even if the reason for their being there was the fight against terrorism, a fight in which Russia stood with the United States. Of particular concern to the Kremlin was the fact that the United States would have to get off its base in Uzbekistan. The Russian press was sure the United States was about to compensate itself for the loss in Uzbekistan by a gain in Turkmenistan of a military presence to facilitate Western action against a resurgent Taliban in Afghanistan. While that might not have been overly controversial, the Iran issue was. In late August and early September 2005, the press sent out the Iran alarm, no doubt reflecting a view of Russian policymakers that the United States needed a military base in Turkmenistan to launch an attack on Iran to remove its ultraconservative anti-American leadership. In this view, an American military base in Turkmenistan would be detrimental to Russian strategic interests in south central Asia, especially if it led to the replacement of existing Iranian leaders sympathetic to the United States.[42]

Making Russian fears plausible was a pronounced deterioration in U.S. relations with Iran during the Summer and Fall of 2005, as the new Iranian government rejected EU's proposals supported by the Bush administration to make substantial economic concessions to Iran in return for a halt in its nuclear experiments. When the Iranian president gave a bellicose speech to the UN General Assembly in mid-September 2005, affirming Iran's decision to defy the West by refusing to halt its program of developing nuclear energy that could be used to make weapons of mass destruction, it seemed to Russia that the danger of a U.S. military confrontation with Iran was all too real and a good reason to prevent a U.S. military base in Turkmenistan.[43]

Further fueling Russian concern over the U.S. interest in an air base and military presence in Turkmenistan in 2005 was Niyazov's weakening of Turkmenistan's role in the CIS at this time. On September 1, 2005, Niyazov made a formal announcement of his decision to downgrade his country's links with the CIS, saying that henceforth Turkmenistan would be an "associate member" with looser links to the organization than those of a full member. This decision communicated at the August 2005 meeting of CIS members in Kazan, Tatarstan, meant, for example, that Turkmenistan no longer would participate in either CIS-sponsored military games and maneuvers or post-Soviet Eurasian military structures. Niyazov defended this policy, saying in effect that it was consistent with and required by his country's policy of "positive neutrality." In addition, Niyazov argued that Turkmenistan's participation in military exercises of the CIS "might send the wrong signals to neighbors."[44]

Niyazov's curtailment of Turkmenistan's links to the CIS deeply troubled the Kremlin because it weakened further an already deeply divided CIS reducing its importance as an instrument of Russian influence-building in the Eurasian republics. According to Mikhail Margelov, chairman of the Federation Council's foreign affairs committee, Niyazov's action confirmed the serious cracks within the CIS and raised more doubt about the survival of the organization. Again, the Kremlin thought it saw the U.S. hand, this time in strengthening ties with Turkmenistan in response to Uzbekistan President Islam Karimov's decision to evict the United States from its military bases on Uzbek territory.[45]

Although, as 2005 drew to a close, the likelihood of a U.S. military base in Turkmenistan seemed as slim as ever, according to Turkmen Foreign Minister Rashid Meredov, who said as much to his Russian counterpart, Sergei Lavrov, the Kremlin could not be sure about Niyazov. There had been a slight sense of annoyance in the tone of Meredov's conversation with Lavrov. The Turkmen foreign minister spoke of all the rumors circulating in Moscow that Turkmenistan had abandoned or was about to abandon its "positive neutrality" in the war against terrorism. He said, "Turkmenistan is bewildered over publications in the Russian press distorting the essence of Turkmenistan's participation in the CIS." Turkmenistan's recent downgrade of its membership in the CIS from "full" to "associate" troubled the Kremlin, which saw the move as a sign of a shift in Turkmenistan's neutrality strategy in favor of the United States and to the disadvantage of Russia in light of U.S. General Abizaid's August summit with Niyazov in Ashgabat.[46]

For his part, Lavrov reflected a continuing suspicion in the Kremlin that Washington in fact ultimately might succeed in "buying off" Niyazov on the base issue. Lavrov said, "Russia was going on Ashgabat's clear statements that Turkmenistan was not participating in military blocs or alliances and would not accommodate foreign military bases on its soil."[47] That said, the likelihood of Turkmenistan allowing the United States a military base on its territory was undercut by the way it knew such a step not only would severely strain relations with Russia, which, after all was said and done, were of prime importance to Turkmenistan, but also would damage relations with China with which Niyazov wanted good relations if only as a counterweight in his dealings with the Kremlin.[48]

TURKMENISTAN TILTS TOWARD RUSSIA

In 2006 and early 2007, the Kremlin found Turkmenistan responsive to its influence-building efforts. In the energy sector, Russia made progress though at a substantial monetary cost. In September 2006, Gazprom agreed to a 40 percent increase for Turkmenistan's natural gas—$100 per 1,000 cubic meters for purchases through 2009. But, with this new deal, Gazprom avoided the risk of an interruption in the flow of Turkmen gas to market through its pipelines, enabling it to continue selling gas at home in Russia as well as to other central Asian republics that strengthened its grip on the energy trade with countries in which it wanted to expand its political influence, in particular Turkmenistan. In return for getting Russia to accept the price increase, Niyazov assured that Turkmenistan would not participate in the U.S.-backed trans-Caspian pipeline that sidelined Russia, making it very clear to the Kremlin that Turkmenistan's gas resources were for Russia and nobody else. The Kremlin now was assured of increased leverage with another ex-Soviet republic strategically and commercially important to its interests in central Asia.[49]

Niyazov's Death

With the sudden demise of Niyazov in December 2006 and the stage-managed election in February 2007 of his successor Gurbanguly Berdimu-khamedov, the deputy prime minister, former finance minister, and a leading member of Niyazov's Democratic Party of Turkmenistan, the only party to field presidential candidates, the Kremlin stepped up its influence-building campaign.[50] Putin invited Berdimukhamedov to visit Moscow. Putin worried that with the end of Niyazov's leadership might come an adjustment of his pro-Russian policy in favor of the West, in particular about the United States. Putin wanted the new Turkmen leader to continue his predecessor's policy of close cooperation between Turkmenistan and Russia in the areas of trade and economic policies and regional security. Putin was concerned in particular how Berdimukhamedov would translate Niyazov's policy of neutrality vis-à-vis Russia and the United States. There was almost a kind of warning, arguably an Aesopian ultimatum, against any sharp changes in Turkmen foreign relations, say in the direct of expanded ties to the West.[51]

Berdimukhamedov assured in early January 2007, a month before his election, when he was acting president, that if elected, he would continue policies abroad of Niyazov. He and his advisers went to great length to reassure Russia about continuity of foreign and trade policy making. Their assurances to the Kremlin had some credibility given their membership in the small oligarchy of leaders serving Niyazov before his death. Indeed, in the weeks following Niyazov's death, they went out of their way to demonstrate their commitment to the pursuit of Niyazov's foreign polices by the excessive praise and adulation of the late leader, which he certainly would have enjoyed and approved if he could have heard them.[52]

That said, ultimate infighting, if not policy alteration, could not be completely ruled out given the existence of a small coterie of disgruntled former officials of the state apparatus. There was also an outspoken but deeply divided reformist political opposition abroad; but it had no power to influence events inside Turkmenistan.[53] And, the new Turkmen leadership wanted to make an explicit statement to the Kremlin at the outset of its rule to the effect that Turkmenistan, indeed, would not slavishly indulge Moscow in a diplomatic form: acting President Berdimukhamedov's first foreign visit was to Saudi Arabia. His second visit was to Moscow.[54]

On the other hand, in the months following his election, Berdimukhamedov was well on his way toward strengthening Turkmenistan ties to Russia to a somewhat greater degree than had ever been true of Niyazov's policy, and with good reason from the Turkmen vantage point. The hypersensitive new Turkmen leadership could hardly miss the less than enthusiastic support of the United States which sent a relatively low-level diplomat, Assistant Secretary of State Richard Boucher, to the funeral of Niyazov in Ashgabat. By contrast with the Americans, Russia sent Prime Minister Mikhail Fradkov and China sent President Hu Jintao's special envoy, State Councillor Tang Jiaxuan.[55]

Despite the uncertainties for their respective interests in Turkmenistan of the transition from Niyazov to Berdimukhamedov, both Russia and the United States, as well as most other countries with interest in Turkmenistan, refrained from interfering in the transition from Niyazov to Berdimukhamedov in the early weeks of 2007. The late Niyazov's closest supporters stage-managed the election of the late leader's successor with little regard to the niceties of liberal democracy. For all intent and purpose, Berdimukhamedov was co-opted into power as president in a manner very close to and reminiscent of leadership succession processes in the era of Communist rule.[56] There may have been a temptation in the West, especially in Washington, to take advantage of Niyazov's death to support a pro-West, pro-democracy reformer but any chances of doing that were at best slim, if not impossible, because Niyazov had done such a thorough job of removing opposition personalities and groups from the country's political environment. Moreover, with its extremist positions and sharp intergroup divisions, the deeply fragmented Turkmen political opposition living abroad was hardly able to play any role whatsoever in the post-Niyazov transition except a strictly rhetorical one.[57]

Berdimukhamedov Moves Closer to Russia in 2007

In May 2007, Berdimukhamedov joined Russia and Kazakhstan in agreeing to the construction of a new natural gas pipeline to run from Turkmenistan to Kazakhstan's Caspian coast and thence north into Russia. This pipeline rivaled the U.S.-sponsored project to construct a trans-Caspian pipeline across the Caspian Sea to Turkey, thus bypassing Russia. The new pipeline agreement between Russia, Turkmenistan, and Kazakhstan was a big win for Russia because it challenged the U.S. strategy in central Asia of encouraging the ex-Soviet republics to indulge their instincts to sideline

Russia. Moreover, Russia's Gazprom stood to benefit enormously in helping to build the pipeline and to market Turkmen gas in the highly lucrative European market. As a consequence, Russia's economic and political influence in the ex-Soviet space and also in the West has been strengthened considerably.[58]

Deteriorating U.S. Prospects in Turkmenistan after Niyazov

Not a very good omen for developing U.S. relations with Turkmenistan in the post-Niyazov era had been Washington's awkward participation in the funeral arrangements for Niyazov. Washington sent only Assistant Secretary of State Richard Boucher. The hypersensitive Turkmen leadership, including soon-to-be President Gurbanguly Berdimukhamedov, considered the Boucher assignment a snub given the high-level representation of Russia and other countries which seemed to outdo themselves in gestures of respect. It was no secret to the Turkmen political elite that the U.S. State Department has about 24 assistant secretaries of state. The central Asian governments were represented by their presidents; Iran sent First Vice President Parviz Davoudi. But, Russia outdid them all by sending Prime Minister Mikhail Fradkov, former Prime Minister Viktor Chernomyrdin, and Gazprom CEO Alexei Miller, who led a delegation of high-ranking officials of Gazprom.[59]

The political fallout of the U.S. apparent faux pas, something akin to what could be called "handwriting on the wall," was an indication that the post-Niyazov leadership might have been considering a reconsideration of Niyazov's recent decision, in late August 2006, to downgrade its status in the Russian-dominated CIS to associate membership in light of the government's decision to send Berdimukhamedov to an upcoming CIS summit in St. Petersburg. There was also an implication of change in Niyazov's policy of "positive neutrality" that would allow a Turkmen tilt toward Russia.[60]

Indeed, Berdimukhamedov's ascendancy may not bring much advantage to the United States. While it is clear to the post-Niyazov leadership that Turkmenistan's interests are served by diversifying its energy export policy rather than relying, as it seems bent on doing, on Russia, in particular Gazprom, it is also true that in 2007 for all intent and purpose Gazprom had a pipeline monopoly leaving Turkmenistan little opportunity for diversification of its energy industry.

Moreover, unlike its virtual "stringless" relationship with Russia, any relationship Turkmenistan has in the future with the United States must involve a credible Turkmen effort to reduce corruption and enhance transparency in the conduct of business, especially involving the United States and other Western countries. It is highly unlikely that the United States will abandon its commitment to democratization of post-Soviet central Asia for reasons of economic and/or strategic expediency despite its need of local co-operation to fight the war against terrorism, for example, in Afghanistan.

Moreover, implementing such a reform agenda may not be what Berdi-mukhamedov has in mind. Old habits of corruption die hard, never mind democratizing a country with virtually no experience with real self-rule. A primary concern of the Berdimukhamedov leadership is political survival which would be jeopardized by the introduction of real democracy that could result in his loss of power, especially if it were to involve not only political freedom and competitive elections but also the release of opposition leaders from jail with permission to reenter national politics.[61]

And, by mid-2008, U.S. efforts to participate in the opening up of Turk-menistan's vast reserve of natural gas seemed to be going nowhere. At the end of February 2008, U.S. Deputy Assistant Secretary of State Steven Mann was in Ashgabat trying to get President Berdimukhamedov to agree to the construction of a pipeline to carry Turkmenistan natural gas to Western markets along a route that excluded Russia. The Berdimukhame-dov regime had reason to consider the U.S. project: Up to the present, most of Turkmenistan gas exports passed through Russian-controlled pipelines run by Gazprom providing the Kremlin with a stranglehold over Turkmen gas exports and enormous leverage to influence not only Turkmenistan but also its customers in the West, which have become increasingly uncom-fortable over their vulnerability to Russia regarding their imported energy.[62]

Driving U.S. policy toward Turkmen gas was the deal Turkmenistan had signed with Kazakhstan and Russia at the end of 2007 to greatly expand an existing pipeline network that runs along the Caspian shoreline on Russian territory. This deal, known as the Prikaspisky agreement, was a blow to a U.S.-sponsored project to build a trans-Caspian pipeline to take gas from Turkmenistan to Azerbaijan and Georgia and then westward under the Caspian excluding Russia. If the Prikaspisky pipeline is built, the Western gas pipeline project would be economically impractical and prob-ably would not be built to the great satisfaction of the Kremlin but to the detriment of Europe and the United States.[63]

The United States, however, was not ready to concede defeat in this aspect of its rivalry with Russia in Turkmenistan and Kazakhstan in the area of energy. In 2008, the U.S. State Department sharpened its focus on the ongoing rivalry with Russia over control of the marketing of Caspian energy resources by creating a new high-level position called the Coordinator of Eurasian Energy Diplomacy and filled by now Assistant Secretary of State Mann. The Bush administration also started looking for a high-profile diplomat to bring more diplomatic muscle to the job of trying to increase U.S. influence with Turkmen President Berdimukhamedov to increase cooperation with the United States and other Western countries in the marketing of his natural gas.[64]

THE IRAN FACTOR

Of special interest to Russia and the United States was the Berdimukhamedov leadership's plans for dealing with Iran as Iran's relations with the United States reached a nadir in 2007, when the Iranian government arrested and imprisoned four American citizens of Iranian extraction along with mounting evidence of Iranian interference against the United States in Iraq and Afghanistan. In July 2006, Berdimukhamedov's predecessor, Niyazov, had laid the groundwork for a strengthening of political and economic ties between Turkmenistan and Iran by welcoming Iranian President Mahmoud Ahmadinejad to Ashgabat to discuss trade between the two countries.[65]

The Iranian leader had other concerns he wanted to discuss with Niyazov, notably finding friends, perhaps even allies, in central Asia to mitigate Iran's increasing international isolation by the West, especially the United States. He also wanted some support in the region for continuing Iran's program of developing nuclear energy despite international hostility this program had caused. At this meeting, Niyazov agreed to increase Turkmenistan's gas exports to Iran to over 10 billion cubic meters, to increase Turkmen oil exports to Iran, and to allow greater participation of Iranian companies in Turkmen oil exploration.[66]

In line with Niyazov's supportive policies, in March 2007, Berdimukhamedov told Iranian Foreign Minister Manouchehr Mottaki in Ashgabat that Turkmenistan recognized Iran's legitimate right to develop nuclear energy for peaceful purposes. Echoing other Iranian views about its nuclear development program, Berdimukhamedov said he agreed with the Iranian position that its nuclear program was consistent with international treaties. He added that Turkmenistan wanted a broadening and a deepening of bilateral ties between the two countries.[67]

In June of 2007, Berdimukhamedov went to Teheran to discuss trade and security issues with President Ahmadinejad. Among other things, the two leaders agreed on a railroad construction project that would link these two countries to one another and Kazakhstan and facilitate trade between Iran and Turkmenistan. In the area of security, they said little publicly, but it was clear that the strengthening of bilateral relations had a strategic goal: to enable them to cooperate in taking advantage of the interests and actions of outsiders toward their country—for Iran, it was the United States, for Turkmenistan, it was Russia.[68]

Ahmadinejad suggested that their best response to outsiders seeking influence in the Caspian region is to encourage the littoral states to strengthen ties with one another for the purpose of presenting a common front instead of trying to deal with the outside Powers individually. Ahmadinejad also spoke of "certain bullying Powers" seeking Caspian oil and other energy resources of the region. He stressed the importance for Iran of Turkmen oil, gas, and petrochemical exports. Ahmadinejad and Berdimukhamedov also discussed border security and an Iranian proposal for cooperation between the two in which Iran could be of help to Turkmenistan in assuring border security.[69]

Finally, at the June 2007 Iranian-Turkmenistan summit in Teheran, Ahmadinejad and Berdimukhamedov discussed Turkmenistan's "neutrality," which the Iranian president highly commended. For Iran, because of its sharp confrontation with the West, especially with the United States, Turkmen neutrality was seen as an obstacle to U.S. efforts to persuade Turkmenistan to play a more active role in alliance with the United States in the war on terrorism in Afghanistan. Rather, in a final joint communiqué, the two countries agreed that they would expand cooperation with one another in the security area as an alternative to working with outsiders. In particular, the Iranian leadership wanted to avoid an American military presence in Turkmenistan. At the same time, Berdimukhamedov emphasized the important role of Iran in preserving regional stability in light of the American occupation of Iraq and the American war against the Taliban in Afghanistan.[70]

Russian and American Reactions

Russia remains highly sensitive to Turkmenistan's policy toward Iran. The Kremlin wants Turkmenistan's post-Niyazov leadership to keep its diplomatic fences with Iran in good repair so as to indirectly enhance Russia's leverage with Teheran and strengthen its hand with the United States in Iranian business. In addition, the Kremlin would like to settle historic differences between Turkmenistan and Iran over conflicting claims of control over portions of the Caspian Sea that threaten the region's stability— Azerbaijan and Kazakhstan already have reached such an agreement with Iran.[71]

For its part, the United States wants Turkmenistan to do nothing to help Iran overcome the international isolation and ostracism imposed by the United States and its allies. But, Berdimukhamedov has demonstrated so far that he does not intend to allow either the United States or Russia to determine his foreign policy though he is proceeding cautiously with Iran in 2007, careful to avoid annoying either Washington or Moscow.[72]

In 2007 and 2008, Berdimukhamedov continued to pursue a balance in its foreign policy, remaining on good terms with both Moscow and Washington. As a counterweight to his obviously close relations with the Kremlin, Berdimukhamedov simultaneously was dialoguing with the United States on security issues. For example, on June 20, 2007, he received Admiral William Fallon, chief of CENTCOM, in Ashgabat. He reportedly spoke of "collaboration between the military establishments of Turkmenistan and the US in order to increase Turkmenistan's capacity to ensure regional security, combat terrorism, curtail the trafficking in drugs, and enhance border protection."[73]

Fallon was responsive to the positive approaches of Berdimukhamedov to Turkmen-U.S. relations, saying in effect that the best way for the Turkmen leader to strengthen Turkmen-U.S. relations was primarily through the continuation of Turkmen exports of energy resources to the region. For its part, according to Fallon, the best way for CENTCOM to maintain good relations with Turkmenistan was not establishing military bases in Turkmenistan but rather building trust between the two countries slowly but steadily and assuring Turkmenistan that it can help restore stability to Afghanistan.[74] Fallon's message to Berdimukhamedov in June 2007 confirmed not only U.S. recognition of its limited capacity at the moment to expand American military and political influence in Turkmenistan but also American appreciation of the Turkmen leader's efforts to keep his country's diplomatic fences with the United States in good repair, despite pressure from Iran to go in the opposite direction, while he preserves good relations with Russia as he obviously had been doing with some success in 2007.

THE CHINA FACTOR

Complicating Russian-American relations is the China factor. For sometime throughout the 1990s and continuing with increased momentum in the opening years of the new century, Niyazov had tried to maintain good relations with China, which had many reasons of its own having to do with strategy and trade to reciprocate his friendly gestures. In May 2005, Chinese President Hu Jintao had told Niyazov—at a meeting with him in Moscow—that China supports Turkmenistan's efforts at neutrality and that China attached great importance to the development of friendly relations between the two countries.[75]

The strengthening of relations between Turkmenistan and China produced agreements on technical and economic cooperation in addition to debt deals and a new agreement between the Turkmen Oil and Gas Ministry and the state-owned China National Petroleum Corporation. China intends to play a major role in helping Turkmenistan to expand lucrative oil exports for its own benefit, as well as for that of Turkmenistan. Chinese engineers want to rejuvenate oil wells in western Turkmenistan. The Chinese have similar interests in the production and marketing of Turkmenistan's huge reserves of natural gas.[76]

Niyazov welcomed these Chinese economic initiatives not only for strategic reasons having to do with his relations with both Russia and the United States but also for economic reasons—Turkmenistan needs the earnings that will come with expanded energy output but lacks the capital needed to access these resources in the short term. Moreover, the Niyazov leadership was annoyed by the fact that it had to ship most of the energy it produced through Russian-owned pipelines. To diminish this dependence, Turkmenistan looked to China and also Kazakhstan as the most promising alternatives to Russia in the energy trade. Chinese President Hu Jintao and Kazakh President Nursultan Nazarbayev had discussed the possibility of a pipeline carrying gas from Kazakhstan and Turkmenistan to China by way of Kazakhstan in July 2005 at a summit in the Kazakh capital of Astana. Both countries are planning the construction through Turkmenistan of a pipeline to carry Kazakh oil headed for the Chinese market.[77]

The strengthening of Turkmen-Chinese ties, especially in the energy trade area, was a source of concern to the Kremlin where there was doubt about Niyazov's ability to live up to delivery pledges if he were also to meet obligations to China. According to the Russian business journal *Kommersant*, a failure of Turkmenistan to deliver promised gas supplies to Gazprom could compromise Russian energy commitments to supplying gas to Western Europe. Putin was so concerned about the reliability of Turkmen gas exports to Russia that he had promised in August 2006 construction of a gas pipeline connecting Russia to China by 2011.[78]

Although the death of Niyazov in December 2006 offered the Chinese an opportunity to escalate their influence-building in Ashgabat to the disadvantage of Russia and the United States, the Chinese leadership had not acted evidently because it did not want to provoke Russia at a time when relations between the two countries had improved significantly as both resisted U.S. policy in the Middle East and west central Asia, that is, Iraq, Afghanistan, and Iran. Moreover, Berdimukhamedov asserted that he intended no change of focus in his country's foreign policy, an important pronouncement for Beijing and also for both Washington and Moscow.[79]

THE GEORGIA FACTOR

While Turkmenistan was not directly involved in the new conflict going on in Georgia, the implications of Russian policy there were obvious and alarming for Ashgabat. The Kremlin was sending a message to ex-Soviet republics in the Caucasus and central Asia that Moscow would use brute military force to prevent them from drawing too close to the West in the Kremlin's view. And in particular the Kremlin was implying that the central Asian republics were treading on dangerous ground insofar as their relations with Russia are concerned by strengthening ties to the United States to the extent of allowing it to establish military bases on their territory. It was as if the Kremlin were saying that the war against terrorism being fought in Afghanistan was not enough to justify the development of military alliances with the United States that allowed the deployment of U.S. military personnel and equipment in countries proximate to the Russian Federation, which saw its security jeopardized by U.S. military expansion in central Asia.

The Kremlin was trying to "message" the central Asian republics that the United States was not a fit partner for them in security or in the management of the energy trade because of all the ways in which the Bush administrations since 2001 had pursued policies in many different parts of the world, notably in central and Balkan Europe as well as in central Asia that challenged and undermined Russian interests.

How broad the impact of Russian policy in Georgia at the end of the Summer of 2008 really is remains to be seen. The leaders of the central Asian republics and other ex-Soviet territories, especially of Ukraine which has had antagonistic relations with Russia for some time that got worse following the election of a pro-West president, Viktor Yushchenko, were watching developments in Georgia carefully and somewhat fearfully. They were not encouraged by the Western response to the events in Georgia because of sharp divisions over what the response should be: the United States favored tough rhetoric accompanied by forceful though nonviolent economic and political sanctions such as evicting Russia from the G-8 unless its troops left Georgia, while the Western and central European states preferred diplomacy to avoid antagonizing and alienating Russia.

In the Summer and Fall of 2008, Turkmenistan had less to worry about than Georgia because its relations with Russia were much stronger than Georgia's relations with the Kremlin for several reasons, notably Turkmen resistance to U.S. efforts to obtain permission to deploy military forces in Turkmenistan to help fight the Taliban in neighboring Afghanistan. The late Niyazov's "positive neutrality," that the Kremlin sometimes found annoying since it justified the Turkmen withdrawal from the CIS, was now seen in a favorable light, at least because it had prevented a U.S. deployment. Moreover, while the Kremlin was at times a bit uncomfortable with the excesses of Niyazov's neo-Stalinistic dictatorship of Turkmenistan, his rule had assured domestic stability and a modicum of Turkmen respect for and friendship with Russia. And last but not least was Turkmenistan's vast energy resources that passed through Russian pipelines to markets in Europe, a lucrative and potentially politically valuable situation for Russia it was not inclined to disrupt.

That said, Turkmenistan's policy of diversifying its energy carrying pipeline by cooperation with Western investors as well as with Gazprom increases its vulnerability to Russian pressure to increase reliance on Russian pipelines. In addition, lingering problems between Russia and Turkmenistan involving allegedly rough treatment of the Russian minority contribute to Turkmenistan's vulnerability to Russian diplomatic if not economic and military "arm-twisting" though it is difficult to see Russia repeating in Turkmenistan its military strategy in Georgia.[80]

CONCLUSIONS

While both Russia and the United States have extensive and compelling interests in Turkmenistan, Russian interests in the Putin era seemed to have outweighed those of the United States. Russian interests are rooted in history, geography, commerce, and culture. Moreover, Russian interests in Turkmenistan are not encumbered by the kind of democratic and human rights considerations that undermine efforts of the United States to build a strong and enduring relationship with the Turkmen government. On the other hand, a nationalist-inspired obliquely anti-Russian sentiment lies just beneath the surface of Turkmen politics and gives the United States an opening to cultivate and strengthen political, economic, and strategic ties with Turkmenistan. Unlike Russia, the United States has no Soviet era skeletons in Turkmenistan's diplomatic closet, a very important consideration for the present Turkmen leadership.

That said, what the United States can do in strengthening ties to Turkmenistan is limited. Real U.S. interest in Turkmenistan began only in the post-9/11 era and were driven by the need of help fighting the radical Islamic government of Afghanistan and al Qaeda. When the war against terrorism winds down, a major reason for U.S. involvement in Turkmenistan will be gone. Moreover, other U.S. ambitions in Turkmenistan, notably encouraging democracy, are less likely to be achieved in the near term, especially since the leaders of the central Asian countries today do not place much value on it. In addition, the chances of Turkmenistan giving the United States an edge over Russia in its production and export of energy resources are slight because of the historic Turkmen ties, especially in trade of all kinds, to Russia. In this regard, the decision of Turkmenistan's new leadership to help build and use a gas pipeline to market energy in Europe that runs through Russia and is strongly opposed by the United States is the most recent of much evidence to indicate Turkmen inclinations to work closely with Russia, while it patronizes the United States for whatever benefit it gets from that policy.

Still, working to the advantage of U.S. influence-building in Turkmenistan is the pragmatic and realistic approach of the post-Niyazov leadership in foreign policy. President Berdimukhamedov wants to keep his diplomatic fences with the United States in good repair for the strategic and other benefits that accrue to Turkmenistan from that policy. Like other central Asian leaders such as those of Kazakhstan, Tajikistan, and Kyrgyzstan, friendship with the United States gives Turkmenistan some modest leverage in resisting growing Russian influence-building and a dream he knows the Putin Kremlin has of reconstituting some of Russia's Soviet status and power.

Also, to its advantage, Washington has learned a lesson about restraint in pushing for democracy. The heavy U.S. focus on democratization strained ties with Niyazov, who feared democratization could cost him his presidency. Niyazov saw the United States with its apparent obsession with democratization of Turkmenistan as being its own way as aggressively intrusive in Turkmen affairs as Russia was—perhaps even more so since it was personally threatening. With these learning experiences in mind, the United States has some continuing interest for wanting influence in the area and every expectation that it will reach some of its goals if only because Turkmenistan's policy of "positive neutrality" is based on a rational estimate of its strategic needs, especially as it serves to keep Russia at some arm's length. If U.S. policy after the Bush administration leaves office in early 2009 were to pay more attention in its dealings with the Berdimukhamedov leadership to strategic issues and less attention to democratization, it could eventually beat the Russians in the influence-building game the two had played throughout the Bush-Putin era from 2000 to 2008.

4

Tajikistan

- Population: 6.3 million (UN, 2005)
- Capital: Dushanbe
- Area: 143,100 sq. km (55,251 sq. miles)
- Major languages: Tajik, Uzbek, Russian
- Major religion: Islam
- Life expectancy: 61 years (men), 66 years (women) (UN)
- Monetary unit: 1 Tajik somoni = 100 dirams
- Main exports: Aluminum, electricity, cotton, fruit, textiles
- GNI per capita: US$330 (World Bank, 2006)

Tajikistan has a special strategic significance for Russia and the United States. As it was located alongside of Uzbekistan and Kyrgyzstan as well as Russia, China, and Afghanistan, inevitably Russia and the United States saw Tajikistan as having a pivotal role because of its geography in the war against terrorism. In addition, Tajikistan has an abundance of unexplored natural gas and oil resources of importance to all its neighbors and to the United States. Finally, Tajikistan, with the lowest annual per capita income of about $1200, is the poorest of the five ex-Soviet central Asian republics and the most vulnerable to external threats to its security and domestic stability. As a consequence of this vulnerability, Tajikistan is especially sensitive to balancing its relationships so as to maximize its political stability and territorial security.

Tajikistan (Courtesy of UN Cartographic Section)

RUSSIA AND TAJIKISTAN UNDER YELTSIN, 1992–1999[1]

Following the collapse of the Soviet Union and the transformation of its central Asian republics into independent sovereign states, Russia under President Boris Yeltsin had two problems in its relations with the Republic of Tajikistan. The first and, arguably, the most serious problem was how to respond when a civil war broke out almost as soon as Tajikistan became independent. The second problem concerned the small Russian minority living permanently in Tajikistan and at risk from the country's rising nationalism driven in part by a strong undercurrent of anti-Russian sentiment. Russian leaders, especially Gennady Zyuganov, head of the Russian Communist Party, Vladimir Zhirinovsky, head of the Liberal Democratic Party of Russia (LDPR), and General Alexandr Labed, head of the Congress of Russian Communities, feared discrimination by the Tajik administration now completely independent of Moscow.

Russia and the Tajik Civil War

Throughout most of the 1990s, Russia was concerned about the appearance of a new Tajik political opposition made up of democratic reformers and Islamic radicals, especially the Islamic Rebirth Party. This opposition wanted to oust from power the pro-Russian leadership of Rahmon Nabiev, head of the Tajik branch of the former Soviet Communist Party. Islamic militants in particular wanted to transform Tajikistan into a Muslim-dominated anti-Russian state. Such a state would be in the Kremlin view a liability for the security and stability of post–Soviet Russia, especially the predominantly Muslim Chechnya, whose anti-Russian insurgency the Kremlin believed was influenced heavily by Islamic fundamentalism.[2]

Opposition parties relentlessly opposed Nabiyev, condemning the corruption and repression of his regime. Fueling the opposition was the poverty of villages in eastern Tajikistan and the evident discrimination against them by the Nabiyev regime. Opposition to Nabiyev came also from Tajiks living in the remote mountainous areas of the country, whose interests had been all but forgotten by Dushanbe in the Soviet era. Support of Nabiyev came mainly from the tribal groups living in the western part of the country in the regions of Kurgan-Tyube, Kulyab, and Khodzhent. Although Nabiyev had won 57 percent in Tajikistan's first presidential election after gaining independence, much of the population soon rejected his leadership.

Nabiyev's refusal to allow democratization of post-Soviet Tajikistan, say in the form of a multiparty system and free elections, was understandable. Real democracy, so he reasoned, as did the Russian leadership which liked and supported him, would weaken his control of Tajikistan by opening the way to an ascendancy of opposition forces that could end with the installation of regimes that would be anti-Russian externally and either theocratic or democratic internally. Indeed, the Yeltsin government early on decided to back Nabiyev against opposition groups challenging his regime in an armed insurgency. Antigovernment demonstrations in 1992 soon turned into an all-out civil war between opponents and supporters of the Nabiyev regime. This full-scale civil war did not abate until the end of the decade.

Scope of Russian Involvement

The Russians offered Tajikistan military support which grew steadily in the early and mid-1990s. By the end of 1992, Russia contributed the major portion of a CIS-sponsored peacekeeping force of about 1,000 troops to try to maintain order in Dushanbe. Sharing Russia's eagerness to keep Nabiyev in power as a bulwark against the expansion of Islamic influence, Kazakhstan, Kyrgyzstan, and Uzbekistan also contributed to the CIS multinational force. Although the Kremlin wanted to make its involvement in Tajikistan collective to avoid the appearance of influence-building, a larger Russian military commitment was inevitable given the increasingly evident weakness of the Nabiyev regime to survive. Subsequently, Russia sent more military personnel to prop up the Nabiyev government. By February 1993, there were about 3,500 Russian troops in Tajikistan and 20,000 additional Russian military personnel. Russia pledged to rebuild the Tajik Army and to provide help at the frontier with Afghanistan. By the mid-1990s, already closely linked to Russia by several treaties, notably the 1992 multilateral Collective Security Treaty and the 1993 bilateral Treaty of Friendship, Cooperation, and Mutual Assistance, Tajikistan had become virtually a satellite of Moscow.[3]

Russia also tightened economic and financial ties to Tajikistan. In a monetary agreement with Russia, Tajik government, now under Emomali Rakhmonov, agreed to turn over control of currency and credit to the Russian Central Bank and to use the Russian ruble as the country's medium of exchange. By 1994, Russia was paying nearly 70 percent of the Tajik state budget and had 25,000 troops deployed in the country to protect the government of President Rakhmonov. During this time, Tajikistan not only faced its own civil war but also incursions from fundamentalists in Afghanistan. In fact, Russian forces occasionally found themselves fighting Islamic insurgents.

Although the Kremlin did have some misgivings about Rakhmonov because of his neo-Stalinistic repressiveness and brutality, it accepted his election to the Tajik presidency in November 1994, as he was the only alternative to a fundamentalist leadership of the country the Russians were determined to prevent. To the dismay of the Kremlin, however, Rakhmonov's hard-line government was unable to fulfill its expectations. By early 1997, Rakhmonov's regime controlled only a few slices of Tajik territory, about 20 percent of the country. It survived mainly because of Russian support and the backing of some local warlords determined to prevent the establishment of an Islamic state led by a fundamentalist—by no means an impossibility.[4]

Russian Goals and Ambitions

A key reason for the Yeltsin government's decision to support Nabiyev and after him Rakhmonov had to do with the security of Russia's southern territory, with its large Muslim minorities. Indeed, Russia and other neighboring republics, in particular Uzbekistan, worried that the Tajik civil strife could spread quickly throughout the region.

Initially, however, Russian President Boris Yeltsin, who preferred to focus Russia's attention on improving relations with the West, was inclined to keep out of the Tajik trouble except to offer mediation between the warring groups. The sooner the civil war came to end, the less threat there would be to Russian interests in Tajikistan and the larger ex-Soviet central Asian region. The Russian commander of military forces deployed in Tajikistan invited the two sides to discuss formation of a government of national reconciliation. But, an agreement fell apart because other Russian military leaders favored a Russian military intervention in Tajikistan to assure the survival of the secular and pro-Russian Tajik leadership.

Russian "Eurasianists," a group of influential political and military leaders, along with policy analysts wanted the Kremlin to pursue a steady policy of Russian influence-building throughout Eurasia, especially in central Asia where most of the political leaders of the region were secular and pro-Russian. They put enormous pressure on Yeltsin to gain a foothold in Tajikistan, and the political justification for intervention in Tajikistan, advocated by the "Eurasianists," was, simply stated, the need to preserve stability, law, and order and prevent Islamic fundamentalism from spreading throughout central Asia and into Russia itself. In their view, if Russia remained aloof and disengaged in Tajikistan, the Kremlin risked destabilization of not only Tajikistan but the entire central Asian region.[5]

From the point of view of these "Eurasianists," Russia had a "head start" in expanding its influence in places like Tajikistan because the anti-Islamic, pro-Russian leadership in not only Tajikistan but other ex-Soviet central Asian republics were sympathetic at least for the time being to maintaining close political, economic, and military ties to Russia. Yeltsin's gradual inclination to accept the thinking of the "Eurasianists" arguably was influenced by increasingly strained Russian relations with the United States and other Western countries, notably over the war in Bosnia where Russian strategic and other interests clashed with those of the West. The Kremlin was sympathetic to and supportive of the Serb side in the Bosnian war, while the West backed the Bosnian Muslim leadership of President Alija Izetbegovic in Sarajevo.[6]

Also, the growing threat of Islamic extremism from Afghanistan and its spread into Russian territory (it was already palpable in the unending war in Chechnya) from Afghanistan influenced Russian policy toward Tajikistan. The political situation in neighboring Afghanistan was especially troubling. In a Russian view, according to the 1994 Foreign Intelligence Service Report, there were political forces in Afghanistan looking to strengthen ties with Tajikistan as part of a large strategy to create a new state of Persian-speaking people living on both sides of the Afghan-Tajik border.[7]

Afghanistan and the Tajik Civil War

The Tajik civil war in the late 1990s was complicated by the radical Islamic fundamentalist Taliban regime in neighboring Afghanistan. The Kremlin and some of its allies in central Asia, in particular Uzbekistan, were terrified by the possibility that Afghan-style fundamentalism was taking root in Tajikistan from where it could spread even as far as Chechnya.

In the Russian view, the Tajik-Afghan border to all intents and purposes was a Russian-Afghan border, and events on that border were of direct importance to Russia. By 1993, the Afghan fundamentalist government had recruited an estimated 65,000 Tajiks in guerrilla training centers for the purpose of returning them to Tajikistan to fight with the Islamists against the Rakhmonov government. There were frequent border clashes, with the Russian troops suffering heavy casualties, prompted a formal protest from the Tajik Foreign Ministry, and from Russia, whose troops were patrolling the Tajik-Afghan frontier.

Through this period, Yeltsin preferred cautious policy but was pressed by hard-liners in the Defense Ministry and the political opposition in the Duma, which wanted to send more Russian troops into Tajikistan. Yeltsin, however, was inclined to proceed cautiously with the Afghan government, fearful of getting Russia into another military involvement with Afghanistan, which the Russian public adamantly opposed. In addition, Yeltsin had to worry about the way in which a growing Taliban influence in the Tajik civil war impacted on Uzbekistan. The Karimov regime was concerned about the safety of the large Uzbek minority in Tajikistan (about 25% of the total Tajik population). With Yeltsin's encouragement, Uzbekistan President Karimov backed the Rakhmonov government, in his view the only political force capable of preventing the establishment of a Taliban-style fundamentalist regime.

To the dismay of the Kremlin, a new phase of Afghan involvement in Tajik affairs began in 1996, when the Taliban took power in Kabul.[8] Most Tajik people were frightened at the prospect of a Taliban approach toward their border, especially those who saw in the Taliban movement a direct threat to the secular character of their state. The Taliban openly encouraged and assisted the Tajik Islamic opposition in its campaign to seize power.

The small Tajik minority living in northern Afghanistan was also at risk. The Taliban were ethnic Pashtun people who wanted to rid Afghanistan of non-Pashtun minorities.

The Taliban were dangerous also because they had the backing of influential outsiders, in particular Pakistan and Saudi Arabia. The Kremlin found Pakistan ready, willing, and able to support the Taliban as leverage with Moscow in its policy toward India. Indeed, the Pakistani government sought to undermine the Russian-Indian partnership, especially to discourage the delivery of Russian military equipment to India. Army General Anatolyi Kvashnin, chief of the Russian General Staff in 2001, advocated priority of Russian attention to regional conflicts like those in Chechnya and Afghanistan, pointing out that Afghanistan under the Taliban was a center of extremism and international terrorism. Gradually, Russian security policy shifted southward, especially toward Tajikistan and its central Asian neighbors.[9]

The Taliban threat to Tajikistan continued into the late 1990s. The Kremlin's fear of long-term negative consequences for both Russia and Tajikistan of the Taliban takeover of Afghanistan was vindicated. Afghan refugees, terrorized by the brutal Taliban rule, streamed into Tajikistan. The Kremlin issued a stern warning to the Taliban about violations of borders of CIS members, with a veiled threat of retaliation if the Taliban did not do something to seal off Afghanistan's frontier with the central Asian republics. As a consequence of the Taliban ascendancy in Afghanistan, Russia continued to protect Rakhmonov's secular government in Dushanbe from subversion by Islamic fundamentalists. About 50,000 uniformed Russian personnel stayed on in Tajikistan after the end of the civil war, 25,000 as part of a CIS peacekeeping force and 25,000 Russian troops helped patrol Tajikistan's borders.

Chechnya and Russian Policy in Tajikistan

The ongoing seemingly unwinnable Russian military conflict in Chechnya in the mid and late 1990s argued for a continued presence of the Russian military in Tajikistan. The Kremlin saw the Chechen insurgency, especially after a Chechen rebel force led by Shamir Basayev invaded Dagestan in August 1999, as expansionist and imperialistic with Basayev seeking to extend Islamic influence and control beyond the confines of Chechnya and other parts of the Russian Caucasus southward to the ex-Soviet republics of central Asia. To prevent this from happening, the Kremlin continued its strong military deployment in neighboring Tajikistan.

Russia Works to End the Tajik Civil War

Meanwhile, Yeltsin wanted an end to the civil war. He called upon Foreign Minister Yevgeni Primakov to get the job done diplomatically.[10] Primakov's direct involvement in what seemed like endless and frequently futile negotiations with the antigovernment opposition seeking a greater voice in national political affairs tightly managed by the Rakhmonov regime eventually led to an agreement providing for a kind of power-sharing arrangement. Rakhmonov remained as president with leadership positions below the presidency shared by neo-Communist secularists and Islamic reformers.

Division of the opposition into different groups and personalities committed to different programs of change allowed Rakhmonov to play the different sides against each other and to keep his political primacy. The large Russian military presence as well as military support from neighboring Uzbekistan, Kyrgyzstan, and Kazakhstan, which had troops deployed in Tajikistan and on its borders under the auspices of the CIS, assured the survival of Rakhmonov.

Primakov's diplomacy was successful with the Islamic constituency because the foreign minister was an "Arabist" expert by training and a diplomat with many years of experience in dealing with the Middle East. Primakov was sympathetic to the Arab-Muslim confrontation with the United States. He wanted restoration of the old Soviet era entente with countries like Syria, Iraq, and Libya. The determination of Primakov to sidestep the CIS and also the United Nations in winding down the war in Tajikistan showed a willingness of the Kremlin to pursue bilateral approaches to the central Asian republics outside the CIS framework in its efforts to strengthen ties to them.[11]

The Russian Minority and Russian-Tajik Relations

Of concern to the Kremlin since the early 1990s was not only this seemingly endless civil strife but also the well-being of the small Russian minority in Tajikistan, which looked to Russia for protection of its interests. Increasingly, they experienced nationalist and anti-Russian-inspired discrimination. The Tajik Russian community had long taken for granted its material well-being, having been encouraged by the Soviet government to take up permanent residence in Tajikistan to strengthen Russian influence in the country when it was one of the 15 constituent (union) republics of the unified Soviet state. The "Eurasianists," advocates of an aggressive influence-building policy on the part of post–Soviet Russia, especially General Labed and his ultranationalist party known as the Congress of Russian Communities, used the tenuous situation of the minority to call for increased Russian involvement in Tajikistan as well as other central Asian republics.[12]

Yeltsin was in no hurry to champion the interests of the Russian minorities, especially in Tajikistan. Tajik Russians had been no friend of his. Tajik Russians had welcomed the conservative anti-Gorbachev coup in August 1991 because they supported preservation of the highly centralized Soviet federal system on which they relied for safety. They took the breakup of the Soviet state that Yeltsin had helped to engineer with great difficulty and disbelief.

In the early and mid-1990s, the Russian community in Tajikistan had much to be worried about. They could read the "handwriting on the wall," so to speak, when the Tajik government had passed in 1989 a new law stipulating the local Tajik tongue as the state language. Many Russians living in Tajikistan for a long time never had learned to speak or read and write the language. Indeed, the Tajik Russians worried about their deteriorating status. Their anxiety was a significant determinant of Russia's effort to expand its influence in Tajikistan from the early 1990s onward though there was never a strong commitment by the Kremlin to interfere directly in Tajik politics for their sake.[13]

An influential component of the Russian-speaking community in Tajikistan were former Soviet military officers who were especially upset over the breakup of the Soviet Union in 1991. They were born, grew up, and trained in Tajikistan and had little sympathy for the democratic revolution in Russia and supported the pro-Communist Popular Front of Tajikistan (PFT) that advocated preservation of the Soviet Union. Eventually, some left the newly independent state of Tajikistan after having helped arm the PFT. They were promoted to leadership positions in the joint command of CIS strategic forces from which they lobbied aggressively for Russian influence-building in the post-Soviet era in Tajikistan.[14]

Uzbekistan and Russian-Tajik Relations

In the 1990s, Uzbekistan's policy toward Tajikistan was still another problem for the Yeltsin Kremlin's policy in Tajikistan, especially when the Karimov government sent troops to end the civil war there. This Uzbek military presence was a source of concern to the Kremlin. Karimov was ambitious for influence-building in the region. By the end of the 1990s, to the Kremlin's chagrin, Uzbekistan had become something of a rival of Russia for influence over the Tajikistan political system and President Rakhmonov. The Tajik civil war had turned out to be a sea of troubles in which the Karimov regime in Uzbekistan could not resist fishing, doubtlessly encouraging the Kremlin to bring the conflict to an end as soon as possible.

Tajikistan was vulnerable to the predatory ambitions of Karimov for several reasons. The Tajik government's authority did not really extend into large parts of the country during the civil war. Throughout the 1990s and in the early years of the new century, political assassinations were a matter of everyday life. The Guarm and Tavildara came under the influence of Islamic insurgents.[15]

In addition, the Uzbek government found a convenient pretext for keeping military forces in Tajikistan after the formal end of the civil war, and when the CIS peacekeeping states except Russia had withdrawn their military forces, Uzbek military personnel remained in Tajikistan, they said, because Islamic insurgents based in Afghanistan might cross into Tajikistan to continue the fight to oust the secular leadership of the country. Moreover, Uzbek authorities accused Tajikistan of providing refuge to anti-Karimov Uzbek extremists given historic Tajik fear and suspicion of Uzbekistan. To make the point, Uzbekistan introduced mandatory visas for Tajiks traveling to Uzbekistan and closed several border-crossing points along the Uzbek-Tajik frontier.[16]

Uzbekistan's interest in northern Tajikistan was of special concern to the Kremlin. For centuries this region had been linked by trade routes to Uzbekistan's lush Ferghama valley with this large geographic space shared by the two countries making up a natural economic unit with a shared transportation and energy infrastructure. Unfortunately, when the Soviet authorities in its early years fixed the state borders in central Asia, they ignored these natural connections. Making this situation worse for Tajikistan in its relations with Uzbekistan was that Tajik depended on Uzbek energy. The Karimov regime used this resource for leverage over the Tajiks. In addition, the main exit roads out of Tajikistan and the only railway connections with the outside world ran through Uzbekistan, further strengthening Karimov's economic leverage over his Tajik neighbor.[17]

The Kremlin monitored Tajik-Uzbek relations because of Tajikistan's strategic importance as an ally of Russia in the war against Islamic extremism. Tajikistan was a major conduit for weapons earmarked for the anti-Taliban forces in northern Afghanistan known as the Northern Alliance. And the role of Tajikistan in Russia's anti-Taliban strategy with the ascendancy of Putin became even more important to the Kremlin because of the increasing reluctance of Uzbekistan and Turkmenistan to confront the Taliban, never mind try to unseat them in Kabul.[18]

By the time Putin was elected President of Russia in March 2000, the domestic situation in Tajikistan had begun to quiet down. The Tajik government had succeeded in extending its administrative control over most of the country weakening the divisive local political "warlords" so that they could not challenge the central authorities. Furthermore, Rakhmonov skillfully preserved the domestic peace of the 1997 agreements by engaging in a limited political liberalization without seriously weakening his dictatorial leadership. Rakhmonov began slowly but steadily to democratize the Tajik political system. For example, an independent media emerged. The Tajik regime also was willing to tolerate an Islamist political group that was more evidence of an emerging political pluralism.

U.S. POLICY IN TAJIKISTAN AFTER 9/11

Perhaps the most serious problem for Russian policy in Tajikistan for Russian President Vladimir Putin was the expansion of U.S. influence. In the aftermath of 9/11, the Bush administration made a concerted effort to enlist Tajikistan, along with other central Asian republics, in its declared war against terrorism, especially the U.S. invasion of Afghanistan to remove the Taliban from power in late 2001.

U.S. Interests

For the United States, Tajikistan's proximity to Afghanistan was of prime importance in its effort to remove the Taliban from power and subsequently keep the Taliban from recovering control. In addition, the United States sought Tajik cooperation in the reconstruction of the debilitated Afghan economy, in particular its infrastructure, as well as fighting terrorism and the drug trade. Ultimately, the United States saw Tajikistan playing a key role along with a Taliban-free Afghanistan in the development of a regional economic-based integration. And last, but certainly not least in importance, was the ideological goal embraced well before 9/11 during the Clinton administrations between 1992 and 2000. The United States was eager to see Tajikistan move more quickly than in the past to a real democratization of its political system that included respect for human rights and accountability of government to the voting public. Both President George Bush and the U.S. Embassy in Dushanbe called relentlessly on the Tajik regime to allow political pluralism and electoral freedom.[19]

Tajik Responsiveness

In the immediate aftermath of 9/11, U.S.-Tajik relations were off to a good start, with the government of President Emomali Rakhmonov willing to grant permission to the United States and its allies to use its airspace for bombing missions in Afghanistan. Rakhmonov also offered NATO and in particular the United States use of bases at the Dushanbe airport, Kulyab, and Kurgan-Tyube. Only one base at Dushanbe was fit for immediate use by the Americans because of its capacity to receive heavy aircraft though it was so run down that it needed about $50 million for repair and upgrading. Other Western military facilities on Tajik territory were located at Khujand, Kulyab, and Kurgan-Tyube. The French stationed up to six Mirage fighters for use in Afghanistan at the Dushanbe facility.[20]

Rakhmonov, however, refused to allow the United States and other Western countries access to some more desirable military bases, while he allowed Russia to deploy a greater amount of military weapons and personnel in Tajikistan. By this concession, Rakhmonov intended to avoid provoking the Kremlin as it strengthened Tajikistan's military and other links to the West, especially the United States.[21]

The United States welcomed Rakhmonov's offer of limited base facilities with periodic financial assistance for food purchases and for other humanitarian purposes. This aid was also to suppress the drug trade and to encourage democratization. Then, in December 2002, Rakhmonov made a first visit ever to Washington where he received a warm welcome to the dismay of the Kremlin. The Americans praised Tajikistan's role in the coalition fighting international terrorism, leading the Tajik Foreign Ministry to ruminate about the "long-term strategic partnership" discussed by both sides.[22]

The United States and Growing Tajik Independence of Russia

On this and other occasions, the Bush administrations encouraged the Tajik leadership to assert itself vis-à-vis the Kremlin to protect and enhance its independence of Moscow. To this end, the administration lifted a ban on the export of weapons to Tajikistan and formally invited Tajikistan to join the Partnership for Peace program enabling it to participate in military games and maneuvers sponsored by NATO.[23]

In 2003, the Tajik government with U.S. support took another step designed to focus attention on its independence. In the Summer of 2003, Rakhmonov came under heavy pressure from the Kremlin to establish a military base on Tajik territory. According to Russian Defense Ministry sources, Rakhmonov refused to accommodate the Kremlin's request except in return for a write-off of Tajikistan's state debt to Russia worth about $300 million with an understanding that this was a "preliminary condition" by the Tajik side. Though the Tajik leadership denied the Russian allegation about the write-off, there was some truth to it because base negotiations between Russian and Tajik officials had been going on for some time but apparently had accomplished little by the time Putin made a visit to Dushanbe in early August to speed things along. The Tajiks also insisted that a Russian military deployment in Tajikistan should be under Tajik command, not Russian. The Russian side rejected out of hand the idea of Russian forces under Tajik command. The base negotiations remained stalemated despite the intercession of Putin.[24]

Tajik intransigence in dealing with the Russians coincided with the United States expanding its military aid program for Tajikistan, and the Russian side seemed to think, with good reason, that the Rakhmonov leadership was trying to ingratiate itself with Americans by cooperating with a U.S. military buildup in Tajikistan, which was making the Kremlin increasingly uncomfortable. In the Russian view, the United States was bribing Rakhmonov with the prospect of loans totaling $1 billion; with the expenditure of $63 million for the construction of a giant diplomatic office complex in central Dushanbe; and with the payment of several thousand dollars for each landing and takeoff of U.S. aircraft from the Dushanbe airport while making plans to upgrade the military airport near Kulyab. The U.S. intent was encouragement of Rakhmonov to block Russia's military buildup aimed at bolstering its own security as well as that of Tajikistan and its central Asian neighbors. According to the Russians, there was a direct relationship between the difficulty the Kremlin was having in developing military cooperation with Tajikistan and the U.S. military buildup.[25]

The Kremlin was much concerned over the difficulty of getting Tajik cooperation on the base issue. For Russia, establishment of a military base in Tajikistan was essential in light of the rapid expansion of U.S. influence not only in Tajikistan but elsewhere in central Asia. The Kremlin wanted to constrain and reverse the U.S. influence-building campaign in the post-9/11 era by setting up the base.[26]

More Tajik independence of the Kremlin was evident in September 2003, when the head of the Tajik border service demanded that Russia withdraw from the joint force patrolling the Tajik-Afghan frontier. The Tajik government, however, was quick to assure the Kremlin that the border service was acting on its own and that its request that Russia turn over its responsibility for helping secure the border to Tajik officials was not formal policy. In fact, the Tajik government agreed that Russian border guards would work with Tajik officials until 2006.[27]

The United States Strengthens Military Ties with Tajikistan, 2005–2006

In response to evident pressure from both Russia and China on Rakhmonov to limit the American military presence in Tajikistan seen as an obstacle to their own interests, there as well was a sense among the Tajik political elite that the United States was an "outsider." The Bush administration sent Defense Secretary Donald Rumsfeld to Dushanbe in late July 2005 to get reassurance from the Tajik government that it would continue to allow an American military presence in the country for the war against terrorism in Afghanistan. Rumsfeld emphasized the importance of the American initiatives for not only terrorism in Afghanistan but also the terrorist threat inside the region to the secular regimes, including the Rakhmonov government, given the susceptibility of their predominantly Muslim societies to militant Islamic terrorist activity. In short, Tajikistan needed the United States as much, if not more, than the United States needed Tajikistan.[28]

Rumsfeld's hard sell on this occasion seemed to be successful. Tajik Foreign Minister Talbak Nazarov said publicly to Rumsfeld that Tajikistan intended to continue active cooperation with the United States. He reaffirmed Tajikistan's continued willingness to grant the United States overflight rights and access to ground facilities. But, as of mid-2005, the United States had no troops stationed in Tajikistan but did have landing rights and what was termed a "gas and go" agreement that permitted U.S. planes to refuel at Tajik airfields on their way to Afghanistan. In return Rumsfeld offered U.S. help in securing Tajikistan's frontier with Afghanistan in the wake of a withdrawal of Russian troops that had served along with Tajik personnel in patrolling the country's borders. The major concern of both sides was the ongoing cross-border traffic in heroin.[29] Overall, the U.S.-Tajik relationship strengthened Tajikistan's security and the Tajik hand in dealing with Russia.[30]

U.S. military diplomacy continued with Rumsfeld's July 2006 visit to Dushanbe to encourage Tajikistan to stand tough against the Taliban's new offensive against American and NATO forces in Afghanistan. By this time as well the United States was countering Taliban use of Tajikistan as a smuggling route in the heroine trade as a means of getting more funds for weapons.[31]

In 2006 and subsequently, the United States kept funds flowing to Tajikistan, providing aid worth about $28.1 million, up from $24.6 million the previous year. The money was to go for democratic and economic reform, to fight infectious diseases, combat extremism, improve education, and improve border control, all of which Rumsfeld discussed with the Tajik leadership in July.[32] And, in 2007, the United States planned to give Tajikistan an estimated $45.2 million worth of assistance with largest portion of this financial package to be spent on security and law enforcement. Other U.S. money was intended to provide humanitarian assistance and fund so-called "democracy programs" that aimed at political liberalization, in particular free speech through an independent media and the fostering of accountability on both local and central government institutions.[33]

Overall, however, U.S. aid to Tajikistan was still quite modest given the large strategic and ideological interests of the United States and its determination to assure stability in the ex-Soviet region. The consequence was that the U.S. Pentagon was unable to reverse an evident decline in American influence-building in central Asia because so much American aid was directed to Iraq and Afghanistan.[34]

Problems in U.S. Relations with Tajikistan

From the outset of the post-9/11 period, the United States had many problems trying to expand U.S. ties with Tajikistan. The most serious problem was an obvious contradiction in U.S. goals. On the one hand, the United States needed and wanted Tajik help in the war against al Qaeda in Afghanistan. On the other hand, the United States pushed for democratization, something its would-be ally, the Rakhmonov regime, resisted and ignored. Other problems concerned the growing interest of Iran, which opposed U.S. policy in Tajikistan and other central Asian countries. Teheran refused to take the war on terrorism seriously and opposed the anti-Taliban policies of the United States in central Asia. China also was a problem for the United States because it too wanted political and economic influence in Tajikistan now that it was independent of Moscow and free to develop its own system of foreign relations. Finally, the United States had to contend with occasionally harsh Russian pressure on the Rakhmonov government to limit its ties to the United States.

Tajikistan's Sluggish Democratization

In the aftermath of 9/11, to the dismay of the Bush administration, Tajikistan became neo-Stalinistic dictatorship under Rakhmonov's increasingly authoritarian leadership. He needed to tighten his grip on power in the face of a threat to his regime from militant Islamic extremism. At the same time, he had the blessing and, indeed, the encouragement of the new Putin Kremlin to embrace a kind of neo-Stalinistic authoritarianism that would enable him to control his society against not only Islamists but also anti-Russian-inspired Tajik nationalism. The United States, nevertheless, found it hard to stomach his perceived reversal of democratic development and pondered what to do as the Kremlin seemed to watch his consolidation of power with none of the qualms the United States had.

Out of fear about the security and survival of his secular leadership in the face of militant Islamic extremism and terrorism, Rakhmonov embraced a new authoritarianism. It was intended to prevent a resurgence of the kind of Islamist challenge he had faced in the 1990s. He tried to amend the Tajik Constitution to extend the term of the president from 5 to 7 years with the possibility of reelection for two additional terms. This change would allow Rakhmonov to remain head of state until 2020. Criticism of these changes was effectively squelched by the government.[35]

Rakhmonov severely restricted political pluralism, limiting the number of parties that could obtain legal recognition and ignoring some opposition parties that said they were willing to play the role of a constructive opposition. Indeed, the appearance of a multiparty system belied reality of an increasingly monolithic political environment reminiscent of the Communist era. The culture supported this authoritarian bias since Tajik society did not take very seriously the role of political parties and, rather, assigned priority to personal ties, kinship relations, and regional affiliations. Nevertheless, some democratization did continue with registration of opposition parties enabling them to compete with the ruling People's Democratic Party of Rakhmonov in parliamentary elections in 2002 though at times it was undermined on the local levels of administration by loyalist officials opposed to political liberalization.[36]

Rakhmonov was extremely skillful in controlling Islamic activities and preserving domestic political stability. While allowing Tajik religious institutions a modicum of autonomy, in particular the heavily Islamist-influenced opposition group known as the Islamic Revival Party, the regime was always on its guard against the appearance of extremism among its Islamic population and minutely regulated it. According to Tajik law, all religious organizations had to register with the state and abide by its strictures like the one that prohibited clerics from joining a political party. In addition, local authorities had a say in the election of the imam of a mosque to make sure block the candidacy of mavericks. In addition, the ruling Ulema was severely limited in what it could say in public on any topic. The Rakhmonov regime contained and restrained religious activities to prevent the appearance of extremism and to that extent made Tajikistan a reliable ally of the Kremlin, keeping a lid on Islamic extremism and opposition.[37]

In another vein, Rakhmonov strengthened his own personal grip on power. He asked the country to allow him to continue as president for a long time into the future in a referendum. Tajik voters accommodated their president in a referendum held in June 2003 that allowed Rakhmonov to be elected for two more seven-year terms following the expiration of his present term in 2006.[38] Tajik voters saw Rakhmonov as founder and savior of an independent and sovereign Tajikistan administered at least in theory by and for and in the interest of ethnic Tajiks, a pleasingly novel situation given the long subjugation of Tajiks to Russians in recent Tajik history.[39]

Despite Rakhmonov's real popularity, the government had gone "overboard" to assure the outcome of the June 2003 referendum, terrifying voters who contemplated not voting. The turnout was 96 percent of eligible voters with 93 percent of them approving the change.[40] The now heavily state-controlled media called on voters to go to the polls and to vote yes. Given a view that Tajik voters lack an understanding of democratic politics and are interested in primarily one issue, stability, the government's intervention was overkill and clearly in violation of the spirit if not the letter of Tajikistan's alleged democratic and parliamentary system of government.[41]

While opposition groups complained that most voters had the wool pulled over their eyes by the charismatic Rakhmonov and had been poorly informed about the package of constitutional changes the government had put through to strengthen the presidency, the Kremlin had no problem with the election and was pleased with Rakhmonov's success. The Tajik leader had become a cooperative friend. Pleased with Russian endorsement of his leadership, Rakhmonov agreed to prolong Russian military assistance to Tajikistan, thereby expanding its already extensive influence in the country.

The American Dilemma

By 2005, to Washington's dismay, it had become evident that Rakhmonov had neither the will nor the capability to pursue the kind of democratization the Bush administration wanted of him as the price of being a U.S. "ally." For example, he manipulated the February 2005 U.S. insistence that these elections be as free and as fair as possible. In fact, the U.S. Embassy in Dushanbe asked the Rakhmonov leadership to relax the political environment to allow a truly open, democratic electoral experience.[42]

The media was of special concern to the United States because it already was heavily influenced by the government making it difficult for opposition groups to appeal to the country as a whole. These concerns certainly did not accord with Rakhmonov's intentions to strengthen and perpetuate his strong grip over the country's already authoritarian political system.

According to the OSCE, the elections were close to a sham with Rakhmonov's party, the People's Democratic Party, winning 80 percent of the votes. Opposition parties, including the pro-government Communist Party, expressed outrage over the obvious fraud that accounted for the striking success of the People's Democratic Party. But the Communists as well as other parties were not inclined to make a crisis over the causes of the Democratic Party's success such as ballot box stuffing and people voting two or three times for the same candidate, divide the country, and restart another civil war that in all probability would bring them no more success than their insurgencies of the 1990s had brought them.[43]

The November 2006 parliamentary elections also were manipulated and there was little surprise over the news that Rakhmonov's supporters had won an overwhelming majority of the popular vote. The OSCE Election Observation Mission then pointed out fault with the holding of the presidential election. The OSCE Mission said among other things that there had been no credible challenger to the incumbent, that the media was under government control, and that the somewhat modest independent private media maintained a self-censorship probably out of fear of retaliation.[44]

Disappointed, the Bush administration refrained from criticism of Rakhmonov's antidemocratic behavior because it needed Rakhmonov's cooperation in the war against terrorism so much. The administration did not want to risk alienating the Tajik political elite. Instead, the United States bided its time until conditions within and around Tajikistan stabilized. Certainly, Bush did not want to risk driving the Tajik government into the arms of the Kremlin. Should it undermine Rakhmonov, the Bush administration could easily open the way for the ascendancy of radical nationalists and religious zealots whose rule could be as troublesome for Washington than Rakhmonov was. Indeed, the United States was unmoved by the fact that Tajikistan under Rakhmonov had become for all important purposes a single-party state. The U.S. ambassador captured the U.S. priority as he reportedly intoned on the eve of the election that Rakhmonov "has done a remarkable job of bringing stability to the country."[45]

Tajik Relations with Iran

Another problem for the U.S. effort to make an ally of Tajikistan in the ongoing war in Afghanistan was Rakhmonov's growing ties to Iran. For some time, Tajikistan had been developing a friendship with Iran. The United States was concerned about this friendship given Iran's special interest in expanding its influence in central Asia now that the "Soviet barrier" is gone. In the official Tajik view, Iran had a decisive role in Tajikistan's defense strategy.[46]

This relationship presented a problem for the United States given its hostile relations with Iran exacerbated by Iran's evident goal to develop nuclear weapons and Iran's opposition to the American presence in Iraq. Moscow was not so alarmed. Moscow accepted Tajikistan and Tajik responsiveness to them. Evidently, Moscow was willing to see Iran play a more active role in central Asia in the aftermath of 9/11 to better check the influence-building of the United States. In addition, the Iranian leadership was extremely careful about its influence-building initiatives in central Asia and in Tajikistan in particular, usually saying something to the effect that Iran envisaged a trilateral partnership with Russia, involving Tajikistan and/or any other central Asian republic.[47]

During the early months of 2005, much to the dismay of Washington, Tajikistan's relations with Iran entered a new more intensive phase. The Rakhmonov government went out of its way to strengthen Tajikistan's relations with Teheran as a means of increasing its leverage with both Russia and the United States. Both the Tajik and Iranian sides had compelling reasons for giving a lift to cooperation between the two countries.[48] Tajikistan wanted help in modernizing its military and looked to Iran for cooperation in the technical, logistical, and educational areas. For his part, Rear Admiral Ali Shamkhani made clear Iran's interest in taking advantage of opportunities to strengthen the capacity of the Eurasian region to resist the influence-building efforts of powerful outsiders, in particular the United States. Iran wanted to provide security to Tajikistan because doing so would strengthen Iranian security also threatened by the United States.[49] On April 20, 2005, Tajik Defense Minister Sherali Khayrulloyev met his Iranian counterpart, Shamkhani, in Teheran where the two signed a memorandum of understanding on the expansion of bilateral defense cooperation.[50]

Beyond its general interest in capitalizing on its relationships in central Asia, Iran was deeply troubled by the readiness of the ex-Soviet central Asian countries to allow the deployment of American military forces on their territory, a policy seen as dangerous to Iran. Shamkhani made clear to Tajikistan that Iran was ready to join others in helping the Rakhmonov government to modernize its military and assist, for example, in strengthening Tajikistan's border guards. And in all of this, Iran accepted Rakhmonov's ongoing autocratization of the Tajik national government and the transformation of it into a single party, single leader dictatorship, a stance that obviously carried great weight with Rakhmonov, encouraging him to take what he could get from the United States while holding it at bay on the issue of democracy.[51]

Tajik leaders continued throughout 2006 to strengthen ties with Iran which wanted to invest in the Tajik economy, in particular in the area of hydroelectricity production where Iran already invested about $200 million in Tajikistan's Sangtuda-2 hydroelectric power station. In return, Tajikistan supported Iran's nuclear program even though it had been condemned by the United Nations and the West, especially the United States. Tajikistan also backed a condemnation of the use of force if Iran ignored UN decrees. Tajikistan also was sympathetic to Iran's pro-Hamas position in the 2006 Israeli-Lebanese conflict.[52]

Iranian President Mahmoud Ahmadinejad's visit to Dushanbe at the end of July 2006, welcomed by the Tajik leadership if not by Washington, punctuated the growing momentum of cooperation between Iran and Tajikistan. Ahmadinejad met with Afghanistan President Hamid Karzai and his host, Tajik President Rakhmonov, to discuss regional problems, cement ties with them, and agree on some concessions to Tajikistan its leadership had been hoping for. Ahmadinejad pledged an investment of up to $180 million in a Tajik hydroelectric power plant. He also promised to attend a ceremony to open a five-kilometer tunnel through the Anzob pass, connecting Dushanbe with the northern Tajik city of Khujand that had been built with Iranian assistance. According to a Tajik political analyst, in 2006, "at the present stage Iran is playing a greater [economic] role than any other country in the region."[53]

Ahmadinejad's meeting with Karzai in Dushanbe seemed like a "double whammy" for the United States, and NATO as well, given their parlous strategic situation in Afghanistan despite the huge military deployment in the south of Afghanistan. While it is true that the current fighting in Afghanistan has affected Tajikistan and Iran less than the Soviet intervention of the 1980s and the Taliban insurgency in the early 1990s, the ongoing drug trade posed a major problem for both countries given Taliban encouragement of Afghanistan's unrelenting drug cultivation and export.[54]

In this instance, as with the case with U.S. complaints about Rakhmonov's antidemocratic policies, Washington was not inclined to make an issue of the growing ties between Iran and Tajikistan, if they remained confined to trade and led to some remedial action in the export of heroin. But, an expansion of Tajik ties with Iran in the strategic and political areas that Washington worried about are not only possible but probable in the future, especially in the context of deteriorating U.S. relations with Teheran throughout 2006. Tajikistan needed foreign investment for sustained economic development and Iran seemed willing to provide it. In return Tajikistan lined up with some policies of Teheran that annoyed the United States. Indeed, the growing international isolation of Iran engineered by the West and the United Nations through the imposition of increasingly severe sanctions has forced the country to look to the ex-Soviet central Asian republics for linkages that diminish its isolation. As it does this in central Asia, Iran becomes a factor in U.S. relations with the region and in the competition between the United States and Russia for influence in the five republics that comprise it.

The significance of the Iranian factor steadily increased in 2007 and 2008 as Ahmadinejad and Rakhmonov continued the practice of holding annual summit meetings in their capital cities. In the May 2007 summit in Teheran, Ahmadinejad took the opportunity to remind Rakhmonov of the strong cultural linkages between Iranians and Tajiks to provide an attractive rationale for the two countries to work together. But, the economic rationale was becoming increasingly important for both countries as Iran's confrontation with the West, especially with the United States, worsened in 2007 and 2008 because of growing determination in Washington and other Western capitals to consider escalation of sanctions against Iran for its intransigence on the nuclear issue.[55]

At the same time, Russia's increasing determination through the use of economic leverage to maintain and expand its influence in the ex-Soviet space could not be dismissed by the Rakhmonov leadership, which strengthened its commitment to diversifying its foreign relation to avoid dependence on not only Russia but also the United States. Indeed, Rakhmonov went out of his way at the May 2007 summit to commend the Iranian leadership for its willingness to expand ties with Tajikistan, especially in the area of trade, with Rakhmonov adding that Tajikistan supported "Iran's stance on international issues" and believed "that negotiations would be the only solution to ongoing stand-off over Iran's nuclear case." Rakhmonov invited Ahmadinejad to meet with him in 2008 in Dushanbe.[56]

While the United States still did not publicly express concern about the growing friendship between Tajikistan and Iran or about the implications of this development for its policy in Tajikistan, in 2007, it certainly had cause to be concerned, especially as the Kremlin made it appear that it had no problem with its two Muslim neighbors developing ties to one another. The Bush administration simply continued to strengthen U.S. relations with Tajikistan in 2007 and 2008, partly by softening its rhetoric on democratization—or rather the lack of it—in Tajikistan as evidenced by the heavy government hand in manipulating the presidential election in 2006 to make sure of Rakhmonov's victory. This restrained U.S. behavior seemed to reflect the negative impact of U.S. criticism of Uzbekistan's crackdown on opposition in Andijon in May 2005 that led to the eviction of the United States from the military base Uzbek President Karimov had allowed the United States to use in the immediate aftermath of 9/11.[57]

Tajik Relations with China

Further to the dismay of Washington and a limit on how far it could get Tajikistan to cooperate with the United States was the Rakhmonov government's policy of improving relations with China, which appreciated Rakhmonov's effort to preserve political stability that was important for Chinese investment. A road link with China was completed in May 2004. On June 27, 2004, a first bus carrying 26 passengers arrived in Khorog, the capital of Tajikistan's Badakhshan province, after a 100-kilometer trip from the Chinese city of Kashgar through treacherous mountain, which took about 24 hours driving time. Then the bus continued on to Dushanbe, another day's drive, symbolizing the new opportunities for trade expansion between Tajikistan and China.[58]

The steadily improving relationship between Tajikistan and China provided Rakhmonov with additional leverage in dealing with both Moscow and Washington.[59] Moreover, presumably because overall Russia's relations with China were less antagonistic than Russian relations with the United States, the Kremlin seemed less concerned about Chinese economic expansion in Tajikistan than about the perceived American military buildup there giving the United States a substantial military presence in Tajikistan but also the overt effort of U.S. policy to discourage Tajikistan's orientation toward Russia. This Chinese diplomacy challenged U.S. efforts to strengthen ties and expand cooperation with Tajikistan.

RUSSIA AND U.S. POLICY AFTER 9/11

Despite the problems the United States was having with Tajikistan, complicating and even undermining its relations with Tajikistan, the Putin Kremlin still was concerned about the Bush administration's efforts to expand its political, economic, and military influence in Tajikistan after 9/11. To the Kremlin, U.S. policy in Tajikistan in this period was aggressive, persistent, and seemingly successful in not only strengthening ties between Dushanbe and Washington but also increasing Tajik independence of Russia and Tajik resistance to the Kremlin's efforts to keep a balance between Russian and American initiatives in Tajikistan.

Concerns about Tajik Independence

In the post-9/11 years, the Kremlin became convinced that the Tajik relationship with the United States, which viewed Tajikistan as an "ally," was encouraging Rakhmonov's assertiveness and independence in dealing with Russia. One event that seems to have especially annoyed the Kremlin was the visit of a delegation of U.S. congressmen to the region in January 2002, an event that seemed at least to the Kremlin to "puff up" Rakhmonov by making Tajikistan appear as a major player in the region against al Qaeda. The annoyance of Moscow took the form of a Russian diplomatic offensive to advertise Russia's leading role in the fight against Islamic extremism and terrorism and to diminish the Tajik role. The Kremlin dispatched high-ranking Russian officials to Tajikistan and other central Asian countries to make the point. Among these politicians was Speaker of the Russian State Duma Gennadi Seleznev. While acknowledging the acceptability of a growing American presence in the region by not criticizing it, despite discomfort over it, Seleznev and others on the team publicly called for an expansion of the Russian military presence in Tajikistan and its neighbors.[60]

The Kremlin also resented U.S. encouragement of the Rakhmonov government to resist the Kremlin's efforts to strengthen Russia's military presence in the country, especially Rakhmonov's interest in cooperation with

the West, in particular NATO and the United States, within the framework
of the Partnership for Peace program. Aside from wanting to build an antiterrorism entente with the United States as an alternative to relying solely
on Russia to resist the expansion of militant Islam, the Tajik government also
wanted Russia to pay a price for its military presence, notably a write-off of
part of the Tajik debt to Russia.[61] And Russia was annoyed by perceived
U.S. encouragement of Rakhmonov's initial resistance in 2003 to a Russian
military base in Tajikistan and his government's demand that Russia forgive
the Tajik debt to Russia of about $300 million.[62] The Kremlin also was
annoyed by the Tajik government's insistence that Russia share command
of its forces that patrolled Tajikistan's border with Afghanistan, viewing
such assertiveness as the result of growing U.S. encouragement.[63] Other
examples of Tajik independence that irritated the Kremlin included Washington's reported allocation of $2.4 million to reconstruct the Dushanbe air-
port and the Pentagon's generous payment to the Tajik government of
between $3,000 and $5,000 for every landing and takeoff of U.S. and NATO
aircraft.[64]

Retaliatory Pressure on Tajik Workers in Russia

A clear sign of a peevish Russian frustration over Rakhmonov's American-
encouraged assertiveness toward Russia in 2003 was the clumsy, mean-
spirited decision of the Kremlin to deport some Tajik migrants living in
Russia. The Tajik leadership responded by raising claims for compensation
from the Kremlin for the presence of Russian troops on its territory, infuriating the Russian side because in its view its military presence was benefiting
the Tajik state.[65]

The Russian deportation, however, was part of a larger strategy of puni-
tive retaliation for Tajikistan's perceived tilt toward the United States after
9/11. The Kremlin tried to escalate the material cost to the Rakhmonov
regime of cooperating with the United States by pressuring Tajik workers
living temporarily in Russia. In other words, Moscow would be tough on
these Tajik workers so long as the Tajik government listened too closely to
the United States. After 9/11 as Tajikistan was strengthening ties to
the United States, about one million Tajik citizens—about a fifth of the total
Tajik population—were working inside Russia and sending money home to
impoverished families. These so-called "remittances" were an important
part of Tajikistan's national income and the country stood to suffer
economic hardship if the Kremlin shut off its labor market or even set
quotas for entering jobless migrants.[66]

As Tajikistan's perceived tilt toward the United States continued, Russia
increasingly treated vulnerable and impoverished Tajik immigrants "in a
rough way" prompting Igor Sattarov, a Tajik Foreign Ministry spokesman,
to protest that many deportees in November 2002 had legitimate if temporary

documents that Russian immigration officials ignored. According to Sattarov, Tajikistan considered the tough Russian actions against Tajik workers an unfriendly act in violation of mutually agreed upon rules governing cross-border travel. Tajik political expert Rustem Samiev believed that Moscow's harsh policies toward Tajik workers were intended to pressure the Tajik government to "more closely align its views with Russian geopolitical policies" or, more bluntly, not get too close to the United States. He suggested that such a policy would not work—it might have worked before 9/11, he argued, but not after that event—Rakhmonov's relationship with the United States gave him new confidence.[67]

Sanobar Shermatova, a Tajik political commentator, noted in the Russian newspaper *Moskovskie Novosti* on November 29, 2002, that "the deportation of Tajik migrants is political pressure and must be seen as a warning." And Shukhrat Sadiev, a lecturer at the Department of History and International Relations at the Russian-Tajik Slavic University, told the Institute for War and Peace Reporting that Moscow fears that improved relations between Tajikistan and the United States will damage Russian interests in the region.[68] Indeed, Rakhmonov was determined to strengthen ties with the West, especially the United States. His planned visit to Washington at the end of 2002 may have pushed the Kremlin to send him a message, perhaps a warning, to limit his closeness to the United States.[69]

As a general matter, Russian officials had little sympathy for—and much prejudice toward—immigrants from other ex-Soviet republics, convinced of the criminal intent of many of them. Russian antipathy toward immigrant workers from the predominantly Muslim central Asian republics was especially strong even though their secular governments were allies of Russia. This firm Kremlin grip on immigration, tightening control of foreign workers living in Russia, was often justified by portraying foreign workers, especially from central Asia and the Caucasus, as criminals and troublemakers. It was also a convenient cover-up for a policy of punishment of poverty-stricken countries like Tajikistan and its central Asian neighbors that expanded ties to the United States.[70]

Russian Military Diplomacy

To counterbalance the American initiatives in central Asia, Kremlin strengthened the CST on the occasion of the 10th anniversary of its founding. The six original signatories agreed on the need to seek international recognition of its security and peacekeeping responsibilities in Eurasia. While it looked like Russia envisaged a rejuvenated CST as a potential partner of the West in the war against terrorism, in reality, the Kremlin intended to have the CST encourage the central Asian republics to rely on Russia rather than on the United States for security. Indeed, the United States and other NATO allies had no interest in the CST as an instrument in fighting terrorism.[71]

The Kremlin said that it was eager to promote a Russian-oriented role in fighting terrorism. But, Tajik officials complained that Russia had not paid much attention to the poverty-stricken Tajik economy, to helping the country expand trade and in other ways stimulate Tajik economic growth. From the Tajik viewpoint, Russia seemed interested only in security issues and other means of justifying and expanding Russia's military role in Tajikistan. The Russian response was that the war on terrorism in Afghanistan, at least, was a more serious problem for both Tajikistan and Russia than Tajik economic growth and for that reason Tajikistan needed Russian military presence in the country.[72]

Limits on Russian Military Diplomacy

Russian military diplomacy was only successful to a point because in response to its pushiness, the Tajik government continued to assert itself in dealing with the Kremlin. For example, in mid-March 2004, the Tajik government decided not to renew the 10-year bilateral agreement with the Kremlin authorizing Russian troops to guard the Tajik border. On this occasion, Tajik Deputy Prime Minister Said Zukhurov reportedly told the Russians, "its time now for Tajikistan to take over guarding its border with Afghanistan." After all, Zukhurov had observed, the Russians had agreed that "when Tajik troops are able to protect their own border, Russian troops would be withdrawn from that border." Again, the independence of the Tajik leadership in dealing with the Russians on the border patrol issue seemed inspired by its awareness of a growing Russian-American rivalry in central Asia that provided Tajikistan with new opportunities to stand up to Russian influence-building.[73]

Furthermore, though the Kremlin continued to expand its military presence in Tajikistan to match and exceed the growing U.S. presence, working the establishment of two Russian bases on Tajik territory, one near Dushanbe and the other at Chkalovsk in northern Tajikistan's Sughd district, the Tajik government seemed to sandbag the effort, expressing qualms over locating a Russian military presence near Dushanbe. Moreover, the Tajik government seemed less willing than in the past to allow the Kremlin to set up military bases thereby giving Russia a much sought-after permanent presence on Tajik territory and jeopardizing any future chances of turning to the United States for security.[74]

A Russian Military Gain

Nevertheless, the Rakhmonov regime eventually accommodated the Kremlin on the base issue. On October 16, 2004, Putin and Rakhmonov signed an agreement establishing a permanent Russian military base that would house the 201st Motorized Rifle Division deployed in the country since the collapse of the Soviet Union. Putin was euphoric about this latest Russian achievement in Tajikistan, intoning that decision to open the base would "create conditions for neutralizing terrorist and extremist attacks," while Rakhmonov called his agreement to set up the base for Russia a "qualitatively new cooperation" between the two countries.[75]

With approximately 7,000 Russian military personnel added to Russia's existing forces deployed in Tajikistan to help the Tajik government patrol its border with Afghanistan, Russia by 2004 had about 20,000 troops in Tajikistan, the largest Russian military deployment on foreign soil. Putin called the new troop deployment a source of regional and local Tajik stability. It was also a means of protecting Russia's security and growing economic interests in the country.[76]

Russian Economic Diplomacy

Russia also took ongoing economic steps to offset the growing American influence in Tajikistan. As of 2003, the Russian state-owned oil and gas cartel Gazprom had a 25-year agreement with Tajik government giving it the right to explore and develop the gas fields of Rangon and Sargazon. Gazprom also was helping to repair Tajikistan's energy infrastructure, including oil and gas wells and pipelines.[77] At a June 2004 summit meeting with Rakhmonov, Putin secured a distinct advantage over the Americans of enormous benefit to Russia. In exchange for writing off approximately $300 million in debt, Tajikistan granted Russia the rights to the Nurek space surveillance center. In addition, Russian companies were to participate in the development of Tajik hydroelectric projects, all this while Russian border guards would remain in charge of guarding Tajikistan's frontier with Afghanistan at least until 2006.[78]

But, the positive fallout of this economic activity for Russian influence-building in Tajikistan was modest because Tajik energy resources were nowhere near as extensive as those in other central Asian republics, notably Uzbekistan and Kazakhstan. Moreover, for the Kremlin to get more political benefit from its economic diplomacy, it had to do far more to help Tajikistan developmentally. Despite granting some economic concessions to Tajikistan sought by the Rakhmonov leadership, the Kremlin ultimately was either unwilling or unable to provide large-scale economic assistance to Tajikistan, at least not to the extent that the United States was able and willing to do.[79]

TAJIKISTAN BETWEEN RUSSIA AND THE UNITED STATES, 2007–2008

By 2007, the Kremlin had come quite far in strengthening ties to Tajikistan to offset expanding U.S. influence in Dushanbe.[80] While both Russia and the United States had a substantial military presence in the country, the Russians seemed to have more of a stake in Tajikistan than the United States. For example, Hamrokhon Zarifi, Tajikistan's foreign minister in early 2007, made clear that "Tajikistan's strategic interests are served mainly through its partnership with Russia," saying that "Russia was, is, and will remain our strategic partner and ally. We have commitments to each other, and, on our part, we will strictly fulfill them."[81]

But, there were limits beyond which Rakhmonov would not go in cultivating Russian friendship. While he was determined to remain close to Russia, he was equally determined not to allow Tajikistan to appear as a cultural extension of Russia and to emphasize his country's sovereignty and independence in foreign and domestic policy, for example, by continuing to strengthen Tajik ties with the West, especially the United States.

A Gesture of Cultural Separation from Russia?

In mid-April, the Tajik government announced to all countries with which it had diplomatic relations that henceforth the president's last name would be "Rahmon," not Rakhmonov. The Tajik government also encouraged the Tajik people to drop endings of their last name that were Slavic such as -ev and -ov and use Persian-sounding last names when registering the birth of their children. The objective of these gestures was to weaken the Slavic cultural influence in Tajikistan to discourage outsiders from viewing Tajikistan as culturally or in any other way an extension of Russia.[82]

A New Tajik Tilt Westward?

In the Spring of 2007, Rakhmonov sought closer bilateral ties with the EU countries. He met Lithuanian Foreign Minister Petras Vaitiekunas in Dushanbe in April 2007 to discuss a strengthening of relations between the two countries, especially in the economic area. For his part, Vaitiekunas said the EU considered Tajikistan important for stability in central Asia and for the fight against terrorism.[83]

At the same time, Rakhmonov looked again to Washington for security assistance given the withdrawal of Russian troops from patrol with Tajik military personnel on the frontier with Afghanistan. Washington was responsive and, in April, sent Deputy Assistant Secretary of State for South and Central Asian Affairs Evan Feigenbaum to Dushanbe to discuss the Tajik role fighting terrorism and the illicit drug trade. Behind the U.S. gesture was eagerness to make sure Tajikistan would continue to cooperate with the United States in the war against the Taliban in Afghanistan in light of the loss of the U.S. military base in Uzbekistan in 2005 and the possibility of losing another military base in 2007 in Kyrgyzstan as a result of political turmoil in those countries and the pressure of Russia on them to terminate the U.S. military presence on their territory. Feigenbaum reassured Rakhmonov that the United States would always be ready to help assure Tajikistan's border security and told him that the U.S. government would provide $40 million for Tajik border security.[84]

The Migrant Workers Issue and Tajik-Russian Relations

It is possible that the Tajik tilt toward the United States and the EU in 2007 has benefited from a continuing irritant in Tajik-Russian relations: the criminalization of Tajik immigrants working in Russia without legal permission. In September 2007, Makhmadsaid Ubaidulloev, speaker of the upper house of the Tajik parliament, announced his government's intention of asking Russian President Putin to grant an amnesty to Tajik citizens working illegally in Russia. Since 2002, when the issue was raised, 50,000 illegal Tajik immigrants were deported to Tajikistan. Given Tajikistan's impoverishment and the importance of remission from Tajik immigrants working in Russia to their families at home to mitigate this poverty, Ubaidulloev wants the Russian government to let the deportees return to Russia to work there before the expiration of the five years Russian law says they cannot return to Russia.[85]

The Kremlin has refused for a long time to address the concern of the Tajik government over the loss of income for its citizens working in Russia largely because of strong bureaucratic opposition to amnesty. The Russian Federal Migration Service has said in effect that it wants to adhere to the law if only because if an exception is made for Tajikistan, exceptions will have to be made to immigrants from other countries and the Service does not want to make exceptions despite Russia's need of workers from abroad. Here is another reason for Tajikistan to resist Russian pressure to limit Tajik ties with the United States.[86]

The Impact of the August 2008 War in Georgia

The Russian invasion of Georgian territory in early August 2008 sent a loud and clear message to the Tajik leadership as it did to other central Asian leaders about the limits beyond which the Kremlin could not be expected to tolerate an increasingly close relationship with the West, especially the United States. But, Tajikistan President Rakhmonov, or Rahmon, as he was now called, is certainly no Mikhail Saakashvili (Georgia's president) in developing ties to the United States, especially in the military sphere, as he had been doing, long after it had become clear that such behavior alarmed Russia. Unlike the provocatively explicit anti-Russian policy Saakashvili had been pursuing since his election in 2003, Tajikistan's Rahmon had been careful in his balancing policy to embrace the West as openly as Saakashvili had done and certainly had kept a lid on any anti-Russian sentiment in the Tajik political elite. His government's reassurance on several occasions that Tajikistan was committed without question to good relations with Russia and looked to Russia for cooperation in the maintenance of Tajikistan's secular government helped him to preserve his country's security vis-à-vis Russia.

That said, in the aftermath of the Russian move into Georgia, Rahmon, as other central Asian leaders, could not dismiss the possibility of a Russian military threat to the territorial integrity of Tajikistan as punishment for its relations with countries with which Russia has difficulties, notably the United States. As has been the case since its achievement of independence in 1991, Tajikistan has been and remains vulnerable to overt Russian interference of the kind that occurred in Georgia. Russia intervened in the early 1990s to help bring an end to the Tajik civil war and in theory could easily intervene again, this time to the detriment of Tajik security and independence. But, should it do so, the Kremlin would surely be taking a risk in Tajikistan that it did not have to take in Georgia: it could inadvertently help the cause of Muslim-inspired extremism and tempt the Taliban forces in neighboring Afghanistan to work for the overthrow of the pro-Russian secular government of Rahmon.

But, at the end of August, another aspect of the Russian move into Georgia ominously appeared: a Russian request for political support of its military policy in Georgia from members of the SCO that included Tajikistan and three other ex-Soviet central Asian republics (Turkmenistan is still not a member of the SCO) as well as Russia and China. The basis of the request was the Russian view that it had had to come to the aid of neighboring South Ossetia, an integral part of the Georgian state but with strong separatist inclinations, because of the Georgian military effort on August 8 to coercively restore fall of Georgian authority to Ossetia and put an end once and for all to its separatist ambitions, which Russia had been tacitly encouraging.

The Russian request did not prompt an immediate response from Rahmon who did not want to endorse any kind of Russian military interference in the internal affairs of Eurasian governments once part of the former Soviet Union.[87] But, at the end of August, Rakhmon felt obliged to make some show of sympathy for the Russian side in the Georgian crisis so as not to appear as if being supportive in any way of the tough U.S. position. When Russian President Dmitry Medvedev openly asked for support of central Asian allies, on August 29, Rakhmon expressed "understanding" of the Russian view of Georgian aggressiveness in seeking the reintegration of South Ossetia into the Georgian state required a tough response, but he was quick to observe that "diplomatic solutions were best."[88]

CONCLUSIONS

The Bush administration's contradictory policy toward Tajikistan of seeking the country's support in the war against terrorism while encouraging democratization helped give an edge to Russian influence-building by mid-2007. Rakhmonov was just as sensitive to U.S. criticism as the leaders of neighboring central Asian countries and perhaps more so. He felt the fragility of his leadership in the aftermath of the long civil war which his side had nearly lost and, probably, would have lost without Russian involvement. The ongoing terrorist threat required him to deal harshly with his political opposition seeking the overthrow of his regime. He also felt threatened by not only his Uzbek neighbor in consequence of its suspected expansionist designs on Tajik territory. Russia also was threatening, supportive of his presidency while simultaneously seeking ways to obtain his loyalty.

Russia also had an edge over the United States in Tajikistan after 9/11 because the United States simply had more problems in cultivating Tajikistan. Some of these problems remain serious obstacles to the consummation of a real, viable, and permanent cooperative relationship between Dushanbe and Washington. In addition to Russia's supersensitivity to the new U.S. influence-building campaign in central Asia after 9/11 and the supersensitivity of the Bush administration to politically repressive acts of the Rakhmonov regime, there were differences between the United States and Tajikistan over Iran. Similarly, Chinese activities in the region put the United States and Tajikistan at odds.

Also playing to Russia's advantage in Tajikistan was the apparent inability of the Bush administration to help Rakhmonov in a predicament that stood in the way of a U.S. effort to strengthen relations after 9/11. Russia was for Rakhmonov and the region's other leaders a foe as well as a friend, hence the importance of ties with the United States which, however, were undermined regularly by Washington in its criticism of his authoritarian rule. Indeed, Rakhmonov wanted U.S. friendship and needed it to bolster his country's newly won sovereignty and independence in its dealings with Russia. But the cost of maintaining good relations with the United States remained high, obliging him to tilt periodically toward Russia and keep his political fences with China in good repair.

One could argue that the United States might have been more cautious and restrained in its criticism of Rakhmonov's dictatorial leadership recognizing, perhaps, how fragile his position was and remains. The United States might have also been more sensitive to the fact that there was no real constituency in the country. If Rakhmonov were to go, the forces of Islamic extremism might well have taken over and provided another refuge for anti-American terrorists. Still, almost under any scenario, Russia would have had a strong hand in the region and the United States a limited but very real role to play.

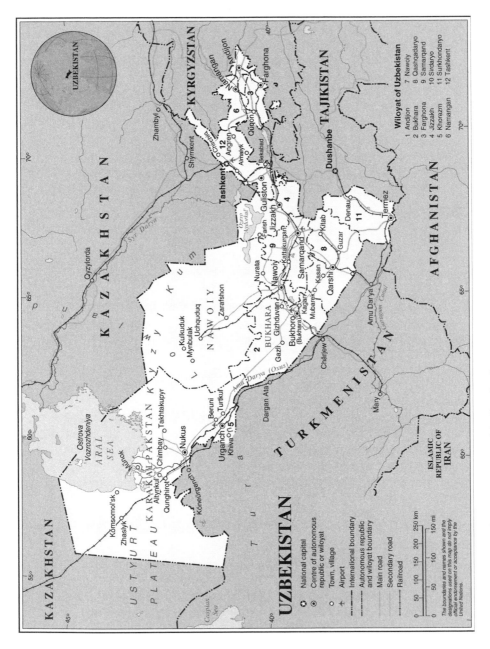

Uzbekistan (Courtesy of UN Cartographic Section)

5

Uzbekistan

- Population: 26.9 million (UN, 2005)
- Capital: Tashkent
- Area: 447,400 sq. km (172,700 sq. miles)
- Major languages: Uzbek, Russian, Tajik
- Major religion: Islam
- Life expectancy: 63 years (men), 70 years (women)
- Monetary unit: 1 Uzbek som = 100 tiyins
- Main exports: Cotton, gold, natural gas, mineral fertilizers, ferrous metals, textiles, motor vehicles
- GNI per capita: US$510 (World Bank, 2006)

Russian relations with Uzbekistan in the early post-Communist era were for the most part stable and relatively trouble-free. The country was, and still is, for that matter as of 2007, run by President Islam Karimov, a neo-Communist dictator with a tight grip over the country. Karimov's leadership has suited the Kremlin by assuring Uzbekistan's respect for and cooperation with Russia.

The Kremlin has not been troubled by Uzbekistan's tightfisted dictatorship, one of the most "neo-Stalinist" in the region. By the end of the 1990s and well into the new century, the Karimov leadership had successfully suppressed almost all the political opposition groups that had emerged in the heady days of Soviet perestroika on the eve of Communist collapse and Soviet disintegration. Karimov transformed his country into a fascist-style police state even as Russia and other ex-Soviet republics in Eurasia were steadily, if somewhat haltingly, democratizing.

The Kremlin welcomed Karimov's opposition to Islamic fundamentalism. Uzbek security police kept a close watch on the local Islamic clergy and severely punished anyone suspected of trying to disseminate fundamentalist ideas. In particular, Karimov's government carefully watched for signs of an Islamic revival in the Ferghama region of Uzbekistan not far from the border with Tajikistan. But, Karimov has shrewdly refrained from overt religious oppression of the kind Communist predecessors might have carried out in the Soviet era. Rather, he has gone out of his way to convince Uzbeks that he is not an atheist and thus has avoided development of an indigenous Islamic-led challenge to his leadership.

RUSSIAN-UZBEK RELATIONS IN THE YELTSIN ERA, 1992–1999

Despite the appearance of stable relations between the two countries in the 1990s, problems did linger and in some instances worsen when Vladimir Putin succeeded Boris Yeltsin as President of the Russian Federation in March 2000. Potentially troublesome to the Kremlin was Uzbekistan's border with Tajikistan where political unrest throughout most of the 1990s threatened to spill over into Uzbek territory. Another issue was Uzbekistan's regional influence-building which the Kremlin linked to its growing independence of Moscow.

And equally troubling for Moscow was the Uzbek diaspora throughout much of the central Asian region that seemed to give rise to an imperialist urge in Tashkent in the 1990s to expand Uzbek influence into neighboring countries the very least to make sure that Uzbek minorities did not suffer discrimination—13 percent of the Tajik population is Uzbek; almost 14 percent of the Kyrgyz population is Uzbek; and 9 percent of Turkmenistan's population is Uzbek. The Karimov leadership was hypernationalistic on this issue, concerned about the well-being of these minorities although the Uzbek leadership did not want these "foreign" Uzbek people to migrate back to Uzbekistan. They prefer to use whatever leverage they have to help the Uzbek diaspora stay where they are.

Uzbek fears were justified. Neighboring countries, in response to pressure from local nationalists, enacted laws making the local language the national language and encouraging minorities to read and speak the local language. Pressures on Uzbek minority communities in neighboring republics led to a kind of forced emigration. The share of the Uzbek population in Tajikistan declined in the 1990s from 24 percent to 13 percent by 2001. As a consequence, tension developed in Uzbekistan's relations with its neighbors, especially with Turkmenistan where President Sepamurad Niyazov was quick to put blame for any popular political disturbance on the Uzbek minority. When he survived an attempted assassination in 2002, Niyazov tried to blame the Uzbeks.[1]

At times out of annoyance, anger, and alarm, the Uzbek government used direct political and/or military pressure to dampen anti-Uzbek sentiment abroad. In one instance, Uzbek officials all but told the Turkmen ambassador to leave the country in protest against Niyazov's perceived harassment of his country's Uzbek-speaking community. Tension between Uzbekistan and Tajikistan escalated when Putin came to power. Putin complicated his predecessor's efforts to bring stability, peace, and some measure of integration to the ex-Soviet central Asian region.

Uzbekistan's External Ambitions

The Karimov leadership was convinced of Uzbekistan's right to claim preeminence in areas where there were sizeable Uzbek minorities to assure their safety and well-being. In addition, in the early 1990s, partly motivated by a fear that the Uzbek minority in Tajikistan of about 5.5 percent of the total population might suffer if the secular Tajik leadership was overthrown in the civil war by Islamists, Karimov offered help to the Tajikistan government. And like other central Asian republics, Uzbekistan logically sought to limit the influence of Russia, despite cooperation and friendship with it, by insisting that Russian troops that served as border guards do so under the aegis of the CIS or the United Nations.[2]

In 1993, Karimov created a small grouping or confederation of Uzbekistan with its near neighbors, Kyrgyzstan and Kazakhstan, calling it the Central Asian Union (CAU). The CAU excluded Russia as its intention was to checkmate the Kremlin's influence in the region as well as to implement a grand plan of Karimov to promote a large grouping of territories inhabited by Turkic people led by Uzbekistan. At first, the leadership of two members of this grouping, Turkmen President Nursultan Nazarbayev and Kyrgyzstan President Askar Akayev, hesitated to join an organization bound to trouble the Kremlin. While they shared Karimov's alarm over the expansion of Russian military strength in central Asia, it was difficult for them to fault the Kremlin, a valuable ally against the Islamic fundamentalist threat. But, before long, Nazarbayev and Akayev became more worried about Russia than the Islamic opposition and therefore backed Karimov's anti-Russian strategy implicit in the plan for the CAU.[3]

To increase his independence of Russia, Karimov also set up Uzbekistan's own border defense service despite the known interest of the Kremlin in deploying Russian troops in border areas to work with the military of the local country in policing its frontier. Uzbekistan built up its national army which barely existed in the immediate post-Communist era because of prior dependence on the Soviet Army. In September 1996, the Uzbek defense

minister declared that henceforth the Uzbek government would not participate in CIS peacekeeping missions, further divorcing itself from Russia.
The Uzbek government bolstered that policy by withdrawing Uzbek military personnel from a CIS peacekeeping mission in Tajikistan.[4] And still
another example of Karimov's will to independence of the Kremlin was pursuit of regional cooperation with ex-Soviet republics outside the central Asian
region. For example, Uzbekistan joined the GUUAM group that included
Georgia, Moldova, and Azerbaijan. Members of this grouping were especially
sensitive to perceived Russian influence-building in the early post-Soviet years
and hoped to have the organization serve as a "counterpoise" to the CIS
dominated by Russia.[5]

Uzbekistan and Tajikistan

Nowhere else were Russian fears about Uzbekistan's nationalistic ambitions more evident than in its forays into Tajikistan's internal affairs. The
very large Uzbek minority in Tajikistan provided the Uzbek government
with a pretext for involvement in the government of Tajikistan President
Emomali Rakhmonov. With about 24 percent of the total Uzbek population
living in the Leninabad region of Tajikistan, Karimov listened to their problems. He especially objected to the Tajik policy known as "Kulyabization,"
which gave senior administrative and political posts in Tajikistan to those
living in the Kulyab region. This policy allowed officeholders from Kulyab
to discriminate against the Uzbek minority.[6]

Trying to influence the Tajik domestic scene, Uzbekistan exploited
Tajikistan's economic and energy dependence on its exports. The Karimov
leadership used energy exports to Tajikistan to gain leverage with the
Rakhmonov government. In addition, Uzbekistan meddled in Tajik tribal
politics, supporting this or that political warlord against the central authority
with the goal of boosting Uzbek power in the region. For example, Uzbekistan
supported Makhmud Khudoberdiev, a Tajik factional leader vehemently
opposed to the Islamist opposition but also critical of Rakhmonov for his
eventual willingness to compromise with the Islamists in a power-sharing
agreement ending the civil war in Tajikistan.[7]

The Russian Minority in Uzbekistan

Uzbek nationalism also underlay a growing Russian concern about the
well-being of the Russian minority living in Uzbekistan. Like other non-
Uzbek ethnic minorities, the Russian minority worried about ethnic-
based discrimination. The Russian minority was vulnerable ironically
because Karimov had tried to avoid discrimination in the case of employment in the Uzbek government, a policy the Uzbek political opposition
resented because it sometimes led to discrimination against ethnic Uzbeks.

Karimov did not want to antagonize the Kremlin, and in 1992, his government allowed the registration of an ethnic-based association of Russian culture to reassure the Kremlin of his respect for the cultural and other special interests of the Russian-speaking community. Nevertheless, nationalists in the Russian parliament were ever ready to use the power of the Russian state to protect the Russian minority in Uzbekistan and other ex-Soviet republics in Eurasia.

But, influential Russian politicians like General Alexandr Labed, leader of the political party devoted to the interests of Russian minorities living in other republics once part of the Soviet Union, called on the Kremlin to play an active role in protecting the interests of these diaspora Russians who were becoming victims of the new local nationalist movements growing up in the 1990s in the central Asian and other ex-Soviet republics. In the Soviet era, the well-being of Russians living abroad had been assured by the Soviet government in Moscow. But, after the collapse of the Soviet Union and with Uzbekistan's achievement of independence, Uzbek citizens of Russian nationality suffered from discrimination.

The Language Issue

In 1989, the Uzbek parliament passed a law requiring that the Uzbek tongue be used by all residents within eight years. The idea was that the Uzbek language be expanded and developed so that it could replace Russian as the language of business, politics, and culture. Then, in 1993, Uzbek nationalists said that the transition toward use of Uzbek as the state language was too slow. In May 1993, the Russian Orthodox Archbishop Vladimir of Tashkent wrote a letter in Russian to the municipal administration. The letter was not acknowledged. Instead, the archbishop was told to communicate with city officials in Uzbek.[8]

Russians had been reluctant to master the difficult Uzbek tongue, convinced that Russian would remain the main language of the educated elite in Uzbekistan and would continue to have primacy, especially since Russian was the only tongue common to all the ex-Soviet states. Thus, they reasoned, Uzbeks would be handicapped in dealings with neighbors should they replace Russian with their own language, which was not spoken widely in the rest of central Asia.

Under strong popular pressure, Karimov could not allow Russian to remain the country's primary language. In particular, educated Uzbek youth, who constituted 50 percent of the population in the 1990s, pushed for the language requirement as a way to gain access to jobs that had gone to those who spoke Russian. As Karimov continued to conciliate the growing number of influential Uzbek nationalists on the language issue, the situation of the Russian minority continues to be a source of possible trouble between the two countries.

Upswing in Russian-Uzbek Relations

In the mid and late 1990s, despite these problems, there was increasing evidence of an improvement in Russian-Uzbek relations. Karimov's efforts to chart an independent course in foreign policy were balanced by concurrent efforts at cooperation with the Kremlin. For example, Uzbekistan backed the Yeltsin government in its conflict with Communist Party hardliners and ultranationalists led by Vladimir Zhirinovsky in Russia's parliament. For its part, the Kremlin offered to help Karimov strengthen Uzbekistan's new military establishment by transferring some Soviet military bases to Uzbekistan and agreeing in 1994 to train 5,000 Uzbek soldiers in Russia and sell it weapons. Karimov welcomed these Russian gestures given the reservations of the Kremlin over the creation of national armies as an alternative to a CIS military force Russia preferred. To the Kremlin's satisfaction, Karimov acknowledged the importance of military cooperation between Uzbekistan and Russia, saying in 1996 that Russia has been and will remain Uzbekistan's "strategic partner" in the face of danger of fundamentalism's onslaught from the south.[9]

Evidence of improving Uzbek relations with Russia during the late 1990s was Karimov's personal support of Yeltsin in his ongoing battle with a conservative communist party–led nationalist opposition to him in the State Duma. In March 1996, this opposition proposed a resolution to the effect that the dissolution of the Soviet Union was unconstitutional. Supporting Yeltsin, the Uzbek parliament condemned the resolution, and Karimov sent a telegram to the Russian president in which he, Karimov, personally rejected the Duma's action and expressed support of Russia's democratic reform program as well as Russia's expanding cooperation with Uzbekistan. Karimov even went so far as to speak positively about the CIS, despite reservations about its future direction, and to affirm Russia's right to play a "leading role" in it—music to the ears of the Kremlin.

In early May 1998, Karimov visited Moscow to discuss regional security, economic relations, and military cooperation. The summit produced a joint communiqué that focused on the threat to both countries of the spread of Islamic extremism from Iran to Afghanistan and the possibility that before long both Russia and Uzbekistan would have to confront and control increases of terrorism, religious militancy, and the illicit trade in arms and drugs.[10]

The communiqué was based on the fact that Uzbekistan faced a serious threat to its stability and security with the appearance in the country of a new militant Islamic organization know as the Islamic Movement of Uzbekistan (IMU) that was trying to make common cause with militants in Kyrgyzstan and Kazakhstan, a very dangerous turn of events in the region from Russia's vantage point. Based in Afghanistan, this group declared in August 1999 its intent to topple the Karimov government and to make its point the IMU took some hostages.[11]

UZBEK-AMERICAN RELATIONS BEFORE AND AFTER 9/11

During the 1990s, while the Uzbek government tried to keep close ties to Russia, it carefully cultivated Washington and was pleased when the United States expressed interest in developing a relationship. Karimov saw friendship with the United States as strategically and economically beneficial. At the very least, it provided him a measure of psychological and political leverage in dealing with the Kremlin. At the same time, the Clinton administration welcomed Uzbek interest in strengthening ties to the United States and saw in friendship with Uzbekistan an opportunity for the United States to encourage democratization in the ex-Soviet space.[12]

In March 1995, Uzbek leaders welcomed a U.S. delegation sent to Tashkent to meet with officials from the ministries of foreign affairs and defense, as well as with Uzbek Prime Minister Utkir Sultanov, to discuss a range of topics, including assistance with the conversion of defense industries to civilian use. That same month, Karimov received official notification that Bill Clinton had submitted a Bilateral Investment Treaty to the U.S. Senate for ratification. In contrast to the U.S. government's past criticisms of Uzbekistan for its lack of democratic reforms, Clinton now said that "our two countries can work together ... Uzbekistan can play a key role [in regional affairs in central Asia]."[13]

In April 1995, Defense Secretary William Perry met with Karimov, Defense Minister Rustam Akhemedov, and Foreign Minister Abdul Aziz Komilov in Tashkent, where they discussed a program of officer training in the United States and the possibility of joint maneuvers. Both sides stressed the need for greater U.S.-Uzbek cooperation in light of possible threats from Islamic fundamentalism. And in October 1995, as part of NATO's Partnership for Peace program, Uzbekistan signed a memorandum of understanding with the United States concerning military relations.[14]

For the first time since gaining independence in 1991, Uzbekistan had an alternative to alliance with Russia in the war against terrorism in central Asia. This strengthening of Uzbek ties to the United States provided Karimov with another means to fight Islamic-inspired terrorism without having to embrace intimacy with Russia. Several terrorist attacks in Uzbekistan by Islamic militants with links to Afghanistan's Taliban regime and al Qaeda network headquartered in and protected by Afghanistan heightened interest of the Karimov regime in cooperation with the United States, in addition to getting help for protection of its security from Russia, on the eve of 9/11.[15]

Cooperation with the United States after 9/11

The Karimov government had the first real opportunity to strengthen ties to the United States after the 9/11 terrorist attack. After 9/11, the American government requested Uzbekistan's help in the war against terrorism. Karimov responded immediately by allowing the United States and its allies to use Uzbek airspace to bomb Afghanistan. Karimov also provided the United States with use of its military bases, notably the air base at Khanabad and others developed and used by the former Soviet Union in the 1980s, in its campaign to control Afghanistan. The initial agreement for the U.S. use of Khanabad was a Status of Forces agreement concluded by the two countries in October 2001. It was a good agreement for the United States: there were no strings attached to the U.S. use of the base.[16] Uzbekistan's military help provided easy access for U.S. planes headed for targets in Afghanistan. By the end of 2001, the U.S. military commander for the Afghan theater, General Tommy Franks, had established his CENTCOM headquarters in Uzbekistan, and the United States had begun to deploy several thousand uniformed military personnel there.

Advantages for Uzbekistan of Cooperation with the United States

Uzbekistan was now in line for a substantial program of American economic and financial aid, a direct consequence of the new strategic situation in Afghanistan. This aid was important for several reasons, not least its usefulness in helping the Karimov regime destroy the IMU which had carried out terrorist attacks in Uzbekistan such as the February 1999 bomb blasts in Tashkent.[17] By 2004, the United States had become one of Uzbekistan's ten largest trade partners with a volume of bilateral trade worth about $335 million.[18]

Another consequence of Karimov's cooperation with Washington was a let up of U.S. criticism of the Uzbek dictatorship.[19] Karimov expected, and for a limited time did receive, a measure of tolerance from the United States about his harsh, antidemocratic rule of Uzbekistan. Also, there was a slight possibility that Karimov might obtain American help in getting a control over the relatively industrialized portions of northern Afghanistan.[20] Also, Karimov's new military relationship with the United States greatly strengthened his legitimacy at home and abroad, especially when he visited Washington in March of 2002 to meet with President George Bush, Secretary of Defense Donald Rumsfeld, and National Security Advisor Condoleeza Rice. Pleased by what he perceived to be U.S. treatment of his country as an equal, Karimov subsequently gave political support in the United Nations to the United States on Iraq and on Israel. In 2002 and 2003, senior U.S. Defense Department officials met regularly with Uzbek leaders.[21]

The new ties between the two countries in the war against terrorism in central Asia seemed to translate into a real bilateral alliance between them. Certainly, this was not an unreasonable perception on Karimov's part when in July 2002 he signed a second bilateral agreement called the Declaration on the Strategic Partnership and Cooperation between the United States and Uzbekistan. The Declaration pleased the Karimov leadership even though it contained references to issues of importance to the Bush administration, such as democratization. No doubt Karimov's pleasure with the Declaration was a U.S. commitment to take seriously any external threat to Uzbekistan security. The Bush administration seemed willing to go to a great length to secure Uzbekistan's cooperation in the war on terrorism by offering a security guarantee to a country in the ex-Soviet space where the Kremlin claimed special privileges. Arguably the United States also had in mind bolstering Uzbekistan's will to independence of the Kremlin. Finally, the Declaration also contained a pledge by Uzbekistan to move forward with democratization. The pledge gave the Bush administration an opportunity to hold Karimov's feet to the fire of political reform.[22]

The Uzbek pledge about democratization also had been intended to assuage Congress where there was a lot of distrust of Karimov for his antidemocratic policies, enumerated in great detail by the State Department in its annual report of human rights violations by countries throughout the world.[23] Despite frequent reassurances about democratizing his country, there was no real evidence of democratic political reform. Still the Bush administration seemed ready to view Karimov's Declaration as an opportunity for the United States to finesse Uzbekistan's transformation into a parliamentary democracy.[24]

Risks and Liabilities for Uzbekistan of Cooperation with the United States

Karimov ran risks in strengthening ties with the United States, especially when he allowed the American military presence on Uzbek territory. Closer Uzbek relations with the United States eventually provoked the hostility of radical Islamic groups inside the country as well as outside, notably the IMU and the Taliban. The danger of a Taliban incursion in Uzbekistan, however, weakened by its defeat by U.S. forces in 2003 could not be ruled out by Uzbek military leaders. Karimov also had to reckon with the possibility of an American failure in Afghanistan that would leave him isolated in central Asia and more dependent than ever on Russia.

Moreover, Uzbekistan could ill afford to antagonize the Kremlin, never mind alienate it, by developing too close a military relationship with the United States. Uzbekistan relied on Russia for the supply of spare parts and maintenance support for all its military equipment and at discount prices. Uzbekistan also was and remains dependent on the rail lines and commercial access routes to the West that go through Russian territory.[25]

RUSSIAN REACTIONS TO U.S. POLICY AFTER 9/11

In the immediate aftermath of 9/11, the Kremlin accepted the risks to its strategic primacy in central Asia of closer U.S. ties to Uzbekistan for the sake of advantages in its own fight against Islamic fundamentalism as well as for the sake of strengthening Russia's own relations with the United States. Given the cost, complexity, and controversiality of Russia's bilateral efforts with individual central Asian countries, and multilaterally through the CIS, of increasing security against the spread of Islamic radicalism in the ex-Soviet central Asian republics, the new and thus far limited American initiatives in central Asia seemed to the Kremlin worthwhile.

The Kremlin also factored in the costs of promoting security in the central Asian countries to prevent the spread of Islamic fundamentalism. Given the drain on its finances of the war in Chechnya, Russia could use the financial help of the United States in the broader anti-fundamentalist effort. It was now quite clear to the Kremlin as well that the CIS was really not up to the task of creating a NATO-style security net for ex-Soviet Eurasia, especially the most vulnerable areas in the south. In sum, in the Russian view, the United States could help with the costs of countering the Islamic fundamentalist threat in central Asia.

The advance of American political and military influence in Uzbekistan inspired a spurt of economic influence-building by the Kremlin, which seemed for the moment to compliment rather than rival the Americans and certainly was welcome by Karimov. The Kremlin focused on cooperation between Russia and Uzbekistan in the areas of energy exploitation and marketing. Although Uzbekistan was an energy importer during Soviet times, it had become self-sufficient in the 1990s and by the end of the decade was exporting gas mostly to Tajikistan, Kyrgyzstan, and Kazakhstan. When Putin became Russia's president at the end of 1999, Uzbekistan was the 10th largest natural gas producer in the world. Putin sought a major Russian role in the exploitation and marketing of Uzbek energy. He wanted in particular to expand Russian purchases of Uzbek gas and to build pipelines to carry the gas to the Russian market. In January 2003, Gazprom, the state-controlled energy consortium, and Uzbekneftgaz, its Uzbek equivalent, agreed to increase deliveries of Uzbek gas to Russia on a long-term basis of 10 years. By August 2003, Russia was a major buyer of Uzbek gas.[26]

Thus, in the immediate aftermath of 9/11, as the Americans made gains in Uzbekistan on the strategic level, Russia seemed to be doing equivalently well in the economic sphere. The energy trade between the two countries grew steadily and tied the two countries closer together in the more durable economic sphere. Indeed, the Russian-Uzbek relationship was built on the exigencies of domestic need that neither side could afford to dismiss.

A Liability for Russia of Uzbek Friendship with the United States

From early 2002 onward, encouraged by his new ties with Washington, Karimov displayed a measure of independence in dealing with the Kremlin.

For example, he responded very cautiously to Russian-led multilateral initiatives to promote security in the region. To the dismay of the Kremlin, Karimov would not allow Uzbek military forces to participate in maneuvers with Russian forces outside the Uzbek territory. In April 2001, again, to the dismay of the Kremlin, Uzbekistan did not join Russia, Kazakhstan, Kyrgyzstan, and Tajikistan in a military exercise by a newly created "Southern Shield" multilateral defense force set up and led by Russia.

Karimov also had a serious disagreement with Russia over the Taliban in Afghanistan. While Russia saw the fundamentalist Taliban as the major threat to the secular, Russian-oriented central Asian republics, Karimov focused on local terrorism groups like the IMU. He also wanted to avoid a confrontation with the Taliban. For its part, the Kremlin was inclined to be aggressive in dealing with the Taliban and wanted to use air strikes against alleged training camps in Afghanistan. Karimov had rejected that tactic on the eve of 9/11.[27]

But, to make himself valuable to the United States after 9/11 in return for U.S. military aid and diplomatic support, Karimov gradually accepted an Uzbek role in the defeat of the Taliban, allowing the United States to use Uzbekistan as a base of operations against the Taliban and al Qaeda, for which he had no affection, seeing it as a threat to his regime and his leadership. Moreover, Karimov appreciated U.S. support of the Uzbek faction of the Northern Alliance, a group of tribes in northern Afghanistan fighting the Taliban ascendancy in Afghanistan for several years.[28]

Karimov's new willingness to resist the Taliban was accepted by Russia but with mixed feelings. On the one hand, the Kremlin was glad to see Karimov do something to weaken the Taliban regime, but doing so in concert with the United States was troublesome to Putin. The Kremlin did not like what appeared to be the making of an Uzbek-American entente against the Taliban. In particular, the Kremlin feared that Uzbekistan and the United States were trying to position themselves to influence the political situation in a post-Taliban Afghanistan that seemed imminent on collapse of Taliban control of Kabul in the beginning of November 2001.

Russian fear of an American ascendancy in Afghanistan that would be a strategic liability for Russia was fully vindicated when the United States installed a new regime in Kabul under the leadership of Hamid Karzai whom the Kremlin considered an American stooge. That Uzbekistan had helped the United States defeat the Taliban and establish a political dominance in Afghanistan, once a virtual satellite of Moscow after the December 1979 Soviet intervention and occupation of the country, was difficult for Moscow to accept. Moreover, to the dismay of the Kremlin, the United States succeeded in Afghanistan in alliance with Pakistan. The Kremlin considered Pakistan a rival for influence in Afghanistan and elsewhere in central Asia and was especially concerned about the sympathy some in the Pakistani military, especially in the Inter-Services Intelligence Agency, had for Islamic fundamentalism that could enhance Pakistani influence. The U.S.-Pakistani alignment advocated opening up the new Karzai regime to moderate ex-Taliban figures, a tactic Russia strongly opposed. But to no avail.

That said, the Kremlin deferred to the United States, in Afghanistan, accepting the Karzai regime and agreeing to provide some material assistance to help the country recover from the years of misrule by the conservative and repressive Taliban leadership. Putin was not ready to disrupt Russian-American cooperation in the aftermath of 9/11. While the new situation in Afghanistan was clearly a "win" for the Americans, thanks in some part to Uzbekistan, the Russians had reason to be cautiously optimistic about a shift in the strategic balance in central Asia in their favor in the next few years because of difficulties the United States would have in its relations with Uzbekistan.[29]

PROBLEMS FOR U.S. POLICY IN UZBEKISTAN AFTER 9/11

By late 2003, the close ties that Uzbekistan had developed with the United States in the aftermath of the post-9/11 attack became frayed. Washington was deeply troubled by the Karimov regime's failure to do much, if anything, to democratize the Uzbek political system, which remained a harsh and abusive dictatorship. In its annual report on human rights practices in Uzbekistan in 2003, the U.S. State Department declared, "Uzbekistan is an authoritarian state with limited civil rights . . . President Islam Karimov and the centralized executive branch of the Uzbekistan national government in Tashkent that serves him dominate political life and exercise nearly complete control over the other branches."[30] The United States also was concerned about a visible strengthening of Uzbek relations with Iran as U.S. relations with that country was deteriorating sharply with the American invasion of Iraq starting in March of 2003. The Kremlin carefully monitored the strain in Uzbek-American relations, waiting for an opportunity to move closer to Karimov.[31]

Uzbek's Sluggish Democratization

The main source of displeasure with Karimov came from the U.S. Congress which disliked the antidemocratic character of Karimov's leadership. Promises of democratization remained unfulfilled prompting recommendations to the Bush administration that henceforth money should be dispersed to Tashkent only if the secretary of state certified progress of democratic change. Congress also insisted that the administration could not waive this criterion in the interest of U.S. national security and thereby enable Bush to do an end run around the stiff certification requirement.[32] Then, in 2003, a State Department human rights report for Uzbekistan criticized the government of President Karimov for persecution of religious Uzbeks and political opponents in its crackdown on Islamic extremism. The report called Uzbekistan's human rights record "very poor." In response to the detailed findings of the State Department's reports on human rights violations in recent years, Congress held hearings on Uzbekistan's alleged violation of the human rights of its citizens. Not much changed for the better in Uzbekistan in 2003. The State Department considered Karimov's leadership a repressive dictatorship.[33]

The U.S. Dilemma over Democratization

Washington was over a barrel, forced to decide whether to punish Uzbekistan to force a change in its repressive domestic behavior by curtailing or terminating an aid program that by 2003 had reached a value of $500 million, or overlook such behavior for the sake of maintaining its valuable strategic relationship.[34] In the Spring of 2003, the United States was willing to continue military and economic assistance to Uzbekistan, according to a report on a meeting on April 14 and 15, 2003, of the United States-Uzbekistan Joint Security Council. While viewing Uzbekistan as a "strategic partner" in central Asia, the report acknowledged the role of Uzbekistan in "establishing a reliable system of regional security," but it also said, "the Uzbek side reaffirms its commitment and intention to further the democratic transformation of society in the political, economic, and spiritual areas."[35]

In 2003, Karimov tried to protect his regime against U.S. criticisms, which he deeply resented. They embarrassed him and gave legitimacy to his political opponents. He sent a personal letter to the White House asking for economic assistance for Uzbekistan in the hope that he could establish a personal relationship with Bush as a means of circumventing the criticisms of the State Department and Congress. This tactic did not work. Bush eventually responded to Karimov by insisting that for a stronger bilateral relationship between Tashkent and Washington, Karimov must introduce political reform involving clear and explicit steps toward democratization, especially with respect for human rights. Eventually, the Bush administration increased the flow of financial help to Uzbekistan, recognizing a serious "downside" if it cut off aid. At the very least, an abrupt curtailment of U.S. aid would benefit Russian influence-building in Tashkent.[36]

Indeed, the Kremlin was ready to exploit any weakening of the American role in Uzbekistan, and the Russians were already making energy investments in the country that could exceed U.S. aid. For example, the Russian energy giant LUKOIL had signed a deal in June 2004 worth $1 billion to explore and market Uzbek gas in a joint venture with Uzbekneftgaz.[37]

Uzbekistan's Ties to Iran

Another source of tension in Uzbek relations with the United States had to do with Iran, which was uncomfortable over Uzbekistan's cooperation with the United States and its perceived link to the large American military presence in Afghanistan. While Iran was not a major player in central Asian politics, Teheran saw a strategic liability for Iran in Karimov's support of the expansion of American influence elsewhere in central Asia. For its part, Uzbekistan sympathized with Iranian anxieties, especially in light of the sharp deterioration of Iranian-American relations under the radical anti-American leadership of President Ahmadinejad, and wanted to keep relations with Iran on an even keel. Also, there was a sense of Islamic solidarity in Uzbek-Iranian relations. One Uzbek official reportedly noted the special attention Tashkent was obliged to pay to relations with other Islamic countries outside the former Soviet space, saying, "Never forget that we are an Islamic nation. We must work to maintain good relations with other Islamic nations. We feel this pressure as we host US forces."[38]

U.S. Reactions to the 2005 Andijon Uprising

In early 2005, the Uzbek domestic situation deteriorated in response to explosions of popular antigovernment demonstrations in Kyrgyzstan following the March parliamentary elections. They seemed to be expressing resentment over not only the repressive political behavior of the Karimov regime but also pervasive poverty. A resurgence of Islamic religious influence also fueled this popular anger. The regime had jailed thousands of Uzbeks who practiced Islam illegally, that is, at mosques that were not officially registered by the state. In the Spring of 2005, protests erupted in Andijon, center of the highly restive Ferghama valley in the southeastern part of Uzbekistan, considered a center of Muslim disaffection for not only reasons of religion but also for economic and political reasons. There was high unemployment. What apparently triggered the explosion of popular protest was the trial of 23 businessmen who were being prosecuted by the government for religious extremism. Protesters attacked the city's police and military posts demanding more democratic freedoms and economic opportunities.[39] Uzbek authorities responded harshly, convinced that armed protestors were insurgents seeking to overthrow Karimov. According to the press reports from Andijon, on May 13, the Karimov regime indiscriminately shot and killed unarmed protestors as well as armed insurgents seeking its overthrow.[40]

The harshness of the crackdown in Andijon strained Karimov's relations with Western nations, especially the United States, which criticized Communist-style intolerance of political dissent and willingness to use torture against opponents. In addition, his opposition to Islamic fundamentalism had given him a reputation as an atheist with little regard or respect for Islam, the faith of a majority of Uzbeks. Indeed, he had used his alliance with the Bush administration as a pretext for hounding the Islamic portion of the opposition to his rule. At the same time, his cooperation with the United States had alienated militant Islamic political groups in Uzbekistan, encouraging them to sympathize with the Taliban regime in Afghanistan and al Qaeda.

Strains in U.S.-Uzbek Relations after Andijon

Through this period of unrest in Uzbekistan, Karimov tried to keep secret exactly what his government had been doing to maintain law and order in Andijon, especially his severe punishment of the political opposition. But, U.S. officials, including Secretary of State Condoleeza Rice, were critical of Karimov, calling on him to compromise with critics and opponents. The United States condemned Karimov for the harshness of his crackdown. In addition, the administration and Congress demanded an investigation of the causes of and circumstances of the Uzbek government's brutal crackdown. Karimov stonewalled, provoking an outcry against him in Congress. In early June, six U.S. Senators (four Republicans and two Democrats) publicly urged the Bush administration to reconsider its relationship with Uzbekistan because of its dictatorship, saying that its methods of political control embarrassed the United States, an ally.[41]

Worse, the United States was implicated in the Karimov regime's actions. For years Washington had been providing training and equipment for U.S. antiterrorist programs. U.S. assistance was intended to improve the skills and capabilities of different Uzbek law enforcement agencies to deal with the rise of Islamic militancy. But, these Uzbek agencies receiving U.S. aid used it against the protestors in the Andijon uprising. Despite U.S. attempts to promote democracy in Uzbekistan, the outside world held the United States culpable for the repressive and brutal tactics by the Karimov regime pursued in the name of the war on terrorism.[42]

Karimov Threatens the U.S. Khanabad Base

During the Summer of 2005, with the United States insisting on an investigation of the May repression, relations between the two countries were going from bad to worse. In early July, in a fit of frustration over the unrelenting U.S. pressure on him to investigate his government's behavior in the Andijon crisis for which he undoubtedly was personally responsible, Karimov threatened to evict the United States from the Khanabad air base. The official Uzbek position was that the U.S. use of the Khanabad was based solely on its importance in waging the war to oust the Taliban from Afghanistan, a mission that appeared almost accomplished by 2005.[43] The Karimov regime also insisted that the United States pay for the use of the base—the base was leased by the Uzbek government free of charge although the United States paid Uzbek authorities for jet fuel and base security. The regime said it needed the money to rebuild infrastructure, repair environmental degradation, and cover other costs.[44]

There were other reasons for Karimov's response. He was concerned that the U.S. military presence had become a political liability for Uzbekistan in its relations with Russia and China. He wanted to avoid straining relations with the hypersensitive Russians who continued to provide welcome support in his confrontation with Washington, carefully refraining from complaints about his failure to live up to pledges of democratization.

To mollify Russian opposition to the U.S. military presence in Uzbekistan, and also score some points with Beijing, which shared Moscow's discomfort over the expanding military cooperation between Uzbekistan and the United States after 9/11, Karimov's government already had imposed some restrictions on U.S. use of the base, banning nighttime operations and limiting the number of flights by the C-17 and other heavy cargo aircraft. The nighttime ban was a real nuisance in the use of HC-130 aircraft used for search and rescue as well as tanker operations, which had to be ready to fly at all hours of the day and night. Consequently, these craft were moved to Bagram air base in Afghanistan where it was difficult to get fuel for them and to repair them since the repair facilities remained in Uzbekistan.[45]

Finally, Karimov feared further American influence-building in the economic sphere. U.S. companies had been investing in Uzbek enterprises, and in Karimov's view, exerting too much influence over them.[46]

Overall, Karimov had become deeply suspicious of the United States despite—and possibly because of—the U.S. military presence on Uzbek territory. Some members of his government were convinced that the United States was using the Khanabad base for political subversion inside Uzbekistan as well as for fighting the war against terrorism in Afghanistan. Uzbek suspicions of the United States had been fed by the perceived U.S. interference in support of democratic groups in Georgia, Ukraine, and Kyrgyzstan in 2003 and 2004. To the Karimov regime, the United States was actively encouraging and supporting political opposition to conservative and pro-Russian leaders throughout the Eurasian region.[47]

A closing of Khanabad to the Americans seemed increasingly to the Karimov regime a logical next step in gradually restricting the U.S. military presence in Uzbekistan, especially in light of a call by the SCO at a meeting in early July 2005 for the removal of U.S.-led antiterrorist forces from central Asia. While SCO members (Russia, China, Kazakhstan, Kyrgyzstan, Tajikistan, and Uzbekistan) reiterated support for the war on terrorism, they noted that the Taliban was defeated making unnecessary the Western, especially American, military presence in Afghanistan and elsewhere in central Asia. Admittedly, the tone of the SCO request was mild, with assurances that the SCO intended no "ultimatum" to the United States; but the intent was clear and the call provided Karimov substantial psychological support in his efforts to limit and eventually terminate the U.S. military presence in his country, enabling him to score points with both the Kremlin and Beijing.[48]

By 2005, Karimov was no longer sure he was safe from American subversion of his government despite the support he had given Washington for the war on terrorism. He knew of opposition to him in the U.S. Congress and in the State Department. The sustained American diplomatic pressure on him following the Andijon crackdown intensified his suspicion and fear of the United States.[49]

On July 29, 2005, the Karimov government formally demanded termination of the U.S. presence at Khanabad within 180 days. But, there was a lot of ambiguity surrounding this demand, suggesting that Karimov did not want a complete, total departure of U.S. forces from his country. He rather seemed to prefer a continuation of the security relationship he had forged with the United States in 2001 in a different guise, one that outwardly would appear more favorable to Uzbekistan and not be considered in any way an example of American influence-building.[50]

Indeed, in a Russian view, Karimov was not wholeheartedly committed to expelling the United States. According to Vladimir Frolov, director for International Analysis Fund for Effective Politics in Moscow in the Spring of 2005, the Uzbek leadership was not as upset as it made out to be by the harsh and unrelenting U.S. criticism of its repressive rule. Frolov said that the Karimov regime in fact depended only minimally, and arguably, not at all, on international legitimacy while appreciating the money it had been getting from Washington. Moreover, Frolov was convinced that, despite its badgering of Karimov on issues of democratization, the United States did not want to push Karimov out of power, especially since there was no alternative to his leadership capable of preventing a possible ascendancy of Islamic fundamentalists. What Frolov seemed to be saying was that Karimov's game playing with the United States was nothing Russia needed to get upset over. U.S. policy in Uzbekistan was not likely to lead to Karimov's replacement by a pro-West democratic reformer at Russia's expense, even though a U.S. military presence of some kind in all likelihood would continue.[51]

The Continuing American Dilemma

Washington once again was faced by the complexity of its dealings with the central Asian republics, wanting their help in the war against terrorism but uncomfortable, indeed, deeply troubled, by their antidemocratic behavior which in some instances, like the crackdown in Andijon, Uzbekistan, was extreme.[52] By July 2005, the Congress had become so concerned by the way in which American money was being used by alleged tyrants in the war against terrorism with little or no heed to the other major objective of American foreign policy in the Eurasian republics, namely democratization. Congress wanted a reassessment of the Bush administration's counterterrorism policies where they seemed to work against democratization.

They wanted the Bush administration to think hard about and resolve this contradiction of goals. The need for a balance was obvious; but creating it was extremely difficult, as the U.S. reaction to the May 2005 events in Uzbekistan demonstrated.[53]

Post-Andijon U.S. Policy

The United States tried to minimize the Uzbek demand to evacuate the Khanabad air base. A State Department official said in effect that while the base had been valuable to the United States, Washington would not back away from its well-established opposition to the Karimov government's disregard of human rights and its refusal to allow an international investigation of its repressive handling of the Andijon uprising. The Americans said that the regime's harshness, bordering on sheer brutality, terrified the local population. It also had provoked a sudden refugee crisis involving the flight of hundreds of Uzbeks from the Andijon region to neighboring Kyrgyzstan. With the help of outside nations, in particular the United States, some of the refugees were airlifted to Romania to ease the financial burden on the Kyrgyz government now under the leadership of President Kurmanbek Bakiyev. U.S. help to the refugees infuriated the Karimov leadership.[54]

By 2006, in surveying the situation overall, the United States concluded that its military could get along without the base and that giving it up was preferable to cutting a deal with the discredited Karimov.[55] The situation in Afghanistan in 2006 was quite different from that in 2001. In 2006, the United States had virtually defeated the Taliban, installed a leadership in Kabul with close ties to Washington, and had seemed to have the logistical requirements for continued fighting in Afghanistan to finish off the Taliban once and for all, though subsequent developments showed that the U.S. military situation was starting to deteriorate with a rejuvenated Taliban insurgency getting help from outside of Afghanistan. But, in early 2006, in addition to the apparent U.S. military predominance, there also was availability of other bases for U.S. forces in neighboring Kyrgyzstan, in particular the Manas base outside of Bishkek. Under these circumstances, the Bush administration was not inclined to go any further in trying to persuade Karimov to let the U.S. continue to use Khanabad.[56] That said, there was another, more pessimistic view of a credible expert on central Asian affairs, Martha Brill Olcott of the Carnegie Endowment for International Peace, who told the U.S. Helsinki Committee in July 2006 that "the loss of Karsi-Khanabad has made the US more dependent upon a weak and at best incompetent regime in Kyrgyzstan."[57]

Not surprisingly, opinion in Washington about the closure of the base remained mixed. On the one hand, in May 2005, Pentagon spokesman Bryan Whitman had called access to the airfield "undeniably critical in supporting our combat operations" and humanitarian deliveries in Afghanistan. But, after the closure was announced by Tashkent, Whitman reiterated that "the U.S. military did not depend on one base in any part of the world."[58]

The Bush administration seemed disappointed by the loss and hoped that a visit to Tashkent of Under Secretary of State Burns to try once more to get Karimov to allow a full investigation of the Andijon uprising and, perhaps, set the stage for a reversal of the Uzbek decision to evict the United States from Khanabad would succeed. Karimov, however, refused to budge on both the investigation of Andijon and the eviction order, which in August 2005 the Kyrgyz parliament ratified, confirming Karimov's policy of diminishing the U.S. military presence in his country.[59]

But, the Bush administration could not retreat on its insistence that Karimov explain his perceived antidemocratic policies in Andijon, having affirmed the promotion of democracy abroad as a key goal of U.S. foreign policy under its leadership. The administration was trapped in its own rhetoric unable to overlook Karimov's brutal dictatorship for the sake of retaining Uzbekistan's cooperation with U.S. policy.[60]

More U.S. Efforts to Reverse the Base Eviction

At the end of September 2005, U.S. Assistant Secretary of State for European and Eurasian Affairs Daniel Fried went to Tashkent to discuss the U.S. departure from the base. On his leaving Washington, State Department spokesman Sean McCormack stated that Fried would try to get Karimov to back off from his closure decision. While in Tashkent Fried agreed to have the United States pay $23 million to Uzbekistan for maintenance of the base, the amount the Karimov government said was due it. But, Fried said nothing publicly about retention of the base, presumably to avoid encouraging Karimov to "dig in his heels" on the issue. In addition, retention of the base in fact had not been on his official agenda. What was on the agenda was U.S. concern about the Uzbek leader's disregard of human rights as well as security matters, in particular the threat of militant Islamic subversion of his government and the outbreak of a civil war of the kind that had plagued Tajikistan for most of the 1990s. Fried seemed to be trying to put the best face on an evident failure of U.S. diplomacy with Tashkent. No doubt Karimov had been under strong Russian, and possibly Chinese, pressure to "stick to his guns" on the base issue and get the Americans out of Uzbekistan, and this pressure worked.[61]

Alienation of the United States carried some risk for Karimov. His strategic options for assuring Uzbekistan's security suddenly were limited. The only place Karimov could look for security was Russia, which he knew had its own ambitions in Uzbekistan. Furthermore, Karimov's decision to oust the Americans from Uzbek territory clearly strengthened the strategic position of Kyrgyzstan, where the United States had a military base. Kyrgyzstan was a country with which Karimov had had difficulties and disagreements from the beginning of the independence era in 1991. American resources now would go from Uzbekistan to Kyrgyzstan, where the Manas air base used by the United States stood to become the most important American base in central Asia, which, in turn, would mean a continued and expanded infusion of U.S. material assistance into Kyrgyzstan. Likewise, another neighbor, Tajikistan, where the Americans were looking for a base stood to benefit from the shift of American strategic resources away from Uzbekistan, further weakening Uzbekistan's security and increasing, as a result, the need to draw closer to Russia.[62]

No doubt planning for diminished support to Uzbekistan—as early as July 2004, citing disappointment over Karimov's neglect of human rights, the United States had announced that it would withhold millions of dollars in security and economic assistance—Karimov allowed an increase in Russian influence, affirmed by the signing of an Uzbek-Russian strategic cooperation pact in June 2004. Then in July 2004, Karimov visited Moscow where he called Russia "a priority partner." There was also an expansion of Uzbek-Russian trade in energy with Russia's Gazprom increasing purchases of Uzbek gas.[63]

A "Nadir" in U.S.-Uzbek Relations in October 2005

In early October 2005, in a sign of the deep trouble in U.S.-Uzbek relations, Secretary of State Rice canceled a planned visit to Tashkent, while she continued her itinerary in the region, going to Kazakhstan, Kyrgyzstan, and Tajikistan. The canceled visit was the clearest indication yet of the Bush administration's dissatisfaction with President Karimov's repressive leadership. According to Assistant Secretary of State Fried, Karimov's government had created a "climate of fear" throughout Uzbek society undermining the already halting progress of Uzbekistan toward democracy.[64] Rice's mission to Uzbekistan's neighbors was to keep them as allies despite strains in relations with them over the repressive behavior of their government. In effect, Rice's decision was an acknowledgement by Washington that maintaining the complicated balance between criticism of and support for these countries had become too much in the case of Uzbekistan.[65]

Uzbek-American relations reached a nadir when the State Department pronounced that the Karimov government had not fulfilled the terms of the 2002 Strategic Partnership Framework Agreement that mandated "substantial and continuing progress on democratization." In addition, in early October 2005, the U.S. Senate voted to block the $23 million payment to Uzbekistan promised by Fried for the air base in retaliation for the Karimov regime's eviction of the United States from the Khanabad base. While the U.S. government again tried to give the impression that the loss of the base was tolerable and in the long term would hardly compromise the ongoing American strategy in Afghanistan, in fact the loss was significant and Washington had difficulty giving the opposite impression.[66]

In October 2005, as the United States prepared to evacuate the Khanabad base, the Pentagon, despite the Congressional vote, made plans to pay Uzbekistan the $23 million. The intent was to show not only Uzbekistan but other central Asian republics that the United States would pay its bills for the war on terrorism and would do so even if it had political differences with some regimes.[67]

The payment also was a message for Kyrgyzstan, which continued to host a U.S. military presence despite persistent pressures at home and externally to cut ties to the United States. But, it is worth noting that a flustered Congress was less worried than the executive branch about the opinion of other central Asian republics, and wanted to cut off funds to Uzbekistan. Congress tried to block payment to Uzbekistan by inserting language in the budget for 2006, denying authorization for the payment of any money to Tashkent for services rendered at Khanabad. Secretary of Defense Rumsfeld, however, found a way to disburse the money anyway.[68] The strong U.S. sentiment against Uzbekistan at this time was well articulated by Republican Senator John McCain who called the harsh Uzbek crackdown on political opposition in Andijon in May so severe as to merit American sanctions against the Karimov government, the opposite of giving it millions of U.S. taxpayer dollars.[69]

Karimov Leaves the Door Ajar for the United States

Karimov's policy on the base eviction did not automatically mean a total rejection of ties to the United States, which he still considered valuable and necessary if only because they helped Uzbekistan wage war against terrorism. Russia lacked power needed to keep the Islamic threat as it affected Uzbekistan contained. In addressing the national parliament in early September 2003, Karimov had said that the "ties with the US remain important as long as the war on terrorism remains in the forefront" and in 2005 he had not changed his mind.[70] Moreover, there was always the suspicion in Tashkent of Russian influence-building at the expense of Uzbek sovereignty. Karimov distrusted the CIS, which Russia dominated, because he viewed the CIS as little more than an instrument of Russian aggrandizement to restore Soviet-style control over Eurasia.

Indeed, Karimov had controlled his emotions and resisted the temptation to "get back at" the Americans for their criticism of his human rights record and preferred a view the Uzbek foreign minister had shared with Assistant Secretary of State Elizabeth Jones during her visit to Tashkent in July 2004 that the Uzbek-American strategic partnership was an "effectively evolving" institution.[71]

Flaws of Post-9/11 U.S. Policy in Uzbekistan

As the problems with Uzbekistan unfolded, the United States saw the need to develop a more nuanced approach to its government.[72] According to Fiona Hill of the Carnegie Endowment for International Peace, the United States may have given too little emphasis in its relations with Uzbekistan to the value of Karimov's help to U.S. policy in the Middle East. She suggested in testimony before the U.S. Helsinki Committee on July 25, 2006 that Karimov could be and was helpful in questions relating to Israel, providing a channel of communication to the Middle East not heavily influenced by Russia.[73]

But, it appeared that it was too late for a nuanced approach. By 2006, Karimov apparently feared that in its denunciation of his repressive responses to the May 2005 Andijon uprising, the United States was covertly and obliquely working for his overthrow. He evidently made this assumption when he saw the United States funding local nongovernmental pro-democracy organizations that supported opposition groups and individuals. Some of these groups wanted him out of office and the U.S. funds were seen as helping them to achieve his ouster. Karimov concluded that the United States also wanted him out. In mid-January 2006, Uzbek authorities suspended the activities of one such organization which was headquartered in Washington D.C. for providing Internet access to the Uzbek public without an official license.[74]

Indeed, Karimov was alarmed by the evident Washington hand in the overthrow in 2005 of Kyrgyzstan President Askar Akayev in what became known as the "tulip revolution." Karimov, and Moscow as well, suspected that the American military presence in central Asia gave Washington an opportunity to interfere in the internal political affairs of the host country to the detriment of any national leadership of which the United States was critical. To protect his power and assure his continuing leadership in the face of U.S. criticism and perceived intrusiveness in supporting antigovernment opposition, Karimov believed he had to rid his country of the U.S. presence.[75]

Furthermore, according to Martha Brill Olcott, the Karimov regime and its supporters had not suffered much from the weakening of its relations with the United States. To begin with, the Islamic threat has been less dangerous than either Karimov or the United States had believed primarily because radical, militant fundamentalist ideas appealed to only a small and youthful minority of Uzbeks with the overwhelming majority of Uzbek society satisfied with the kind of secularism Karimov practiced in his day-to-day leadership. Furthermore, the U.S. and Western effort to isolate and ostracize Karimov because of his brutal policies in Andijon was substantially mitigated by new foreign investors in Uzbekistan's energy trade, largely from Russia and China, which were eager to work with Karimov to limit the U.S. presence in central Asia after 9/11.[76] Certainly, Russia under Putin had been working for years to counterbalance the growing U.S. influence in Tashkent and was encouraged to intensify this policy as Uzbek-U.S. relations became increasingly strained over the issue of Karimov's perceived disinterest in real democratization.

Finally, Karimov has been successful maintaining his power base and preserving his leadership of the country despite his authoritarian bent and the persistence of a resilient opposition. He was reelected to the presidency in 1999 by a 92 percent majority though the regime had worked to minimize opposition to his candidacy. One of the contenders in that election had observed that, though a candidate, he had voted for Karimov. And in the next presidential election in December 2007, Karimov ran again despite a limit of two consecutive terms for any president. His government ignored this restriction and argued further that in fact the recent referendum of 2002 extending the president's term from five to seven years left Karimov with "a clean slate." An overwhelming majority of Uzbek citizens both fear and admire Karimov, enabling him to lead the country without much concern about the opposition, which he continually harasses. Karimov, obviously, has not been weakened—and may well have been strengthened— by his tough policies toward the United States in the wake of Andijon. Certainly, the Kremlin appreciated Karimov's frequently prickly relations with Washington.[77]

IMPROVING RUSSIAN-UZBEK RELATIONS, 2003–2008

While the United States had been struggling in the aftermath of 9/11 to strengthen military and other ties to Uzbekistan, the Kremlin had gone on an offensive of its own to checkmate the Americans and expand their own influence over Karimov. Indeed, as Uzbekistan's relations with the United States steadily deteriorated with the virtual explosion of U.S. criticisms of Akayev's rule after the crackdown on opposition in Andijon, its relations with Russia improved. In particular, the Putin Kremlin made a point of continuing to support Karimov's oppressive rule while the United States continued to denigrate it as "antidemocratic."

The August 2003 Samarkand Summit

At a summit meeting between Putin and Karimov in mid-August 2003 in Samarkand, Russia's effort to counter U.S. influence-building was evident. Though the meeting lasted only three hours of one day, a lot was accomplished, confirming a new Russian-Uzbek diplomatic effort at strengthening relations between the two countries in the aftermath of 9/11, particularly in the areas of regional security and trade, especially in oil and gas.[78]

On the security front, the two leaders discussed counterterrorism measures being developed under the aegis of the SCO. Russia and Uzbekistan agreed to join other SCO states in holding military maneuvers involving simulated attacks on terrorist groupings. Karimov won Russia's support for the establishment of a counterterrorism center in Tashkent rather than elsewhere, such as Bishkek, Kyrgyzstan. This strategic cooperation suggested a major improvement in the Uzbek attitude toward Russia, which in the past had been defined by Uzbek fears of Russian expansionism in central Asia.[79]

Trade was another item on the summit agenda. Russia wanted to expand its economic influence in Uzbekistan. In part, Russia's interest also was driven by the need to counter aggressive American efforts to construct pipelines in the Caspian region that bypassed Russia but served Uzbekistan by setting the stage for an expansion of direct U.S. investment in Uzbek energy development. At the summit, Putin made a point of saying that the Kremlin backed the effort of Gazprom to develop joint gas projects with Uzbekistan. Gazprom would help exploit Uzbekistan's energy resources and expand its gas exports.[80]

This Samarkand meeting did not bode well for the United States, marking, as it did, the beginning of a long period of decline in Uzbek-American relations. The Kremlin undoubtedly was elated by the opportunity it now had to reverse the sudden advance of American influence in Uzbekistan after 9/11.[81]

Another top-level meeting between Russian and Uzbek leaders occurred in April 2004. Karimov went to Moscow to discuss trade and security issues. Then in June 2004, it was reported that the three largest Russian energy companies, Gazprom, LUKOIL, and Soyuzneftgaz, had opened offices in Tashkent. At the same time, there was a conspicuous suspension of Uzbek media criticism of Russia. Then Russia and Uzbekistan signed a Strategic Partnership Agreement affirming and defining their cooperation in the war against terrorism and providing for the right of each signatory to use military facilities on the territory of the other in counterterrorist initiatives. For all intent and purpose, this Strategic Partnership Agreement gave Russia the same permission to maintain a military presence on Uzbek territory as had been given the United States in 2002.[82]

Putin Encourages the Uzbek Tilt toward Russia

One major reason for a revival of interest in strengthening Uzbek relations with Russia was unquestionably the U.S. decision to trim its aid to Uzbekistan as a penalty for the Karimov regime's human rights violations. In addition was Karimov's incurable suspicion of the United States, no doubt fed by U.S. criticisms of his leadership, that he and his country were just being used and not really valued for what they could offer the United States. He thought that the United States was condescending and demeaning in its interaction with him. Typical, in his view, was in an incident during his visit to Washington in 2002, when, at least in his opinion, he had been snubbed by the Bush administration in its decision to send only an assistant secretary of state to meet him on his arrival at Andrews Air Force Base for talks with U.S. officials. He believed that Washington attached less importance to its new post-9/11 relationship with Uzbekistan than it deserved. In his mind, Uzbekistan with a population of 25 million people and valuable energy resources deserved more respect than the Americans were showing.[83]

The Kremlin's support of Karimov as U.S. criticism of his rule continued was psychologically important for the Uzbek leader. Taking a far different tack than the Americans that was seen as respectful of his leadership, the Kremlin had called his crackdown on antigovernment demonstrations during and after Andijon "an internal matter" with which outsiders should not interfere. Here Putin was not only going out of his way to ingratiate Russia with Karimov, hopefully at the expense of the Americans, but also echoing a dismissal of outside complaints about his own harshness in dealing with the Chechnya insurgents carrying the message that leaders in Moscow and in Tashkent were on the same "wavelength," so to speak, when it came to dealing with threats to the stability and security of their respective countries. Moreover, the Kremlin blamed the Andijon protest partly on terrorists based in Afghanistan, seeming to endorse Karimov's justification for using draconian measures against Uzbek protestors.[84]

The Putin Kremlin thus encouraged Karimov's inclination to strengthen ties with Russia by not only avoiding criticism of his repressive rule but also indicating acceptance of the rightness of authoritarian rule that Putin himself seemed to be pursuing in Russia for reasons good and sufficient to himself. The Kremlin believed Karimov's dictatorship was the best defense against any kind of Islamic-inspired militant opposition. From this perspective, Karimov had dealt promptly and effectively with the Andijon uprising that conceivably could have destabilized the country and threatened an unwanted (at least on the part of the Kremlin) regime change.[85] Equally important for the Kremlin, as well as for Karimov himself, of course, was the absence of any alternative to him as a protector of his country against Islamic fundamentalism.

That said, Putin was forever pragmatic in his strategic thinking about Russian relations with Karimov's Uzbekistan. The Kremlin was never completely dismissive of the increasingly antidemocratic behavior of Karimov, if only because it obviously ran counter to the Kremlin's stated goal of developing democracy in post-Communist Russia. Openly and insistently condoning Karimov's brutality would have strained the creditability of Putin's frequent assertions of his loyalty to the democratization of post-Communist Russia.[86]

Moreover, should Karimov be overthrown, it would be difficult to deal with new government, especially if it were democratically inclined and tolerant of political opposition. Putin had early examples of this kind of regime change that had brought democratic leaders to power in Georgia in 2003 and Ukraine in 2004.

Continuing Russian Support of Karimov

The Kremlin welcomed Karimov's decision on closure of the U.S. base at Khanabad. At the end of June 2005, Putin and Russian Defense Minister Sergei Ivanov met with Karimov in Moscow to discuss military cooperation and affirm Russia's backing of the beleaguered Uzbek leader. Ivanov announced that Russia would conduct joint military exercises with Uzbekistan, the first such activity since Uzbekistan became independent in late 1991. In addition, Putin was receptive to a suggestion by Karimov that there may well have been an American hand in the uprising in Andijon, music to Russian ears since Putin had been insisting off and on for some time that the United States was aggressively supporting antigovernment political opposition groups in post-Soviet Eurasian republics.[87]

Putin and Karimov undertook a joint military exercise involving Russian and Uzbek forces on September 21–23, 2005, in southern Uzbekistan. Russia contributed a reinforced airborne company and a contingent of "special forces" known as the Spetsnaz, while Uzbekistan deployed two companies of special mountain troops. Although the exercises consisted of no more than about 400 troops, the timing of them was significant. They were occurring when a decisive rupture in Uzbek-American relations seemed imminent. So rejuvenated did the Russian-Uzbek relationship seem to the Kremlin that Defense Minister Ivanov intimated that Uzbekistan need not change past policies and join the CIS, CSTO, and its Rapid Deployment Force for good relations between the two countries to flourish.[88]

But, at the end of 2005, Uzbekistan in fact rejoined the CSTO and became an active member of other Russian-led groupings such as the SCO and the Eurasian Economic Community. Further to the Kremlin's satisfaction was Karimov's decision to take Uzbekistan out of the pro-Western GUUAM organization to which Georgia, Ukraine, Azerbaijan, and Moldova belonged.

In October 2005, Ivanov made it plain that there would be no Russian sanctions against Uzbekistan for Andijon or any other of Karimov's human rights violations as the West was imposing. For Russia the bottom line was that Karimov's repression was the only effective guarantee of Uzbek stability, important for Russia's own domestic stability, as well as its security vis-à-vis the threat of Islamic militancy which Uzbekistan's dictatorship was determined to resist.[89]

Something of a climax in Russia's conciliatory diplomacy with Uzbekistan occurred with the signing of a treaty of alliance between the Kremlin and Karimov on November 14, 2005, in Moscow. The alliance had the standard phraseology that was equivalent to saying that an attack on one was an attack on both and that each signatory would render assistance to the other.[90]

Karimov took the opportunity to emphasize the shift of his focus from the United States to Russia, saying in effect that if Uzbekistan were endangered in any way, a transgressor against Uzbekistan now would have to face Russia as well. He called the alliance "a reliable guarantee of peace and stability in the region," adding that "no one will ever be able to dispute Russia's presence in the region" and casting the new alliance as a long-term strategic choice by Uzbekistan.[91]

Uzbek officials believed they had made a crucial choice in favoring Russia over the United States in their foreign policy strategy. Karimov intoned in the Kremlin that "by signing this treaty . . . we showed once again with whom we build our future. Russia is our most reliable partner and ally." The Uzbek gesture clearly was a setback for U.S. influence-building in central Asia in the post-9/11 years and a conspicuous reversal of the strong relationship the two countries had achieved only a year before.[92]

The Russian side was equally ebullient. The treaty opened the way for a substantial Russian military presence on Uzbek territory, as well as for Russian assistance to Uzbekistan to upgrade and strengthen its modest military establishment, leaving little doubt about the U.S. strategic setback.[93] Oksana Antonenko, a senior fellow at the International Institute of Strategic Studies, provided some insight into the Kremlin's diplomacy with Uzbekistan, observing that Russia was supportive of Karimov because Uzbekistan was "one of the few places left where Russia can maintain its status as a great power that it has lost elsewhere."[94]

A Downside of Russian Diplomacy

Although Russian Defense Minister Ivanov said in November 2006 that he "could not care less" about the contrast between Russian and Western, especially American, policies toward Uzbekistan, the growing disagreement between Karimov and Washington complicated Russia's relations with the United States, which saw the Kremlin's hand in the base eviction. At the same time, the rejuvenated Russian relationship with Uzbekistan in 2005 posed risks to Russian relations with Turkmenistan president, Sepamurad Niyazov, who did not appreciate a perceived Russian favoritism toward Uzbekistan. The Kremlin could not rule out an effort by the hypersensitive and quixotic Niyazov to retaliate against the Kremlin to discourage its playing favorites in central Asia, though it was never clear how Niyazov could do this. Finally, the Kremlin could find itself in an unpleasant political situation should Karimov be forced out of office given its evident support of his leadership, an improbable though by no means impossible development. In any event, Karimov won an overwhelming victory in Uzbek presidential election in December 2007, assuring his grip on power at least for the next several years and a Russian expectation of his continuing friendship and cooperation with Russia.[95]

Russia Bests the United States in 2007?

Throughout 2007 and 2008, Russian relations with Uzbekistan in fact steadily improved. The Kremlin persistently stood by Karimov in his war of words with the United States over its complaints about how he had lapsed in democratizing his country. The Kremlin also continued to refrain from criticism of Karimov's antidemocratic leadership, reassuring him of Russia's sympathy for and support of him. For example, in a visit to Tashkent in March 2007, Russian Prime Minister Mikhail Fradkov called Uzbekistan "Russia's closest partner in central Asia," telling the Uzbek leadership that he had come to Tashkent to achieve a broader and deeper cooperation between the two countries.[96]

Karimov reciprocated Fradkov's gesture, calling attention to the dynamic, fast-paced improvement in relations between Uzbekistan and Russia on both the bilateral and multilateral levels. Indeed, it seemed that by 2007, Uzbekistan's tough internal controls and pro-Russian policies had made it a role model for its neighbors in their relations with Russia, weakening the United States not only in Uzbekistan but elsewhere in the ex-Soviet central Asian region. Indeed, Fradkov's effusive diplomacy with the Uzbek leadership was intended to send a message to other central Asian republics to the effect that diminishing U.S. influence in their country would automatically strengthen their relations with Russia in ways that would yield immediate material advantage, say in the form of expansion of trade.[97]

Further evidence of increasing Russian influence in Uzbekistan was the Moscow summit of Putin and Karimov in February 2008, when Karimov took the opportunity to remind the Kremlin of Uzbekistan's closeness to Russia, speaking of "special relations between the two countries" and of "Uzbekistan's high respect for Russia," no doubt in response to Putin's continuing support of his regime as Western criticism of it for its political repression in the aftermath of Andijon in 2005 continued unabated.[98] There, however, a definite softening of the Western attitude toward Uzbekistan was evident in late 2007 and throughout 2008, as the military situation in Afghanistan deteriorated for NATO troops fighting against a seemingly resurgent Taliban.

It is worth noting that Putin had promptly congratulated Karimov on his reelection on December 23, 2007, despite aspects of the contest that were fraudulent. The December 2007 election occurred in much the same way as earlier contests Karimov had won with overwhelming majorities. In these presidential elections, Karimov had left no stone unturned in denying the political opposition opportunities to communicate with voters and offer them an alternative to his leadership.[99]

At the February 2008 Moscow summit, Putin was as effusive as Fradkov had been months earlier in praising the Russian-Uzbek relationship. He said that Karimov's presence in Moscow was a sign that "our relations are going to develop further, as they have been developing in previous years." In particular, Putin called attention to an expansion of Russian-Uzbek trade worth $2 billion at the end of 2006, an indication of the importance of trade as a means of strengthening Russian influence in Uzbekistan.[100]

At the summit, there also was a concern for security vis-à-vis the continuing struggle of the United States and its NATO allies to defeat a resilient Taliban. According to Sergei Luzyanin, a professor at the Moscow State Institute for International Relations, the so-called "Afghanistan-Pakistan problem has become extremely acute." In Luzyanin's view, Afghanistan in 2008 could fall apart along with the collapse of President Hamid Karzai's leadership, events that "will directly impact Uzbekistan and other central Asian countries and, therefore, Russia." A successful return to power of the Taliban with the encouragement of certain military elements in Pakistan would constitute a major threat to the stability of the secular regimes in central Asia, as well as to Russia itself, and a basis for bilateral cooperation.[101]

But, according to Yuri Fedorov, a senior regional analyst at the London-based Chatham House, Moscow does not consider Karimov a trustworthy partner. "Relations between Russia and Uzbekistan," he said, "are not sincere." He did not think Moscow really trusted Karimov because of his foreign policy "zigzags," namely, his flirtations with the United States since 9/11 and his steadfast refusal to break Uzbekistan's static relations with Washington. He may not be happy with Uzbekistan's ties to the United States but he is also suspicious of Moscow, viewing Russia, according to Fedorov, "as an unwanted partner with which he must deal given the absence of other allies," a diplomatic situation that works to the advantage of the United States.[102]

A U.S.-UZBEK RECONCILIATION IN THE MAKING IN 2008?

Meanwhile, in late 2007 and early 2008, there was reason to believe that there was a reconciliation in the making between the United States and Uzbekistan, with the United States taking the lead in bringing it about and with a surprising willingness of the Uzbek side to respond positively to this new development. For example, in September 2007, a new U.S. ambassador to Uzbekistan, Richard Norland, presented his credentials to Uzbek President Karimov. He was seen in Tashkent as interested in repairing and strengthening the debilitated U.S.-Uzbek relationship severely compromised by the relentless U.S. criticism of the Karimov regime's repressiveness, especially in the Andijon crackdown in 2005. Norland had a meeting with an Uzbek human rights official in which he acknowledged that the United States was guilty of human rights violations at the Abu Ghraib prison in Iraq, seeming to say that no nation, not even the United States, had an unblemished record on respect for human rights.[103] Subsequently, Norland made unmistakable signals to Karimov of U.S. interest in strengthening relations between the two countries.[104]

Karimov's response to the new U.S. hints was positive. In December 2007, he said in a speech commemorating Uzbekistan's "Constitution Day" that he saw no problems in Uzbek relations with the West, in particular the United States, strained for a long time by the repressiveness of his leadership for which he had been criticized by not only the United States but also the EU with which he wanted to remain on good terms.[105] In early 2008, there was more evidence, at least in the American view, of a modest warming of Uzbek-U.S. relations. Karimov seemed to be easing up on repression of political dissent. The regime reportedly pardoned six jailed human rights activists. Karimov also was alleged to have promised a liberalization of Uzbekistan's rigid financial system. He was also credited with a softening of criticism of the West.[106] Moreover, Norland was quoted in March 2008 saying that "since January 2008, the [Uzbek] government is making small but significant steps to improve the human rights situation."[107]

The Bush administration tried to make the most of this perceived change in Karimov's political behavior. In late January, the administration sent CENTCOM chief Admiral William Fallon to Tashkent to discuss issues in U.S.-Uzbek relations. He reviewed a large number of substantive issues in areas of mutual interest and regional security that included some Uzbek concession on use of a military facility in Uzbekistan. Fallon seems to have handled the mission very well because on March 5 the United States was informed that NATO troops, in particular U.S. forces, would soon be able to use the southern air base in the city of Termez located on Uzbekistan's frontier with Afghanistan.[108]

Driving the U.S. initiatives seeking a reconciliation with Uzbekistan were several considerations, not least having to do with Afghanistan. The reality of Uzbekistan's importance to U.S. strategy in Afghanistan and the larger war on Islamic extremist terrorism had not changed since 2001. According to the U.S. Ambassador to the United Nations Zalmay Khalilzad, U.S. plans to expand its military deployment in Afghanistan in light of the dismaying resilience of the Taliban made a base in Uzbekistan to facilitate the expanded U.S. deployment more valuable than ever.[109]

For his part, Karimov had reason to reciprocate continuing U.S. efforts to strengthen ties with Uzbekistan and expand cooperation in the war against terrorism, in particular the fighting in Afghanistan. By 2008, it was absolutely clear to Karimov, as well as to other central Asian leaders, especially those of countries that bordered Afghanistan, that the stability of that country was crucial to their survival and material well-being and that insecurity in Afghanistan in 2008 was no good for them. Moreover, Karimov wants Uzbekistan to have some influence over the political development of post-Taliban Afghanistan and realizes the only way this can happen, if it happens at all, is through cooperation with the West, in particular the United States.[110]

Karimov was interested in repairing ties to the West also to gain some leverage in coping with Russia's aggressive influence-building strategy in Uzbekistan. In particular, there seemed to be some tension in Uzbek relations with the Putin Kremlin, with Karimov seeking access to the Prikaspisky pipeline project, under construction by Russia, Kazakhstan, and Turkmenistan, that will skirt the Caspian Sea to carry natural gas north starting in 2012. Uzbekistan was conspicuously excluded from the project.[111]

In April 2008, Karimov tried to strengthen relations with NATO, offering increased cooperation in Afghanistan. But NATO responded cautiously, mindful of the way in which Karimov severely curtailed Uzbekistan's cooperation with the United States in the Summer of 2005. Moreover, there is little chance that Karimov's effort to stabilize Afghanistan through a revival of the "6+2" idea of the preceding decade will work. Since the United States dominates the Western military campaign for control of Afghanistan, Karimov has to seek improved relations with Washington.[112]

Whether this promise of improving relations between the United States and Uzbekistan continues after 2008 remains to be seen. From the Kremlin's point of view, Karimov now joins Kyrgyz President Bakiyev in making clear to neighbors in ex-Soviet central Asia as well as to the Russians that neither want to disrupt ties with the United States no matter how strongly Moscow lobbies Tashkent for an anti-American strategy. The resilience of the Taliban in Afghanistan and the prospect, however improbable in 2008, of a Taliban return to power and resumption of the severe Islamicization of that country by the Taliban when they first took power in the mid-1990s may be the only plausible reason for a revitalization of U.S. ties to Uzbekistan and even a slight softening of Karimov's repressive leadership to ensure the fulfillment of this revitalization.

A KAZAKHSTAN FACTOR

A potential "wild card" in Uzbekistan's diplomacy with Russia and the United States in 2007–2008 was Kazakhstan because of an ill-concealed rivalry for influence and power in central Asia between Nazarbayev and Karimov. Kazakhstan has "skillfully" used a "multi-vector" foreign policy to its strategic advantage and Karimov of late has been doing the same thing. The term "multi-vector" refers to the way in which Kazakhstan President Nursultan Nazarbayev has been able to maintain good relations with the Kremlin while doing the same with the United States. A key aspect of this Kazakh trilateral diplomacy is the way in which Nazarbayev has cultivated China. Karimov has done the same in recent years.[113]

A CHINA FACTOR

Like Russia, China was uncomfortable over the growing U.S. presence in central Asia in the post-9/11 years, especially in light of Beijing's long-term strategic interests in the region. Occasionally making common cause with Russia, despite the persistence of outstanding differences between the two countries, not least aggressive Russian influence-building in the ex-Soviet states, especially in central Asia, the Chinese cooperated with the Russians within the framework of the SCO to contain and restrain the expanding American role in central Asia after 9/11.[114]

As Russia, China supported Karimov in differences with the United States over his antidemocratic rule. The Chinese did not want to criticize the harshness of his repression of political opponents. Partly, the Chinese sympathized with Karimov's problem of preserving power against popular efforts to take it away from him, especially in the Andijon uprising. From Beijing's vantage point, Karimov did in Andijon what the Chinese leadership had had to do in its response to the June 1989 Tiananmen Square uprising against the Communist Party's dictatorship, that is, ruthlessly suppress it. For China, as for Russia, stability created by political authoritarianism was needed for security, a view opposed by the United States, which always maintained that stability comes from democracy, strengthening it by legitimizing it.[115]

In addition, supporting Karimov's rule of Uzbekistan offered the Chinese an opportunity to do some influence-building of their own in Uzbekistan, an important consideration in light of its on-again, off-again rivalry with Russia and the United States for the friendship and cooperation of the newly independent ex-Soviet republics. In addition, both Russia and China had the same regional enemy shared by Uzbekistan, notably the powerful and subversive influence of Islamic militancy which they feared and opposed as much as their resources would allow them and which tended to diminish their rivalry by encouraging their cooperation. Karimov at times seemed to be their "point man" in the war against terrorism.[116]

At the core was China's concern with security. According to Ding Peihua, a central Asia expert in the Shanghai Academy of Social Sciences, "if Uzbekistan is not stable, that will have a big impact on China's (own) security situation." Peihua called attention in this regard to the way in which Uzbekistan for a long time had served as one of the key hideouts of ethnic Muslim separatists seeking to create an independent state in Xinjiang. China also appreciated the fact that Karimov could keep a lid on East Turkestan separatists in China with links to Uzbekistan's Islamic extremist groups. Karimov was in a position to cooperate with China in restraining the growth of these separatist groups, and China did not care how much repression he used.[117]

For his part, Karimov went out of his way to cultivate China. As Uzbekistan's relations with the United States steadily deteriorated, Karimov increasingly looked to China as well as to Russia to counterbalance this development. In mid-May 2005, Karimov went to Beijing to discuss shared security and trade interests. Chinese leaders, including President Hu Jintao, warmly welcomed him.[118]

This meeting, at which he was received warmly by the Chinese leadership, symbolized the opportunities available to Karimov to pursue his strategy of cultivating powerful friends abroad to strengthen whatever leverage he had in dealing with the Kremlin. Indeed, the Chinese leadership could not have done more to express its support of Karimov. President Hu Jintao emphasized the importance for China of friendship and cooperation with Uzbekistan, clearly willing to help Karimov hold his own in the strategic shifts taking place in Uzbekistan's relations with Russia and the United States. Hu underscored China's complete acceptance of his tough political line on dissent, saying, "China respects the way the Uzbek people choose to develop their country and their efforts in safeguarding national independence, sovereignty, and territorial integrity." The leaders of the two countries ended their summit emphasizing a friendly and cooperative partnership between the two countries. Agreements on economic cooperation in the fields of oil, gas, mining, telecommunications, transportation, and infrastructure development were signed. Beijing also pledged to support the admission of Uzbekistan into the World Trade Organization.[119]

In July 2006, in high-level meetings between Uzbek and Chinese officials, Karimov reiterated the new Chinese cooperation in the area of security. Uzbekistan hoped that good relations with China would help offset the negative economic as well as strategic impact of the closure of the American air base at Khanabad and the cutoff of U.S. aid. Moreover, China as well as Russia would help mitigate the loss of American help in the war against terrorism.[120]

A NEW IRAN FACTOR

In 2005 and after, Iran welcomed the decline of U.S. influence in Uzbekistan. It was Iran's intent to block any expansion of American military power in Uzbekistan and other central Asian countries for reasons of Iranian territorial security threatened by the sharp deterioration in its relations with the United States and EU countries throughout 2006 and early 2007. In the early months of 2007, the Iranian regime took advantage of the Uzbek decision to evict the United States from the Khanabad military base. The Teheran regime allegedly proposed to Uzbekistan and other central Asian countries in which the United States had developed a military presence that it would sign with them a new security and defense agreement to send weapons and technology. So far these offers have not amounted to much. For Uzbekistan, too close a relationship with Iran would further complicate its relations with the United States. And so far this possibility limits what Iran can do.[121]

A GEORGIAN FACTOR

Karimov's careful tilt back toward the West may have influenced his cautious response to the explosion of turmoil in Georgia in early August 2008. He seemed in no rush to give strong Uzbek backing to Russia's military moves into Georgia and in particular Russian recognition in early September of the independence of South Ossetia. The Georgian government had provoked the Russian military action in South Ossetia by using military force to end once and for all the province's strong separatist inclinations and restore control of Georgia's central government in Tbilisi. The Kremlin was concerned about Uzbek behavior in the Georgian crisis, fearful that it could signal a further strengthening of Uzbek relations with the United States, which had severely criticized the Russian military penetration of Georgian territory.[122]

CONCLUSIONS

As of 2008, the United States seemed stymied in Uzbekistan, trapped by the Karimov regime's limits on democratization. The Bush administration has had no strategy beyond rhetoric and the threat of sanctions. In particular, Washington cannot turn to a strong indigenous pro-democracy opposition to lead the way to change. No such opposition has survived Karimov's tightly run dictatorship.

The Karimov regime does not see that it has any choice in its repressive policies. It sees democratization as a threat to its survival and this is a realistic assessment. Karimov's leadership surely would have been weakened, if not destroyed, by the political pluralism democracy required. For Karimov, this price of achieving security, as well as leverage, in dealing with Russia and China, by developing close ties with the United States was too high. Further constraining U.S. relations with Uzbekistan is the U.S. Congress which has shown no inclination to cultivate Karimov for the sake of an alliance with him in the war against terrorism even if the Bush administration might have been willing, as on occasion it seemed to be, to look the other way at Karimov's antidemocratic policies.

This U.S. predicament in Uzbekistan has benefited Russia enormously, leaving it for the moment, at least, ahead of the United States in the rivalry over influence-building in Tashkent. Moreover, working to Russia's advantage, and encouraged by the Putin Kremlin, is Karimov's fear that if he loses control of Uzbekistan by paying more attention to safeguarding human rights and in other ways promoting real democratization in his country, he would be too weak to stop radical Islamic forces that want to take over from him. Also, in his relations with the United States, Karimov always worries that the United States is plotting his overthrow just as it did with Kyrgyzstan President Askar Akayev who was ousted from power in mid-2005 by an aggressive, anti-regime, American-backed political opposition. Closeness to the United States for Karimov always carried a risk—at least in his view—of subversion and destruction of his rule of Uzbekistan, and so for now, he remains close to Russia and distrustful, though attentive, to the overtures of the United States.

Still, Karimov remains careful to avoid a permanent rupture with Washington. The value of Uzbek friendship with the United States is still very high, despite embarrassing and unrelenting U.S. criticisms of his rule. Karimov in 2008 still had not ended in a definitive way the U.S. military presence in his country though under Russian pressure to do so. The U.S. base in Khanabad is still being used for refueling of aircraft with targets in Afghanistan. It looks as if Karimov intends to keep the diplomatic door with the United States ajar, if not fully open, indefinitely as he continues to strengthen ties to Russia.

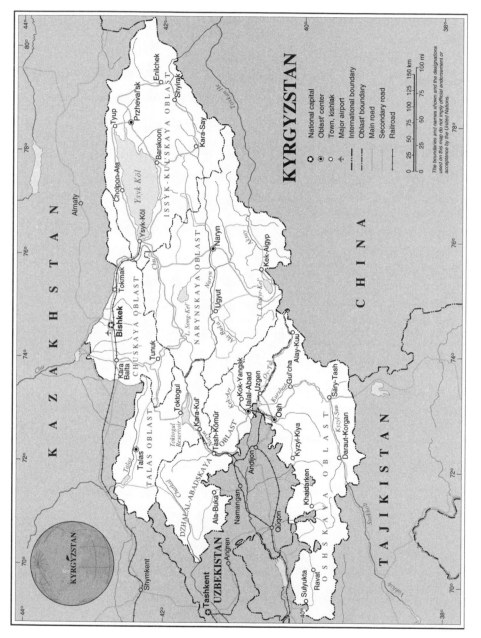

Kyrgyzstan (Courtesy of UN Cartographic Section)

6

Kyrgyzstan

Full name: Kyrgyz Republic

- Population: 5.1 million (UN, 2006)
- Capital: Bishkek
- Area: 199,900 sq. km (77,182 sq. miles)
- Major languages: Kyrgyz, Russian
- Major religions: Islam, Christianity
- Life expectancy: 63 years (men), 71 years (women) (UN)
- Monetary unit: 1 Kyrgyz som = 100 tiyins
- Main exports: Fruit, vegetables, gold, tobacco
- GNI per capita: US$440 (World Bank, 2006)

Both Russia and the United States pursued policies of influence-building in Kyrgyzstan throughout the 1990s and well into the first decade of the new century. Under Russian presidents Boris Yeltsin (1992–1999) and Vladimir Putin (2000–2008) Russia strengthened ties to Kyrgyzstan with the goals of halting the expansion of militant Islam, controlling its energy sector, and assuring the material well-being of Kyrgyzstan's Russian-speaking minority.

In this same period, under the presidential administrations of Bill Clinton and George W. Bush, the United States promoted democracy as Kyrgyzstan moved away from Communist rule and Soviet control and tried to prevent

Russia from reestablishing a Soviet-style dominance over Kyrgyzstan. In the wake of 9/11, the Bush administration enlisted Kyrgyz military cooperation in the war against terrorism.

The United States had several advantages in cultivating Kyrgyz friendship and cooperation, not least the perennial effort of the Kyrgyz leadership to use the United States as a counterweight with Russia. For its part, the United States was willing to invest a lot of money to promote its interest in Kyrgyzstan, especially to secure a military base for use against the Taliban regime in Afghanistan. U.S. money was welcome in a country that was, like others in central Asia, underdeveloped and impoverished.

The Kremlin also had advantages in its efforts to orient Kyrgyzstan to Russia, including a long history of political, economic, and military closeness between the two dating back through the era of Communist and Soviet rule to the time of the czars. Another advantage for the Kremlin was its open acceptance of the authoritarian rule of Kyrgyz President Askar Akayev in power throughout the 1990s to his ouster from power on the eve of the 2005 presidential election. Akayev's repressive control over the Kyrgyz political environment played well with the Kremlin because it unified the country, kept it stable, and discouraged anti-Russian sentiment which in any event was never as strong as it was and is elsewhere in the ex-Soviet space. Finally, working to Russia's strategic advantage was the Kyrgyz leadership's willingness to allow a substantial Russian military presence on Kyrgyz territory to protect its security when threatened from challenges abroad as well as at home.

RUSSIA AND KYRGYZSTAN IN THE YELTSIN ERA, 1992–1999

From the early 1990s, under the leadership of President Boris Yeltsin, Russia had at least two major concerns about the post-Soviet development of Kyrgyzstan. One was the status of Kyrgyzstan's large Russian minority which today makes up almost 14 percent of the total population. The second was Kyrgyzstan's relations with central Asian neighbors, especially China, which sought political influence over the Kyrgyz leadership once Kyrgyzstan had become independent of Moscow. For its part, Russia wanted Kyrgyz friendship and strategic cooperation in the early post-Soviet era. For reasons of his country's security and domestic stability, Kyrgyz President Askar Akayev reciprocated Russia's interest in good relations between the two countries.

The Russian Minority

The Yeltsin government had good reason to worry about the status of the Russian minority in Kyrgyzstan. With the advent of independence, the Russian minority of the Kyrgyz population found their privileged status in jeopardy. Nationalist politicians in the Kyrgyz parliament insisted that the newly independent republic was a "national homeland" of the Kyrgyz people, whose interests should be considered ahead of the minorities, including the Russians. They wanted to restrict the presidency of the country to an ethnic Kyrgyz. They also insisted that the land of the republic belonged to the Kyrgyz people—a principle that, if accepted into law, would deprive non-Kyrgyz people of ownership rights. They fought against dual citizenship sought by both Russian and German minorities. Kyrgyz nationalists also criticized the loyalty of the country's Russian residents pointing out that most of them had never bothered to develop a working knowledge of the Kyrgyz language.

President Akayev, leader of the Kyrgyz branch of the Soviet Communist Party and president of the Kyrgyz republic in the last decade of the Soviet Union's existence, was pro-Russian and resisted these nationalistic pressures. But, a strong undercurrent in Kyrgyz society held strong anti-Russian sentiment, partly fueled by the privileged status of the Russian-speaking community in the period of Soviet rule. Akayev tried to block the efforts of Kyrgyz nationalists to harass and embarrass Russian residents and other minorities in his country. He did not want to antagonize the Kremlin, and he certainly did not want to destabilize his multinational society, in which only about 60 percent of the population are ethnic Kyrgyz.

Throughout the 1990s, Akayev deftly parried the nationalists in the parliament and succeeded in preventing them from achieving their provocative political agenda. A new Constitution promulgated in 1993 explicitly opened the process of selecting the head of state to all Kyrgyz citizens, regardless of ethnicity. But Akayev did not succeed in getting the parliament to approve of dual citizenship. Nor did the growing discrimination against Russians and other minorities stop. Indeed, a Kyrgyz government declaration that Kyrgyz is the state language was accompanied by an increasing Islamicization of the society, and preferential treatment was given to ethnic Kyrgyz workers.

Tired of being relegated to second-class status by the political leadership of post-Soviet Kyrgyzstan, about 15 percent of the Russian minority departed for Russia, even though some came from families that had deep roots in Kyrgyz territory dating back almost a century. This flight hurt the Kyrgyz economy, depriving it of skilled labor in the construction and other industries.

Akayev was alarmed and tried to reverse this trend—and the Kremlin had qualms about it as well because the fragile, unstable post–Soviet Russian economy lacked the resources needed to integrate the new Kyrgyz refugees of Russian descent. In September 1994, with Akayev's prodding, the Kyrgyz government declared Russian the "second state language" for a 10-year period, a move that opened the way for the temporary use of Russian in all areas of national administration and provided Russians with the time many said they needed to master the difficult Kyrgyz language.

Other policies gradually revitalized the economy, such as the introduction of a modern banking system. Akayev also pursued a careful policy to assure the secular character of Kyrgyzstan in the face of pressure from a religious elite to give more official attention to Islamic practices. Apparently these policies have had a positive outcome. By the end of the 1990s, the emigration of non-Kyrgyz minorities had declined.

Russia and Kyrgyz Relations with Central Asian Neighbors

Another problem for Russia in the era of Yeltsin's leadership concerned the stability of Kyrgyzstan's relations with other central Asian republics. There was friction between Kyrgyzstan and Uzbekistan over the Uzbek minority in Kyrgyz territory. Almost 13 percent of the Kyrgyz population are Uzbeks, and ethnic Kyrgyz people resented competition from these Uzbeks, whom they considered foreigners, for scarce jobs, land, and other resources. For their part, the Uzbek minority resented discrimination and believed correctly that the Kyrgyz majority thought that they were not entitled to equality. Complicating matters, and to Russian discomfort, Uzbek President Islam Karimov proclaimed himself the protector of Uzbeks living abroad, opening up the possibility of Uzbek interference in internal Kyrgyz affairs. Indeed, Kyrgyz nationalists feared that he might support claims by some in Uzbekistan that territory in Kyrgyzstan inhabited primarily by Uzbeks in the Ferghama valley, including the cities of Osh and Uzgen, should really be part of Uzbekistan.

China

In the 1990s, Russia was concerned also about Kyrgyzstan's relations with China. Although Kyrgyz-Chinese relations appeared stable, a small minority of Uighurs in Kyrgyzstan worried about the well-being of Uighurs in the neighboring Chinese Xinjiang-Uighur Autonomous Region. Radical Kyrgyz Uighurs complained that Beijing had a "colonial policy" toward its Uighur minority, keeping them second-class citizens. The Kyrgyz Uighurs called for increased administrative autonomy for Uighurs in China.

The Chinese leadership was hypersensitive to this Uighur issue, calling this behavior of Kyrgyz Uighurs "subversive." Beijing complained to the Kyrgyz government, which responded by trying to limit the expansion of Uighur nationalism inside its borders—for example, by refusing to legalize a nationalist party known as the Uighur Organization for Freedom, which was committed among other things to the establishment of a separate republic of Uighurstan.

The Kremlin watched this situation and was satisfied with the way in which Akayev seemed to be keeping it under control. The last thing in the world Russia wanted was a conflict between one of the ex-Soviet central

Asian republics and China, especially given its known influence-building ambitions in the region. Akayev, to the Kremlin's satisfaction, had little sympathy for radical Uighur nationalists using Kyrgyzstan as a base from which to badger the Chinese leadership. Indeed, expelling them from Kyrgyzstan, he sent them back across the border to certain and severe punishment by Chinese authorities.

Kyrgyz-Russian Relations in the 1990s

The political situation in Bishkek remained stable and favorable to Russian interests throughout the 1990s. President Akayev managed to survive sharp political battles between ex-Communists and non-Communist politicians for influence over the future direction of the country, and he supported political and economic reform with Russia as a model of change. To the satisfaction of the Yeltsin Kremlin, Akayev's impressive popularity with voters seemed to cut across tribal, ethnic, regional, and ideological lines. He was elected president in 1991 by an overwhelming majority and an overwhelming turnout of 96 percent. Akayev won on a platform of political and economic democracy. He won the same kind of support in a referendum in 1994, in which he asked voters to back market reforms that, to use his own words, would turn Kyrgyzstan into the "Switzerland of Central Asia."[1]

By the end of the 1990s, Russia had good relations with Kyrgyzstan. Akayev was a close ally of the Kremlin in central Asia, supporting most of Russia's influence-building initiatives in the region, including efforts to promote Russian-initiated and Russian-led collective security agreements providing for diplomatic and military cooperation. Indeed, in the aftermath of a series of car bombs in Tashkent, Uzbekistan, that nearly killed Uzbek President Karimov, Akayev approved the opening of a Russian military base in Kyrgyzstan in 1999 within the framework of the CIS peacekeeping mandates to protect and preserve Kyrgyz international security and domestic stability.

RUSSIA, THE UNITED STATES, AND KYRGYZSTAN IN THE PUTIN ERA

In the Putin era, Russia confronted a new challenge in Kyrgyzstan: an expansion of U.S. political and military influence after 9/11.[2] Immediately following its declaration of war against terrorism and its invasion of Afghanistan, the United States wanted Kyrgyzstan military assistance in its campaign to remove the Taliban regime in Afghanistan. As was true in other ex-Soviet central Asian republics, it was difficult for the Kremlin to fault Kyrgyzstan's willingness to cooperate with the United States against militant Islamist extremism—even Russia considered itself an ally of the United States in the war against terrorism—the fact remained that Kyrgyz relations with the United States in the post-9/11 years grew stronger, especially in the military sphere, and as this happened, the Russian government now led by President Vladimir Putin became increasingly frustrated and angered by the U.S. presence in a significant corner of Russia's strategic backyard.

Akayev Conciliates the United States after 9/11

Akayev was ready to offer some help to the United States in Afghanistan in the immediate aftermath of 9/11. By the end of 2001, the United States had struck a deal with Akayev to allow the United States and its allies to use the Manas International Airport outside of Bishkek to refuel and service aircraft on military missions in the war against the Taliban regime in Afghanistan. Akayev in fact was happy to have an American military presence with a limited mission on Kyrgyz territory to counterbalance Russian political and military influence-building in Kyrgyzstan. The Kremlin was driven increasingly by a determination not to allow the United States to have more influence in Kyrgyzstan than Russia.

There were at least three objectives of U.S. policy in Kyrgyzstan in the aftermath of 9/11. An ideological component had to do with continued U.S. promotion of democratization on the authoritarian political system under Akayev. An economic component focused on development of a free market economy and curtailing pervasive impoverishment throughout most of Kyrgyzstan where average annual per capita income was recently around $440. A strategic component involved the security of Kyrgyzstan as it faced a growing threat of militant Islamic fundamentalism much as its neighbors as well as Kyrgyzstan's role as an ally of the United States in the war against the Taliban in Afghanistan. On February 15, 2002, Kyrgyz and U.S. officials signed a memorandum of understanding on a planned expansion of bilateral relations between the two countries. By mid-2002, about 1,000 American troops and other coalition forces were stationed at the Manas base, now unofficially renamed Ganci after Fire Chief Peter J. Ganci of New York City Fire Department who died in the 9/11 attack.[3] A joint statement by U.S. President Bush and Kyrgyz President Akayev on September 23, 2002, echoed and reconfirmed the February 2002 memorandum.[4]

Russian Post-9/11 Initiatives

In the aftermath of 9/11, Putin strengthened bilateral relations with Kyrgyzstan for two reasons. He wanted to protect the Akayev regime against domestic opposition that threatened its survival. He also wanted to checkmate U.S. influence-building by blocking and reversing it.

Russia Supports a Besieged Akayev in 2002

In the Spring of 2002, there was an outbreak of popular antigovernment demonstrations by nationalists and Islamists. The nationalists opposed

Akayev's closeness to Russia and the Islamists were thought to be seeking common cause with the IMU, a potentially dangerous grouping of religious militants. In the government's view, the IMU threatened to destabilize the fragile tranquility of Kyrgyzstan fostered by the tightfisted Akayev dictatorship.[5]

Putin stood by Akayev's harsh crackdown on his political opponents,[6] despite qualms about its severity, which was bound to catch the attention of the West and lead to sharp Western criticism of his leadership and Russia's support of it. Akayev was pro-Russian and determined to do whatever possible to protect his secular and pro-Russian leadership against liberal reformers and militant Islamists, a course that could only gratify the Kremlin. Subsequently, however, Putin was inclined to be more careful and restrained in his backing of Akayev because the Kyrgyz leader's political excesses could prove to be a liability for Russia, especially his appearance of using the threat of Islamic extremism as a means of justifying the brutality of crackdown on political opponents.

The Akayev government welcomed Russian support. In December 2002, it approved the Kremlin's deployment of additional air planes at the Kant air base. But, the Kremlin paid a big financial price for this concession from Kyrgyzstan. It rescheduled Kyrgyzstan's debt of about $58 million of the total $171 million over a 20-year period with a Russian pledge to protect the environment around Kant. One-fifth of the debt was converted into Russian investments in environmental protection projects as well as in the Kant airfield base for use by the Russian military.[7] The December 2002 agreement also provided for a resumption of joint Russian-Kyrgyz production of military goods like torpedo rockets. In May 2003, Gazprom signed a 25-year agreement with Kyrgyzstan to repair and modernize existing gas pipelines and to develop joint enterprises to produce oil and gas. The benefits to Kyrgyzstan of these agreements were substantial, opening the way for a diversification of its energy sources to assure reliable deliveries of oil and for a lessening of its dependence on Uzbek gas. In October 2003, Putin went to Kyrgyzstan to open a Russian military base in Kant and sign agreements providing for an expansion of Russian investment in the Kyrgyz economy.[8]

Russia Responds to U.S. Policy

While initially sympathetic to closer Kyrgyz ties to the United States to facilitate the war on terrorism, the Kremlin was concerned by the extent of the U.S. penetration of this central Asian country, the United States more or less had ignored in the 1990s. In June 2002, the Kremlin dispatched a number of top security officials, including Defense Minister Sergei Ivanov, to Bishkek to discuss how Russia and Kyrgyzstan could work together to bolster each other's security in the central Asian region. In particular, the talks concerned the terrorist efforts of the IMU allegedly headed by Juma Namangani. Gunmen in this IMU organization had been intruding into Afghan, Kyrgyz, and Uzbek territories from their mountain bases in Tajikistan. They sought to unseat Uzbek President Islam Karimov.[9]

At the June 2002 meeting, Ivanov underlined Russia's interest in strengthening military links to Kyrgyzstan, and Akayev acknowledged that he could use Russian help. Russia and Kyrgyzstan concluded security arrangements, including a Status of Forces agreement regulating the deployment of Russian military personnel on Kyrgyzstan territory. Russian Security Council Chief Vladimir Rushailo affirmed Russia's support of Akayev's efforts to preserve the stability of his country against terrorist threats, which meant that the Kremlin would refrain from criticizing his strong arm measures against the political opposition. The Russians would not object to Akayev's determination to maintain a firm control over the power hungry clans in the south, including a small Uzbek minority angry over his refusal to share power with them—the Uzbeks felt that Akayev discriminated against them.[10]

Russia's goals in the June 2002 meeting with Akayev were part of its regional policy objectives and intended to set the stage for an extensive strategic and economic regional alliance among the central Asian republics with Russia dominating and directing such an alliance. During the June meeting, Russian Defense Minister Ivanov told Kyrgyz Defense Minister Esen Topayev that Russia anticipated Bishkek becoming an emerging "capital of military structures" of many post-Soviet groupings, an Aesopian reference to the next military and security alignments the Kremlin planned throughout Eurasia, especially in central Asia.[11]

The Russian Military Base at Kant

Russia's military leadership viewed the U.S. post-9/11 policy in Kyrgyzstan in the context of rivalry and set about the completion of a Russian military base at Kant to counter an expansion of U.S. influence in Kyrgyzstan, notably the new U.S. base at Manas.[12] The Russian base also would provide Russia, Kyrgyzstan, and other central Asian republics with a rapid response force to consist of a substantial Russian contribution of troops and weapons.[13] Underlying this policy was the conviction in the Kremlin that Russia not the United States should lead the central Asian states in the war against Islamic-inspired terrorism.

The Kant base also was inspired by Russian concerns about China's policy in central Asia. For the Kremlin, China had become, by 2002, potentially more dangerous to Russian interests in ex-Soviet central Asia than the United States, if only because it was easier for the Chinese to strike deep roots in the region, especially in Kyrgyzstan, with which it shared a border. For its part, China felt threatened by the rise of Taliban-style militant Islamic extremism in central Asia and worried about the aggressive influence-building agenda of the Putin Kremlin. As did Russia and other central Asian republics, China saw the United States as an "outsider" and believed that it should not be allowed to establish a military presence in the region.[14]

With the Kant base in Kyrgyzstan, the Kremlin now had the means of intervening in Uzbekistan to protect the Karimov government from militant Islamists or from some other threat to its security and stability.[15] To this end, the Kremlin intended to deploy several hundred uniformed military personnel on the base.[16]

For the moment, the Kant base did not strain Russian relations with the United States. There seemed to be no reason why Kant could not coexist with the U.S. military base at Manas even though for the Kremlin, Kant was intended as a response to and a check on the perceived expansion of U.S. military and political influence in Kyrgyzstan. For its part, the United States did not see the new Russian base as a threat. According to a U.S. view, the Russian military deployment at Kant was much weaker than the U.S. deployment at Manas. Russian planes deployed there did not seem combat ready and the poor quality of Kyrgyz fuel did not help the cause of Russian military preparedness. The American-led force in Kyrgyzstan in the beginning of 2003 was in fact qualitatively and quantitatively superior to the Russian military deployment. It included 20 F-16 fighters and over 2,000 troops ready to serve as a backup for the deployments in Afghanistan.[17]

Both Russia and Kyrgyzstan agreed that Manas and Kant could coexist. Indeed, the Kyrgyz Ministry of Defense said that each base had a separate and independent military mission: the mission of Kant was regional self-defense and the mission of Manas was to fight terrorism, which involved not just U.S. forces but Russian and Kyrgyz troops as well. Kyrgyz Foreign Minister Askar Aitmatov went even further, saying in April 2003, "this region and Kyrgyzstan are in the sphere of strategic interests of both Russia and the United States" and the two bases run by the two Powers separately and independently of one another "will complement one another."[18]

Russian Economic Influence-Building

The Putin Kremlin continued the economic dimension of Russian influence-building begun in the Yeltsin era, especially in the energy trade. Putin shrewdly understood that while Kyrgyzstan itself did not have large oil and gas resources, it could serve as an effective transit country for the reserves of these resources in neighboring Kazakhstan, Turkmenistan, and Uzbekistan. In mid-May 2003, Kyrgyzstan and Gazprom signed several subsequent agreements to explore and develop Kyrgyz oil and gas resources and, importantly, cooperate in the repairing and building of gas pipelines. While this agreement was another signal of Russia's attempts to restore its influence in Kyrgyzstan and the other ex-Soviet central Asian republics, it was welcomed by Kyrgyzstan as a means of reducing its vulnerability to occasional cutoffs of gas from Uzbekistan. The Karimov regime, like the Kremlin, used an occasional cutoff of energy deliveries to expand its influence over neighbors like Kyrgyzstan. In restraining Uzbek expansionist tendencies, the Kremlin had a strategic advantage in Bishkek not shared by the United States.[19]

There was an economic dimension of Russian influence-building under Putin. For example, the Kremlin granted concessions to allow most Kyrgyz migrant workers to remain working in Russia when Kyrgyz Prime Minister Nikolai Tanyev said a planned forced return of Kyrgyz migrant workers would cause a "social explosion" in his country. Russia also offered help to the Kyrgyz government to rebuild plants and repair planes, helicopters, and aircraft engine manufacturing facilities. Russia also encouraged representatives of Siberian and Ural textile enterprises to buy cotton, woolen fabrics, and antimony from Kyrgyzstan. In exchange, Kyrgyzstan got household chemicals, fertilizers, sawn timber, and medical equipment from Russia.[20]

RUSSIA, THE UNITED STATES, AND THE OUSTER OF AKAYEV

Opposition to Akayev inside Kyrgyzstan was a prime cause of his political downfall. By the time of parliamentary elections in early 2005, opposition to Akayev's rule was pervasive and deep-seated. The Akayev regime's blatant manipulation of the electoral process by infuriating an angry electorate provoked an explosion of popular wrath that seemed to portend a violent revolution to force his ouster.

Both the Kremlin and Washington had a hand in his loss of power. While the Putin Kremlin would have preferred that he continue in power despite pervasive and popular opposition to his rule, it opted for caution and restraint, carefully avoiding outright backing of him. By contrast, the United States was eager for his ouster and the ascendancy of political leaders willing to move forward with democratization and willing to strengthen military ties with the West in the war against terrorism in Afghanistan. And while Akayev's ouster seemed to favor U.S. influence-building in the short term, in the long term it was Russia that benefited, more so than the United States.

Roots of Akayev's Fall

Akayev was done-in partly by his own repressive political behavior, a departure from his initially liberal and democratic path in the mid-1990s, when outsiders in the West, especially the Clinton administration, viewed his rule as a promising model of democratization in the post-Communist era in ex-Soviet central Asia. But, Akayev was not committed to a rapidly paced and extensive democratization of Kyrgyzstan. He feared that the more open political environment democracy required was dangerous for his country's unity and that it would give too many opportunities for the political opposition to mount an offensive against him. As parliamentary elections in February and March 2005 approached, Akayev strengthened his undemocratic hold on authority and tried in every way he could to undermine the opposition despite warnings from U.S. Ambassador Stephen Young to the effect that "significant problems in the conduct of the elections will harm the image and reputation of Kyrgyzstan as a country that is a leader in conducting democratic reforms." The ambassador's comments were denounced as "an attempt to interfere in the country's internal affairs."[21]

The 2005 Parliamentary Elections

On February 27 and March 13, 2005, the outcome of parliamentary elections led eventually to Akayev's ouster from power.[22] The elections were manipulated by the Akayev regime to assure the retention of a government majority. The outcome was an overwhelming victory for candidates who were government supporters. According to OSCE, election monitors found fraud on a massive scale to make sure of the government's victory despite pervasive and deep-seated hostility to Akayev. Candidates bribed voters and the state-controlled media denied opposition candidates' opportunity to mobilize voters. Following the elections there was an explosion of popular wrath against the cheating that had taken place. Between the first and second ballots from February 27 to March 13, and after the second ballot on March 13, Kyrgyzstan suddenly was on the threshold of a violent civil war, with popular calls for Akayev's immediate resignation. An armed insurgency in the south threatened Akayev's ouster, which occurred on March 24, 2005.[23]

After the first round of elections on February 27, there was widespread civil disobedience by people angered by overt and pervasive electoral fraud for which they blamed Akayev. The embattled Kyrgyz leader infuriated the public by calling critics of the elections enemies of democracy, ready to throw the country into civil war. The second round of elections were just as dishonest as the first and put Akayev's supporters in control.[24]

Driving popular anger over how the elections had been managed and over their "staged" outcome, it was now clear, were other considerations. People had become fed up with Akayev himself, who had been in power for 15 years, since the beginning of the country's newly won independence of Moscow in 1991. Many younger Kyrgyz voters really wanted him out of office because they were fed up with the poor economy.[25] While the economy had been growing by 5 percent, this had still left most Kyrgyz people in poverty. The creation of wealth seemed to benefit only a small minority of the population that included Akayev and his numerous relatives.

Finally, Kyrgyz voters in March 2005 were already thinking about upcoming presidential election and the possibility that the unpopular Akayev somehow would finesse his retention of the country's leadership. Popular pressure was on him to resign or give assurances that he would not run for a third term, a possibility if the parliamentary majority loyal to Akayev changed the rules governing presidential elections.[26]

Russia and Akayev's Fall

With the spread of antigovernment demonstrations throughout the country, an intimidated Akayev fled the country for Russia, hoping for a temporary refuge until things quieted down in his country and for the Kremlin's help in his return to power.[27] But, Putin refused to give Akayev any real political backing though the Russian leader assured his Kyrgyz counterpart of a safe haven in Russia. Evidently, the Kremlin was inclined to wait and see how much real opposition there was in Kyrgyzstan to Akayev's rule before backing him. Before long it was clear that Akayev's cause was lost when demands for his resignation came from leading Kyrgyz politicians, including some of his own supporters.

Following the parliamentary elections, the Kremlin continued to proceed very cautiously with Akayev. While affording him safe haven, Putin was reluctant to give him the kind of support he had given Viktor Yanukovich in the Fall 2004 Ukrainian presidential election. When Yanukovich lost the election, Putin was embarrassed, and, worse, on the wrong side of the new Ukrainian president, Viktor Yushchenko. Putin did not want to back the wrong horse in Kyrgyzstan in the Spring of 2005. Russian Foreign Ministry spokesman Alexander Yakovenko blandly explained Kremlin policy, saying Russia "does not interfere in Kyrgyzstan's internal political affairs. Moscow wants political processes in that country to be legitimate."[28]

The Putin Kremlin bided its time in deciding what to do about Akayev's untenable political situation in Bishkek. For his part, Akayev could not return to his country's capital and resume his leadership without risk of personal danger; but, neither was he willing to accept the reality of his political collapse and resign. The Kremlin did not push Akayev to resign, probably hoping for a change in the political situation in Bishkek to Akayev's advantage.

The United States and Akayev's Fall

By contrast, the United States was deeply involved in Kyrgyz politics before, during, and immediately after the 2005 parliamentary elections, unabashedly helping pro-democratic opposition groups to sell their reformist message to Kyrgyz voters. The United States supported the opposition press and financed the American University in Kyrgyzstan whose stated mission was in part to promote development of a civil society through exchange programs that sent students and nongovernmental organization leaders to the United States.[29]

During the campaign for the 2005 parliamentary elections, the United States helped the political opposition to discredit Akayev and undermine him by finding and paying newsprint media to publicize the corruption of his regime. One newspaper with American financial support ran photographs of a palatial Akayev home; this while the rest of the country was in poverty. Without American support a gesture of this kind would not have been possible given government control of printing presses and paper supplies.[30]

The political opposition also got American help in reaching voters unable to read Russian or get possession of a newspaper. People could listen to the Kyrgyz language Radio Azattyk, which summarized articles from opposition newspapers. Radio Azattyk was the local franchise of the U.S.-financed Radio Free Europe/Radio Liberty. Other independent radio stations also broadcast talk shows funded by the United States, as was the case with a local station in Osh, in the south of the country where antigovernment demonstrations were especially vehement. By mid-March of 2005, when the parliamentary elections were held, a good part of Kyrgyz society had become politicized after a long history of passivity promoted by the Communist regime before 1991 and by the Akayev leadership.[31]

In part, it could be said that the United States was influential in weakening Akayev's political control of Kyrgyzstan by its encouragement of democratization, especially political pluralism. In response to American prodding backed by a modest program of economic assistance, Akayev early in his leadership had allowed a somewhat free press and some political opposition. While this policy had won him plaudits from Washington, it eventually weakened his hold on power and led to his political demise, especially when an unusually unrestrained media disseminated information about his personal corruption and ineptitude. In early July 2005, Akayev openly accused the United States of having financed the Kyrgyz opposition, weakening him, and eventually causing his political collapse.[32] More to the point, the people of Kyrgyzstan had developed political instincts which, along with an active press, put Akayev out of power. But, in Akayev's view, the United States did all this to him because of his ongoing friendship with Russia, its rival in cultivating the cooperation and backing of the ex-Soviet central Asian republics since the early 1990s.[33]

China and Akayev's Fall

China was somewhat troubled by the seemingly abrupt collapse of the Akayev regime in the Spring of 2005, since Akayev had been a strong advocate of close Kyrgyz relations with China as a means of counterbalancing the aggressive influence build of Russia in the Putin years, climaxed in 2003, by the establishment of a Russian air base at Kant reluctantly approved by Bishkek. That said, the Chinese decided to back the new Bakiyev leadership, which insisted it had no intention of deviating from the foreign policy of the Akayev regime which meant continuing constructive relations with China which, for its part, assumed this meant renewal of Akayev's clampdown on the Uighur diaspora inside Kyrgyz territory. The Chinese were fearful that Bakiyev's pledges about pursuing democratization after years of Akayev's repressive, antidemocratic rule might involve assuming a tolerant approach to the Uighurs living in eastern Kyrgyzstan.[34]

The Chinese leadership also was surprised by the failure of the Kremlin to prop up Akayev similar to the way it had supported Karimov in Uzbekistan when his regime was severely criticized by the West, especially the United States, for the severity of its crackdown on antigovernment demonstrators in the Andijon uprising. From the vantage point of Beijing, Russia seemed to lack the will and, arguably, the resources to protect its interests in a consistent way in central Asia.

RUSSIA, THE UNITED STATES, AND BAKIYEV'S ASCENDANCY, 2005–2006

With the Kremlin aloof and the United States eager for a replacement of Akayev with a less pro-Russian, more pro-democracy political leadership, the opposition leader, Kurmanbek Bakiyev, gained the ascendancy in the immediate aftermath of the March parliamentary elections. Bakiyev's election as president "pro-tempore" and acting prime minister by the parliament—the old one, not the new one, which was temporarily prevented from taking its seats by the Kyrgyz Supreme Court because of complaints about the election rigging—forced Akayev to acknowledge his loss of political power and to resign, opening the way to a formal success through presidential election to be held in July.[35] But, Bakiyev's ascendancy was complicated by the Court's unwillingness for the moment to allow the seating of the new parliament, which, in-fact, was still influenced by Akayev's supporters, but not to the extent that these deputies were willing to welcome Akayev back to the presidency.

Russia and Bakiyev's Ascendancy

Kurmanbek Bakiyev was not an unknown quantity in Moscow. Indeed, the Putin Kremlin knew him better than the Americans—Bakiyev had been educated in Russia and had married a Russian woman. There was a sense among the Russian leadership that if Akayev could not serve Russian interests in Bishkek, Bakiyev might be able to do. In April 2005, Bakiyev had been hospitably received in Moscow, if in a somewhat informal way, by former Russian Foreign Minister Igor Invanov, who had close ties to the Putin leadership, which was still inclined to play its Kyrgyz card close to its vest while waiting to see who might be the successor of Akayev.[36]

Despite the key role the United States had played in helping to undermine the Akayev regime, the new leadership was determined to keep Kyrgyzstan on good terms with the Kremlin. Bakiyev was very careful to reassure Moscow that existing agreements and linkages with Russia, as well as with those with the United States, would continue. A day after coming to power Bakiyev reportedly declared, "we do not see our future without Russia." Bakiyev asked the Russians for financial support to the republic, in particular for agriculture and for rebuilding of Bishkek's infrastructure. Putin was quick to respond to Bakiyev's pro-Russian initiatives, sending a plane with humanitarian aid to Bishkek on March 30.[37]

Acting Kyrgyz Foreign Minister Rosa Otunbaeva went to Moscow in April 2005, making Russia the first diplomatic destination of the new Kyrgyz leadership. When she left Bishkek, Bakiyev observed, "Russia was and remains the closest strategic partner for us."[38] Otunbaeva met with Russian Minister Sergei Lavrov who immediately raised the issue of the well-being of the small Russian-speaking community in Kyrgyzstan. Otunbaeva reassured him that they were safe and that the new government would assure an improvement in their economic situation. She also promised government efforts to promote the Russian language and culture in Kyrgyzstan. She also said that the presence of the Americans in Kyrgyzstan was temporary, observing that the contract the Kyrgyz government signed each year with the United States was "not forever."[39]

In early April 2005, Bakiyev continued to reassure the Russians that his government was committed to good, close, and cooperative relations with Russia. *Izvestia* quoted him saying that he promised "to do everything to strengthen relations between Kyrgyzstan and Moscow" and Otunbaeva confirmed that Kyrgyz relations with Russia "remained a priority of foreign policy" for Bishkek. Subsequently, he was as good as his word. For example, Bakiyev undertook closer cooperation with Russia in multilateral regional organizations in which they were both members. He took steps to promote Russian business interests in the republic and supported the idea of Russian companies helping to construct two hydroelectric power stations on the Kambar-Ata river in central Kyrgyzstan.[40]

The United States and Bakiyev's Ascendancy

Though he had the support of the United States, which thought he would embrace the West and accelerate Kyrgyzstan's democratization in the political and economic spheres, Bakiyev kept Washington at "arm's length" to assuage Kremlin's concern about the vitality of Kyrgyzstan's friendship with Russia. He wanted to appear willing to limit and contain U.S. efforts to expand its military presence in Kyrgyzstan but he also wanted to reassure the United States that he did not want to lose its friendship. Bakiyev's position was inspired no doubt by a desire to avoid antagonizing a sensitive and defensive Kremlin opposed to the expansion of U.S. influence in Kyrgyzstan.[41]

Bakiyev soon had an opportunity to pursue this difficult strategy. In April 2005, the Bush administration sent Defense Secretary Donald Rumsfeld to Bishkek with one goal among others to gain assurance that the United States could continue to use the Manas, a base the Kremlin wanted the Americans to evacuate. Rumsfeld assured the Bakiyev leadership of U.S. support and praised the Kyrgyz government's past cooperation with the United States in the war on terrorism in Afghanistan. Bakiyev responded to Rumsfeld that the bilateral cooperation with the United States initiated by the Akayev government would continue.[42]

But, partly as a gesture to Russia, Bakiyev refused to accommodate the U.S. request to deploy AWACS aircraft, a new weapon in the war against terrorism which were known for their detection capabilities. The planes, Bakiyev suggested, were not directly related to the fighting in Afghanistan. Bakiyev seemed to be telling the Americans that Kyrgyzstan could not allow them to develop an information gathering capability that could be used to the detriment of Russia, China, and other central Asian republics with which Kyrgyzstan wanted friendly and cooperative relations. Nor was Bakiyev willing to allow the United States to increase the number of coalition troops who could deploy at Manas.[43] And in what seemed to be a move to ingratiate himself with Russia, after having told Rumsfeld that arrangements to allow the United States to use the Manas base would continue in force, Bakiyev went on television on April 19 to remind the Bush administration that he was the new boss of Kyrgyzstan, warning that he could still terminate the U.S. presence at Manas.[44]

Furthermore, Bakiyev was disappointing to the United States on the ideological front. In the weeks and months following his ascendancy in the aftermath of the parliamentary elections, Bakiyev showed himself in no rush to accelerate his country's halting process of political democratization despite Bush administration's calls for progress. Bakiyev clearly was concerned about maintaining his power base that would be threatened by the introduction of a real, Western-style political pluralism. Moreover, Bakiyev's resistance to democratic reform had the sympathy of the Kremlin which obliquely encouraged his resistance to the United States. In particular, the Kremlin was in no hurry to see a pro-Islamic anti-Russian ascendancy in Bishkek as a result of a loosening of control of the Kyrgyz political environment.

There were other reasons for Washington to doubt Bakiyev's stated commitment to democratization. Friends, supporters, and relatives of Akayev were members of the newly elected parliament and Bakiyev needed to work with them. In fact, Bakiyev himself and many of his allies had been at one time or another allies of Akayev and had broken with him not necessarily over democratic principles but rather over their eagerness for more power than he had been willing to allow them.[45] It would appear that Bakiyev had used the political turmoil of the parliamentary elections to rid the country of Akayev, rather than to install democracy.

Indeed, Kyrgyzstan's real democrats also were disappointed by the failure of the change in leadership to bring about a real democratic transformation. As matters stood, the new leadership was only "different" not really "new" in terms of goals and policies, or at least that is how it seemed to the country's disappointed democrats following Akayev's ouster. There was no real guarantee of political freedom coming out of the replacement of Akayev by Bakiyev.[46]

Russia, the United States, and the July 2005 Presidential Election[47]

As the date of the presidential election approached in early Summer of 2005, the country remained deeply divided over the shape of its political future with much of the north, where Akayev had drawn most of his political strength, impoverished and conservative on the issue of change while the south, where Bakiyev drew his political support and where the capital, Bishkek, was located, somewhat better off economically and more open to real political reform. A youthful urban-based opposition offered some hope for change. For example, students at the American University in Bishkek had developed a reform movement that resembled the Serbian youth movement Otpur that had helped oust Serbian President Slobodan Milosevic from power in October 2000. The Kyrgyz university youth wanted real political democratization, not the "old wine in new bottles" leadership symbolized by the ascendancy of Bakiyev.[48]

In the meantime, and with some oblique Russian encouragement inspired by a still vain hope that somehow he could finesse a return to power given the continuing influence of his personal political supporters in high places in the Kyrgyz government, Akayev remained a contender in the presidential race. Akayev did have some sympathy among constituencies such as government employees and officials and others in a newly developing professional middle class that had benefited from his leadership. The exiled Kyrgyz leader thus continued in the early Summer of 2005 to hold off his resignation.[49]

Bakiyev responded by depriving Akayev of some privileges that gave him a special status as the first leader of the independent Kyrgyzstan state, in particular the prerogative of addressing parliament and of attending meetings of government agencies from the cabinet on down, and free access to the media.[50] In turn Akayev in a state of frustration and anger used some of the enormous wealth he had accumulated while in office to pay thugs and vandals to disturb the peace by looting and by other criminal activity. Evidently, in the melee he hoped to create, he would find an avenue to return to power.[51]

But, in a surprising and sudden shift of tactics, in the beginning of July, just days before the election, Akayev publicly supported Bakiyev, saying that he was well suited to lead the country to democracy and political stability.[52] This turnabout suggested that Akayev had correctly gauged the political situation in his country as far as he was concerned. But, beyond that it is also probable that with little or no chance of Akayev regaining power in Bishkek, the Kremlin had advised him against challenging Bakiyev and, rather, to support him as the inevitable choice for the presidency. Indeed, by early July, it was clear that without direct Russian interference in the presidential election on behalf of Akayev, Bakiyev was likely to win. Since the Kremlin was determined not to interfere, Akayev was doomed to lose, hence his last-minute endorsement of Bakiyev. Although the election results closed off at least for the time being his return to power in Bishkek, Russia was at least able to avoid alienating Bakiyev.[53]

There were about a half dozen candidates for the office but only Bakiyev who was also acting president had the best chance of winning. In terms of credentials he seemed to many Kyrgyz voters the best choice, having successfully restored a measure of normality to the country. Then, his most likely rival Felix Kulov, a former security general, vice president, and governor who had been jailed for apparently political reasons by the Akayev regime on corruption and embezzlement charges in 2001, and who had a strong popular political base in the south, cut a deal with Bakiyev. Kulov agreed to withdraw from the presidential race and support Bakiyev in return for being appointed Prime Minister following a Bakiyev victory.[54]

In the presidential election held on July 11, Bakiyev won by a landslide. He garnered 88 percent of votes. The turnout was almost 75 percent of eligible voters, a big plus for Bakiyev personally. Moreover, the election appeared to be mostly free, and fair to a point. There were fewer electoral shenanigans and a substantial amount of freedom of voters and political groups to assemble and campaign and only a minimum of vote buying, a widespread practice in past Kyrgyz parliamentary elections. But turnout seemed to be higher than outside observers such as Kimmo Kiljunen, head of the observer delegation from the OSCE, thought was the case. The official count was almost 75 percent of eligible voters though Kiljunen thought fewer people had voted.[55]

With free expression and only a minimum of vote buying, the July 2005 presidential campaign and the election contrasted sharply with the March parliamentary elections where there had been large-scale fraud. Outsiders saw the election as a promising step toward further democratization in Kyrgyzstan.[56]

U.S. Problems with Bakiyev

Beyond his mixed feelings about democratic political reform and his determination to continue Kyrgyzstan's traditional closeness to Russia, Bakiyev disagreed with other U.S. policy recommendations. One disagreement had to do with the humanitarian problem of Uzbek refugees in Kyrgyzstan. These refugees had fled Uzbekistan President Islam Karimov's brutal crackdown during and after the Andijon political uprising in May 2005. The Bush administration advised Bakiyev not to repatriate these refugees because they would in all likelihood be severely punished by the retributive Karimov government. Bakiyev, however, had his own agenda, which was to avoid provoking Uzbekistan. He sent many of the refugees back to Uzbekistan, knowing what their ultimate fate would be and showing to the somewhat disillusioned U.S. policymakers that he had little concern with human rights.

Controversy over the U.S. Base at Manas

Other problems were of greater concern to the Bush administration, notably new doubt about the willingness of the new Bakiyev leadership to continue to allow the United States to use the Manas base given demands by both Russia and China Bakiyev could not ignore to evict the United States. The other problem concerned democratization of Kyrgyzstan's heavily authoritarian governmental system with its severe limits on basic liberties.

Bakiyev and the Americans also disagreed on how the Manas base should be used. Bakiyev was under pressure from both China and Russia to evict the United States from the base, having endorsed the SCO demand he get from Washington not only a deadline for the withdrawal of U.S. forces in Iraq but also a timetable for an evacuation of the 1,000 U.S. Air Force personnel at Manas. He told the Americans that since the situation in Afghanistan seemed to be stabilizing, continuation of the base did not seem as necessary as it had been in the wake of the 9/11 attack.[57]

But, Bakiyev was in no rush to evict the United States from Kyrgyzstan or, for that matter, take any further steps in implementing the SCO declaration on Iraq that would weaken Kyrgyzstan's good working relationship with Washington. He was determined to preserve this relationship as a counterweight to the Kremlin and to Beijing which both kept up their pressure to get the United States out of Manas. Accordingly, in mid-April 2005, he told U.S. Secretary of Defense Donald Rumsfeld in Bishkek that "bilateral cooperation in the political, military, and economic spheres will continue."[58]

For its part, the United States thought that the situation in Afghanistan still needed the backup of its forces in Kyrgyzstan. Accordingly, in July 2005, the Bush administration sent Secretary of State Rumsfeld back to Bishkek to underline the importance the United States attached to good relations between the two countries, an always welcome strategy for states simultaneously being cultivated by the Kremlin. U.S. Defense Department officials made the point that American military action was still needed in Afghanistan because of the continuing threat of international terrorism.[59]

The Bakiyev government at the moment was somewhat sympathetic to the U.S. pitch. Apart from sharing the U.S. view that both countries should continue to cooperate in the war against terrorism—the Kyrgyzstan government has been taken aback by the terrorist bombings in London on July 9, 2005—Kyrgyz Acting Defense Minister Ismail Isakov acknowledged that the situation in Afghanistan in fact was still parlous and that the United States should continue to maintain its base in Kyrgyzstan.[60] By the end of July 2005, it was more than apparent that Bakiyev was strongly inclined to keep Kyrgyzstan's fences with the United States in good repair so as to maintain a balance between the United States and Russia in their competition for influence in Kyrgyzstan in the post-9/11 era.[61]

A New Agreement on Manas

Bakiyev eventually resolved the base problem to the immediate, if not long-term, satisfaction of the United States. Determined to maintain what was becoming known as a "pragmatic balance" between Russian and American interests in Kyrgyzstan, Bakiyev assured Secretary of State Condoleeza Rice in October 2005 that the U.S. lease could continue for servicing military aircraft on missions to Afghanistan "until the situation in Afghanistan is stabilized." The new agreement was a noteworthy accomplishment for the United States, especially in light of the demand of Uzbekistan President Karimov for the United States to evacuate the Khanabad base in Uzbekistan.[62] Bakiyev asked the United States to pay Kyrgyzstan more rent than before and the Bush administration ultimately agreed to the terms.[63] The United States agreed to increase payment for use of the Manas base by $18 million annually and gave Kyrgyzstan $150 million as an aid and compensation package.[64]

Still, Bakiyev felt intense pressure from the Kremlin to rely solely on Russia for security and to oust the Americans from Manas. In response, Bakiyev upped still further the financial price he wanted the United States to pay Kyrgyzstan for using the base. He insisted on a jump of the annual rate of rent to $200 million. Bakiyev's objective here seemed to be scoring points with the Kremlin. He wanted to look as if he was really trying to get rid of the U.S. military presence in his country without really doing so.[65]

More Democratization Unlikely

Bakiyev's administration failed to make much progress with democratization. Instead, his leadership was marked by high-profile killings of government critics and opponents, a weak economy, and a refusal to initiate promised political reform. In April 2006, large antigovernment demonstrations in Bishkek demanded limits on presidential power and a strengthening of the role of parliament. In response, Bakiyev promised changes, including amendments to the Kyrgyz Constitution designed to prevent oppressive and corrupt rule.[66]

In November 2006, the Kyrgyz parliament approved reforms introducing changes in the executive and legislature to prevent abuse of power. Bakiyev went along with reforms even though they were weakening the presidential office, fearing that resistance to them would provoke a confrontation with an alienated public and lead to his ouster in a "flower"-type revolution of the kind experienced in Georgia in 2003 (the "rose" revolution that brought Mikhail Saakashvili to power), in Ukraine in 2004 (the orange revolution that brought Viktor Yushchenko to power), and in Kyrgyzstan itself in 2005 (the "tulip" revolution that brought him to power). Each of these revolutions had given power to politicians who were suspicious of Russia, sympathetic to the West, especially the United States, and interested in further democratization of their country. In each of the "flower" revolution, the United States was known to have had a hand that influenced the outcome to the advantage of the West.[67]

A Weakening of U.S. Influence

By the Spring of 2006, there were signs that U.S. influence in Bishkek had declined. For example, the Bakiyev regime showed little enthusiasm for what appeared to be a well-intentioned gesture toward Kyrgyzstan by the Bush administration. The proposal, made to the Kyrgyz government by the U.S. Ambassador to Kyrgyzstan Marie Yovanovitch, suggested Kyrgyz membership in a Western-sponsored organization known as the Heavily Indebted Poor Countries Initiative (HIPC), which had a program managed by the World Bank and the International Monetary Fund to help poor countries manage their international debt.[68]

While Kyrgyz Prime Minister Felix Kulov liked the idea, saying that Kyrgyzstan was interested in joining, the Kyrgyz Foreign Ministry thought differently, denouncing the ambassador's proposal as "beyond the scope of diplomatic relations." The ministry seemed annoyed by what it considered an unwarranted interference by a foreigner in Kyrgyz internal affairs. For his part, Bakiyev, though reluctant to ruffle the Americans needlessly, was by no means positive. He told Yovanovitch that her proposal would be given some consideration in light of the severity of Kyrgyzstan's debt problem and a need to do something about it in the short term.[69]

The Kremlin also was unimpressed. Russian Ambassador to Kyrgyzstan Yevgeni Shmagin was dismissive of the U.S. idea, saying somewhat haughtily that it warranted no comment though he was careful to avoid ruffling the Americans despite his evident suspicion of what they were up to in proposing HIPC membership to the Kyrgyz.[70]

Furthermore, the United States was still having difficulty achieving a mutually acceptable deal on the Manas base. For example, Kyrgyz Foreign Minister Alikbek Jekshenkulov observed in mid-2006 that the differences between the two sides were not confined to money but rather involved, as he put it, "ecology, security, and taxes."[71] To the U.S. side, it looked like a classic case of stonewalling encouraged by the Kremlin in its determination to assert Russia's political and strategic interests in central Asia while blocking the expansion of U.S. influence and doing so by using economic rather than overt political and military power.

By the end of 2006, domestic developments did not favor the U.S. position in Kyrgyzstan. The same groups opposed to Bakiyev were also critical of the American military presence in Kyrgyzstan. Indeed, even the national parliament opposed the U.S. military base at Manas and urged the Kyrgyz leadership to close down the base for the Americans.[72] These opponents were not altogether pro-Russia, but rather highly nationalistic, sympathetic to the idea that Kyrgyzstan, with a predominantly Muslim population, should pay more attention to religion, making domestic and foreign policy more in accordance with at least their version of Islamic thought and practice.[73] This meant at the least keeping the United States at arm's length, if not actually terminating the U.S. military presence in Kyrgyzstan, a move that Bakiyev in fact was unwilling to make despite the enormous pressure inside of Kyrgyzstan as well as abroad.

Russian Influence-Building and Bakiyev

As the Kyrgyz government waffled on the issue of evicting the United States from the Manas base, the Kremlin escalated its pressure on Bishkek to allow an increase in Russia's military presence already in theory agreed to in 2003. The Kremlin had in mind doubling the number of Russian troops at the Kant air base. The goal of the Russian initiative seemed to be to reassure the Kyrgyz government that if they got the United States to close down the Manas base, Russia could and would pick up the slack to assure Kyrgyzstan's security and stability.[74]

By the end of the Summer of 2005, however, it looked as if the Kremlin had hit a road block in its influence-building strategy in Kyrgyzstan: Bakiyev could not be moved from his determination to maintain a military balance of power between Russia and the United States. In addition, there was some tension in Kyrgyz-Russian relations coming from a deterioration of the condition of the Russian minority in Kyrgyzstan. Russian-speaking Kyrgyz citizens suffered from the nationalism increasingly evident in the country. Under nationalistic local authorities, the Russian minority had lost business concerns, and many were unemployed and living in poverty. A small minority of Kyrgyz

Russian residents considered migration back to Russia, a development the Kremlin wanted to avoid given Russia's own economic problems and its high unemployment rate, not least the escalating rate of unemployment in recent years. As Bakiyev seemed unwilling to do much about their deteriorating situation, there was a sense in the Russian minority that his regime was not as solicitous of their interests as Akayev's had been.[75]

In any event, Russian Air Force Commander General Vladimir Mikhailov along with CSTO Secretary Nikolas Bordyuzha met with Bakiyev in February 2006 to firm up arrangements for the Russian presence at the Kant base. But, when Mikhailov arrived in Bishkek, he was not very subtle in communicating Russian objectives for the base to Bakiyev. He reportedly said: "Our base is here forever." Moreover, he added that Russia planned to increase troop strength at the Kant base from 300 personnel to about 750 and that more military equipment would be added.[76]

At the end of April 2006, Putin met Bakiyev in Moscow and announced Russia's intention of expanding its military presence in Kyrgyzstan, no doubt in response to concurrent U.S. influence-building. Prior to this Moscow meeting, Russian military officials indicated Moscow's intention to double the number of planes and personnel at the Kant base. And at the summit, the two leaders revealed plans for the scheduling of joint Russian-Kyrgyz antiterrorism exercises. In addition, Putin and Bakiyev agreed to enhance Kyrgyz participation in the SCO as well as the CSTO. The Moscow summit signaled a continuing Kyrgyz movement toward Russia on security matters, in particular the war on terrorism. And further evidence of Russian influence-building at this juncture were discussions and agreements on energy at the Putin-Bakiyev April 2006 summit. For example, Russia promised to assist Kyrgyzstan in the completion of two power plants, while Bakiyev agreed with Gazprom Chief Alexei Miller to mount a joint venture involving the Kyrgyz national energy company, Kyrgyzneftigaz, and Gazprom.[77]

Putin remained cautious about offering public political backing to a besieged Bakiyev facing a renewal of popular unrest among both voters and politicians critical of and impatient with his leadership. Putin was unwilling to give Bakiyev the support needed to face down his domestic opposition, waiting to see how far the Kyrgyz leadership was willing to go in response to his pressure to lessen the American presence in Kyrgyzstan. Putin's caution and restraint was no doubt attributable to his recognition that supporting or opposing Eurasian leaders was risky for Russia, as had been the case with the Kremlin's overt opposition to Mikhail Saakashvili, the winner of the 2003 presidential election in Georgia, and Viktor Yanukovich, the loser in the 2004 presidential election in Ukraine.[78]

In addition, Putin's careful handling of Bakiyev, arguably, was influenced by the existence in Kyrgyz domestic politics of a potential alternative to him, namely the popular Prime Minister Felix Kulov, though Kulov was known to be sympathetic to the West and an unknown quantity I, the political calculation in Bishkek. Putin was inclined to be neutral in what seemed to be a developing rivalry between Bakiyev and Kulov. In the Spring of 2006, Putin continued to proceed cautiously but sympathetically in his dealings with Bakiyev, eager to discourage his relationship with the United States but not quite ready to accept him as a reliable ally though he wanted to build on the gains Russia thus far had made in strengthening economic links between the two countries that provided Russia with substantial political leverage in Bishkek.[79]

BAKIYEV BETWEEN MOSCOW AND WASHINGTON SINCE 2006

Bakiyev tried hard to resist Russian pressures on him to give the United States an Uzbek-style base eviction notice. He carefully refrained from calling for the Americans to evacuate Manas, saying on June 1, 2006, that "given the positive development of U.S.-Kyrgyz relations," the Kyrgyz government was willing to extend the lease of the Manas base and resume talks about payment "in the nearest future." Moreover, according to a Bishkek-based political analyst, Sadyrbek Cherikov, two sides ultimately would conclude an agreement on the Manas base because it was mutually advantageous to do so. For its part, the Kyrgyz leadership, despite its cultivation of the Kremlin, in fact continued to want the United States to stay at Manas. Certainly, the Kyrgyz government needed the money the United States would pay for the lease, as well as the strategic advantage of having the United States as a friend in Bishkek's dealing with the overbearing Russians.[80]

U.S. influence in Kyrgyzstan nevertheless had been weakened. Continued U.S. use of Manas air base was not as certain as the United States would have liked, especially in light of the exorbitant fee the Kyrgyz government wanted from Washington. A resumption of bilateral talks on the status of the Manas base though resumed on July 12, 2006. These talks went nowhere and again were suspended.[81]

More Strain on U.S.-Kyrgyz Relations

In mid-August 2006, building on whatever slight signals there were of Kyrgyz interest in allowing the United States to keep the Manas base for the time being, the Bush administration sent Assistant Secretary of State Richard Boucher to Bishkek to tell the Bakiyev leadership that the United States still needed the Manas base and that relations between the two countries would improve in the closing months of 2006 with "a lot of cooperation between the two countries."[82] But, on this, as on so many other occasions, the optimism of the U.S. side was tempered by Kyrgyz caution about upsetting Russia. Aibek Moldogaziev, a top Kyrgyz Foreign Ministry official, observed that Russia would continue to figure prominently in Kyrgyzstan's foreign policy making for the foreseeable future.[83]

U.S. relations with Kyrgyzstan suffered something of a setback in the beginning of December 2006. At the Manas base, an American guard shot an ethnic Russian fuel truck driver because he waved at him in a threatening manner. The Kyrgyz government demanded that the American be tried in a Kyrgyz court, but the United States refused, claiming a kind of extraterritorial-type jurisdiction covering the base facility. Bakiyev called for an annulment of this implicit American immunity to Kyrgyz laws. He said his government would soon propose a revision of the agreement to address the issue of their legal status in Kyrgyzstan.[84] Overall, the incident set back U.S. relations with Kyrgyzstan and put the base closing again on the agenda.

The shooting incident placed Bakiyev in a difficult political position. The opposition was critical of him for not doing something to push the Americans off the base. Although Bakiyev did not want to lose the American presence in his country—it was too valuable strategically and financially— he had a hard time defending continued American use of the base given the way in which the opposition was going after him, never mind the known sentiments of the Kremlin. And, Bakiyev did not want to annoy the Russians.[85]

On December 15, the Kyrgyz parliament passed a resolution calling on the government to review the "expediency" of the U.S. base in Kyrgyzstan, saying that the shooting "added to the list of incidents connected with airbase that have provided a negative image among our country's population."[86] The parliament's action indicated that a considerable portion of the Kyrgyz public favored improving relations with Russia.

This apparent pro-Russian bias was not surprising given the fact that most Kyrgyz got their news through Russian mass media outlets and as a consequence have had a significant impact on the formation of Kyrgyz public opinion, especially about world politics. Indeed, playing to Russia's advantage in its competition with the United States for influence in Kyrgyzstan was and is the continuing dominance of the Russian media throughout the country, helping to create a highly critical and unflattering image of the United States. Orozbek Moldaliyev, director of Bishkek's Research Center on Politics, Religion, and Society, reportedly observed that "the Russian media plays a major role in the formation of political consciousness" in Kyrgyzstan, often inciting anti-American sentiment.[87] In addition, since Bakiyev came to power in March 2005 and because of the series of agreements he had signed with Russia, there was an expansion of the Russian economic impact on Kyrgyzstan, especially in the energy and industrial sectors.[88]

Also, pro-Russian sentiment in Kyrgyzstan was probably enhanced by the intrusive activities of several U.S.-funded organizations to promote democratization in Kyrgyzstan, notably the National Democratic Institute and the International Republican Institute, which complicated U.S. relations with the Kyrgyz government. These organizations supported pro-democracy groups and individuals, encouraging them to lobby the Kyrgyz government for more political democratization. Kyrgyz officials considered them almost politically subversive because they had reportedly backed opposition demands for Bakiyev's resignation. But, Kyrgyz officials kept a low profile, saying that they did not want to "unleash a conflict with the US."[89]

Indeed, by 2007, it was clear that despite the enormous pressure to evict the United States from the Manas base, Bakiyev was unwilling to do so. Rather, he wanted a resolution of the issue of the Manas base that would not alienate the United States and disrupt its relations with Kyrgyzstan. He had an opportunity to conciliate the United States on the base issue in early June 2007, when, desperate over the prospect of losing the base at Manas so soon after losing the U.S. base in Uzbekistan in 2005, the Bush administration sent Secretary of State Robert Gates to Bishkek to confirm that Bakiyev would continue to let the United States use the base in return for a U.S. payment of $150 million in rent, a figure agreed upon in 2006. This figure was roughly the equivalent of 7 percent of Kyrgyzstan's gross domestic product and more than 7 times the rent of $20 million the United States had agreed to pay prior to 2006.[90]

But, Gates's diplomacy with Bishkek was not as successful as Washington would have liked. While Bakiyev was willing at this point to resist growing domestic opposition to the U.S. military presence in Kyrgyzstan, along with the opposition of his SCO partners, Russia and China, he showed little concern for U.S. strategic interests in central Asia, in particular continuing the war against terrorism. During Gates's visit, there were anti-American demonstrations in Bishkek affirming how fragile the U.S. role in Kyrgyzstan had become by 2007.[91]

Nevertheless, during 2007 and into 2008, Bakiyev was determined to avoid alienating the United States for strategic and economic reasons. Friendship with the United States continued to provide Kyrgyzstan with some leverage in dealing with Russia and China both of which wanted a de-escalation of Kyrgyz ties to the United States, especially in the military sphere. In the long term, Bakiyev hoped that good working relations with the United States would help Kyrgyzstan enhance its role as a bridge between the West and central and east Asia. Moreover, it was economically expedient for Kyrgyzstan to remain on good terms with the United States. The Bakiyev government sought an expansion of trade with the United States, especially an increase in U.S. foreign investment in Kyrgyzstan.[92]

Increasing Russian Influence in Kyrgyzstan

In 2007, the Kremlin made substantial headway in luring Bakiyev closer to Russia. In part this was true because of Russian initiatives. But, it was also true that the Bakiyev leadership was increasingly becoming pro-Russian in response to Russian initiatives and a growing pro-Russian sentiment among the political elite critical of and opposed to the continuing U.S. military presence.

In February 2007, the Kyrgyz government said once and for all, it would not join the HIPC, which anti-U.S. groups had severely criticized, saying the HIPC membership would jeopardize Kyrgyz sovereignty.[93] This Kyrgyz opposition to the HIPC reflected a growing disagreement with the U.S. policies in central Asia and reflected Kyrgyz concern with the sharp deterioration of U.S. relations with Iran as a whole. Also, the Kyrgyz government disapproved of the Iraq war and of U.S. policy toward Iran. Kyrgyz relations with Iran had been steadily improving throughout 2007. In September 2007, the Kyrgyz ambassador to Iran reportedly stated that the people and government of his country assigned great importance to ties with Iran. While Iranian First Vice President Parviz Davoudi expressed equivalent sentiments, noting his country's readiness to cooperate with Bishkek in the areas of trade, technology, and engineering.[94] Kyrgyz policy experts, notably Emil Juraev, deputy director of the OSCE Academy, and Orozbek Moldaliyev of Bishkek's Research Center on Politics, Religion, and Society, attributed the growing popular dislike of the United States not so much to U.S. policy in Kyrgyzstan as to U.S. policy elsewhere, notably in Iraq and Iran. Kyrgyz parliament speaker Marat Sultanov reportedly declared that the government would close down the U.S. base at Manas, if it were used in any way for military action against Iran.[95]

A Kyrgyz Tilt toward Russia in 2008–2009?

Working to the advantage of Russia's influence-building in Kyrgyzstan were strains in Kyrgyz relations with the United States, especially as a result of the U.S. military base at Manas, which seemed to have become quite controversial, doubtlessly with the Kremlin's oblique encouragement. For example, following his May 27, 2007, meeting in Bishkek with CSTO General Secretary General Nikolai Bordyuzha, Bakiyev ordered his government to form a special commission to determine the compatibility of the Manas base with Kyrgyzstan's national interests, identifying both advantages and disadvantages for Kyrgyzstan of continuing to allow the U.S. military presence.[96]

Indeed, working to the Kremlin's advantage was pressure on Bakiyev from within his government to oust the United States from Manas, a step which for several years both China and Russia had been aggressively urging the Kyrgyz government to take. The Kyrgyz political elite questioned the rationale of the base from possible ecological damage to use of the base in a U.S. war against Iran. Questions had been raised in the Kyrgyz media about possible Iranian retaliation against Kyrgyzstan for allowing the United States to use the Manas base to attack Iran. Kyrgyz leaders were very sensitive to the ongoing deterioration in U.S. relations with Iran with fear of an imminent U.S. strike against Teheran.[97]

During 2007 and 2008, the killing of a Kyrgyz truck driver, Alexander Ivanov, by a U.S. soldier on December 6, 2006, was another source of growing Kyrgyz dissatisfaction with the U.S. military presence at Manas.[98] When it was discovered that Ivanov, an ethnic Russian and longtime employee of a base contractor, had not been armed, the Kyrgyz media had a field day portraying the U.S. military as "reckless and callous." Adding insult to injury in the Kyrgyz view, U.S. officials refused to allow the soldier accused of shooting of Ivanov to be tried in a Kyrgyz court and instead sent him back to the United States. The Kremlin undoubtedly watched as the Kyrgyz media generated intense popular dislike of American use of the Manas base, portraying the United States as hypocritical, calling for a renegotiation of the country's relationship with the United States.[99]

By 2007, moreover, at least in an American view, the Kyrgyz government was becoming increasingly reliant on Russia in security matters. In mid-May, citing internal security concerns and the constant threat from Islamist militants, the Kyrgyz parliament officially requested that Russia increase its troop presence on Kyrgyzstan's southern border and expand Russian personnel at the Kant air base.[100]

Other evidence of expanding Russian influence in Kyrgyzstan in 2007 and 2008 was Prime Minister Felix Kulov's proposal for a confederation between Russia and Kyrgyzstan. It would be a loose administrative entity with both states retaining their statehood and sovereignty but the confederation would have a common budget, customs policy, economic territory, and, possibly, a common currency. Proponents of a confederation argued its economic advantages for future Kyrgyz economic growth.[101]

The confederation idea, however, was dismissed for practical reasons, not least an absence of Russian interest in it. Moreover, the Kyrgyz government, for all the criticism of the U.S. use of the Manas base, exemplified by Bakiyev's statement in February 2008 that Bishkek eventually would demand that the United States close down Manas, seemed to have no intention of evicting the United States from the base, at least because of important economic considerations. Kyrgyzstan's impoverished economy desperately needed the money it received for the U.S. use of the base. In addition, the base had generated much needed jobs.[102]

Still, Kulov was critical of the United States and pushed for close ties to Russia, calling attention to Kyrgyz workers in Russia who benefited the economy of both Russia and Kyrgyzstan as one reason for close political ties between the two countries. According to Kulov, the confederation would provide for close and joint cooperation between Russia and Kyrgyzstan in say budgetary and customs policies that could include even a common currency. Though Bakiyev was still far from considering anything like an alliance with Russia that would effectively end cooperation with the United States, the mere suggestion of such a policy confirmed in still another way, at least at the moment, a substantial pro-Russian sentiment in Kyrgyzstan.[103]

Responding to the Kremlin's desire to limit U.S. influence, Orozbek Moldaliyev suggested that Russia could be more effective in persuading the Bakiyev leadership to severely limit American influence in Kyrgyzstan by providing Bishkek with an attractive economic package that could replace $850 million from the United States for use of the Manas base and for other economic and humanitarian purposes.[104] The Kremlin took the idea of a generous aid package to Kyrgyzstan seriously and ultimately offered Bakiyev an aid package exceeding $2 billion, including an emergency $300 million loan, $180 million in debt write-off, and $1.7 billion worth of financing for Kyrgyzstan's hydroelectric industry. This funding was worth far more than the aid programs Washington was willing to offer in ongoing negotiations with the Bakiyev government over continued U.S. use of the Manas base.[105]

The Russian economic tactic bore fruit. At a summit meeting with Russian President Dmitry Medvedev in Moscow in early February 2009, Bakiyev announced the Kyrgyz government's intention of terminating the use of the Manas base by the United States and its coalition allies fighting the Taliban in Afghanistan. The possible loss of the Manas base could not have come at a worse time for the United States given Taliban military advances in the early weeks of 2009, that included a strike against Kabul itself in early February, and the decision of newly elected U.S. President Barack Obama to deploy another 30,000 U.S. troops in Afghanistan.[106]

THE CHINA FACTOR

China has had the same goal as Russia in Kyrgyzstan in blocking the expansion of radical Islamic political forces. China fears that the expansion of militant Islamic radicalism in central Asia may spillover its western frontier with Kyrgyzstan into China itself. China already senses its presence in its increasingly restive Muslim minorities, notably the Uighurs living in Xinjiang province near the Sino-Kyrgyzstan border. The Uighur minority has sought administrative autonomy of Beijing and remains susceptible to the appeal of Islamic fundamentalism in the pursuit of its separatist goal. At the same time, militant Uighurs have fled the Chinese authorities into eastern Kyrgyzstan, though they have not been well received by the Kyrgyz government, which wants no trouble with Beijing. Indeed, to avoid antagonizing the China, Kyrgyz governments frequently deported illegal Uighur migrants into Kyrgyzstan sought by Chinese authorities.[107]

Furthermore, while China and Russia are rivals for influence in Bishkek, they also have cooperated in blocking the expansion of U.S. influence in central Asia, especially in Kyrgyzstan because of its proximity to Chinese territory and because of the Uighur minority problem. Indeed, China is hypersensitive to U.S. influence-building in an area that could easily be called China's western "backyard," where the United States is considered an intrusive and unwanted interloper. Russia can be and has been helpful to China in efforts to checkmate the development of ties between Kyrgyzstan and the United States. Indeed, at recent meetings of the SCO, there seemed to be an entente between Moscow and Beijing in pursuit of the shared commitment to constrain and restrain U.S. policy in Kyrgyzstan and elsewhere in central Asia.

Advantages for Chinese Influence-Building in Kyrgyzstan

In response to China's overtures, Bakiyev, much like Akayev before him, has promoted friendship and cooperation with Beijing to balance his relations with an overbearing Kremlin and Washington. China is delighted to do whatever it can to encourage Kyrgyz leadership to stand up to these other two powerful outsiders. Moreover, the Chinese leadership in recent years had been willing to invest "big bucks" in Kyrgyzstan to nudge it closer to China. For example, in 2002, China offered Kyrgyzstan $970 million in military aid at a moment when the Kyrgyz national debt was almost equal to the value of GDP of $10.8 billion.[108]

Also, China has benefited from the growing popular aversion to the United States provoked by unpopular policies toward Iraq and Iran. Indeed, it is something of a symbol of an unwanted and unwarranted U.S. intrusion subversive of the country's sovereignty and national independence. While for the time being at least Russia seems to be the chief beneficiary of this public anti-American sentiment, China stands to benefit from it as well.

So far, Beijing has skillfully avoided any criticism of Kyrgyz politics, in particular the sluggish movement toward democracy. Beijing, like Moscow, prefers a strong centralized government under an authoritarian leader to keep in check any possible encroachments of Islamic fundamentalism, to which Kyrgyzstan remains vulnerable because of its pervasive poverty. Under these circumstances, Kyrgyz leaders see China as a friend that can help it develop a foreign policy independent of Moscow and also Washington. Moreover, in certain situations like the war on Islamic-inspired terrorism, China finds itself in alignment with Russia, despite its rivalry with the Kremlin on many other issues in the region. They have a collective clout vis-à-vis the Americans, as seen in the SCO, which has had a growing appeal to the newly independent central Asian countries.

Disadvantages and Difficulties for Chinese Policy in Kyrgyzstan

Chinese diplomacy has to contend with the fact that Russia has the upper hand when dealing with Kyrgyzstan given the long history of closeness between the two countries. China also has to contend with the fact that Kyrgyzstan's economic and military ties with the United States are important for Bakiyev who is not ready to diminish them in response to pressure from China or Russia or for that matter statements in his own parliament. China needs to buy energy from Kyrgyzstan. It relies on the electricity generated by Kyrgyz hydroelectric power stations and therefore has to cater somewhat to Kyrgyzstan's preferences.[109]

There is much anti-Chinese sentiment in Kyrgyzstan. Kyrgyz politicians and voters resent what they perceive to be a great power patronizing of them. In 2002, the Chinese consul in Bishkek was murdered and there have been other incidents of anti-Chinese sentiment. So while the Chinese have made respectable progress in Kyrgyzstan, both Russia and the U.S. presence dominate the diplomatic front.[110] And, if there were something of a Sino-Russian entente in central Asia outside the SCO framework, it had not worked for either Russia or China. Moreover, the SCO, which the Kremlin would like to be a major help to Russian policy in central Asia in the post-9/11 period, has been only marginally useful.[111]

By early 2008, the most successful of the three outside Powers competing for influence in Kyrgyzstan was undoubtedly, and, not surprisingly, Russia. The United States runs a close second because of the resources it has given Kyrgyzstan in return for its cooperation with American policy in the Afghan theater of the war on terrorism. China with limited resources and narrower, primarily economic, interests in Kyrgyzstan, at least for the moment, exerts much less influence than either the United States or Russia.

THE GEORGIA FACTOR

The Russian military invasion of Georgian territory in early August 2008 to block efforts of the government of President Mikhail Saakashvili to restore Georgian state authority in the separatist region of South Ossetia placed Bakiyev in a difficult position. As other central Asian leaders, Bakiyev wanted to keep both Russia and the United States somewhat placated. Bakiyev was mildly sympathetic to Russian complaints about the independent and implicitly anti-Russian foreign policies of the Saakashvili government; but, like other central Asian leaders, he resisted giving overt support to the Kremlin's harsh crackdown on Georgia in part because he did not want to be on the wrong side of the United States and other Western countries which severely condemned the Russian action.

Bakiyev's Dilemma

Following the Russian invasion, Georgia had withdrawn from the CIS. Bakiyev as current chair of the CIS and responsible for organizing a summit meeting slated for October would have to take a stand on the Russian action congenial to Moscow but hardly so to Washington and likely to compromise Kyrgyz relations with the United States.

Making matters even more complicated for Bakiyev in responding to Russian policy in Georgia was domestic political pressure, in particular the influence of the Russian media on Kyrgyz society which was full of pro-Russian commentary on the Georgian crisis. Kyrgyz politicians also generally endorsed Russian policy. But, other groups, notably the Kyrgyz NGO "Citizens Against Corruption," openly supported the Georgian decision to leave the CIS and urged Kyrgyzstan also to leave the organization.[112] Meanwhile, a group of pro-Moscow Kyrgyz lawmakers visited South Ossetia after the Russian invasion to express support of the Ossetians in their ongoing confrontation with the Georgian central government and Moscow's effort to protect them.[113] Then, U.S. Vice President Dick Cheney during visits to both Tbilisi and Kiev in early September 2008 denounced Russian policy.[114]

Kyrgyzstan and its neighbors had to confront another aspect of the Georgian crisis, namely the Kremlin's recognition of the independence of both South Ossetia and Abkhazia, another separatist enclave within the legal boundaries of the Georgian republic. At the SCO summit in early September 2008, the Bakiyev leadership refused to endorse Russia's recognition of independence for the Georgian separatist enclaves. But it emphasized the importance for Kyrgyzstan of good and close relations with Russia. Following the lead of Nazarbayev, Bakiyev was not going to slavishly back Russian policy as he had done in February 2008 in condemning Kosovo's declaration of independence and the West's approval of it. And Russia's vehement opposition to even the thought of ex-Soviet republics such as Ukraine and Georgia joining NATO.[115]

In the early months of 2009, it was still too early to determine with any certainty the full impact of the Russian move against Georgia on Kyrgyz relations with Russia and the United States, in particular the nearness to, or the distance from, each of the two outside Powers. On the one hand, former Prime Minister Felix Kulov, now in the political opposition, did not think that Kyrgyzstan would make any changes in the status of the Russian and U.S. military bases on its territory. At the same time, political scientist Marat Kazakbaev said Kyrgyzstan remains a "strategic partner and main political ally" of Russia within the framework of the CIS and CSTO and "will never dare for complete integration with the West."[116]

In the Shadow of the Georgian War: The 2009 Flap over Manas

In a way, Kazakbaev's view was plausible and seemed to explain Bakiyev's February 3, 2009, announcement in Moscow of the closing of the Manas base to the United States.[117] The Kyrgyz parliament was ready to start discussion of and vote on the closure but agreed to postpone a vote until the end of February. Iskhak Masaliyev, a Communist Party deputy in the

Kyrgyz parliament, observed that "Kyrgyzstan had to make its choice. And it has now made its strategic choice."[118] While Washington noted that there had been no formal advice from the Kyrgyz government about the closure of Manas and that the United States would continue to use the base as it tried to negotiate a new agreement with Kyrgyzstan on fees,[119] on February 6, Adakhan Madumarov, secretary of the Kyrgyz Security Council, said, "the air base's fate had been decided."[120]

The Kremlin had a right to celebrate what looked like a diplomatic coup for Russia in its ongoing rivalry with the United States in Kyrgyzstan. Dmitry Rogozin, Russia's envoy to NATO, crowed that the U.S. departure will allow Manas to be run for the benefit of CSTO rather than for "foreign troops who don't respect Kyrgyzstan's sovereignty."[121] In addition, refuting an argument that Russia had bribed Kyrgyzstan to oust the United States from Manas by offering an aid program worth over $2 billion, the Bakiyev leadership claimed that the base was no longer needed as it had been in 2001, because Afghanistan had become "almost a functioning" state. Grigori Kerasin, a Russian Foreign Ministry spokesman, insisted that the United States view that Russia had bribed the Kyrgyz leadership to oust the U.S. military from the Manas base and that the Kyrgyz decision to close Manas was "absolutely independent and predictable."[122]

Other reasons for the closure of Manas stated in the draft parliamentary law closing the base included the growing popular opposition to the base as well as popular hostility to the U.S. refusal to allow Kyrgyzstan to punish the U.S. soldier accused of killing the Russian truck driver Ivanov at the end of 2006. And, Kyrgyz political scientist Nur Omarov observed that the Kyrgyz government had to somehow assuage Russia which along with China long had opposed U.S. use of the base.[123]

At the same time, however, another issue that may have contributed to the closure was simply Bakiyev's difficulty getting the United States to pay more money for use of Manas. Unwilling to accommodate the Kyrgyz leadership, negotiations for more rent money went nowhere, offering the Kremlin an opportunity to cut its own deal with Bakiyev in the form of a substantial aid offer which was worth more than the United States had been willing to offer.[124]

Finally, a highly critical analysis of U.S. public affairs strategy in managing the Manas base offers still another explanation of not only Bakiyev's announcement in Moscow on February 3 of closure of Manas but also the mounting popular Kyrgyz dissatisfaction with the U.S. presence. Alexander Cooley, an associate professor of political science at Columbia University's Barnard College, points out among other things that the U.S. Embassy in Bishkek made little effort to counter the highly critical views about Manas and the Americans in the Russian language media in Kyrgyzstan. "Overall," he writes, "the US perspective about Manas and its operations was not adequately presented to the Kyrgyz public," as was the case of the Ivanov killing.[125]

An American Dilemma?

If the firm and final closing of Manas does eventually occur, the United States would have to look elsewhere for a replacement of Manas, which had become virtually invaluable in the war against the Taliban in Afghanistan. About 15,000 personnel and 500 tons of cargo passed through Manas each month, and the base was used for large tanker aircraft for the in-air refueling of fighter planes on combat missions over Afghanistan.[126] The United States and its European allies rejected the idea that the base was no longer needed because the situation in Afghanistan had improved. Even the Kremlin acknowledged that "the number of radicals in Afghanistan is not declining." A possible alternative to Manas for the United States was Tajikistan, which was willing to help the United States, but the country was still unstable after a decade of civil war. Nor was Uzbekistan a realistic alternative—dealing with Uzbek President Islam Karimov always had been difficult because of his repressive leadership which the United States had frequently criticized. While Russia expressed willingness to allow "nonlethal" supplies for Afghanistan to cross its territory, it would hardly tolerate a U.S. effort to set up another "Manas"-like base elsewhere in central Asia, never mind on its own territory.[127]

By the end of February 2009, it remained to be seen whether the Bakiyev leadership in fact would close down the Manas base. Kyrgyz political analyst Nur Omarov did not think the closure would happen. Omarov observed, "in the past five years, the president has talked a lot about closing the base and it never happened. I doubt that it will happen this time either."[128]

In addition, there was some opposition to closing the base to the Americans from the Kyrgyz Green Party. Kanybek Sarymsakov, a party spokesman, called Bakiyev's decision against the Americans "shortsighted" and based on immediate financial needs rather than on the longer term economic picture and that the policy will alienate the United States. Strategic and other reasons for Kyrgyz friendship and cooperation with the United States were as valid in 2009 as a decade earlier, and especially after 9/11. Sarymsakov declared that it was not a good time for Kyrgyzstan "to spoil relations with America." Bakyt Beshimov, leader of the Kyrgyz Social Democratic Party in the Bishkek parliament, was another high-level Kyrgyz official with concerns about damaging Kyrgyz relations with the United States for the sake of pleasing Russia. He predicted a vigorous opposition to the base closing bill. Moreover, Beshimov thought it was quite possible that Bakiyev could easily change his mind about the closure if he felt like doing so. The end of the flap was nowhere in sight by the beginning of March 2009.[129]

Finally, the United States could expect that Bakiyev might indeed continue to allow its use of the Manas base as a counterweight to Russian influence-building in Kyrgyzstan as well as elsewhere in the central Asian region. Perhaps the lesson of the Soviet military incursion in Georgia in

August 2008 and the continuing Russian presence in the South Ossetian and Abkhazian provinces of the Georgian state is and will be the need of Kyrgyzstan and its neighbors of U.S. friendship and support indefinitely. In any event, the United States left the door open for further negotiations about payment of a higher rent for use of Manas.

CONCLUSIONS

While Kyrgyz President Kurmanbek Bakiyev does not like and does not support a meaningful military, political, and economic relationship with the United States, in dealing with the Americans he has been a skillful, ambitious pragmatist. Despite pressure to do otherwise, Bakiyev has maintained a U.S. military presence and kept a significant advantage in his dealings with the Kremlin. In the event of a military clash with Iran, Bakiyev has made it plain the base was not to be used against Iran, only against the Taliban insurgency in Afghanistan. The United States eventually did agree in 2006 to pay a little more money to Kyrgyzstan for use of the base. Clearly, the United States has benefited from Bakiyev's unwillingness to shut the United States out of his country and thereby increase its vulnerability to Russia. By the beginning of 2008, U.S.-Kyrgyz relations were not as strained as the Putin Kremlin hoped they would be.

But, the American opportunity is a limited one. The influence of Russia in Kyrgyzstan is much stronger than that of the United States. Russia together with other members of the SCO have called for the U.S. military to leave Kyrgyzstan. While these calls have been carefully worded to avoid provoking the United States, which the Kremlin has not wanted to do for its own reasons, they have been persistent and the Kyrgyzstan government and people are sympathetic to them. In particular, the Kyrgyz people remain critical of the U.S. war in Iraq and of its hostility toward Iran, motivated, the people believed, by strong anti-Muslim sentiments.

The Russians also have strengthened their position politically in Kyrgyzstan because they are giving more economic support to Kyrgyzstan in return for its willingness to strengthen ties to Russia. Indeed, the Kremlin is considering writing off some of the Kyrgyz debt to Russia though it is unlikely that Russia would be as generous as the United States.

There were other disadvantages and difficulties for U.S. post-9/11 policies in Kyrgyzstan that benefited Russia, notably the outspoken U.S. advocacy of democratization. Kyrgyz leaders believe, probably correctly, that the democratic process would weaken their personal grip on power, open the way to power for political groups heavily influenced by militant Islamic radicalism emanating from Iran and Afghanistan, and both de-secularize and destabilize the country.

While one might say, the Kremlin and Washington shared a common goal, that of preventing militant Islamists from gaining a foothold in Kyrgyz domestic politics, Putin always supported Kyrgyz leaders' dictatorial actions. Putin also insisted that Kyrgyzstan look to and rely on Russia, not the United States, for security in central Asia. To make the point clear, he insisted on a substantial expansion of Russian military capability at the Kant base given to Russia by Akayev.

Over time the U.S. situation might improve should Kyrgyzstan move in a more democratic direction and should the threat of radical Islam subside. For now, however, the trend seems to be in the opposite direction toward more authoritarian rule in order to maintain stability that has meant close relations with Russia.

7

Conclusion

Post-Soviet era Russia saw the former Soviet republics of central Asia as a part of a large region in which it had a privileged sphere of influence. The region was important to Russia for many reasons, not least is proximity—all five republics were contiguous to Russian territory. All of them had Russian-speaking minorities. They had valuable natural resources, especially in the energy area. All had a long history of close relations with Russia, having been conquered, occupied, and administered by Russia back at least to the eighteenth century and the rule of imperialistic czars, notably Peter the Great and Catherine, and their close association with Russia continued in the Soviet/Communist era from 1917 until 1991. For Russia the region was key to its internal stability and external security. Both post-Communist presidents of Russia, Boris Yeltsin (1990–1999) and Vladimir Putin (2000–2008), believed and, indeed, insisted on the international acceptance of Russia's paramount and privileged political, economic, and geostrategic interests in ex-Soviet central Asia.

At the very least, the post-Soviet Kremlin was determined to bind the central Asian republics, along with other former Soviet states such as Belarus, Ukraine, Georgia, Moldova, Armenia, and Azerbaijan, close to Russia in every possible area of their national life starting with their membership in the CIS founded on the eve of the Soviet collapse in late 1991. After the establishment of the CIS, the Kremlin sought membership of the central Asian republics in other organizations set up explicitly to foster closer ties with them, especially in the area of security and trade. At first, the policy drew some skepticism in the Russian political elite about assigning priority to the achievement of this ambition in the early years of Yeltsin's presidency, say at the expense of relations with the West, which opposed any apparent Russian effort to recreate in any shape or form the defunct Soviet Union. But, by the end of the Yeltsin era, that skepticism had dissipated. With Putin's election by a large majority to the Russian presidency in March 2000, the Kremlin proceeded with a policy meant to bring effective Russian influence over the post-Soviet, post-Communist internal and external development of the ex-Soviet central Asian republics.

Other considerations were behind Russia's influence-building foreign policy in the central Asian republics. Russian strategists had concluded that there was a better chance Russia would be successful in expanding its influence in the Near Abroad than in strengthening ties with the West, especially the United States. In their view, Russia had too many differences with the West and, again, with the United States. The West evidently opposed Russia's dominance in the ex-Soviet space even though it gave lip service in the mid-1990s to the Kremlin's claim that Russia, before all other countries, had a special interest in and responsibility for maintaining peace and stability in the ex-Soviet region. Moreover, Russia saw a loss of influence in central and Eastern (Balkan) Europe, as these states gradually linked up with Western Europe's institutions such as NATO and the EU. In response, the Putin leadership was increasingly sensitive about maintaining its preeminence in central Asia and skeptical about the economic and strategic benefits of friendship and cooperation.

At first, the United States was interested primarily in assuring that the ex-Soviet central Asian republics would remain independent of Russia and begin to develop ties to the West. The Clinton administration made clear that it opposed any Russian effort to weaken the sovereignty and undermine the independence of the new republics. The Clinton administration also went out of its way to cultivate the friendship of the ex-Soviet republics to bolster them in their dealings with the Russians. Moreover, the United States encouraged the republics to move quickly away from their Communist-style dictatorship to some version of Western-style democracy. Finally, as the Clinton era was coming to a close in the late 1990s, the United States moved to participate in the exploration, transit, and marketing of the huge energy resources in the region, especially in Kazakhstan and Turkmenistan, as world demand for energy was expanding, forcing the price of energy upward.

The 9/11 terrorist attack on the New York World Trade Center spiked U.S. interests and led to an American campaign to enlist the support of the central Asian republics in the war on terrorism declared by U.S. President George W. Bush in late 2001. From the vantage point of Washington, the cooperation of the central Asian countries in this war was absolutely necessary given their geographic proximity to where the United States thought the attack had originated, namely Afghanistan, the known headquarters of al Qaeda. Since then the Bush administration has worked aggressively to strengthen U.S. political, economic, military, and strategic ties to the five central Asian republics.

At first, and only briefly, Russia welcomed an opportunity to work with the United States against the Taliban government in Afghanistan and international terrorist activity, which for the Russians involved their own war in Chechnya. The central Asian republics also initially welcomed the chance to strengthen ties to the United States, if only for psychological benefits of having the Bush Administration call them "allies." But the Russians soon became wary of the U.S. presence. They were troubled in particular as the United States acquired military bases on the territory of the central Asian republics. The benefits of having U.S. cooperation in ousting the Taliban, especially as it became clear that it and al Qaeda were supporting Muslim extremist groups in the central Asian republics, eventually were outweighed by what the Kremlin perceived as the negative consequences of the U.S. military deployments and other aspects of the U.S. strengthening of ties with central Asian leaders.

What also worried and alarmed the Kremlin beyond the development for the first time of a U.S. military presence in countries Russia considered its "backyard" were collateral U.S. tactics not necessarily connected to fighting the war against terrorism in Afghanistan. The United States on its own, though with the cooperation of the Western European countries, was building pipelines to carry the oil and gas exports of countries like Kazakhstan and Turkmenistan to Western markets, bypassing Russia and its pipeline system. These Western efforts were in conflict with the Russian goal of creating a Russian monopoly of energy marketing facilities in central Asia. With this monopoly, Russia would have leverage with not only the central Asian countries but also with powerful outsiders like China and the Western European countries that were buying more and more oil and gas from Russia and central Asia.

Another source of Russian irritation with the United States in central Asia concerned the Bush administration's focus on, almost an obsession with, the political democratization of the authoritarian and often harshly repressive governments in the region. A major concern of Putin in this regard was that real democracy in the central Asian republics would endanger their secular governments led by political dictators who valued friendly and cooperative relations with Russia with a sort of "you scratch my back and I will scratch yours" relationship. Russian strategic and economic interests were well served by these post-Soviet leaders, and the Kremlin did not want them voted out of power with the introduction of pluralistic democracy. Also, Putin worried that Islamic fundamentalists might use any democratic process to gain power in some of the republics. Indeed, what Putin had been doing in Russia since coming to power as president in March 2000 and what he probably wanted for the central Asian republics was development of what he called "managed" democracy or a democracy with a minimum of political pluralism or with "fake" pluralism, that is, the holding of elections for legislative and executive posts with almost no challenges from a political opposition that was "kept in line" through frequent harassment involving violations of human rights.

As U.S. influence-building in central Asia progressed, the Kremlin tried to maintain a kind of balance of influence in the region with the United States. For example, as the United States acquired bases and basing rights in different central Asian republics, the Kremlin insisted that the central Asian leaders provide an equivalent accommodation to Russia, which now began to develop an enhanced military presence in several of the central Asian republics. Also, the Kremlin tried to discourage the central Asian republics from expanding the new U.S. military presence at frequent bilateral and multilateral summit meetings between Kremlin leaders. Russia used the framework of the CIS, the CSTO, and similar Russian-led organizations to foster integration in economic and security areas of the different ex-Soviet republics with Russia. At these meetings, Russian leaders emphasized the importance for the central Asian leaders of looking to Russia and not to the United States for the security of their borders and for the maintenance of their domestic political stability, especially against Islamic political radicalism and terrorism. The Kremlin insisted that Russia, not the West or the United States, was the best and most reliable ally of the ex-Soviet republics.

Another aspect of the Russian campaign to rival and reverse where possible the expansion of U.S. influence in central Asia after 9/11 had to do with the energy trade. Under Putin, Russian policy was to exclude outsiders from participating in the exploration, processing, and exportation of the abundant energy resources of central Asia, notably its oil and natural gas resources. The more control Russia had over the distribution and marketing of central Asian energy, the more influence it would have over not only the domestic and foreign policy making of the central Asian republics but also the policies of customers of central Asian energy, especially in Western Europe which was quickly becoming dependent on that energy.

Russian policy could not stop the opening of the Baku-Tbilisi-Ceyhan (Turkey) pipeline financed by Western investors and championed by the United States in 2005, with a route that bypassed Russian territory. But, since 2005, the Russian-controlled oil and gas cartel Gazprom, a tool of Russian foreign policy toward central Asia, has aggressively floated and consummated a variety of pipeline projects to enhance Russia's influence in the transit of oil to foreign as well as regional markets.

The Russian responses to U.S. influence-building in central Asia after 9/11 have been complicated by the ambitions and actions of other interested parties in the greater central Asian region, notably China and Iran. On some occasions, these outside countries supported Russian resistance to the expansion of U.S. influence, especially in the military and economic areas. But, on other occasions, their ambitions were in conflict with Russian policy, making them competitors of Russia in central Asia.

For example, China has had its own influence-building agenda in the region for reasons of border security, their expanding need for energy, and a concern about cultural threats to its domestic stability such as ties between Chinese and Kyrgyz Uighurs and the possibility of Islamic extremism from the west penetrating Chinese territory. But, China has been at all times sympathetic to and willing to support the Russian effort to limit and reverse the expansion of U.S. influence. At meetings of the SCO, China has joined Russia along with several central Asian republics in calling upon the United States to pull its military personnel out of the region where, as a real "foreigner," it did not belong. Still, China's relationship with Russia in central Asia was not always positive in the Kremlin's view and one could hardly speak of a Sino-Russian entente in central Asia just because the Powers shared a common dislike and a fear of U.S. influence-building so close to their home territory.

Iran has been especially sensitive to the growing U.S. military presence in central Asia, fearful that base facilities or their equivalents in some central Asian countries constituted a direct threat to its security given the extreme tension in Iranian-U.S. relations. The Iranian leadership has been concerned that the United States was expanding its military presence in central Asia not only to fight the Taliban in Afghanistan but also to prepare for an attack on Iran. To Iranian President Ahmadinejad, the Russian strategy to checkmate and undermine the U.S. military presence in central Asia was welcome. But, Iranian support had caveats. Russia has watched for the most part in an anxious silence how Iran has cultivated several central Asian republics like Turkmenistan and Kyrgyzstan to encourage them as predominantly Muslim countries to reach out to Iran economically, culturally, and politically in a strategy to moderate the international isolation of the country by the United States and its allies.

Overall, the Kremlin was ill at ease with Chinese and Iranian policies which might, as U.S. policy seemed to be doing, strengthen the will to independence of Russia on the part of the central Asian republics. Indeed, the bilateral Chinese and Iranian policies of cultivating the central Asian republics have diminished a kind of none-too-subtle isolation the Kremlin seemed bent on imposing on the republics as a means of keeping them closely linked in economic, strategic, and other ways to Russia.

Despite the varying pressures on them, in their policymaking toward Russia and the United States in the Putin-Bush era, the five central Asian republics differ very little in their policies toward Russia and the United States in the post-9/11 era. All the republics were committed to some form of postindependence foreign policy diversification in bringing to an end a long period in which they had been closely linked in all possible ways to

Russia. They all shared a view of the necessity of remaining good and cooperative friends with Russia regardless of any feelings of resentment toward Russia because of the harshness of its past policies of the czars and the Communists toward them. None of them has been prepared to defy Russia, never mind provoke, as some nationalists in all the republics wanted their governments to do. There has been uniform determination to keep whatever anti-Russian feelings there were in each country well below the surface. At the same time, they all seem willing, though in somewhat varying degrees, to implement foreign policy diversification starting with a steady cultivation of Western countries with which all the central Asian countries had had little to do prior to their achievement of independence in 1991. And all responded in a positive way to the U.S. call for help in fighting terrorism in Afghanistan in the aftermath of 9/11, especially as they all shared the concern expressed by the United States about the danger to their national security of Islamic-inspired terrorism, which looked like it could strike anywhere, anytime, in any mode since all the central Asian countries had Muslim majorities vulnerable to the appeal of Islamic fundamentalism of which all these secular governments were very fearful. Also of great importance was the shared strategic advantage as well as economic advantages of strengthening ties with other countries, especially Western ones. The so-called "lure of the West," no matter how sharply Western democratic systems differed from their own, was powerful. Central Asians also admired Western culture with its emphasis on material affluence and sociocultural and political individualism. These commonalities strengthened the ex-Soviet central Asian republics in the pursuit of their postindependence national destiny and in particular their will to have good relations with the West, especially the United States.

That said, some distinctions among the central Asian republics in their response to the Russian-American rivalry for influence over them in the post-9/11 years have been noticeable. For example, Kazakhstan, Turkmenistan, and Tajikistan have been very careful to limit the U.S. military presence on their territory, refusing to give Western forces actual military bases, preferring mere "landing rights." Turkmenistan's President Niyazov considered any kind of military help to the United States as a violation of his policy of positive neutrality vis-à-vis Russia and the United States. Kazakh President Nursultan Nazarbayev and Tajik President Emomali Rahmon were supersensitive to Russia's growing disquiet over their military ties with the United States and disinclined to provoke the Kremlin even though they were sympathetic to the U.S. need for their military cooperation in the fighting in Afghanistan. They also resented the U.S. criticism of their antidemocratic authoritarian rule. They offered cooperation to the United States but drew the line when asked to allow the United States to have a military base on their territories.

Uzbekistan and Kyrgyzstan were somewhat less worried than their central Asian neighbors about the impact of expanding military and economic ties to the United States. Both of these countries allowed the United States to lease military base facilities in return for generous rental agreements. But, both countries by 2005 had begun to have second thoughts about costs and benefits of base concessions to the United States. Uzbek President Karimov was provoked by unrelenting U.S. criticism of his crackdown on the political opposition before and especially after the antigovernment uprising in the Andijon area of Uzbekistan. His government approved the eviction, though not complete exclusion, of the U.S. military from the Khanabad military base. As a result, Karimov scored points with the Kremlin, which saw him as an ally in the campaign to reduce and terminate the U.S. military presence in the region. Kyrgyzstan had also given the United States base rights on its territory, but after the ascendancy of President Bakiyev in the Spring of 2005, the Kyrgyz government was inclined to pay more attention to Russian complaints about the U.S. base on Kyrgyz territory that were shared up by China, Kyrgyzstan's eastern neighbor. Bakiyev wanted good relations with both Powers and was also inclined to send a message to the Americans to hold back their criticisms of his increasingly dictatorial regime. So far, Bakiyev has not ruptured his working relationship with Washington and shown no indication of making the U.S. military leave his country.

In the post-9/11 period, the central Asian republics have aided and exploited this great power rivalry in the region. Whatever their pro-Russian inclinations, all the leaders of the central Asian republics have worried about the possibility of their country's loss of independence and sovereignty as a result of Russian ambitions to restore control over the region in the post-Soviet era. It was with some anxiety and reluctance that they agreed to Russia's request to join Russian-founded and Russian-led collective organizations such as the CIS and the CSTO. Despite Russia's insistence in the post-9/11 Putin era that the major threat to the well-being of the central Asian republics came from Islamic fundamentalism, the central Asian leaders knew—but none said publicly—that as far as they were concerned the chief threat to their country's independence in fact was Russia. This vulnerability to Russian power starts with their proximity to Russian territory and includes Russia's superiority in military power, population, natural resources, military capability, and territorial size. This fear and suspicion of Russia is also grounded in their history with Moscow's dominance of the area. It has been brought home and devastatingly demonstrated to them by the Russian invasion of Georgia in August 2008, revealing how far Russia will go to protect its interests in the greater ex-Soviet region. Despite their many reservations, the leaders of the region have concluded that some degree of friendship and cooperation with the United States provides them with a modest amount of leverage in relating to the Kremlin. They have developed a vested interest in keeping their diplomatic fences with the United States at all times in good repair despite sometimes sharp differences with the Americans.

By 2008, the balance of power between Russia and the United States in central Asia appeared to have shifted somewhat to Russia's advantage, partly because of U.S. policymaking, in particular its criticism of the sluggish pace of democratization throughout all the countries in the region. The central Asian leaders have resisted the Bush administration's insistence that to be a genuine ally of the United States, the central Asian leaders have to democratize faster than they think is in their best interests. For example, in Uzbekistan since 2005, relations between Uzbek President Islam Karimov and the Bush administration have been nearly ruptured several times because of U.S. criticism of Karimov's harshly repressive leadership and his unwillingness to liberalize his authoritarian government. He has punished the United States by restricting use of an air base by Allied forces fighting against the Taliban in Afghanistan. He did this despite the fact that he wanted the Taliban out of power in Kabul, knowing that the only way that this could be achieved was by U.S.-led Western military forces.

Clearly, the Russian side benefited from the heavy American focus on democratization because it was a policy all the central Asian leaders feared would put them out of office. The Bush administration helped the Russian cause by seeming to ignore the fact that what the United States wanted in the way of political change in Uzbekistan and its ex-Soviet neighbors was simply not practical, at least in part because it did not take into account the fragile stability of these regimes and the threat that radical Islamic fundamentalism could use free parliamentary elections to put them out of power. The Kremlin supported the secular and autocratic leaders in their ideological differences with the United States and asked them in return to accept Russian, not Western and especially American, leadership.

The Russian side also benefited from the strong inclination of the central Asian leaders not to go too far in developing ties to the United States when Russia was in opposition. After all, Russia was "next door" to them while the United States was far away and also considered to a degree unpredictable and unreliable in its relations with foreign countries, especially those with what the United States considered alien governmental regimes, that is, nondemocratic. The central Asian leaders were encouraged in holding this view by the continuous opposition in the U.S. Congress to close and supportive U.S. relations with them because of their nondemocratic political behavior and their unwillingness to accommodate U.S. demands to change that behavior in return for U.S. friendship.

Washington has been aware of the limits on U.S. policy, and since 2007, there has been a realization in Washington that the ideological component of its policy toward the central Asian republics in the post-9/11 years was undermining U.S. strategic objectives in the region. Criticizing and thereby weakening the central Asian leaders for their antidemocratic behavior had the unintended effect of tempting them, against their better instincts, to strengthen ties to the Kremlin. By 2008, there seemed to be a softening of

U.S. policy toward Karimov to which he has been artfully responsive. He has continued to have close relations with Russia but he also has steadfastly refused to terminate the U.S. military presence in his country, as both the Kremlin and Beijing had been telling him to do.

The central Asian leaders are undoubtedly weighing these relationships in light of the Russian intervention in Georgia in early August 2008. Russian ground forces suddenly moved into South Ossetia to prevent a Georgian military effort to restore Georgian central authority over the province and put an end to its separatist ambitions. Russian troops went beyond South Ossetia as far as the Georgian city of Gori, less than 50 miles from Tbilisi, the Georgian capital. With this move, Russia appeared to want not only to protect the South Ossetians from Georgian authority but also to send a message to the government of Georgian President Mikhail Saakashvili that Russia opposed his steady strengthening of ties with the West, especially with the United States, and his stated ambition to join NATO.

The message in effect was that Russia was prepared to use overwhelming power to prevent ex-Soviet republics from pursuing policies believed injurious to Russian strategic and other external interests. The message was not lost on the central Asian republics. At a meeting of the SCO in early September 2008, central Asian leaders acknowledged the legitimacy of Russian grievances against Georgia, refused to endorse Russian military intervention, and called for the use of diplomacy to resolves differences between the two. They remained as ever careful to avoid provoking Russia with any expressions of concern about the preservation of Georgia's political independence and territorial integrity; but, they displayed an independence that no matter how circumscribed was clear. Moreover, the central Asian republics have consequently expressed no intention of suspending their military and other ties to the United States, though they continue to limit them to assuage the Kremlin. It would appear that the Russian military deployment on Georgian territory has made them wary; but it has also encouraged them to keep their lines of communication with Washington open and operational, a plus for the U.S. side in the ongoing competition for influence with Russia in the ex-Soviet central Asian region.

Finally, as is true for other ex-Soviet republics in the Caucasus and western Caspian, and especially for Ukraine as well as for the five central Asian republics, the Russian military penetration of Georgian territory in August 2008 was message-laden. By sending troops into Georgia and threatening the continuation in power of Georgian President Mikhail Saakashvili and his government, the Kremlin was telling the countries once integral parts of the former Soviet Union that Russia will not tolerate a reorientation of their foreign relations Westward for any reason. That for security, trade, and the course of overall political development, these supposedly sovereign states, emancipated from Russian control with the collapse of the Soviet state in 1991, must look to the Russian Federation and must accept the

Russian strategic view that Russia and no other country is paramount in the ex-Soviet space. And, in particular, Russia will not tolerate the membership of these countries in the Western alliance system known as NATO which was still considered by the Kremlin as a threat to the security and stability of Russia in the post-Communist, post-Soviet era.

And, if the five central Asian republics thought otherwise, they should now, beginning in the late Summer of 2008, accept the reality of Russian dominance starting with a commitment to keeping their relationship, especially in the military sphere, with the United States to a careful and cautious limit. And even if none of them has publicly, diverging from Georgia and Ukraine, expressed interest in joining NATO to assure their security vis-à-vis Russia, they are still under suspicion of Russia, which, in occupying Georgian territory, has made it clear that Russia will not countenance a strategic shift of any of the countries toward the United States and will punish the countries in the ex-Soviet space that dismisses this message.

On the one hand, the central Asian countries obviously have been aware and fearful of Russia long before the Russian moves against Georgia in August 2008 and have behaved in the post-Soviet era accordingly. In sharp contrast with Georgia, they have reiterated their loyalty to Russia and their reliance on Russia in addressing their own political, economic, and strategic problems. And, they all have carefully structured their relations with the West since 9/11 to reassure Russia that cooperation with the United States does not mean a willingness to allow the United States to exercise undue influence over them or a willingness to allow large U.S. military deployments. As preceding chapters show, the central Asian republics have carefully avoided the provocative behavior of Georgian President Mikhail Saakashvili and carefully restrained the Washington in developing relations with the U.S. leadership to avoid provoking, never mind infuriating, the Kremlin, as Saakashvili had done, and thereby risk the kind of Russian crackdown Georgia experienced in August 2008 and afterward.

On the other hand, Russia is limited in what it can do to keep the central republics as loyal to Russian policy as the Kremlin would like. A heavy Russian hand has serious political, economic, and strategic liabilities, not least an explosion of Islamic extremism to which more than a minority in all likelihood would subscribe and for which it would support leading eventually to the removal from power of the current generation of pro-Russian secular leaders now in power. In addition, Russian coercion of the central Asian republics of the kind used in Georgia in August 2008 would disrupt the near complete Russian monopoly of the transit of the region's oil and gas to foreign markets, a situation that could wreak economic havoc in the West and that the United States could and would exploit to the fullest. Finally, were the central Asian republics threatened by the kind of Russian interference in their internal affairs suffered by the Georgians, they would look for economic and territorial security abroad, no doubt from the West, a situation that today's Russian state, despite its wealth and military power, would be hard put to block.

In late August 2008, the Kremlin asked the central Asian members of the SCO along with China to endorse Russian military action in Georgia earlier in the month. To its dismay, the SCO refused to accommodate this Russian request and adopted a kind of neutrality in the ongoing dispute between Russia and Georgia, this despite—or, possibly because of—U.S. support of Georgia. The position of the central Asian republics was driven by several considerations, not least a reluctance to endorse a policy that conceivably could be used against them, namely Russian military intervention to block the expansion of U.S. influence. Also, the central Asian republics did not want to prejudice their efforts to remain on good terms with the United States for whatever leverage it would provide them in their dealings with Russia. As the Fall of 2008 approached, it looked like Russia was not prepared to make an issue of the central Asian refusal to back Kremlin policy toward the turmoil in Georgia.

Notes

CHAPTER 1

1. For a brief overview of Russian policy in central Asia, see Arun Sahgal, "Growing Russian Influence in Central Asia," *Pravda* (November 5, 2004), pp. 1–4; for a brief but thoughtful analysis, see Lena Jonson, *Vladimir Putin and Central Asia: The Shaping of Russian Foreign Policy* (London: I. B. Tauris, 2005), pp. 23–42; Gail W. Lapidus, "Central Asia in Russian and American Foreign Policy after September 11, 2001," Presentation from "Central Asia and Russia: Responses to the 'War on Terrorism,'" sponsored by the Institute of Slavic, East European, and Eurasian Studies, the Berkeley Program in Soviet and Post-Soviet Studies, the Caucasus and Central Asia Program, and the Institute of International Studies at University of California, Berkeley, October 29, 2001, pp. 1–7, especially pp. 1–4.

2. Sahgal, "Growing Russian Influence in Central Asia"; Daniel Kimmage, "Central Asia: The Mechanics of Russian Influence," *Radio Free Europe/ Radio Liberty* (September 16, 2005), pp. 1–4, especially p. 1, hereafter cited as *RFE/RL*.

3. Stephen Foy, "Russia and the Near Abroad," *Post-Soviet Prospects* Vol. III, No. 12 (December 1995); see also Mark Webber, *The International Politics of Russia and the Successor States* (Manchester: Manchester University Press, 1996), p. 98.

4. Martha Brill Olcott, Anders Aslund, and Sherman W. Garnett, *Getting It Wrong: Regional Cooperation and the Commonwealth of Independent States* (Washington DC: Carnegie Endowment for International Peace, 1999), pp. 4–7.

5. Webber, *The International Politics of Russia*, p. 62; for more about the arguments favoring an expansionist Russian policy in the Near Abroad, see Andranik Migrainian, "Russia and the Near Abroad" and "Geopolitics and the Near Abroad: The Entire Space of the Former USSR Is a sphere of Russia's Vital Interests," *Nezavisimaya Gazeta* (January 12, 1994), pp. 1, 4 and (January 18, 1994), pp. 4–5, 8, respectively, in *Current Digest of the Post-Soviet Press*, Vol. XLVI, No. 6 (January 12, 1994), pp. 1–6 and (January 18, 1994), pp. 6–11, respectively.

6. Jonson, *Vladimir Putin and Central Asia*, pp. 143–44; see also Pauline Jones Luong (ed.), *The Transformation of Central Asia: States and Societies from Soviet Rule to Independence* (Ithaca: Cornell University Press, 2004), *passim*; Martha Brill Olcott, *Central Asia's Second Chance* (Washington DC: Carnegie Endowment for International Peace, 2005), *passim*; Yaacov Ro'i, *Democracy and Pluralism in Muslim Asia* (London: Frank Cass, 2004), *passim*.

7. Sahgal, "Growing Russian Influence in Central Asia," p. 1; Lapidus, "Central Asia in Russian and American Foreign Policy after September 11, 2001," pp. 1–3; see also Boris Rumor, *Central Asia: A Gathering Storm* (Armonk, NY: M. E. Sharpe, 2002), *passim*; and Adeeb Khalid, *Islam after Communism: Religion and Politics in Central Asia* (Berkley: University of California Press, 2007), *passim*.

8. See Freedman, "Russia and Central Asia under Yeltsin"; see also Roy Allison, "Strategic Reassertion in Russia's Central Asia Policy," *International Affairs*, No. 2 (2004), pp. 277–78.

9. Olcott, Aslund, and Garnett, *Getting It Wrong*, p. 21; see also Graham Smith, *The Post Soviet States: Mapping the Politics of Transition* (London: Arnold, 1999), p. 67.

10. Freedman, "Russia and Central Asia under Yeltsin"; see also Ro'i, *Democracy and Pluralism in Muslim Asia, passim*.

11. Jonson, *Vladimir Putin and Central Asia*, pp. 56–57.

12. Ibid., p. 57.

13. Ibid.

14. Ibid.

15. Ibid., pp. 58–59.

16. Ibid.

17. Ibid., pp. 73–74.

18. Ibid., p. 75.

19. Ibid., pp. 79–80.

20. Ibid., 78–79; see also Lapidus, "Central Asia in Russian and American Foreign Policy after September 11, 2001," pp. 9–10.

21. Jonson, *Vladimir Putin and Central Asia*, p. 75.

22. Vadim Trukhachev, "Russia to Cooperate with the West in the former USSR?" *Pravda* (August 24, 2005).

23. Jonson, *Vladimir Putin and Central Asia*, pp. 79–80.

24. Ibid., p. 50; see also pp. 43–51, *passim*.

25. Ibid., p. 63.

26. Lapidus, "Central Asia in Russian and American Foreign Policy after September 11, 2001," p. 2.

27. Jonson, *Vladimir Putin and Central Asia*, pp. 84–85.

28. Allison, "Strategic Reassertion in Russia's Central Asia Policy," p. 293.

29. Jonson, *Vladimir Putin and Central Asia*, pp. 84–85.

30. Ibid.

31. Ibid., pp. 191–94.

32. Ibid., pp. 8–17; Allison, "Strategic Reassertion in Russia's Central Asia Policy," pp. 277–78; Roger McDermott, "Russia Reclaiming Central Asia as Sphere of Influence," *Eurasia Daily Monitor* (March 13, 2007).

33. Fiona Hill, "The United States and Russia in Central Asia: Uzbekistan, Tajikistan, Afghanistan, Pakistan, and Iran," The Brookings Institution, Paper Delivered to the Aspen Institute Congressional Program (August 15, 2002), http://www.brookings.edu/views/speeches/hillf/20020815.htm; see also Allison, "Strategic Reassertion in Russia's Central Asia Policy," pp. 278–80.

34. Jonson, *Vladimir Putin and Central Asia*, pp. 63–68.

35. Ibid.

36. Allison, "Strategic Reassertion in Russia's Central Asia Policy," p. 278; see also commentary about a neo-Russian imperialism in the Near Abroad in Kimmage, "Central Asia: The Mechanics of Russian Influence," pp. 1–4, especially pp. 2–3.

37. Hill, "The United States and Russia in Central Asia: Uzbekistan, Tajikistan, Afghanistan, Pakistan, and Iran"; Gregory Gleason, "Turkmenistan's Neutrality and Russia's New Southern Policy," *Eurasia Daily Monitor*, Vol. 1, No. 120 (November 4, 2004).

38. Allison, "Strategic Reassertion in Russia's Central Asia Policy," p. 290.

39. Ibid.

40. Kimmage, "Central Asia: The Mechanics of Russian Influence," pp. 1–4, especially p. 1; Sergei Gretsky, "Russia's Policy toward Central Asia," *Journal of Social and Political Studies*, p. 6, http://www.ca-c.org/dataeng/GRETSKY.shtml; see also Hill, "The United States and Russia in Central Asia: Uzbekistan, Tajikistan, Afghanistan, Pakistan, and Iran," pp. 1–5, especially p. 2.

41. See Jonson, *Vladimir Putin and Central Asia, passim.*

42. Gretsky, "Russia's Policy toward Central Asia," p. 19.

43. See Hill, "The United States and Russia in Central Asia: Uzbekistan, Tajikistan, Afghanistan, Pakistan, and Iran," p. 4; Joshua Kucera, "US Aid to Central Asia: The Rhetoric and the Numbers Are at Odds with One Another," *EURASIANET.org* (February 6, 2007), http://eurasianet.org/departments/insight/articles/eav020607_pr.shtml.

44. Ibid.

45. Ibid.

46. Keely Lange, "Intervention and Conflict Resolution in Central Asia"; see also Allison, "Strategic Reassertion in Russia's Central Asia Policy," pp. 284–85.

47. Gretsky, "Russia's Policy toward Central Asia," p. 17; Hill, "The United States and Russia in Central Asia: Uzbekistan, Tajikistan, Afghanistan, Pakistan, and Iran," p. 4; Kucera, "US Aid to Central Asia: The Rhetoric and the Numbers Are at Odds with One Another."

48. Hill, "The United States and Russia in Central Asia: Uzbekistan, Tajikistan, Afghanistan, Pakistan, and Iran," p. 4; Kucera, "US Aid to Central Asia: The Rhetoric and the Numbers Are at Odds with One Another."

49. Jonson, *Vladimir Putin and Central Asia, passim.*

50. Gretsky, "Russia's Policy toward Central Asia," p. 17.

51. Allison, "Strategic Reassertion in Russia's Central Asia Policy," pp. 285–86.

52. Ibid.

53. Ibid.

54. For recent and detailed analyses of Chinese policy in the ex-Soviet republics of central Asia, see Niklas Swanstrom, "China and Central Asia: A New Great Game or Traditional Vassal Relations," *Journal of Contemporary China*, Vol. 14, No. 45 (November 2005), pp. 569–84; Xuanli Liao, "Central Asia and China's Energy Security," *China and Eurasia Forum Quarterly*, Vol. 4, No. 4 (2006), pp. 61–69; Hill, "The United States and Russia in Central Asia: Uzbekistan, Tajikistan, Afghanistan, Pakistan, and Iran"; Robert M. Cutler, "Central Asia: Emerging Triangles: Russia-Kazakhstan-China," *Asian Times Online* (January 15, 2004), http://www.atimes.com/atimes/Central_Asia/FA15Ag03.html.

55. Swanstrom, "China and Central Asia: A New Great Game or Traditional Vassal Relations," p. 580.

56. Ibid.; for trade statistics, see Liao, "Central Asia and China's Energy Security," pp. 61–69, *passim*.

57. Swanstrom, "China and Central Asia: A New Great Game or Traditional Vassal Relations," p. 584.

58. Heinz Kramer, "Will Central Asia Become Turkey's Sphere of Influence?" *Perceptions*, Vol. 1 (March–May 1996), http://www.sam.gov.tr/perceptions/volume1/march-may1996/willcentralAsiabecometurkey.pdf; Gareth M. Winrow, "Turkey and the Newly Independent States of Central Asia and the Transcaucasus," *Middle East Review of International Affairs*, Vol. 1, No. 2 (July 1997), pp. 1–10; Ziya Onis, "Turkey and Post-Soviet States: Potential and Limits of Regional Power Influence," *Middle East Review of International Affairs*, Vol. 5, No. 2 (June 2001), pp. 1–10, especially pp. 1–3.

59. Onis, "Turkey and Post-Soviet States: Potential and Limits of Regional Power Influence," pp. 1–3.

60. Ibid.

61. Ibid., pp. 3–4.

62. Amberin Zaman, "Turkey Moves to Expand Central Asian Ties," *EURASIANET.org* (October 26, 2000), http://www.eurasianet.org/departments/insight/articles/eav102600_pr.shtml.

63. Onis, "Turkey and Post-Soviet States: Potential and Limits of Regional Power Influence," pp. 5–6.

64. See Olivier Roy, "The Iranian Foreign Policy toward Central Asia," *EURASIANET.org*, pp. 1–16, especially pp. 9–12, http://www.eurasianet.org/resource/regional/royoniran.html; Golnaz Esfandiari, "Central Asia: Iran, Turkey Struggle to Influence Region," *RFE/RL* (October 25, 2005).

65. Esfandiari, "Central Asia: Iran, Turkey Struggle to Influence Region."

66. Freedman, "Russia and Central Asia under Yeltsin."

67. Esfandiari, "Central Asia: Iran, Turkey Struggle to Influence Region."

68. For a thorough and thoughtful analysis of American interests in central Asia, see S. Neil Macfarlane, "The United States and Regionalism in Central Asia," *International Affairs*, Vol. 80, No. 3 (2004), pp. 447–61; see also Ariel Cohen, "Security, Energy, and Democracy: US Interests in Central Asia," *EURASIANET.org* (December 6, 2006), http://www.eurasianet.org/departments/insight/articles/eav120606a_pr.shtml.

69. Macfarlane, "The United States and Regionalism in Central Asia," p. 454.

70. Ibid.; see also Martha Brill Olcott, "The War on Terrorism in Central Asia and the Cause of Democratic Reform," *Demokratizaya*, Vol. II, No. 1 (Winter 2003), p. 94, cited in Macfarlane, "The United States and Regionalism in Central Asia," p. 448; Eugene Rumer, "The US Interests and Role in Central Asia after K2," *Washington Quarterly*, Vol. 29, No. 3 (Summer 2006), pp. 141–54, especially 141–53.

71. Allison, "Strategic Reassertion in Russia's Central Asia Policy," pp. 278–79.

72. Rumer, "The US Interests and Role in Central Asia after K2," pp. 149–50.

73. Ibid., p. 148.

74. Dan Burghart, "The New Nomads? The American Military Presence in Central Asia," *China and Eurasia Forum Quarterly*, Vol. 5, No. 2 (2007), pp. 5–19, *passim*, http://www.silkroadstudies.org/new/docs/CEF/Quarterly/May_2007/Burghart.pdf; see also Vladimir Socor, "US Military Presence at Risk in Central Asia," *Eurasia Daily Monitor* (July 8, 2005).

75. Ibid.

76. Macfarlane, "The United States and Regionalism in Central Asia," p. 450, footnote 1.

77. Cohen, "Security, Energy and Democracy: US Interests in Central Asia," p. 1.

78. Allison, "Strategic Reassertion in Russia's Central Asia Policy," p. 279.

79. Macfarlane, "The United States and Regionalism in Central Asia," pp. 450–53.

80. Ibid.

81. Jad Mouawad, "Conflict Narrows Oil Options for West," *New York Times* (August 14, 2008).

82. Macfarlane, "The United States and Regionalism in Central Asia," pp. 456–57; Allison, "Strategic Reassertion in Russia's Central Asia Policy," p. 280.

83. Allison, "Strategic Reassertion in Russia's Central Asia Policy," pp. 281.

84. Ibid.

85. Ibid.

86. Ibid., p. 282; see also Ian Bremmer and Samuel Charap, "The Siloviki in Putin's Russia: Who Are They and What They Want," *Washington Quarterly*, Vol. 30, No. 1 (Winter 2006–2007), pp. 83–92, especially pp. 86–90, http://www.twq.com/07winter/docs/07winter_bremmer.pdf.

87. Bremmer and Charap, "The Siloviki in Putin's Russia: Who Are They and What They Want," pp. 83–92.

88. Ibid.

89. Socor, "US Military Presence at Risk in Central Asia."

90. Stephen Blank, "Its Time to Pay Attention to Russian Military Reforms," *EURASIANET.org* (January 4, 2007), http://www.eurasianet.org/departments/insight/articles/eav010407a_pr.shtml.

91. See Sergei Blagov, "Eurasia Insight: Russian Leaders Mull Geopolitical Moves in 2005," *EURASIANET.org* (January 4, 2005), http://www.eurasianet.org/departments/insight/articles/eav010405_pr.shtml.

92. Sahgal, "Growing Russian Influence in Central Asia."

CHAPTER 2

1. See Vitaly Naumkin, "Russian Policy toward Kazakhstan," in Robert Legvold (ed.), *Thinking Strategically: The Major Powers, Kazakhstan, and the Central Asian Nexus* (Cambridge, MA: MIT Press, 2003), pp. 39–65, cited in Allison, "Strategic Reassertion in Russia's Central Asia Policy," pp. 282; see also Sahgal, "Growing Russian Influence in Central Asia," pp. 1–4, especially p. 2.

2. For a detailed explanation of Russia's relations with Kazakhstan in the early and mid-1990s, see Mikhail Alexandrov, *Uneasy Alliance: Relations between Russia and Kazakhstan in the Post-Soviet Era 1992–1997* (Westport, CT: Greenwood Press, 1999), especially the overview in chapter 2, pp. 57–97.

3. Gretsky, "Russia's Policy toward Central Asia," p. 19; for a recent study of the larger "Eurasian" context of Russian policy toward Kazakhstan, see Herman Pirchner, Jr., *Reviving Greater Russia: The Future of Russia's Borders and Belarus, Georgia, Kazakhstan, Moldova* (Lanham, MD: University Press of America, 2005), especially the coverage of Kazakhstan.

4. Olcott, Aslund, and Garnett, *Getting It Wrong*, pp. 24, 112, 116, 118; for an extensive analysis of Nazarbayev's thinking about integration within the framework of the CIS in the 1990s, especially in the economic sphere, see Alexandrov, *Uneasy Alliance*, chapter 4, pp. 155–202.

5. Olcott, Aslund, and Garnett, *Getting It Wrong*, pp. 24, 112, 116, 118.

6. Ibid., p. 117; for a detailed study of the impact of Kazakhstan's Russian minority on Kazakh politics, see Bhavna Dave, *Kazakhstan: Ethnicity, Language and Power* (London: Routledge, 2007), *passim*; and Sebastien Peyrouse, "The 'Imperial Minority': An Interpretive Framework of the Russians in Kazakhstan in the 1990's," *Nationality Papers*, Vol. 36, No. 1 (March 2008), pp. 105–24, *passim*.

7. Alexandrov, *Uneasy Alliance*, pp. 99, 108.

8. Ibid., pp. 118–19.

9. Ibid., p. 124.

10. William Ratliff, "Oil-rich Kazakhstan Could Ease U.S. Pain," *San Jose Mercury News* (April 4, 2000), http://www.hubbertpeak.com/caspian/Kazakhstan/; see also Ibragim Alibekov, "Kazakhstan Tilts toward Russia," *EURASIANET.org* (February 18, 2004), http://www.eurasianet.org/departments/insight/articles/eav021804a.shtml.

11. "Autocratic Kazakh Leader Ousts His Reformist Premier," *New York Times* (October 11, 1997), hereafter cited as *NYT*.

12. Ibid.

13. James Risen, "Gore to Meet Kazakh Leader after MIG Case," "Gore and Kazakh Vow Cooperation," *NYT* (November 24, December 21, 1999, respectively).

14. Ibid.

15. "Kazakhs Try 2 for Jet Sales to North Korea," *NYT* (January 11, 2000).

16. For a detailed discussion of Russian concern in the 1990s about the beginnings of international competition for Kazakhstan's energy resources, see Alexandrov, *Uneasy Alliance*, chapter 6, pp. 260–308; see also Olcott, Aslund, and Garnett, *Getting It Wrong*, pp. 53–55.

17. Ratliff, "Oil-rich Kazakhstan Could Ease U.S. Pain."

18. Sergei Blagov, "Georgia: A Small Pawn in the Great Game," *Asia Times Online* (2004), http://www.atimes.com/atimes/Central_Asia/FA07Ag03.html.

19. Ibid.

20. Ibid.

21. Ibid.

22. Cutler, "Central Asia: Emerging Triangles: Russia-Kazakhstan-China."

23. Jim Nichol, "Kazakhstan: Current Developments and U.S. Interests," *CRS Report for Congress* (May 4, 2004), p. 6.

24. Office of the Press Secretary, "Joint Statement by President G. W. Bush and President Nursultan Nazarbayev on the New Kazakhstan–American Relationship" (December 21, 2001).

25. U.S. Department of State, "Joint Press Conference with Nursultan Nazarbayev, President of the Republic of Kazakhstan" (Presidential Administration Building, Astana, Kazakhstan, December 9, 2001); see also Office of the Press Secretary, "Joint Statement by President Bush and Kazakhstan President" (The White House President George W. Bush, December 21, 2001).

26. Nichol, "Kazakhstan: Current Developments and U.S. Interests"; see also U.S. Department of State, Bureau of Democracy, Human Rights, and Labor, "Kazakhstan—Country Reports on Human Rights Policies—2001" (May 4, 2004), pp. 1–19.

27. "Kazakh Parliament Votes to Send Peacekeepers to Iraq," *Central Asia Caucasus Institute Analyst* (May 30, 2003), http://www.cacianalyst.org/?q=node/1226/print.

28. "Speech by NATO Secretary General, Jaap de Hoop during His Visit to Kazakhstan," *NATO/OTAN* (October 19, 2004), http://www.nato.int/docu/speech/2004/s041019a.htm.

29. Blagov, "Georgia: A Small Pawn in the Great Game."

30. Office of the Press Secretary, "Joint Statement by President G. W. Bush and President Nursultan Nazarbayev on the New Kazakhstan–American Relationship."

31. See Nichol, "Kazakhstan: Current Developments and U.S. Interests," pp. 4–6.

32. Douglas Frantz, "World Briefing Asia: Kazakhstan: Bribery Sentence" (September 6, 2001); Andrew E. Kramer, "Mix of Nepotism and Nationalism Rules Kazakhstan's Oil Industry," *NYT* (December 23, 2005).

33. "Kazakhstan: Human Rights Developments," Human Rights Watch World Report (2003), http://www.hrw.org/wr2k3/europe8.html; see also Kseniy A. Kaspari, "Kazakh Journalist Convicted," *Boston Globe* (January 29, 2003), hereafter cited as *BG*; "Kazakhstan Government Critic Sentenced" (January 29, 2003); Michael Wines, "Kazakhs Reject Appeal of Editor Who Says He Was Framed for Rape," *NYT* (March 13, 2003); see also U.S. Department of State, Bureau of Democracy, Human Rights, and Labor, "Kazakhstan—Country Reports on Human Rights Policies—2002" (March 31, 2003), pp. 1–24.

34. Sabrina Tavernise and Christopher Pala, "Energy-Rich Kazakhstan Is Suffering Growing Pains," *NYT* (January 4, 2003); see also Jeff Gerth, "U.S. Businessman Is Accused of Oil Bribes to Kazakhstan," *NYT* (April 1, 2004); see also Nichol, "Kazakhstan: Current Developments and U.S. Interests," p. 5; U.S. Department of

State, Bureau of Democracy, Human Rights, and Labor, "Kazakhstan—Country Reports on Human Rights Policies—2002" (February 25, 2004).

35. For a brief but highly detailed account of corruption in Kazakhstan, see Ron Stodghill, "Oil, Cash, and Corruption," *NYT* (November 5, 2006); see also Kramer, "Mix of Nepotism and Nationalism Rules Kazakhstan's Oil Industry."

36. Christopher Pala, "Intimidation Alleged in Vote in Kazakhstan," *NYT* (September 9, 2004); U.S. Department of State, Bureau of Democracy, Human Rights, and Labor, "Kazakhstan—Country Reports on Human Rights Policies—2004" (February 26, 2005), pp. 11–12.

37. Christopher Pala, "Kazakh President Takes Steps to Ensure Easy Re-election," *NYT* (June 26, 2005).

38. Christopher Pala, "Election in Kazakhstan Failed Democracy Test, Europeans Say," *NYT* (September 9, 2004).

39. Pala, "Kazakh President Takes Steps to Ensure Easy Re-election"; C. J. Chivers, "Signs of Big Win for Kazakhstan President in Peaceful Election," "Kazakh President Re-Elected; Voting Flawed, Observers Say," *NYT* (December 5, 6, 2005, respectively).

40. Ibragim Alibekov, "Eurasia Insight: Kazakhstan's Leader Clears the Decks for Another Presidential Run," *EURASIANET.org* (September 9, 2005), http://www.eurasianet.org/departments/insight/articles/eav090905_pr.shtml.

41. Ibid.

42. "Kazakhstan: Presidential Election Fell Short of International Standards—OSCE," *IRIN* (Ankara, December 5, 2005).

43. Alibekov, "Kazakhstan Tilts toward Russia."

44. Sergei Blagov, "Economic Union Slips from View at Russia-Kazakhstan Summit," *EURASIANET.org* (January 15, 2004), http://www.eurasianet.org/departments/business/articles/eav011504_pr.shtml.

45. Ibid.

46. Alibekov, "Kazakhstan Tilts toward Russia."

47. Blagov, "Economic Union Slips from View at Russia-Kazakhstan Summit"; "Russia Puts Business before Politics," *Asia Times Online* (2004).

48. "Russia, Kazakhstan: Chronicle of New Cooperation," *Kazinform* (June 13, 2005).

49. Ibid.

50. "US Lawmakers Commend Kazakhstan's Non-Nuclear Choice," *Kazakhstan's Echo*, a publication of the Embassy of Kazakhstan to the United States and Canada (April 29, 2005).

51. Ibid.

52. "Ambassador John Ordway Transcript of Interview with Khabar Television Chief of Mission Residence, Almaty, Kazakhstan, February 27, 2005," pp. 2–3.

53. Adam Ereli, "Kazakhstan: Presidential Election," U.S. Department of State (December 7, 2005).

54. Ibid.

55. Ibid.

56. Ibid.

57. Heather Maher, "Kazakhstan: President to Visit Bush in Washington," *RFE/RL* (September 25, 2006); see also Office of the Vice President, "Vice President's Remarks in a Press Availability with President Nursultan Nazarbayev of the Republic of Kazakhstan" (The Presidential Palace, Astana, Kazakhstan, May 5, 2006), pp. 1–4; Steven Lee Myers and Ilan Greenberg, "US Sees a Friend in Kazakh Leader," *International Herald Tribune* (September 28, 2006).

58. Lionel Beehner, "The White House's Kazakh Dilemma," *Council on Foreign Relations* (September 29, 2006), http://www.cfr.org/publication/11553/whitehouses kazakhdilemma.html?breadcrumb=...; for a detailed review of the bribe case, see Stodghill, "Oil, Cash, and Corruption"; see also Office of the Press Secretary, "President Bush Welcomes President Nazarbayev of Kazakhstan to the White House" (September 29, 2006).

59. Joanna Lillis, "Nazarbayev Visit to Washington: Looking for Recognition as Regional Leader," *EURASIANET.org* (September 26, 2006); see also Maher, "Kazakhstan: President to Visit Bush in Washington"; Beehner, "The White House's Kazakh Dilemma."

60. Myers and Greenberg, "US Sees a Friend in Kazakh Leader."

61. Ibid.

62. Beehner, "The White House's Kazakh Dilemma."

63. See U.S. Embassy, Astana, Kazakhstan, "Transcript of Press Conference Given by U.S. Ambassador to Kazakhstan John Ordway" (February 14, 2007), p. 3.

64. Myers and Greenberg, "US Sees a Friend in Kazakh Leader"; see also Roger McDermott, "Kazakhstan Questions US Military Role in Central Asia," *Eurasia Daily Monitor*, Vol. 2, No. 160 (August 16, 2005), pp. 1–3, especially p. 1.

65. Office of the Vice President, "Vice President's Remarks in a Press Availability with President Nursultan Nazarbayev of the Republic of Kazakhstan," pp. 1–4.

66. Ibid.

67. McDermott, "Kazakhstan Questions US Military Role in Central Asia," p. 1.

68. Ilan Greenberg, "Russia Will Get Central Asian Pipeline," *NYT* (May 13, 2007).

69. Ibid.

70. Andre E. Kramer, "Kazakhs Suspend Permits for Oilfields," *NYT* (August 28, 2007); see also "Pressure Builds on ENI as Kazakh Government Threatens Kashagan Halt Due to Environmental Violations," *Global Insight*, pp. 1–3, http://www.globalinsight.com/SDA/SDADetail10361.htm.

71. Greenberg, "Russia Will Get Central Asian Pipeline."

72. Wikipedia, "Kazakstan-China Oil Pipeline," pp. 1–2, http://en.wikipedia.org/wiki/Kazakhstan-China_oil_pipeline.

73. See Marat Yermukhanov, "China's Relations with Kazakhstan Are Warming, But to What End?" *Association for Asian Research (AFAR)* (July 9, 2004), http://www.asianresearch.org/articles/2185.html; "China Calls for Substantiation of China-Kazakhstan Strategic Partnership," *People's Daily Online* (January 1, 2006); for a detailed review of Chinese policy in ex-Soviet central Asia, see Swanstrom, "China and Central Asia: A New Great Game or Traditional Vassal Relations?" pp. 569–84, especially pp. 576–79 for energy-based interest in central Asia.

74. See Yermukhanov, "China's Relations with Kazakhstan Are Warming, But to What End?" "China Calls for Substantiation of China-Kazakhstan Strategic Partnership."

75. Eurasia Insight, "Uighur Issues May Become Factor in China-Kazakhstan Relations," *EURASIANET.org* (January 2, 2003); see also Swanstrom, "China and Central Asia: A New Great Game or Traditional Vassal Relations?" pp. 571–74.

76. Ibraghim Alibekov, "Khatami, in Kazakhstan, Asserts Iran as a Critical Partner for Kazakhstan," Gerghana Information Agency (April 27, 2002), http://enews.ferghana.ru/article.php?id=29&print=1&PHPSESSID=97691f499006399effad...45.

77. Ibid.

78. Ibid.

79. "Kazakh President Leaves for Iran for Official Visit," *Itar-Tass* (October 15, 2007).

80. Marat Yermukhanov, "Kazakhstan Seeks Iran's Reconciliation with the West," *Eurasia Daily Monitor* (June 16, 2008).

81. Ibid.

82. Ibid.

83. For further brief commentary on the long-term impact of the Russian military action in Georgia in August 2008 on the central Asian republics, in particular, Kazakhstan, see "Russia's Asia Allies Fail to Back Georgia Action," *Asharq Alawsat* (August 28, 2008), http://www.asharq-e.com/print.asp?artid=id13873; Oksana Antonenko, "Central Asia Watches Warily (the Russian Military Action in Georgia)," *International Herald Tribune* (August 29, 2008).

84. Kazakhstan, neweurasia.net, "Kazakh Perspectives on the Russian-Georgian War" (August 13, 2008).

CHAPTER 3

1. Martha Brill Olcott, "Challenges in the Transport of Turkmen Gas," a draft paper prepared for Stanford University Program on Energy and Sustainable Development (November 2003), pp. 1–47, *passim*, especially p. 29.

2. See Gleason, "Turkmenistan's Neutrality and Russia's New Southern Policy," pp. 1–3.

3. "Turkmenistan: Role of Russia and the CIS," AllREFER (March 1996).

4. Olcott, Aslund, and Garnett, *Getting It Wrong*, p. 19.

5. Ibid., p. 22.

6. For a detailed discussion of Russia's role in the transit and marketing of Turkmen gas, see Olcott, "Challenges in the Transport of Turkmen Gas," pp. 22–25.

7. See "Russians in Turkmenistan," *Minorities at Risk* (December 10, 2001), http://www.cidcm.umd.edu/inscr/mar/data/turruss.htm.

8. Ibid.

9. "Turkmen Decree to Annul Citizenship in Force," *Interfax*, BBC Monitoring (June 24, 2003); "Envoy Says People in Turkmenistan Hold Onto Their Russian Citizenship," ITAR-TASS (June 24, 2003), cited in *Weekly News Brief on Turkmenistan* (Turkmenistan Project, June 20–26, 2003).

10. Igor Torbakov, "Russian–Turkmen Pacts Mark Strategic Shift for Moscow in Central Asia," *EURASIANET.org* (April 15, 2003); see also "Turkmen Decree to Annul Dual Citizenship in Force" and "Envoy Says People in Turkmenistan Hold Onto Their Russian Citizenship."

11. Ibid.

12. "President Putin Says Russians in Turkmenistan Have Nothing to Fear," *RTR Russia TV* (BBC Monitoring Service, June 3, 2003), cited in *Weekly News Brief on Turkmenistan* (Turkmenistan Project, June 20–26, 2003).

13. See Gleason, "Turkmenistan's Neutrality and Russia's New Southern Policy."

14. For an extensive review of Turkmen gas pipeline construction initiatives from the late 1990s and early years of the new century and in particular the discussion of a gas pipeline that would bring Turkmen gas to Afghanistan and Pakistan without Russian involvement, see Energy Information Administration, "Caspian Sea Region: Natural Gas Export" (July 2002), pp. 1–6, *passim*, especially p. 4, http://www.eia.doe.gov/emeu/cabs/caspgase.html.

15. Daniel Kimmage, "Central Asia Provides Window on Russia-US Relations," *RFE/RL Newsline* (February 24, 2005); Blagov, "Russian Leaders Mull Geopolitical Moves in 2005."

16. Ibid.

17. See Kimmage, "Central Asia Provides Window on Russia-US Relations."

18. Lapidus, "Central Asia in Russian and American Foreign Policy after September 11, 2001," p. 4.

19. Steven Lee Meyers, "World Briefing/Asia: Turkmenistan: Military Aid from US," *NYT* (August 28, 2002).

20. Kenley Butler, "Central Asian Military Bases," *Monterey Institute of International Studies* (October 11, 2001), http://cns.miis.edu/research/wtc01/cabases.htm; see also Gleason, "Turkmenistan's Neutrality and Russia's New Southern Policy."

21. See Commission on Security and Cooperation in Europe of the United States House of Representatives Hearing (March 21, 2000), "Democratization and Human Rights in Turkmenistan," pp. 3–5.

22. Butler, "Central Asian Military Bases"; see also Gleason, "Turkmenistan's Neutrality and Russia's New Southern Policy."

23. Commission on Security and Cooperation in Europe of the United States House of Representatives Hearing, "Democratization and Human Rights in Turkmenistan," pp. 3–5; see also Ariel Cohen, "Advancing American Interest in Central Asia," *Heritage Foundation* (January 17, 2007), http://www.heritage.org/Press/Commentary/ed020907c.cfm?Renderforprint=1.

24. Sabrina Tavernise, "Show Trials Like Stalin's in Turkmenistan," *NYT* (January 27, 2003); see also Sergei Blagov, "Turkmenistan: A Study in Democracy Denial," *Asia Times* (December 6, 2003), http://www.atimes.com/atimes/Central_Asia/EL06Ag02.html.

25. "United States Comes Close to Slapping Economic Sanctions on Turkmenistan," *News Central Asia* (August 9, 2003).

26. "Eurasia Insight: Is Washington Exploring a Base Deal with Turkmenistan," *EURASIANET.org* (August 31, 2005).

27. Mike Whitney, "Washington's Game in Turkmenistan," Information Clearing House (December 26, 2006), http://www.informationclearinghouse.info/article15987.htm; see also Jim Nichol, "Central Asia's Security: Issues and Implications for US Interests," *CRS Report for Congress* (April 3, 2003), pp. 5–6, https://www.policyarchive.org/bitstream/handle/10207/954/RL30294_20030403.pdf?sequence=1.

28. Torbakov, "Russian–Turkmen Pacts Mark Strategic Shift for Moscow in Central Asia."

29. Jonson, *Vladimir Putin and Central Asia*, p. 147.

30. Ibid., p. 148.

31. Ibid., pp. 146–47.

32. Ibid., p. 148.

33. Ibid.

34. Torbakov, "Russian–Turkmen Pacts Mark Strategic Shift for Moscow in Central Asia."

35. Jonson, *Vladimir Putin and Central Asia*, p. 106.

36. Ibid.

37. "Russia, Turkmenistan Sign a 25 Year Gas Cooperation Agreement," *Pravda* (April 10, 2003), http://newsfromrussia.com/economis/2003/04/10/45916.html; Torbakov, "Russian–Turkmen Pacts Mark Strategic Shift for Moscow in Central Asia."

38. Torbakov, "Russian–Turkmen Pacts Mark Strategic Shift for Moscow in Central Asia."

39. "Is Washington Exploring a Base Deal with Turkmenistan."

40. "Potential U.S. Base in Turkmenistan Alarming for Russia—Expert," *RIA Novosti* (September 6, 2005); Roger McDermott, "Turkmenistan Pulls Back from CIS," *Eurasia Daily* (September 1, 2005).

41. "Is Washington Exploring a Base Deal with Turkmenistan."

42. "Potential U.S. Base in Turkmenistan Alarming for Russia—Expert."

43. See Islamic Republic of Iran—Permanent Mission to the United Nations, "Address by H. E. Dr. Mahmood Ahmadinejad President of the Islamic Republic of Iran before the Sixtieth Session of the United Nations General Assembly New York—September 17, 2005," pp. 1–10, especially pp. 7–10.

44. McDermott, "Turkmenistan Pulls Back from CIS"; Ivan Shmelev, "Commonwealth of Independent States, the Former USSR, Likely to Collapse and Take a Different Form," *Pravda* (August 29, 2005), p. 65; State Information Agency of Turkmenistan, "Turkmen Neutrality Serves National Interests and Tasks of Peaceful Development" (September 4, 2005).

45. McDermott, "Turkmenistan Pulls Back from CIS."

46. See "Turkmenistan Does Not Want US Military Base on Its Territory," *RIA Novosti* (September 8, 2005).

47. Ibid.

48. Ibid.

49. Sergei Blagov, "Russia Bows to Turkmenistan's Gas Pricing Demand," *EURASIANET.org* (September 6, 2006); see also Gregory Gleason, "Turkmenistan Tilts Toward Russia," *Eurasia Daily Monitor* (January 2, 2007).

50. See C. J. Chivers, "Intrigue Follows Death of a President," *NYT* (December 22, 2006).

51. Roger McDermott, "Putin Seeks Closer Ties with Turkmenistan," *Eurasia Daily Monitor* (February 20, 2007); see also John C. K. Daly, "Turkmenistan Back in Former USSR's Orbit," *Eurasia Daily Monitor* (June 8, 2007).

52. Gleason, "Turkmenistan Tilts Toward Russia"; see also Breffni O'Rourke, "Turkmenistan: President's Death Brings Muted World Reaction," *RFE/RL* (December 21, 2006); C. J. Chivers, "Turkmen Exile Urges Interim President to Step Down," *NYT* (December 30, 2006).

53. Gleason, "Turkmenistan Tilts Toward Russia"; see also O'Rourke, "Turkmenistan: President's Death Brings Muted World Reaction"; Chivers, "Turkmen Exile Urges Interim President to Step Down."

54. Vladimir Dubov, "Turkmenistan, Russia and the West: Two's Company, Three's a Crowd," *RIA Novosti*.

55. Daly, "Turkmenistan Back in Former USSR's Orbit."

56. Ilan Greenberg, "Turkmenistan Limits Election to Soviet Style Slate," "Turkmen Leader Proposes Vast Change to Lift Isolation," *NYT* (December 27, 2006, January 5, 2007, respectively).

57. Ibid.; see also C. J. Chivers, "Little Doubt on Result of Turkmenistan Vote," "Turkmenistan Hails Leader and New Era after Election," *NYT* (February 12, 15, 2007, respectively).

58. See "Russia, Kazakhstan, Turkmenistan Agree on Caspian Gas Pipe," *RIA Novosti* (May 12, 2007), http://en.rian.ru/world/20070512/65373780 .html; "Russia, Kazakhstan, and Turkmenistan Agreed on Construction of Caspian Pipeline," *Regnum* (May 14, 2007), http://www.regnum.ru/English/826354 .html; for more analysis of the Putin visit to Ashgabat in May 2007, see Mikhail Peresplesnin, "Russia's Comeback to Central Asia Is Not Just Pipe Dream," *RIA Novosti* (May 8, 2007), http://en.rian.ru/analysis/20070508/65139688.html; "Putin to Lobby Gas Pipe Via Russia in Turkmenistan, Kazakhstan," *RIA Novosti* (May 10, 2007); and "Putin in Turkmenistan to Preserve Gas Exports-1," *RIA Novosti*.

59. Daly, "Turkmenistan Back in Former USSR's Orbit."

60. Ibid.

61. Ariel Cohen, "US Opportunity in Turkmenistan," *EURASIANET.org* (January 17, 2007); Cohen, "Advancing American Interest in Central Asia"; see also Whitney, "Washington's Game in Turkmenistan."

62. Joshua Kucera, "US Sets Its Sights on Turkmenistan Gas," *enerpub* (January 29, 2008), http://www.energypublisher.com/print.asp?idarticle=14075; Okzhas Auyezov, "US Envoy Discusses Energy Ties with Turkmenistan," *Reuters—UK* (February 28, 2008).

63. Auyezov, "US Envoy Discusses Energy Ties with Turkmenistan."

64. Ibid.

65. "Ahmadinejad in Turkmenistan Looking for Gas and Allies," *AsiaNews.it* (July 25, 2006), http://www.asianews.it/view4print.php?1=en&art=6791; Gulnoza Saidzimova, "Turkmenistan: Iranian President Pays First Visit to Ashgabat," *RFE/RL* (July 24, 2006).

66. Ibid.

67. "Turkmen President Supports Iran's Peaceful Nuclear Program," *Islamic Republic News Agency* (March 16, 2007).

68. "Turkmenistan and Iran Consolidate, Expand Bilateral Relations," *News Central Asia* (June 18, 2007), http://www.newscentralasia.net/print/42.html; Roger McDermott, "Turkmenistan and Iran Strengthen Relations," *Eurasia Daily Monitor* (June 26, 2007).

69. Ibid.

70. McDermott, "Turkmenistan and Iran Strengthen Relations."

71. Saidzimova, "Turkmenistan: Iranian President Pays First Visit to Ashgabat"; see also Olcott, "Challenges in the Transport of Turkmen Gas."

72. Daly, "Turkmenistan Back in Former USSR's Orbit."

73. McDermott, "Turkmenistan and Iran Strengthen Relations."

74. Ibid.

75. "China, Turkmenistan to Further Bilateral Ties," *Xinhua News Agency* (May 9, 2005).

76. Firket Ertan, "Turkmenistan-China Cooperation," *Zaman Daily Newspaper* (September 17, 2005); see also Whitney, "Washington's Game in Turkmenistan."

77. Can Karpat, "Tired of Russia, Turkmenistan Is Due to Choose China," *Axis Information and Analysis* (August 30, 2005), http://www.axisglobe.com/article.asp ?article=356; Ertan, "Turkmenistan-China Cooperation."

78. Igor Torbakov, "Russia Watches Warily as Turkmen-Chinese Economic Cooperation Expands," *EURASIANET.org* (August 29, 2006).

79. See Frederico Bordonaro, "Moscow Moves to Consolidate Control in Belarus and Turkmenistan," *Power and Interest News Report* (January 5, 2007).

80. For further brief commentary on the long-term impact of the Russian military action in Georgia in August 2008 on Turkmenistan, see "Russia's Asia Allies Fail to Back Georgia Action"; Antonenko, "Central Asia Watches Warily (the Russian Military Action in Georgia)"; Michael A. Reynolds, "Russia and Georgia at War" (August 9, 2008), pp. 1–2, especially p. 2.

CHAPTER 4

1. For a comprehensive but concise and thoughtful review of Russian relations with Tajikistan during the era of Russian President Boris Yeltsin (1992–1999), see Lena Jonson, "Russian Policy and Tajikistan," *Central Asia*, Vol. 8, No. 2 (1997), pp. 1–6. At the time of writing this article, Dr. Jonson was a Senior Research Fellow at the Swedish Institute of International Affairs.

2. Gretsky, "Russia's Policy toward Central Asia," pp. 1–7.

3. Jonson, *Vladimir Putin and Central Asia*, p. 51.

4. Jonson, "Russian Policy and Tajikistan," pp. 3–4.

5. Gretsky, "Russia's Policy toward Central Asia," p. 7; Jonson, *Vladimir Putin and Central Asia*, p. 50.

6. Gretsky, "Russia's Policy toward Central Asia," p. 5.

7. Jonson, *Vladimir Putin and Central Asia*, pp. 50–51.

8. Michael Jasinski, "Russian Policy toward Afghanistan," *Center for Non-Proliferation Studies* (September 15, 2001), pp. 1–3, especially p. 1, http://cns.miis.edu/research/wtc01/rusafg.htm.

9. Ibid., pp. 1–3, especially p. 2.

10. Gretsky, "Russia's Policy toward Central Asia," pp. 11–14; Jonson, *Vladimir Putin and Central Asia*, pp. 52–54.

11. Gretsky, "Russia's Policy toward Central Asia," pp. 13–14.

12. Ibid., pp. 4–5.

13. Ibid.

14. Ibid., p. 5.

15. Jonson, *Vladimir Putin and Central Asia*, p. 72.

16. Ibid.

17. Ibid., p. 73.

18. Ibid.

19. See Office of the Press Secretary, "Joint Statement by President Bush and President Rakhmonov on the Relationship between the United States and the Republic of Tajikistan" (December 20, 2002); "US Ambassador Tracey Ann Jacobson's Remarks at the International Conference on Afghanistan and Regional Security," *Embassy of the United States—Dushanbe* (December 11, 2006).

20. "Tajik Military Facilities," *Global Security*, http://globalsecurity.org/military/world/centralasia/tajikistan.htm; "US Defense Secretary to Make Surprise Tajik Visit," *Peyvand's Iran News* from *RFE/RL* (July 10, 2006).

21. "Tajik Military Facilities"; "US Defense Secretary to Make Surprise Tajik Visit"; Sgt. Sara Wood, USA American Forces Press Service, "Tajikistan Important to War on Terrorism," *American Forces Press Service NEWS ARTICLES* (July 10, 2006).

22. See Rashid G. Abdullo, "Tajikistan Turns to the West," *Institute for War and Peace* (January 10, 2003).

23. Jonson, *Vladimir Putin and Central Asia*, pp. 90–91.

24. Vladimir Mukhin, "Russian and American Interests Clash in Tajikistan: Tajikistan's Military Infrastructure Will Depend on the US Dollar," *Nezavisimaya Gazeta* (August 12, 2003), http://www.cdi.org/Russia/269-13.cfm.

25. Ibid.

26. Zafar Abdullayev, "Tajikistan, Russia Probe Military Partnership," *EURASIANET.org* (March 4, 2003), http://www.eurasianet.org/departments/insight/articles/eav030404_pr.shtml.

27. Jonson, *Vladimir Putin and Central Asia*, p. 108.

28. "Secretary Rumsfeld, Tajik Foreign Minister Talbak Nazarov Brief Press" (July 26, 2005); Ann Scot Tyson, "Rumsfeld Wins Assurances in Central Asia: Kyrgyzstan, Tajikistan Say U.S. Can Still Use Bases," *Washington Post* (July 27, 2005); Tyson, "Rumsfeld Wins Assurances in Central Asia"; for more detail, see also "United States, Tajikistan to Continue Active Military Cooperation," *AVESTA Tajikistan News* (August 19, 2005).

29. "Secretary Rumsfeld, Tajik Foreign Minister Talbak Nazarov Brief Press"; Tyson, "Rumsfeld Wins Assurances in Central Asia"; for more detail, see also "United States, Tajikistan to Continue Active Military Cooperation."

30. Tyson, "Rumsfeld Wins Assurances in Central Asia."

31. Wood, "Tajikistan Important to War on Terrorism"; David S. Cloud, "Rumsfeld in Tajikistan, Urges Tough Stand against Taliban," *NYT* (July 11, 2006).

32. Kucera, "US Aid to Central Asia: The Rhetoric and the Numbers Are at Odds with One Another."

33. "US Assistance to Tajikistan—Fiscal Year 2007," *Embassy of the United States—Dushanbe* (October 28, 2007).

34. Kucera, "US Aid to Central Asia: The Rhetoric and the Numbers Are at Odds with One Another."

35. Jonson, *Vladimir Putin and Central Asia*, pp. 149–51.

36. Ibid.

37. Ibid., p. 160.

38. Dmitry Solovyov, "Tajikistan Adds Years to Power of Leader," *BG* (June 24, 2003).

39. Zafar Abdullahaev and Saida Nazarova, "Tajikistan: Referendum Result Controversy," *Institute for War and Peace* (June 28, 2003).

40. Ibid.

41. Ibid.

42. Richard E. Hoagland, "Democracy and Tajikistan," *United States Embassy in Dushanbe Press Release* (March 2, 2004).

43. See Bruce Pannier, "OSCE: Tajik Elections Fall Short of Standards," *RFE/RL* (February 28, 2005); Embassy of the United States Dushanbe, Tajikistan, "Press Releases: US Embassy Statement on Parliamentary Elections in Tajikistan" (February 28, 2005).

44. OSCE Election Observation Mission, Presidential Election, Republic of Tajikistan—November 6, 2006, "Statement of Preliminary Findings and Conclusions," pp. 1–12, especially pp. 1–2; see also Bruce Pannier, "Tajikistan: Experts Say Incumbent President Will Be Easily Re-Elected," *EURASIANET.org* (October 8, 2006), http://www.eurasianet.org/departments/insight/articles/pp100806_pr.shtml; Joanna Lillis, "Tajikistan: No Surprises in Presidential Election," *EURASIANET.org* (November 6, 2006).

45. Christopher Pala, "Tajikistan and Kyrgyzstan Vote, Observers See Trouble," "A Lopsided Victory Is Seen for Tajikistan's Ruling Party," *NYT* (February 28, March 1, 2005, respectively).

46. Roger McDermott, "Tajikistan Fosters Security Links with Iran," *Eurasia Daily Monitor* (May 10, 2005).

47. "Iran Seeks Expanding Military Presence in Central Asia," *Iran Press Service* (March 10, 2001); "Iran, Tajikistan to Join Hands against Shared Danger: President Khatami," *Pravda* (March 4, 2004), http://newsfromRussia.com/world/2004/03/04/52627.html.

48. McDermott, "Tajikistan Fosters Security Links with Iran."

49. Ibid.

50. Ibid.

51. Ibid.

52. Roger McDermott, "Iran Builds Partnership with Tajikistan," *Eurasia Daily Monitor* (July 25, 2006).

53. Bruce Pannier, "Rakhmonov Hosts Iranian, Afghanistan Presidents," *RFE/RL* (July 25, 2006).

54. Ibid.; see also "Ahmadinejad Is Visiting Tajikistan," *NEWEURASIA.NET* (July 26, 2006).

55. "Iran-Tajikistan Enhanced Ties in Favor of the Region," "Iran, Tajik Presidents Stress Enhanced Ties," *Islamic Republic News Agency* (May 8, 9, 2007, respectively).

56. Ibid.

57. Daniel Kimmage, "Tajikistan: No Surprises Expected in Presidential Election," *RFE/RL* (November 3, 2006).

58. Kambiz Arman, "US Loses Grip on Geopolitical Position in Tajikistan: As Tajikistan Has Strengthened Its Ties with Both Russia and China, the Appeal of Strategic Cooperation with the U.S. Seems to Be Fading," *ISN* (August 20, 2005); Antoine Blua, "Tajikistan: Traders Look to China for Brighter Fortunes," *RFE/RL* (August 20, 2004).

59. Australian Government, Department of Foreign Affairs and Trade, "Tajikistan Country Brief" (January 21, 2005).

60. Jonson, *Vladimir Putin and Central Asia*, pp. 94–95.

61. Ibid., p. 108.

62. Mukhin, "Russian and American Interests Clash in Tajikistan."

63. Ibid.

64. Ibid.

65. Ibid.

66. Vladimir Davlatov, "Russia: Tajiks Face Deportation," *Institute for War and Peace* (November 19, 2002); Sanobar Shermatova, "Tajik Snub to Russia?" *International Eurasian Institute for Economic and Political Research* (December 4, 2002); see also Catherine Davis, "Moscow Deports Tajik Migrants," *BBC News* (November 24, 2002).

67. Ibid.

68. "Russia, Tajikistan Spar Over Illegal Labor Migration," *Tajikistan Development Gateway* (January 9, 2003); Abdullo, "Tajikistan Turns to the West."

69. Davlatov, "Russia: Tajiks Face Deportation"; Shermatova, "Tajik Snub to Russia?" see also Davis, "Moscow Deports Tajik Migrants."

70. "Russia Tightens Rules on Migrants," *BBC News* (November 16, 2006).

71. Jonson, *Vladimir Putin and Central Asia*, pp. 94–95.

72. Bruce Pannier, "Tajikistan: Relations with Moscow Appear to Have Reached an Impasse," *RFE/RL* (March 15, 2004).

73. See Davlatov, "Russia: Tajiks Face Deportation."

74. Jonson, *Vladimir Putin and Central Asia*, pp. 94–95.

75. Abdullayev, "Tajikistan, Russia Probe Military Partnership"; "Tajikistan: First Permanent Military Base Opened," *RFE/RL* (October 17, 2004); "Russian Military Base in Tajikistan to Ensure Regional Security," *MOSNEWS* (October 18, 2004).

76. "Tajikistan: First Permanent Military Base Opened."

77. Russ Oil-Gas, "Gazprom Gets Gas, Oil Prospect License in Tajikistan" (Moscow, December 29, 2006).

78. "This Week at a Glance," *RFE/RL Central Asia Report*, Vol. 4, No. 4 (June 8, 2004), pp. 1–6, especially p. 2.

79. For a Russian view of the enormity of potential U.S. aid to Tajikistan, see Mukhin, "Russian and American Interests Clash in Tajikistan."

80. "Zarifi Hails Russian-Tajik Cooperation," *New Europe*, http://www.neurope.eu/print.php?id=79137.

81. Roger McDermott, "Tajikistan Restates Its Strategic Partnership with Russia, While Sending Mixed Signals," *Eurasia Daily Monitor*, Vol. 4, No. 81 (April 25, 2007).

82. Ibid.

83. Ibid.

84. Ibid.

85. "Tajikistan to Ask Putin for Amnesty," *Kommersant* (September 18, 2007), http://www.kommersant.com/p805527/r_immigration_policy/.

86. Ibid.

87. "Russia's Asia Allies Fail to Back Georgia Action."

88. John Boyle, "Russia's Medvedev Looks East for Support on Georgia," *Star Online Worldupdates* (August 28, 2008); LiveMint.com, "Russia Wins Some Support from Tajik Ally Over Georgia," *Reuters* (August 29, 2008); see also Patrick Goodenough, "Moscow Looks East for Support," *CNSNews.com* (August 27, 2008), http://www.cnsnews.com/public/content/article.aspx?RsrcID=34664.

CHAPTER 5

1. Jonson, *Vladimir Putin and Central Asia*, pp. 162–63.

2. Lange, "Intervention and Conflict Resolution in Central Asia."

3. Gretsky, "Russia's Policy toward Central Asia," p. 20.

4. Jonson, *Vladimir Putin and Central Asia*, p. 54.

5. Fiona Hill, "Prospects for Political Change," Testimony before the U.S. Helsinki Committee (July 25, 2006).

6. Jonson, *Vladimir Putin and Central Asia*, p. 54.

7. Ibid.

8. Paul Kolstoe, *Russians in the Former Soviet Union* (Bloomington, Indiana: University of Indiana Press, 1995), footnote 76, p. 223; for more detail on the language issue for the Russian minority in Uzbekistan as well as the larger context in which it has developed in the postindependence period, see David Macfayden, *Russian Culture in Uzbekistan: One Language in the Middle of Nowhere* (New York: Routledge Publishers, 2006), *passim*.

9. Peter Trunscott, *Russia First: Breaking with the West* (London: I. B. Taurus, 1997), p. 93.

10. Jonson, *Vladimir Putin and Central Asia*, pp. 54–55; see also Sharam Akbar-zadeh, *Uzbekistan and the United States: Authoritarianism, Islamism, and Washington's New Security Agenda* (New York: Palgrave, 2005), *passim*.

11. Ibid.

12. For a brief analysis of the development of Uzbek relations with the United States, see John C. K. Daly, Kurt H. Meppen, Vladimir Socor, and S. Frederick Star, *Anatomy of a Crisis: US-Uzbekistan Relations 2001–2005* (Washington DC: Central Asia-Caucasus Institute & Silk Road Studies Program, 2006), pp. 5–12.

13. Ibid.

14. Ibid.

15. Ibid.; see also Bruce Pannier, "Central Asia: Odd Couple Crashes NATO Summit," *RFE/RL* (April 1, 2008).

16. Daly, Meppen, Socor, and Star, *Anatomy of a Crisis: US-Uzbekistan Relations 2001–2005*, p. 21.

17. Ibid., p. 15.

18. Yuri Fedorov, "Washington Pushes Karimov Closer to Moscow," *Eurasia Daily Monitor*, Vol. 1, no. 57 (July 24, 2004), http://www.cdi.org/Russia/315-12.cfm.

19. For an extensive documentation of Karimov's repressive rule, see U.S. Department of State, "Uzbekistan: Country Reports on Human Rights Practices—2004," *Bureau of Democracy, Human Rights, and Labor* (February 28, 2005), pp. 1–19, *passim*.

20. Daly, Meppen, Socor, and Star, *Anatomy of a Crisis: US-Uzbekistan Relations 2001–2005*, pp. 15–16; Kenley Butler, "Uzbekistan's Alliance with the United States: Benefits and Risks," *CNS* (Monterey Institute of International Studies, October 11, 2001) http://cns.miis.edu/research/wtc01/uzbek1.htm.

21. Daly, Meppen, Socor, and Star, *Anatomy of a Crisis: US-Uzbekistan Relations 2001–2005*, pp. 22–23, 28.

22. For a review of U.S. concern about Karimov's authoritarian leadership, see Rumer, "The US Interests and Role in Central Asia after K2," pp. 141–54, especially p. 145.

23. U.S. Department of State, "Uzbekistan: Country Reports on Human Rights Practices—2002 (for 2001), 2003 (for 2002)," *Bureau of Democracy, Human Rights, and Labor* (March 4, 2002, March 31, 2003), pp. 1–18, 1–22, respectively, *passim*.

24. Daly, Meppen, Socor, and Star, *Anatomy of a Crisis: US-Uzbekistan Relations 2001–2005*, pp. 22–23.

25. Ibid., pp. 17, 27; Butler, "Uzbekistan's Alliance with the United States: Benefits and Risks."

26. Jonson, *Vladimir Putin and Central Asia*, pp. 110–11.

27. Ibid., pp. 70–71.

28. For a review of U.S. concern about Karimov's authoritarian leadership, see Rumer, "The US Interests and Role in Central Asia after K2," pp. 141–54, especially p. 144.

29. Brian Grodsky, "Direct Pressures for Human Rights in Uzbekistan: Understanding the US Bargaining Position," Central Asia Survey (December 2004), pp. 327–44, especially p. 335; see also Jonson, *Vladimir Putin and Central Asia*, pp. 86–88.

30. U.S. Department of State, "Uzbekistan: Country Reports on Human Rights Practices—2003," *Bureau of Democracy, Human Rights, and Labor* (February 24, 2004), p. 1, http://www.state.gov/g/drl/rls/hrrpt/2003/27873.htm.

31. Rumer, "The US Interests and Role in Central Asia after K2," p. 145.

32. Daly, Meppen, Socor, and Star, *Anatomy of a Crisis: US-Uzbekistan Relations 2001–2005*, p. 24.

33. U.S. Department of State, "Uzbekistan: Country Reports on Human Rights Practices—2002, 2003, 2004, 2005," *Bureau of Democracy, Human Rights, and Labor* (February 28, 2005), pp. 1–22, 1–25, 1–19, respectively, *passim*.

34. For the U.S. dilemma, see Butler, "Uzbekistan's Alliance with the United States: Benefits and Risks."

35. Philip T. Reeker, "United States–Uzbekistan Joint Security Cooperation Consultations," U.S. Department of State, Press Statement (April 15, 2003); see also Rumer, "The US Interests and Role in Central Asia after K2," pp. 141–54, especially p. 146.

36. Daly, Meppen, Socor, and Star, *Anatomy of a Crisis: US-Uzbekistan Relations 2001–2005*, p. 31.

37. "Lukoil Signs a Production Sharing Agreement on the Kandym-Khausak-Ahady Project in Uzbekistan" (June 16, 2004); "RUSSIA—LUKoil Leads in External E&P Investment," *APS Review Downstream Trends* (September 6, 2004).

38. Daly, Meppen, Socor, and Star, *Anatomy of a Crisis: US-Uzbekistan Relations 2001–2005*, p. 26.

39. Steven Lee Myers, "At Least 10 Die as Conflict Erupts in Restive Uzbek Area," *NYT* (May 14, 2005); Paul Tumelty, "Analysis: Uzbekistan's Islamists," *BBC News* (May 15, 2005); "Uzbekistan Politics: Cracks in the Karimov Regime—Update," *EIU* (Economist Intelligence Unit) ViewsWire (May 16, 2005).

40. Myers, "At Least 10 Die as Conflict Erupts in Restive Uzbek Area"; see also Burt Herman, "Uzbek Leader Defies Calls for Probe," *BG* (May 21, 2005); C. J. Chivers, "Survivors and Toe Tags Offer Clues to Uzbeks' Uprising," *NYT* (May 23, 2005).

41. C. J. Chivers, "Uzbekistan Shaken by Unrest, Violence and Uncertainty," "Six Senators Urge Reassessment of Ties with Uzbekistan Ruler," "Under Pressure, Uzbek President Raises Toll from Deadly Unrest," *NYT* (May 16, 18, 2005, June 9, 2005, respectively); see also Daly, Meppen, Socor, and Star, *Anatomy of a Crisis: US-Uzbekistan Relations 2001–2005*, p. 35.

42. C. J. Chivers, "Uzbek Ministries in Crackdown Received American Aid," *NYT* (June 18, 2005).

43. Ethan Wilensky-Lanford, "Uzbeks Threaten to Evict U.S. from an Air Base Near Afghanistan," *NYT* (July 8, 2005).

44. Daly, Meppen, Socor, and Star, *Anatomy of a Crisis: US-Uzbekistan Relations 2001–2005*, pp. 47, 50; "Limits on Uzbek Air Base Spur Shift," *BG* (June 15, 2005); Wilensky-Lanford, "Uzbeks Threaten to Evict U.S. from an Air base Near Afghanistan"; "Uzbekistan Wants U.S. to Pay for Airbase," *Moscow News* (July 8, 2005).

45. Wilensky-Lanford, "Uzbeks Threaten to Evict U.S. from an Air Base Near Afghanistan."

46. Gulnoza Saidazimova, "What Does Closure of U.S. Military Base in Uzbekistan Mean?" *Iran News* (August 2, 2005).

47. Rumer, "The US Interests and Role in Central Asia after K2," pp. 148–49.

48. Daly, Meppen, Socor, and Star, *Anatomy of a Crisis: US-Uzbekistan Relations 2001–2005*, p. 45.

49. Ibid., pp. 52–53.

50. Ibid.

51. Peter Lavelle, "Analysis: Experts on Uzbekistan's Fate," *UPI.com* (May 20, 2005), http://www.upi.com/Security_Industry/2005/05/20/Analysis-Experts-on-Uzbekistans-fate/UPI-18261116599609/print/.

52. See Mathew Davis, "Uzbek Crisis Poses Dilemma for US," *BBC News* (Washington, May 16, 2005), http://news.bbc.co.uk/1/hi/world/asia-pacific/4552463.stm.

53. Thom Shanker and C. J. Chivers, "Crackdown in Uzbekistan Reopens Long-Standing Debate on U.S. Military Aid," *NYT* (July 13, 2005).

54. Steven Weisman and Thom Shanker, "Uzbeks Order US from Base," *NYT* (July 31, 2005); Eric Schmitt, "No Harm Seen in Loss of Base in Uzbekistan," *NYT* (August 8, 2005); Ann Scott Tyson and Robin Wright, "Uzbek Crackdown Puts U.S. in a Quandary," "U.S. Evicted from Uzbek Base," *BG* (June 5, July 31, 2005, respectively).

55. Schmitt, "No Harm Seen in Loss of Base in Uzbekistan"; Tyson and Wright, "Uzbek Crackdown Puts U.S. in a Quandary," "U.S. Evicted from Uzbek Base."

56. Rumer, "The US Interests and Role in Central Asia after K2," p. 147.

57. Martha Brill Olcott, "Prospects for Political Change in Uzbekistan," Testimony before the U.S. Helsinki Committee, Briefing on Prospects for Political Change (July 25, 2006).

58. Tyson and Wright, "U.S. Evicted from Air Base in Uzbekistan," *WP* (July 30, 2005).

59. Ibid.

60. Rumer, "The US Interests and Role in Central Asia after K2," p. 148.

61. Bruce Pannier, "Uzbekistan: Departure from Base Underlines US-Uzbek Tensions," *RFE/RL* (September 28, 2005); Daly, Meppen, Socor, and Star, *Anatomy of a Crisis: US-Uzbekistan Relations 2001–2005*, p. 60.

62. Saidazimova, "What Does Closure of U.S. Military Base in Uzbekistan Mean?"

63. "United States Cuts Off Aid to Uzbekistan," *EURASIANET.org* (July 14, 2004).

64. "The US Administration Tries to Isolate the Former Soviet Republic from the Rest of the World," *Pravda* (October 8, 2005).

65. Robin Wright, "Rice Signals Rift with Uzbekistan," *BG* (October 11, 2005).

66. Schmitt, "No Harm Seen in Loss of Base in Uzbekistan."

67. Daly, Meppen, Socor, and Star, *Anatomy of a Crisis: US-Uzbekistan Relations 2001–2005*, p. 37; Saidazimova, "What Does Closure of U.S. Military Base in Uzbekistan Mean?"

68. Joshua Kucera, "One Year after Andijan: US Lawmakers Take Action to Punish Uzbekistan," *EURASIANET.org* (May 11, 2006), http://www.eurasianet.org/departments/insight/articles/eav051106_pr.shtml.

69. "U.S. Senate Blocks Uzbek Payment," *BBC News* (October 8, 2005).

70. See Charles Carlson, "Uzbekistan: Karimov Says Improved Relations with Russia Not at the Expense of US ties," *EURASIANET.org* (September 6, 2003), http://www.eurasianet.org/departments/insight/articles/pp090603_pr.shtml.

71. Jonathan Beale, "Rice's Soft Tone in Central Asia," *BBC News* (October 11, 2005); Wright, "Rice Signals Rift with Uzbekistan"; see also Robert McMahon, "Central Asia: Russia and US Often at Odds," *RFE/RL* (October 25, 2005).

72. Ibid.

73. Hill, "Prospects for Political Change."

74. "Uzbek Court Suspends Work of US Group," *NYT* (January 14, 2006).

75. Sarah Shenker, "Struggle for Influence in Central Asia," *BBC News* (January 27, 2005); McMahon, "Central Asia: Russia and US Often at Odds in Region."

76. Olcott, "Prospects for Political Change in Uzbekistan."

77. "Uzbekistan Is Expected to Re-Elect Its President," *NYT* (December 24, 2007).

78. Adam Albion, "Putin in Samarkand: The 'Old Friend' Returns," *RFE/RL Newsline* (August 11, 2003), http://www.cdi.org/Russia/Johnson/7285-16.cfm.

79. Ibid.

80. Ibid.; Carlson, "Uzbekistan: Karimov Says Improved Relations with Russia Not at the Expense of US Ties."

81. Albion, "Putin in Samarkand: The 'Old Friend' Returns."

82. Yuri Fedorov, "Uzbekistan Looks toward Russia," *Eurasia Daily Monitor*, Vol. 1, No. 7 (June 23, 2004).

83. Fedorov, "Washington Pushes Karimov Closer to Moscow."

84. Herman, "Uzbek Leader Defies Calls for Probe."

85. See "Russia Closely Following Uzbekistan Unrest," *People's Daily* (May 14, 2005).

86. Ibid.

87. "Uzbekistan: Support from Russia," *NYT* (June 30, 2005); "Uzbek President Tells Putin of Foreign Link in Recent Riots," *MOSNEWS* (June 29, 2005), http://www.mosnews.com/news/2005/06/29/karimovreveals.shtml; "President of Uzbekistan and Russia Meet," *Embassy of Uzbekistan in the United States* (June 29, 2005), http://www.uzbekistan.org/news/archive/236/?print=1.

88. Bruce Pannier, "Uzbekistan: Military Exercises with Russia Timely for Tashkent," *RFE/RL* (September 23, 2005); Daly, Meppen, Socor, and Star, *Anatomy of a Crisis: US-Uzbekistan Relations 2001–2005*, pp. 58–59.

89. "U.S.A. Intends to Bring Economic Sanctions against Uzbekistan and Jail Uzbek President," *Pravda* (October 3, 2005); McMahon, "Central Asia: Russia and US Often at Odds."

90. Erich Marquardt and Yevgeny Bendersky, "Uzbekistan's New Foreign Policy Strategy," *Power and Interest News Report* (November 23, 2005); Daly, Meppen,

Socor, and Star, *Anatomy of a Crisis: US-Uzbekistan Relations 2001–2005*, pp. 63–64.

91. Ibid.

92. Shenker, "Struggle for Influence in Central Asia."

93. Marquardt and Bendersky, "Uzbekistan's New Foreign Policy Strategy"; Daly, Meppen, Socor, and Star, *Anatomy of a Crisis: US-Uzbekistan Relations 2001–2005*, pp. 63–64.

94. Shenker, "Struggle for Influence in Central Asia."

95. Ignor Torbakov, "Russia's Warming toward Uzbekistan May Damage Relations with the West," *Eurasia Daily Monitor*, Vol. 2, no. 214 (November 16, 2005).

96. Roger McDermott, "Russia Reclaiming Central Asia as a Sphere of Influence," *Eurasia Daily Monitor* (March 13, 2007).

97. Ibid.

98. Gulnoza Saidazimova, "Uzbekistan: President Karimov Meets with Close Ally Putin," *RFE/RL* (February 6, 2008), http://www.rferl.org/articleprintview/1079440.html.

99. Ibid.

100. Ibid.

101. Ibid.

102. Ibid.

103. "Uzbekistan: New US Ambassador, New Policy?" *EURASIANET.org* (November 13, 2007), http://www.eurasianet.org/departments/insight/articles/eav111307a_pr.shtml.

104. "US-Uzbekistan Relations: Another Step Toward Rapprochement?" *EURASIANET.org* (January 23, 2008).

105. Ibid.

106. Shamil Baigin, Olzhas Auyezov, Dmitry Solovyov, and Mary Gabriel, "US Urges Uzbekistan to Open Up for Dialogue," *Reuters* (March 27, 2008), http://www.reuters.com/articlePrint?articleId=USL2782922520080327.

107. Shamil Baigin, Maria Golovnina, and Elizabeth Piper, "US Praises Uzbekistan for Rights Improvement," *Reuters* (March 27, 2008), http://www.reuters.com/articlePrint?articleId=USL1365963520080313.

108. Erkin Akhmadov, "A Thaw in Relations between West and Uzbekistan," *Central Asia-Caucasus Institute Analyst* (March 19, 2008); see also "Uzbekistan May Let the United States Use a Military Airbase for Operations in Afghanistan," *Reuters* (March 5, 2008), http://www.reuters.com/articlePrint?articleId=USL0593284.

109. Akhmadov, "A Thaw in Relations between West and Uzbekistan."

110. Baigin, Golovnina, and Piper, "US Praises Uzbekistan for Rights Improvement"; Bruce Pannier, "Uzbek, Turkmen Presidents Offer Cooperation," *RFE/RL* (April 4, 2008).

111. "US-Uzbekistan Relations: Another Step Toward Rapprochement?" see also "Soviet Era Ends as Gazprom Pays Market Price," *Petroleum Economist* (2008).

112. Pannier, "Uzbek, Turkmen Presidents Offer Cooperation."

113. Daniel Kimmage, "Uzbekistan: Is Tashkent's Foreign Policy Going Multi-vector?" *RFE/RL* (March 9, 2007).

114. Daly, Meppen, Socor, and Star, *Anatomy of a Crisis: US-Uzbekistan Relations 2001–2005*, pp. 27; see also Eugene Rumer, "US Military Presence at Risk in Central Asia," *Eurasia Daily Monitor* (July 8, 2005).

115. See McMahon, "Central Asia: Russia and US Often at Odds in Region."

116. C. J. Chivers, "China Backs Uzbek, Splitting with U.S. on Crackdown," Joseph Kahn and Chris Buckley, "China Gives a Strategic 21 Gun Salute to Visiting Uzbek President," "China Honors a Friend," *NYT* (May 25, 26, 28, 2005, respectively); see also "China to Help Uzbekistan Struggle against Revolutions," *Pravda* (May 28, 2005), http://English.pravda.ru/world/20/02/373/15553_Uzbekistan.html.

117. "Uzbekistan Seeks China's Help against Terrorism," *Daily Times* (May 26, 2005), http://www.dailytimes.com.pk/default.asp?page=story_26-5-2005_pg4_7; "Karimov in China: Uzbekistan Reaches Out to a Rare Ally," *Current Affairs: Archive by Region: Central Asia* (May 26, 2005).

118. "President of Uzbekistan Starts China Visit," *People's Daily* (May 25, 2005), http://English.people.com.cn/200505/25/eng20050525_186761.html; "Karimov in China: Uzbekistan Reaches Out to a Rare Ally."

119. "China, Uzbekistan Sign Friendship Treaty," *ZEENEWS* (May 25, 2005); "China, Uzbekistan Agree Further Cooperation in Regional Security," *Xinhua* (May 26, 2005); "China Against 'External Influence' in Uzbekistan's Affairs—Envoy," *Interfax* monitored by BBC (June 21, 2005).

120. See Roger McDermott, "Uzbekistan's Relations with China Warming," *Eurasia Daily Monitor* (July 22, 2005).

121. Brad Macdonald, "US Diplomatic Rescue Mission Secures Military Base, for Now," *TheTrumpet.com*.

122. Antonenko, "Central Asia Watches Warily (the Russian Military Action in Georgia)"; "Uzbek Senior Deputy Premier Rustam Azimov Is Expected in Moscow," *Ferghama Information Agency* (August 25, 2008).

CHAPTER 6

1. *Freedom of the World Ratings 1989–1998, Kyrgyz Republic*, "Political Process 5.00/7," p. 325; Ella Akerman (ed.), *Political Culture Case Studies* (Conflict Studies Research Center #M27, March 2003); Rafis Abazov, "The Political Culture of Central Asia," pp. 43–56, especially p. 47.

2. "Joint Statement by President George W. Bush and President Askar Akayev on the Relationship between the United States and the Kyrgyz Republic," Office of the Press Secretary (September 23, 2002).

3. "Manas International Airport, Ganci Air Base, Bishkek, Kyrgyzstan," *GlobalSecurity.org*, http://www.globalsecurity.org/military/facility/manas.htm.

4. "Joint Statement by President George W. Bush and President Askar Akayev."

5. See "Kyrgyzstan Police Crush Protest Detaining 100," *NYT* (November 11, 2007).

6. Jonson, *Vladimir Putin and Central Asia*, p. 146.

7. Sanobar Shermatova, "Russia's Motives in Kyrgyzstan: Russia's Intent in Building an Air Base in Kyrgyzstan Is Clearly to Counterbalance U.S. Forces Stationed in the Region," *Russia Weekly* No. 13 (December 25–31, 2002); see also Jonson, *Vladimir Putin and Central Asia*, p. 103.

8. Sabrina Tavernise, "Kyrgyzstan and Russia Sign New Pact," *NYT* (December 7, 2002); see also Jonson, *Vladimir Putin and Central Asia*, pp. 103–4.

9. Sergei Blagov, "Russia Boosts Military Ties with Kyrgyzstan," *Asia Times* (June 15, 2002), http://www.atimes.com/c-asia/DF15Ag02.html; Shermatova, "Russia's Motives in Kyrgyzstan: Russia's Intent in Building an Air Base in Kyrgyzstan Is Clearly to Counterbalance U.S. Forces Stationed in the Region."

10. Blagov, "Russia Boosts Military Ties with Kyrgyzstan."

11. Ibid.

12. Allison, "Strategic Reassertion in Russia's Central Asia Policy," p. 288.

13. Ariel Cohen, "New Russian Deployment Marks Changed Strategy," *Russia Weekly* No. 236 (December 17, 2002), http://www.cdi.org/Russia/236-15-pr.cfm.

14. Ibid.

15. Allison, "Strategic Reassertion in Russia's Central Asia Policy," p. 288.

16. Ibid., p. 287.

17. Cohen, "New Russian Deployment Marks Changed Strategy."

18. Jonson, *Vladimir Putin and Central Asia*, p. 104.

19. Hamid Toursunof, "Opening the Door to Gazprom," *International Eurasian Institute for Economic and Political Research* (Transitions On Line, June 2, 2003).

20. Shermatova, "Russia's Motives in Kyrgyzstan: Russia's Intent in Building an Air Base in Kyrgyzstan Is Clearly to Counterbalance U.S. Forces Stationed in the Region."

21. "Revolution in Kyrgyzstan," *RFE/RL* (March 25, 2005), p. 7.

22. Ibid.; Roman Ginzburg, "The Parliamentary Elections in Kyrgyzstan," *Carnegie Endowment for International Peace* (March 22, 2005).

23. See "Protests in Kyrgyzstan," *Human Rights Watch*; "The Parliamentary Elections in Kyrgyzstan"; Scott Parish and Margarita Sevcik, "Kyrgyz Government Ousted," *CNS* (March 24, 2005), pp. 1–4, *passim*, http://cns.miis.edu/pubs/week/050324.htm.

24. Ibid.; see also Christopher Pala, "Cries of Fraud Give Election in Kyrgyzstan Aura of Ukraine," *NYT* (March 14, 2005).

25. Christopher Pala, "Denouncing Elections, Protesters Gather for Rallies in Kyrgyzstan," *NYT* (March 15, 2005); Michael Steen, "Violence Rocks South Kyrgyzstan," *BG* (March 21, 2005).

26. Ibid.

27. Parish and Sevcik, "Kyrgyz Government Ousted," pp. 1–4, *passim*.

28. "Russia Says Not to Interfere in Kyrgyzstan's Internal Affairs," *XINHUANET* (Moscow, March 31, 2005), http://www.klasney.com/kyrgyzrevolution/2005/03/Russia-says-not-to-interfere-in.html; see also Minton F. Goldman, "Polish-Russian Relations and the 2004 Ukrainian Presidential Elections," *East European Quarterly*, Vol. 40, No. 4 (Winter 2006), pp. 409–28, *passim*.

29. Craig Smith, "U.S. Helped to Prepare the Way for Kyrgyzstan's Uprising," *NYT* (March 30, 2005).

30. Ibid.

31. Ibid.

32. See Erica Marat, "Tensions Rising Ahead of Kyrgyz Presidential Elections," *Eurasia Daily Monitor*, Vol. 2, No. 129 (July 5, 2005).

33. Ibid.

34. Stephen Blank, "After the Tulip Revolution: Are Sino-Kyrgyz Relations Still Alive and Kicking?" *Eurasia Daily Monitor*, Vol. 2, No. 203 (November 1, 2005); Mathew Oresman, "Assessing China's Reaction to Kyrgyzstan's 'Tulip Revolution,' " *Central Asia-Caucasus Analyst* (April 6, 2005).

35. Craig Smith, "Crisis Grips Kyrgyzstan; Ousted Chief Is in Russia," *NYT* (March 27, 2005); Kadry Toktogulov, "Kyrgyz Officials Striving for Order," *BG* (March 27, 2005).

36. Ulugbek Djuraev, "The Battle for Kyrgyzia: The Kremlin Is leading 1:0," *Axis Information and Analysis* (May 9, 2005).

37. Ibid.

38. Djuraev, "The Battle for Kyrgyzia: The Kremlin Is leading 1:0."

39. Ibid.

40. Djuraev, "The Battle for Kyrgyzia: The Kremlin Is leading 1:0"; see also Kimmage, "Central Asia: The Mechanics of Russian Influence"; Ulugbek Djuraev, "Kyrgyzstan Attacks the USA Counting on Russia and China," *Axis Information and Analysis* (April 20, 2005), http://www.axisglobe.com/print_article.asp?article=804.

41. Gulnoza Saidazimova, "Kyrgyzstan: Old Actors, New Priorities—Or Are They Old Priorities?" *RFE/RL* (April 14, 2005).

42. Ibid.

43. Djuraev, "Kyrgyzstan Attacks the USA Counting on Russia and China."

44. Ibid.

45. Craig S. Smith, "Kyrgyzstan's Shining Hour Ticks Away and Turns Out to Be a Plain, Old Coup," *NYT* (April 3, 2005); see also Djuraev, "Kyrgyzstan Attacks the USA Counting on Russia and China."

46. For a thorough assessment of the July 2005 presidential elections in Kyrgyzstan, see Linda Kartawich and Espen Eftedal Svensen, "Kyrgyzstan: Early Presidential Election July, 2005," *Nordem Report* (July 13, 2005), pp. 1–24, *passim.*

47. Smith, "Kyrgyzstan's Shining Hour Ticks Away and Turns Out to Be a Plain, Old Coup"; see also Djuraev, "Kyrgyzstan Attacks the USA Counting on Russia and China."

48. Ibid.

49. C. J. Chivers, "Interim Kyrgyz President Is Expected to Win a Quiet Election," "Leader Wins 88 Percent of Vote in Kyrgyzstan," *NYT* (July 11, 12, 2005, respectively); UN Office for the Coordination of Humanitarian Affairs, "Kyrgyzstan: Focus on Major Players Ahead of Presidential Polls," *IRINnews* (April 27, 2005); see also Marat, "Tensions Rising Ahead of Kyrgyz Presidential Elections."

50. Smith, "Kyrgyzstan's Shining Hour Ticks Away and Turns Out to Be a Plain, Old Coup"; see also Djuraev, "Kyrgyzstan Attacks the USA Counting on Russia and China."

51. Chivers, "Interim Kyrgyz President Is Expected to Win a Quiet Election," "Leader Wins 88 Percent of Vote in Kyrgyzstan"; UN Office for the Coordination of Humanitarian Affairs, "Kyrgyzstan: Presidential Polls Show Significant Improvements in Democracy Building," *IRINnews* (August 21, 2005); "Akayev Backs Political Opponents for Upcoming Election," *RFE/RL* (July 1, 2005).

52. Ibid.

53. "Bakiyev Wins Landslide in Kyrgyzstan, Courts Controversy with the United States," *EURASIANET.org* (July 11, 2005), http://www.eurasianet.org/departments/insight/articles/eav071105_pr.shtml.

54. Chivers, "Leader Wins 88 Percent of Vote in Kyrgyzstan"; UN Office for the Coordination of Humanitarian Affairs (August 21, 2005); "Focus on Many Players Ahead of Presidential Polls," *IRINnews* (Bishkek, April 27, 2005); see also Djuraev, "Kyrgyzstan Attacks the USA Counting on Russia and China"; see also Kartawich and Svensen, "Kyrgyzstan: Early Presidential Election July, 2005," p. 4.

55. Chivers, "Interim Kyrgyz President Is Expected to Win a Quiet Election," "Leader Wins 88 Percent of Vote in Kyrgyzstan."

56. UN Office for the Coordination of Humanitarian Affairs (August 21, 2005); "Bakiyev Wins Landslide in Kyrgyzstan, Courts Controversy with the United States."

57. "USA to Keep Its Army Bases in Post-Soviet States to Control Afghanistan and Put Pressure on China," *Pravda* (July 27, 2005); see also Joldosh Osmonov, "The US Kyrgyz Military Base Negotiations," *Central Asia-Caucasus Institute* (June 9, 2006), pp. 1–3, especially p. 2.

58. Ibid.; see also Saidazimova, "Kyrgyzstan: Old Actors, New Priorities."

59. Gulnoza Saidazimova, "Bishkek Assures Rumsfeld That U.S. Air Base Can Stay," *EURASIANET.org* (July 26, 2005), http://www.eurasianet.org/departments/insight/articles/pp062605.shtml.

60. Ibid.

61. "USA to Keep Its Army Bases in Post-Soviet States to Control Afghanistan and Put Pressure on China."

62. Barbara Slavin, "Kyrgyzstan Will Allow US to Keep Using Air Base," *USA TODAY* (October 12, 2005); Joel Brinkley, "Rice Reaches Pact on Keeping Central Asia Base," *NYT* (October 12, 2005).

63. Ibid.

64. "American Military Base in Kyrgyzstan: Afterthoughts" (August 26, 2006), http://kyrgyzstan.neweurasia.net/?p=88.

65. Bruce Pannier, "Kyrgyzstan: Russian, US Military Bases on Opposite Tracks," *EURASIANET.org* (February 20, 2006), http://www.eurasianet.org/departments/insight/articles/pp022006_pr.shtml; "US Military Base in Kyrgyzstan Comes into Play as Domestic Political Confrontation Brews," *EURASIANET.org* (April 20, 2006), http://www.eurasianet.org/departments/insight/articles/eav042006_pr.shtml.

66. "US Military Base in Kyrgyzstan Comes into Play as Domestic Political Confrontation Brews"; "Big Protests in Kyrgyzstan," *NYT* (April 30, 2006).

67. Leila Saralayova, "Proposal Pacifies Kyrgyz Protests," *BG* (November 8, 2006); "Kyrgyzstan: Parliament Curbs President's Powers," *NYT* (November 9, 2006).

68. "US Military Base in Kyrgyzstan Comes into Play as Domestic Political Confrontation Brews."

69. Ibid.

70. Ibid.

71. The Hill Staff, "Kyrgyz-Russian Ties Could Affect the US," *The Hill* (May 9, 2006); Jean-Christophe Peuch, "Kyrgyzstan: Negotiations Over US Base End Inconclusively," *RFE/RL* (June 1, 2006); Elena Chadova, "Negotiations on US Military Base in Kyrgyz Raise Transparency Concerns," *EURASIANET.org* (June 5, 2006), http://www.eurasianet.org/departments/insight/articles/eav060506_pr.shtml.

72. Brad Macdonald, "US Diplomatic Rescue Mission Secures Base, for Now."

73. Brinkley, "Rice Reaches Pact on Keeping Central Asia Base."

74. Antoine Blua, "Kyrgyzstan: Russia Hopes to Double Troops at Base as Future of U.S. Base in Doubt," *EURASIANET.org* (July 16, 2005), http://www.eurasianet.org/departments/insight/articles/pp071605.shtml; "Russia Ratifies Air Base Agreement with Kyrgyzstan," *RFE/RL* (July 8, 2005).

75. "Immigration from Kyrgyzstan to Russia on the Rise—Ambassador," *Central Asia-Caucasus Institute* (August 2, 2006); see also Chivers, "Leader Wins 88 Percent of Vote in Kyrgyzstan"; UN Office for the Coordination of Humanitarian Affairs (August 21, 2005); "Kyrgyzstan: Focus on Major Players Ahead of Presidential Polls."

76. Pannier, "Kyrgyzstan: Russian, US Military Bases on Opposite Tracks"; Sergei Blagov, "Russian Economic and Strategic influence in Kyrgyzstan Set to Expand," *EURASIANET.org* (April 25, 2006).

77. Blagov, "Russian Economic and Strategic Influence in Kyrgyzstan Set to Expand."

78. Ibid.; The Hill Staff, "Kyrgyz-Russian Ties Could Affect the US"; see also "US Military Base in Kyrgyzstan Comes into Play as Domestic Political Confrontation Brews."

79. Blagov, "Russian Economic and Strategic influence in Kyrgyzstan Set to Expand"; The Hill Staff, "Kyrgyz-Russian Ties Could Affect the US."

80. The Hill Staff, "Kyrgyz-Russian Ties Could Affect the US"; Peuch, "Kyrgyzstan: Negotiations Over US Base End Inconclusively"; see also Chadova, "Negotiations on US Military Base in Kyrgyz Raise Transparency Concerns."

81. See Erica Marat, "Kyrgyz Government Risks Relations with the US before the G-8 Summit," *Eurasia Daily Monitor* (July 13, 2006).

82. "US-Kyrgyz Relations Back on Solid Ground—But for How Long?" *EURASIANET.org* (August 23, 2006); Roger McDermott, "Boucher Visit to Bishkek Reveals Widening Gap in US-Kyrgyz Relations," *Eurasia Daily Monitor* (August 15, 2006).

83. "US-Kyrgyz Relations Back on Solid Ground—But for How Long?" McDermott, "Boucher Visit to Bishkek Reveals Widening Gap in US-Kyrgyz Relations."

84. Daniel Sershen, "Kyrgyzstan: Base Shooting Sours US-Kyrgyz Relations," *EURASIANET.org* (December 19, 2006), http://www.eurasianet.org/departments/insight/articles/eav121906_pr.shtml.

85. Ibid.

86. Ibid.

87. Ibid.

88. See Marat, "Kyrgyz Government Risks Relations with the US before the G-8 Summit."

89. Sershen, "Kyrgyzstan: Base Shooting Sours US-Kyrgyz Relations."

90. Macdonald, "US Diplomatic Rescue Mission Secures Base, for Now."

91. Ibid.

92. McDermott, "Boucher Visit to Bishkek Reveals Widening Gap in US-Kyrgyz Relations"; see also "Gates and Boucher Visits to Kyrgyzstan, Muted Responses," *Institute for the Study of Conflict, Ideology, and Policy* (June 28, 2007).

93. Daniel Sershen, "Anti-Western Direction," *Transition on Line* (May 24, 2007).

94. "Davoudi Calls for Upgrading Iran-Kyrgyz Ties," *Islamic Republic News Agency* (September 29, 2007).

95. Sershen, "Anti-Western Direction."

96. Erica Marat, "Kyrgyz Officials, Citizens Oppose US Base," *Eurasia Daily Monitor*, Vol. 4, No. 102 (May 24, 2007).

97. Ibid.

98. Ibid.; "US Airbase in Kyrgyzstan Says No Sign of Closure" (February 4, 2009).

99. Alexander Cooley, "How the US Lost Its Kyrgyzstan Air Base," *International Herald Tribune* (February 10, 2009).

100. Macdonald, "US Diplomatic Rescue Mission Secures Base, for Now."

101. "Felix Kulov Suggests a Confederation with Russia: Kyrgyzstan," *Turkish Weekly* (June 1, 2007).

102. Ibid.; "Kyrgyzstan Says Russians Will Retain Military Presence," *REA Novosti* (March 25, 2008).

103. "Felix Kulov Suggests a Confederation with Russia: Kyrgyzstan."

104. Daniel Sershen, "Kyrgyzstan: An Anti-Western Mood Gains Strength," *EURASIANET.org* (May 22, 2007), http://www.eurasianet.org/departments/insight/articles/eav052207_pr.shtml; see also "American Military Base in Kyrgyzstan: Afterthoughts."

105. Cooley, "How the US Lost Its Kyrgyzstan Air Base."

106. "Kyrgyzstan President Orders US Air Base Closed: Announcement Comes Amid Russia Offered Millions to Kyrgyz Government," Anti-War.com (February 3, 2006); Ellen Barry, "Russia Offers Kind Words But Its Fist Is Clenched," *NYT* (February 6, 2009).

107. Rustam Mukhamedov, "Uyghurs in Kyrgyzstan under Careful Government Supervision," *Central Asia—Caucasus Analyst* (January 28, 2004); "China: Border Security Tightened Amid 'Terrorist Infiltration,'" *RFE/RL* (January 11, 2007).

108. John C. Daly, "Sino-Kyrgyz Relations after the Tulip Revolution," *China Brief*, Vol. 5, No. 9 (April 26, 2005).

109. Ibid.

110. Blank, "After the Tulip Revolution: Are Sino-Kyrgyz Relations Still Alive and Kicking?"

111. Ibid.

112. Erica Marat, "Conflict in South Ossetia Confuses Kyrgyz Government Ahead of CIS Summit," *Eurasia Daily Monitor* (August 14, 2008); "Kyrgyz Rights Activists Support Georgia's Withdrawal from CIS," *Turkish Weekly* (Ferghama News, August 14, 2008).

113. Patrick Goodenough, "Post-Soviet States May Be Pulled Towards Moscow after Georgian Crisis," *CNSNews.com* (August 22, 2008), http://www.cnsnews.com/public/content/article.aspx?RsrcID=34495.

114. Marat, "Conflict in South Ossetia Confuses Kyrgyz Government Ahead of CIS Summit"; "Kyrgyz Rights Activists Support Georgia's Withdrawal from CIS."

115. Erica Marat, "Can Nazarbayev Help Kyrgyzstan Escape Moscow's Pressure?" *Eurasia Daily Monitor* (September 5, 2008).

116. Goodenough, "Post-Soviet States May Be Pulled Towards Moscow after Georgian Crisis."

117. Ellen Barry and Michael Schwirtz, "Kyrgyzstan Wants to Close US Base Used for Afghan War," *NYT* (February 4, 2009); see also "USA Loses Air Base in Kyrgyzstan to Russia," *Pravda* (February 4, 2009).

118. "Kyrgyzstan Delays Vote on US Base," *BBC News* (February 5, 2009).

119. "US Airbase in Kyrgyzstan Says No Sign of Closure."

120. "Kyrgyzstan Says US Base Decision Is Final," *International Herald Tribune* (February 6, 2009).

121. Deidre Tynan, "Kyrgyzstan Mulls US Air Base Closing Bill," *ISN Eth Zurich* (February 5, 2009).

122. Elisabeth Bumiller and Ellen Barry, "US Searches for Alternative to Central Asian Base" *NYT* (February 5, 2009); Alexander Cooley, "Kyrgyzstan: The Five Lessons of the Great American Air Base Debate," *EURASIANET.org* (February 12, 2009).

123. Ibid.

124. Cooley, "Kyrgyzstan: The Five Lessons of the Great American Air Base Debate."

125. Ibid.

126. Ibid.; see also Bumiller and Barry, "US Searches for Alternative to Central Asian Base."

127. Vladimir Isachenkov, "Russia Says It Wants to help US in Afghanistan," *Yahoo News* (February 4, 2009); Nathan Hodge, "Air Base Loss Could Hobble Afghan War Effort," *Danger Room* (February 5, 2005); "Russia Allows Transit of US Supplies for Afghanistan," *Fox News* (February 6, 2009).

128. "Kyrgyz Parliament Mulls US Air Base Closing Bill."

129. Ibid.

Bibliography

CHAPTER 1: INTRODUCTION

Roy Allison, "Strategic Reassertion in Russia's Central Asia Policy," *International Affairs*, No. 2 (2004), pp. 277–93.

Sergei Blagov, "Eurasia Insight: Russian Leaders Mull Geopolitical Moves in 2005," *EURASIANET.org* (January 4, 2005).

Ian Bremmer and Samuel Charap, "The Siloviki in Putin's Russia: Who Are They and What They Want," *Washington Quarterly*, Vol. 30, No. 1 (Winter 2006–2007), pp. 83–92.

Dan Burghart, "The New Nomads? The American Military Presence in Central Asia," *China and Eurasia Forum Quarterly*, Vol. 5, No. 2 (2007), pp. 5–19, http://www.silkroadstudies.org/new/docs/CEF/Quarterly/May_2007/Burghart.pdf.

Ariel Cohen, "Security, Energy, and Democracy: US Interests in Central Asia," *EURASIANET.org* (December 6, 2006), http://www.eurasianet.org/departments/insight/articles/eav120606a_pr.shtml.

Robert M. Cutler, "Central Asia: Emerging Triangles: Russia-Kazakhstan-China," *Asia Times Online* (January 15, 2004), http://www.atimes.com/atimes/Central_Asia/FA15Ag03.html.

Golnaz Esfandiari, "Central Asia: Iran, Turkey Struggle to Influence Region," *Radio Free Europe/Radio Liberty* (October 25, 2005).

Stephen Foy, "Russia and the Near Abroad," *Post-Soviet Prospects*, Vol. 3, No. 12 (December 1995).

Sergei Gretsky, "Russia's Policy toward Central Asia," *Journal of Social and Political Studies*, http://www.ca-c.org/dataeng/GRETSKY.shtml.

Fiona Hill, "The United States and Russia in Central Asia: Uzbekistan, Tajikistan, Afghanistan, Pakistan, and Iran," The Brookings Institution, Paper Delivered to the Aspen Institute Congressional Program (August 15, 2002), http://www.brookings.edu/views/speeches/hillf/20020815.htm.

Lena Jonson, *Vladimir Putin and Central Asia: The Shaping of Russian Foreign Policy* (London: I. B. Tauris, 2005).

Daniel Kimmage, "Central Asia: The Mechanics of Russian Influence," *Radio Free Europe/Radio Liberty* (September 16, 2005), pp. 1–4.

Heinz Kramer, "Will Central Asia Become Turkey's Sphere of Influence?" Perceptions, Vol. 1 (March–May 1996), http://www.sam.gov.tr/perceptions/volume1/march-may1996/willcentralAsiabecometurkey.pdf.

Joshua Kucera, "US Aid to Central Asia: The Rhetoric and the Numbers Are at Odds with One Another," *EURASIANET.org* (February 6, 2007), http://eurasianet.org/departments/insight/articles/eav020607_pr.shtml.

Keely Lange, "Intervention and Conflict Resolution in Central Asia."

Gail W. Lapidus, "Central Asia in Russian and American Foreign Policy after September 11, 2001," Presentation from "Central Asia and Russia: Responses to the 'War on Terrorism,' " a panel discussion held at the University of California, Berkeley, on October 29, 2001, pp. 1–7.

Xuanli Liao, "Central Asia and China's Energy Security," *China and Eurasia Forum Quarterly*, Vol. 4, No. 4 (2006), pp. 61–69.

S. Neil Macfarlane, "The United States and Regionalism in Central Asia," *International Affairs*, Vol. 80, No. 3 (2004), pp. 447–61.

Roger McDermott, "Russia Reclaiming Central Asia as Sphere of Influence," *Eurasia Daily Monitor* (March 13, 2007).

Andranik Migrainian, "Geopolitics and the Near Abroad: The Entire Space of the Former USSR Is a Sphere of Russia's Vital Interests," *Nezavisimaya Gazeta* (January 18, 1994), in *Current Digest of the Post-Soviet Press*, Vol. 46, No. 6 (January 18, 1994), pp. 6–11.

———, "Russia and the Near Abroad," *Nezavisimaya Gazeta* (January 12, 1994), in *Current Digest of the Post-Soviet Press*, Vol. 46, No. 6 (January 12, 1994), pp. 1–6.

Jad Mouawad, "Conflict Narrows Oil Options for West," *New York Times* (August 14, 2008).

Martha Brill Olcott, Anders Aslund, and Sherman W. Garnett, *Getting It Wrong: Regional Cooperation and the Commonwealth of Independent States* (Washington DC: Carnegie Endowment for International Peace, 1999).

Ziya Onis, "Turkey and Post-Soviet States: Potential and Limits of Regional Power Influence," *Middle East Review of International Affairs*, Vol. 5, No. 2 (June 2001), pp. 1–10, especially pp. 1–3.

Olivier Roy, "The Iranian Foreign Policy toward Central Asia," *EURASIANET.org*, pp. 1–16, http://www.eurasianet.org/resource/regional/royoniran.html.

Eugene Rumer, "The US Interests and Role in Central Asia after K2," *Washington Quarterly*, Vol. 29, No. 3 (Summer 2006), pp. 141–54.

Arun Sahgal, "Growing Russian Influence in Central Asia," *Pravda* (November 5, 2004), pp. 1–4.

Graham Smith, *The Post Soviet States: Mapping the Politics of Transition* (London: Arnold, 1999).

Vladimir Socor, "US Military Presence at Risk in Central Asia," *Eurasia Daily Monitor* (July 8, 2005).

Niklas Swanstrom, "China and Central Asia: A New Great Game or Traditional Vassal Relations," *Journal of Contemporary China*, Vol. 14, No. 45 (November 2005), pp. 569–84.

Vadim Trukhachev, "Russia to Cooperate with the West in the Former USSR?" *Pravda* (August 24, 2005).

Mark Webber, *The International Politics of Russia and the Successor States* (Manchester: Manchester University Press, 1996).

Gareth M. Winrow, "Turkey and the Newly Independent States of Central Asia and the Transcaucasus," *Middle East Review of International Affairs*, Vol. 1, No. 2 (July 1997), pp. 1–10.

Amberin Zaman, "Turkey Moves to Expand Central Asian Ties," *EURASIANET .org* (October 26, 2000).

CHAPTER 2: KAZAKHSTAN

Mikhail Alexandrov, *Uneasy Alliance: Relations between Russia and Kazakhstan in the Post-Soviet Era 1992–1997* (Westport, CT: Greenwood Press, 1999).

Ibragim Alibekov, "Eurasia Insight: Kazakhstan's Leader Clears the Decks for Another Presidential Run," *EURASIANET.org* (September 9, 2005), http:// www.eurasianet.org/departments/insight/articles/eav090905_pr.shtml.

———, "Kazakhstan Tilts toward Russia," *EURASIANET.org* (February 18, 2004), http://www.eurasianet.org/departments/insight/articles/eav021804a .shtml.

———, "Khatami, in Kazakhstan, Asserts Iran as a Critical Partner for Kazakhstan," Ferghana Information Agency (April 27, 2002), http://enews.ferghana.ru/ article.php?id=29&print=1&PHPSESSID=97691f499006399effad.…

"Ambassador John Ordway Transcript of Interview with Khabar Television Chief of Mission Residence, Almaty, Kazakhstan, February 27, 2005."

Oksana Antonenko, "Central Asia Watches Warily (the Russian Military Action in Georgia)," *International Herald Tribune* (August 29, 2008).

"Autocratic Kazakh Leader Ousts His Reformist Premier," *New York Times* (October 11, 1997).

Lionel Beehner, "The White House's Kazakh Dilemma," *Council on Foreign Relations* (September 29, 2006), http://www.cfr.org/publication/11553/ whitehouseskazakhdilemma.html?breadcrumb=.…

Sergei Blagov, "Economic Union Slips from View at Russia-Kazakhstan Summit," *EURASIANET.org* (January 15, 2004).

———, "Georgia: A Small Pawn in the Great Game," *Asia Times Online* (2004), http://www.atimes.com/atimes/Central_Asia/FA07Ag03.html.

"China Calls for Substantiation of China-Kazakhstan Strategic Partnership," *People's Daily Online* (January 1, 2006).

C. J. Chivers, "Kazakh President Re-Elected; Voting Flawed, Observers Say," *New York Times* (December 6, 2005).

———, "Signs of Big Win for Kazakhstan President in Peaceful Election," *New York Times* (December 5, 2005).

Robert M. Cutler, "Central Asia: Emerging Triangles: Russia-Kazakhstan-China," *Asia Times Online* (January 15, 2004), http://www.atimes.com/atimes/Central_Asia/FA15Ag03.html.

Adam Ereli, "Kazakhstan: Presidential Election," U.S. Department of State (December 7, 2005).

Eurasia Insight, "Uighur Issues May Become Factor in China-Kazakhstan Relations," *EURASIANET.org* (January 2, 2003).

Douglas Frantz, "World Briefing Asia: Kazakhstan: Bribery Sentence," *New York Times* (September 6, 2001).

Jeff Gerth, "U.S. Businessman Is Accused of Oil Bribes to Kazakhstan," *New York Times* (April 1, 2004).

Ilan Greenberg, "Russia Will Get Central Asian Pipeline," *New York Times* (May 13, 2007).

Kseniy A. Kaspari, "Kazakh Journalist Convicted," *Boston Globe* (January 29, 2003).

"Kazakh Parliament Votes to Send Peacekeepers to Iraq," *Central Asia Caucasus Institute Analyst* (May 30, 2003), http://www.cacianalyst.org/?q=node/1226/print.

"Kazakh President Leaves for Iran for Official Visit," *Itar-Tass* (October 15, 2007).

"Kazakhs Try 2 for Jet Sales to North Korea," *New York Times* (January 11, 2000).

"Kazakhstan Government Critic Sentenced," *New York Times* (January 29, 2003).

"Kazakhstan: Human Rights Developments," Human Rights Watch World Report (2003), http://www.hrw.org/wr2k3/europe8.html.

Kazakhstan, neweurasia.net, "Kazakh Perspectives on the Russian-Georgian War" (August 13, 2008).

"Kazakhstan: Presidential Election Fell Short of International Standards—OSCE," *IRIN* (Ankara, December 5, 2005).

Andre E. Kramer, "Kazakhs Suspend Permits for Oilfields," *New York Times* (August 28, 2007).

———, "Mix of Nepotism and Nationalism Rules Kazakhstan's Oil Industry," *New York Times* (December 23, 2005).

Joanna Lillis, "Nazarbayev Visit to Washington: Looking for Recognition as Regional Leader," *EURASIANET.org* (September 26, 2006).

Heather Maher, "Kazakhstan: President to Visit Bush in Washington," *Radio Free Europe/Radio Liberty* (September 25, 2006).

Roger McDermott, "Kazakhstan Questions US Military Role in Central Asia," *Eurasia Daily Monitor*, Vol. 2, No. 160 (August 16, 2005), pp. 1–3, especially p. 1.

Steven Lee Myers and Ilan Greenberg, "US Sees a Friend in Kazakh Leader," *International Herald Tribune* (September 28, 2006).

Vitaly Naumkin, "Russian Policy toward Kazakhstan," in Robert Legvold (ed.), *Thinking Strategically: The Major Powers, Kazakhstan, and the Central Asian Nexus* (Cambridge, MA: MIT Press, 2003), pp. 39–65.

Jim Nichol, "Kazakhstan: Current Developments and U.S. Interests," *CRS Report for Congress* (May 4, 2004).

Office of the Press Secretary, "Joint Statement by President G. W. Bush and President Nursultan Nazarbayev on the New Kazakhstan–American Relationship" (December 21, 2001).

———, "President Bush Welcomes President Nazarbayev of Kazakhstan to the White House" (September 29, 2006).

Office of the Vice President, "Vice President's Remarks in a Press Availability with President Nursultan Nazarbayev of the Republic of Kazakhstan" (The Presidential Palace, Astana, Kazakhstan, May 5, 2006), pp. 1–4.

Martha Brill Olcott, Anders Aslund, and Sherman W. Garnett, *Getting It Wrong: Regional Cooperation and the Commonwealth of Independent States* (Washington DC: Carnegie Endowment for International Peace, 1999).

Christopher Pala, "Election in Kazakhstan Failed Democracy Test, Europeans Say," *New York Times* (September 9, 2004).

———, "Intimidation Alleged in Vote in Kazakhstan," *New York Times* (September 9, 2004).

———, "Kazakh President Takes Steps to Ensure Easy Re-Election," *New York Times* (June 26, 2005).

"Pressure Builds on ENI as Kazakh Government Threatens Kashagan Halt Due to Environmental Violations," *Global Insight*, pp. 1–3, http://www.globalinsight.com/SDA/SDADetail10361.htm.

James Risen, "Gore and Kazakh Vow Cooperation," *New York Times* (December 21, 1999).

———, "Gore to Meet Kazakh Leader after MIG Case," *New York Times* (November 24, 1999).

"Russia, Kazakhstan: Chronicle of New Cooperation," *Kazinform* (June 13, 2005).

"Russia's Asia Allies Fail to Back Georgia Action," *Asharq Alawsat* (August 28, 2008), http://www.asharq-e.com/print.asp?artid=id13873.

"Speech by NATO Secretary General, Jaap de Hoop During His Visit to Kazakhstan," *NATO/OTAN* (October 19, 2004), http://www.nato.int/docu/speech/2004/s041019a.htm.

Ron Stodghill, "Oil, Cash, and Corruption," *New York Times* (November 5, 2006).

Niklas Swanstrom, "China and Central Asia: A New Great Game or Traditional Vassal Relations?" *Journal of Contemporary China*, Vol. 14, No. 45 (November 2005), pp. 569–84.

Sabrina Tavernise and Christopher Pala, "Energy-Rich Kazakhstan Is Suffering Growing Pains," *New York Times* (January 4, 2003).

U.S. Department of State, Bureau of Democracy, Human Rights, and Labor, "Kazakhstan—Country Reports on Human Rights Policies—2001" (May 4, 2004), pp. 1–19.

———, Bureau of Democracy, Human Rights, and Labor, "Kazakhstan—Country Reports on Human Rights Policies—2002" (March 31, 2003), pp. 1–24.

———, Bureau of Democracy, Human Rights, and Labor, "Kazakhstan—Country Reports on Human Rights Policies—2003" (February 25, 2004).

———, "Joint Press Conference with Nursultan Nazarbayev, President of the Republic of Kazakhstan" (Presidential Administration Building, Astana, Kazakhstan, December 9, 2001).

U.S. Embassy, Astana, Kazakhstan, "Transcript of Press Conference Given by U.S. Ambassador to Kazakhstan John Ordway" (February 14, 2007).

"US Lawmakers Commend Kazakhstan's Non-Nuclear Choice," *Kazakhstan's Echo*, a publication of the Embassy of Kazakhstan to the United States and Canada (April 29, 2005).

Michael Wines, "Kazakhs Reject Appeal of Editor Who Says He Was Framed for Rape," *New York Times* (March 13, 2003).

Marat Yermukhanov, "China's Relations with Kazakhstan Are Warming, But to What End?" *Association for Asian Research (AFAR)* (July 9, 2004), http://www.asianresearch.org/articles/2185.html.

———, "Kazakhstan Seeks Iran's Reconciliation with the West," *Eurasia Daily Monitor* (June 16, 2008).

CHAPTER 3: TURKMENISTAN

Oksana Antonenko, "Central Asia Watches Warily (the Russian Military Action in Georgia)," *International Herald Tribune* (August 29, 2008).

Okzhas Auyezov, "US Envoy Discusses Energy Ties with Turkmenistan," *Reuters— UK* (February 28, 2008).

Sergei Blagov, "Russia Bows to Turkmenistan's Gas Pricing Demand," *EURASIANET .org* (September 6, 2006), http://www.eurasianet.org/departments/business/articles/eav090606_pr.shtml.

———, "Russian Leaders Mull Geopolitical Moves in 2005," *EURASIANET.org* (January 4, 2005), http://www.eurasianet.org/departments/insight/articles/eav010405_pr.shtml.

———, "Turkmenistan: A Study in Democracy Denial," *Asia Times* (December 6, 2003), http://www.atimes.com/atimes/Central_Asia/EL06Ag02.html.

Frederico Bordonaro, "Moscow Moves to Consolidate Control in Belarus and Turkmenistan," *Power and Interest News Report* (January 5, 2007).

Kenley Butler, "Central Asian Military Bases," *Monterey Institute of International Studies* (October 11, 2001), http://cns.miis.edu/research/wtc01/cabases.htm.

C. J. Chivers, "Intrigue Follows Death of a President," *New York Times* (December 22, 2006).

———, "Little Doubt on Result of Turkmenistan Vote," *New York Times* (February 12, 2007).

———, "Turkmen Exile Urges Interim President to Step Down," *New York Times* (December 30, 2006).

———, "Turkmenistan Hails Leader and New Era after Election," *New York Times* (February 15, 2007).

Ariel Cohen, "Advancing American Interest in Central Asia," *Heritage Foundation* (January 17, 2007), http://www.heritage.org/Press/Commentary/ed020907c.cfm?Renderforprint=1.

———, "US Opportunity in Turkmenistan," *EURASIANET.org* (January 17, 2007).

Commission on Security and Cooperation in Europe of the United States House of Representatives Hearing (March 21, 2000), "Democratization and Human Rights in Turkmenistan," pp. 3–5.

John C. K. Daly, "Turkmenistan Back in Former USSR's Orbit," *Eurasia Daily Monitor* (June 8, 2007).

Vladimir Dubov, "Turkmenistan, Russia and the West: Two's Company, Three's a Crowd," *RIA Novosti*.

Energy Information Administration, "Caspian Sea Region: Natural Gas Export" (July 2002), pp. 1–64, http://www.eia.doe.gov/emeu/cabs/caspgase.html.

Firket Ertan, "Turkmenistan-China Cooperation," *Zaman Daily Newspaper* (September 17, 2005).

"Eurasia Insight: Is Washington Exploring a Base Deal with Turkmenistan," *EURASIANET.org* (August 31, 2005).

Gregory Gleason, "Turkmenistan Tilts toward Russia," *Eurasia Daily Monitor* (January 2, 2007).

———, "Turkmenistan's Neutrality and Russia's New Southern Policy," *Eurasia Daily Monitor* Vol. 1, No. 120 (November 4, 2004).

Ilan Greenberg, "Turkmen Leader Proposes Vast Change to Lift Isolation," *New York Times* (January 5, 2007).

———, "Turkmenistan Limits Election to Soviet Style Slate," *New York Times* (December 27, 2006).

"Is Washington Exploring a Base Deal with Turkmenistan," *EURASIANET.org* (August 31, 2005).

Islamic Republic of Iran—Permanent Mission to the United Nations, "Address by H. E. Dr. Mahmood Ahmadinejad President of the Islamic Republic of Iran before the Sixtieth Session of the United Nations General Assembly New York—September 17, 2005," pp. 1–10.

Can Karpat, "Tired of Russia, Turkmenistan Is Due to Choose China," *Axis Information and Analysis* (August 30, 2005), http://www.axisglobe.com/article.asp?article=356.

Daniel Kimmage, "Central Asia Provides Window on Russia-US Relations," *Radio Free Europe/Radio Liberty Newsline* (February 24, 2005), http://www.rferl.org/articleprintview/1057645.html.

Joshua Kucera, "US Sets Its Sights on Turkmenistan Gas," *enerpub* (January 29, 2008), http://www.energypublisher.com/print.asp?idarticle=14075.

Roger McDermott, "Putin Seeks Closer Ties with Turkmenistan," *Eurasia Daily Monitor* (February 20, 2007).

———, "Turkmenistan and Iran Strengthen Relations," *Eurasia Daily Monitor* (June 26, 2007).

———, "Turkmenistan Pulls Back from CIS," *Eurasia Daily* (September 1, 2005).

Steven Lee Meyers, "World Briefing/Asia: Turkmenistan: Military Aid from US," *New York Times* (August 28, 2002).

Jim Nichol, "Central Asia's Security: Issues and Implications for US Interests," *CRS Report for Congress* (April 3, 2003), pp. 5–6, https://www.policyarchive.org/bitstream/handle/10207/954/RL30294_20030403.pdf?sequence=1.

Martha Brill Olcott, "Challenges in the Transport of Turkmen Gas," a draft paper prepared for Stanford University Program on Energy and Sustainable Development (November 2003).

Breffni O'Rourke, "Turkmenistan: President's Death Brings Muted World Reaction," *Radio Free Europe/Radio Liberty* (December 21, 2006).

Mikhail Peresplesnin, "Russia's Comeback to Central Asia Is Not Just Pipe Dream," *RIA Novosti* (May 8, 2007), http://en.rian.ru/analysis/20070508/65139688.html.

"Potential U.S. Base in Turkmenistan Alarming for Russia—Expert," *RIA Novosti* (September 6, 2005).

"President Putin Says Russians in Turkmenistan Have Nothing to Fear," *RTR Russia TV* (BBC Monitoring Service, June 3, 2003), cited in *Weekly News Brief on Turkmenistan* (Turkmenistan Project, June 20–26, 2003).

"Putin to Lobby Gas Pipe Via Russia in Turkmenistan, Kazakhstan," *RIA Novosti* (May 10, 2007).

"Putin in Turkmenistan to Preserve Gas Exports-1," *RIA Novosti*.

Michael A. Reynolds, "Russia and Georgia at War" (August 9, 2008), pp. 1–2.

"Russia, Kazakhstan, Turkmenistan Agree on Caspian Gas Pipe," *RIA Novosti* (May 12, 2007), http://en.rian.ru/world/20070512/65373780.html.

"Russia, Kazakhstan, and Turkmenistan Agreed on Construction of Caspian Pipeline," *Regnum* (May 14, 2007).

"Russia, Turkmenistan Sign a 25 Year Gas Cooperation Agreement," *Pravda* (April 10, 2003), http://newsfromrussia.com/economis/2003/04/10/45916.html.

"Russia's Asia Allies Fail to Back Georgia Action," *Asharq Alawsat* (August 28, 2008), http://www.asharq-e.com/print.asp?artid=id13873.

Ivan Shmelev, "Common-wealth of Independent States, the Former USSR, Likely to Collapse and Take a Different Form," *Pravda* (August 29, 2005).

State Information Agency of Turkmenistan, "Turkmen Neutrality Serves National Interests and Tasks of Peaceful Development" (September 4, 2005).

Sabrina Tavernise, "Show Trials Like Stalin's in Turkmenistan," *New York Times* (January 27, 2003).

Igor Torbakov, "Russia Watches Warily as Turkmen-Chinese Economic Cooperation Expands," *EURASIANET.org* (August 29, 2006).

———, "Russian–Turkmen Pacts Mark Strategic Shift for Moscow in Central Asia," *EURASIANET.org* (April 15, 2003).

"Turkmen Decree to Annul Citizenship in Force," *Interfax*, BBC Monitoring (June 24, 2003), "Envoy Says People in Turkmenistan Hold Onto Their Russian Citizenship," ITAR-TASS (June 24, 2003), cited in *Weekly News Brief on Turkmenistan*, Turkmenistan Project (June 20–26, 2003).

"Turkmen President Supports Iran's Peaceful Nuclear Program," *Islamic Republic News Agency* (March 16, 2007).

"Turkmenistan Does Not Want US Military Base on Its Territory," *RIA Novosti* (September 8, 2005).

"Turkmenistan and Iran Consolidate, Expand Bilateral Relations," *News Central Asia* (June 18, 2007), http://www.newscentralasia.net/print/42.html.

"Turkmenistan: Iranian President Pays First Visit to Ashgabat," *Radio Free Europe/Radio Liberty* (July 24, 2006).

"Turkmenistan: Role of Russia and the CIS," *AllREFER* (March 1996).

"United States Comes Close to Slapping Economic Sanctions on Turkmenistan," *News Central Asia* (August 9, 2003).

Weekly News Brief on Turkmenistan, "Turkmen Decree to Annul Dual Citizenship in Force," June 24, 2003, BBC Monitoring, *EURASIANET.org* (June 20–26, 2003).

Mike Whitney, "Washington's Game in Turkmenistan," Information Clearing House (December 26, 2006), http://www.informationclearinghouse.info/article15987.htm.

CHAPTER 4: TAJIKISTAN

Zafar Abdullayev, "Tajikistan, Russia Probe Military Partnership," *EURASIANET.org* (March 4, 2003), http://www.eurasianet.org/departments/insight/articles/eav030404_pr.shtml.

Zafar Abdullayev and Saida Nazarova, "Tajikistan: Referendum Result Controversy," *Institute for War and Peace* (June 28, 2003).

Rashid G. Abdullo, "Tajikistan Turns to the West," *Institute for War and Peace* (January 10, 2003).

"Ahmadinejad Is Visiting Tajikistan," *NEWEURASIA.NET* (July 26, 2006).

Kambiz Arman, "US Loses Grip on Geopolitical Position in Tajikistan: As Tajikistan Has Strengthened Its Ties with Both Russia and China, the Appeal of Strategic Cooperation with the US Seems to Be Fading," *ISN* (August 20, 2005).

Australian Government, Department of Foreign Affairs and Trade, "Tajikistan Country Brief" (January 21, 2005).

Antoine Blua, "Tajikistan: Traders Look to China for Brighter Fortunes," *Radio Free Europe/Radio Liberty* (August 20, 2004).

John Boyle, "Russia's Medvedev Looks East for Support on Georgia," *Star Online World Updates* (August 28, 2008).

David S. Cloud, "Rumsfeld in Tajikistan, Urges Tough Stand against Taliban," *New York Times* (July 11, 2006).

Catherine Davis, "Moscow Deports Tajik Migrants," *BBC News* (November 24, 2002).

Vladimir Davlatov, "Russia: Tajiks Face Deportation," *Institute for War and Peace* (November 19, 2002).

Embassy of the United States Dushanbe, Tajikistan, "Press Releases: US Embassy Statement on Parliamentary Elections in Tajikistan" (February 28, 2005).

Patrick Goodenough, "Moscow Looks East for Support," *CNSNews.com* (August 27, 2008), http://www.cnsnews.com/public/content/article.aspx?RsrcID=34664.

Richard E. Hoagland, "Democracy and Tajikistan," *United States Embassy in Dushanbe Press Release* (March 2, 2004).

"Iran Seeks Expanding Military Presence in Central Asia," *Iran Press Service* (March 10, 2001).

"Iran, Tajik Presidents Stress Enhanced Ties," *Islamic Republic News Agency* (May 9, 2007).

"Iran-Tajikistan Enhanced Ties in Favor of the Region," *Islamic Republic News Agency* (May 8, 2007).

"Iran, Tajikistan to Join Hands against Shared Danger: President Khatami," *Pravda* (March 4, 2004), http://newsfromRussia.com/world/2004/03/04/52627.html.

Michael Jasinski, "Russian Policy toward Afghanistan," *Center for Non-Proliferation Studies* (September 15, 2001), pp. 1–3, http://cns.miis.edu/research/wtc01/rusafg.htm.

Daniel Kimmage, "Tajikistan: No Surprises Expected in Presidential Election," *Radio Free Europe/Radio Liberty* (November 3, 2006).

Joanna Lillis, "Tajikistan: No Surprises in Presidential Election," *EURASIANET.org* (November 6, 2006).

LiveMint.com, "Russia Wins Some Support from Tajik Ally Over Georgia," *Reuters* (August 29, 2008).

Roger McDermott, "Iran Builds Partnership with Tajikistan," *Eurasia Daily Monitor* (July 25, 2006).

———, "Tajikistan Fosters Security Links with Iran," *Eurasia Daily Monitor* (May 10, 2005).

———, "Tajikistan Restates Its Strategic Partnership with Russia, While Sending Mixed Signals," *Eurasia Daily Monitor*, Vol. 4, No. 81 (April 25, 2007).

Vladimir Mukhin, "Russian and American Interests Clash in Tajikistan: Tajikistan's Military Infrastructure Will Depend on the US Dollar," *Nezavisimaya Gazeta* (August 12, 2003), http://www.cdi.org/Russia/269-13.cfm.

Office of the Press Secretary, "Joint Statement by President Bush and President Rakhmonov on the Relationship between the United States and the Republic of Tajikistan" (December 20, 2002).

OSCE Election Observation Mission, Presidential Election, Republic of Tajikistan—November 6, 2006, "Statement of Preliminary Findings and Conclusions," pp. 1–12.

Christopher Pala, "A Lopsided Victory Is Seen for Tajikistan's Ruling Party," *New York Times* (March 1, 2005).

———, "Tajikistan and Kyrgyzstan Vote, Observers See Trouble," *New York Times* (February 28, 2008).

Bruce Pannier, "OSCE: Tajik Elections Fall Short of Standards," *Radio Free Europe/Radio Liberty* (February 28, 2005).

———, "Rakhmonov Hosts Iranian, Afghanistan Presidents," *Radio Free Europe/Radio Liberty* (July 25, 2006).

———, "Tajikistan: Experts Say Incumbent President Will Be Easily Re-Elected," *EURASIANET.org* (October 8, 2006), http://www.eurasianet.org/departments/insight/articles/pp100806_pr.shtml.

———, "Tajikistan: Relations with Moscow Appear to Have Reached an Impasse," *Radio Free Europe/Radio Liberty* (March 15, 2004).

Russ Oil-Gas, "Gazprom Gets Gas, Oil Prospect License in Tajikistan" (Moscow, December 29, 2006).

"Russia Asks Asian Alliance for Support on Georgia," *Washington Times*.

"Russia, Tajikistan Spar Over Illegal Labor Migration," *Tajikistan Development Gateway* (January 9, 2003).

"Russia Tightens Rules on Migrants," *BBC News* (November 16, 2006).

"Russian Military Base in Tajikistan to Ensure Regional Security," *MOSNEWS* (October 18, 2004).

"Russia's Asia Allies Fail to Back Georgia Action," *Asharq Alawsat* (August 28, 2008), http://www.asharq-e.com/print.asp?artid=id13873.

"Secretary Rumsfeld, Tajik Foreign Minister Talbak Nazarov Brief Press" (July 26, 2005).

Sanobar Shermatova, "Tajik Snub to Russia?" *International Eurasian Institute for Economic and Political Research* (December 4, 2002).

Dmitry Solovyov, "Tajikistan Adds Years to Power of Leader," *Boston Globe* (June 24, 2003).

"Tajik Military Facilities," *Global Security*, http://globalsecurity.org/military/world/centralasia/tajikistan.htm.

"Tajikistan to Ask Putin for Amnesty," *Kommersant* (September 18, 2007), http://www.kommersant.com/p805527/r_immigration_policy/.

"Tajikistan to Continue Active Military Cooperation," *AVESTA Tajikistan News* (August 19, 2005).

"Tajikistan: First Permanent Military Base Opened," *Radio Free Europe/Radio Liberty* (October 17, 2004).

"This Week at a Glance," *Radio Free Europe/Radio Liberty Central Asia Report*, Vol. 4, No. 4 (June 8, 2004), pp. 1–6.

Ann Scot Tyson, "Rumsfeld Wins Assurances in Central Asia: Kyrgyzstan, Tajikistan Say U.S. Can Still Use Bases," *Washington Post* (July 27, 2005).

"US Ambassador Tracey Ann Jacobson's Remarks at the International Conference on Afghanistan and Regional Security," *Embassy of the United States— Dushanbe* (December 11, 2006).

"US Defense Secretary to Make Surprise Tajik Visit," *Payvand's Iran News* from *Radio Free Europe/Radio Liberty* (July 10, 2006).

Sgt. Sara Wood, USA American Forces Press Service, "Tajikistan Important to War on Terrorism," *American Forces Press Service NEWS ARTICLES* (July 10, 2006).

CHAPTER 5: UZBEKISTAN

Erkin Akhmadov, "A Thaw in Relations between West and Uzbekistan," *Central Asia–Caucasus Institute Analyst* (March 19, 2008).

Adam Albion, "Putin in Samarkand: The 'Old Friend' Returns," *Radio Free Europe/ Radio Liberty Newsline* (August 11, 2003), http://www.cdi.org/Russia/Johnson/7285-16.cfm.

Oksana Antonenko, "Central Asia Watches Warily (the Russian Military Action in Georgia," *International Herald Tribune* (August 29, 2008).

Shamil Baigin, Olzhas Auyezov, Dmitry Solovyov, and Mary Gabriel, "US Urges Uzbekistan to Open Up for Dialogue," *Reuters* (March 27, 2008), http://www.reuters.com/articlePrint?articleId=USL2782922520080327.

Shamil Baigin, Maria Golovnina, and Elizabeth Piper, "US Praises Uzbekistan for Rights Improvement," *Reuters* (March 27, 2008), http://www.reuters.com/articlePrint?ArticleId=USL1365963520080313.

Jonathan Beale, "Rice's Soft Tone in Central Asia," *BBC News* (October 11, 2005).

Kenley Butler, "Uzbekistan's Alliance with the United States: Benefits and Risks," *CNS* (Monterey Institute of International Studies, October 11, 2001), http://cns.miis.edu/research/wtc01/uzbek1.htm.

Charles Carlson, "Uzbekistan: Karimov Says Improved Relations with Russia Not at the Expense of US Ties," *EURASIANET.org* (September 6, 2003), http://www.eurasianet.org/departments/insight/articles/pp090603_pr.shtml.

"China against 'External Influence' in Uzbekistan's Affairs—Envoy," *Interfax*, monitored by BBC (June 21, 2005).

"China to Help Uzbekistan Struggle against Revolutions," *Pravda* (May 28, 2005), http://English.pravda.ru/world/20/02/373/15553_Uzbekistan.html.

"China Honors a Friend," *New York Times* (May 28, 2005).

"China, Uzbekistan Agree Further Cooperation in Regional Security," *Xinhua* (May 26, 2005).

"China, Uzbekistan Sign Friendship Treaty," *ZEENEWS* (May 25, 2005).

C. J. Chivers, "China Backs Uzbek, Splitting with U.S. on Crackdown," *New York Times* (May 25, 2005).

———, "Six Senators Urge Reassessment of Ties with Uzbekistan Ruler," *New York Times* (May 18, 2005).

———, "Survivors and Toe Tags Offer Clues to Uzbeks' Uprising," *New York Times* (May 23, 2005).

———, "Under Pressure, Uzbek President Raises Toll from Deadly Unrest," *New York Times* (June 9, 2005).

———, "Uzbek Ministries in Crackdown Received American Aid," *New York Times* (June 18, 2005).

———, "Uzbekistan Shaken by Unrest, Violence and Uncertainty," *New York Times* (May 16, 2005).

Ariel Cohen, "Advancing American Interest in Central Asia," *Heritage Foundation* (January 17, 2007), http://www.heritage.org/Press/Commentary/ed020907c.cfm?Renderforprint=1.

John C. K. Daly, Kurt H. Meppen, Vladimir Socor, and S. Frederick Star, *Anatomy of a Crisis: US-Uzbekistan Relations 2001–2005* (Washington DC: Central Asia-Caucasus Institute & Silk Road Studies Program, 2006).

Mathew Davis, "Uzbek Crisis Poses Dilemma for US," *BBC News* (Washington, May 16, 2005), http://news.bbc.co.uk/1/hi/world/asia-pacific/4552463.stm.

Brian Grodsky, "Direct Pressures for Human Rights in Uzbekistan: Understanding the US Bargaining Position," Central Asia Survey (December 2004), pp. 327–44.

Burt Herman, "Uzbek Leader Defies Calls for Probe," *Boston Globe* (May 21, 2005).

Fiona Hill, "Prospects for Political Change," Testimony before the U.S. Helsinki Committee (July 25, 2006).

Joseph Kahn and Chris Buckley, "China Gives a Strategic 21 Gun Salute to Visiting Uzbek President," *New York Times* (May 26, 2008).

"Karimov in China: Uzbekistan Reaches Out to a Rare Ally," *Current Affairs: Archive by Region: Central Asia* (May 26, 2005).

Daniel Kimmage, "Uzbekistan: Is Tashkent's Foreign Policy Going Multivector?" *Radio Free Europe/Radio Liberty* (March 9, 2007).

Paul Kolstoe, *Russians in the Former Soviet Union* (Bloomington, Indiana: University of Indiana Press, 1995), footnote 76, p. 223.

Peter Lavelle, "Analysis: Experts on Uzbekistan's Fate," *UPI.com* (May 20, 2005), http://www.upi.com/Security_Industry/2005/05/20/Analysis-Experts-on-Uzbekistans-fate/UPI-18261116599609/print/.

"Limits on Uzbek Air Base Spur Shift," *Boston Globe* (June 15, 2005).

"Lukoil Signs a Production Sharing Agreement on the Kandym-Khausak-Ahady Project in Uzbekistan" (June 16, 2004).

Erich Marquardt and Yevgeny Bendersky, "Uzbekistan's New Foreign Policy Strategy," *Power and Interest News Report* (November 23, 2005).

Roger McDermott, "Russia Reclaiming Central Asia as a Sphere of Influence," *Eurasia Daily Monitor* (March 13, 2007).

———, "Uzbekistan's Relations with China Warming," *Eurasia Daily Monitor* (July 20, 2005).

Brad McDonald, "US Diplomatic Rescue Mission Secures Military Base, for Now," *TheTrumpet.com.*

Robert McMahon, "Central Asia: Russia and US Often at Odds," *Radio Free Europe/Radio Liberty* (October 25, 2005).

Martha Brill Olcott, "Prospects for Political Change in Uzbekistan," Testimony before the U.S. Helsinki Committee, Briefing on Prospects for Political Change (July 25, 2006).

Bruce Pannier, "Central Asia: Odd Couple Crashes NATO Summit," *Radio Free Europe/Radio Liberty* (April 1, 2008).

———, "Uzbek, Turkmen Presidents Offer Cooperation," *Radio Free Europe/Radio Liberty* (April 4, 2008).

———, "Uzbekistan: Departure from Base Underlines US-Uzbek Tensions," *Radio Free Europe/Radio Liberty* (September 28, 2005).

———, "Uzbekistan: Military Exercises with Russia Timely for Tashkent," *Radio Free Europe/Radio Liberty* (September 23, 2005).

"President of Uzbekistan Starts China Visit," *People's Daily* (May 25, 2005), http://English.people.com.cn/200505/25/eng20050525_186761.html.

"Presidents of Uzbekistan and Russia Meet," *Embassy of Uzbekistan in the United States* (June 29, 2005), http://www.uzbekistan.org/news/archive/236/?print=1.

Philip T. Reeker, "United States–Uzbekistan Joint Security Cooperation Consultations," U.S. Department of State, Press Statement (April 15, 2003).

Eugene Rumor, "The U.S. Interests and Role in Central Asia after K2," *Washington Quarterly*, Vol. 29, No. 3 (Summer 2006), pp. 141–154.

"Russia Closely Following Uzbekistan Unrest," *People's Daily* (May 14, 2005).

"RUSSIA—LUKoil Leads in External E&P Investment," *APS Review Downstream Trends* (September 6, 2004).

Gulnoza Saidazimova, "Uzbekistan: President Karimov Meets with Close Ally Putin," *Radio Free Europe/Radio Liberty* (February 6, 2008), http://www.rferl.org/articleprintview/1079440.html.

———, "What Does Closure of U.S. Military Base in Uzbekistan Mean?" *Payvand's Iran News* (August 2, 2005).

Eric Schmitt, "No Harm Seen in Loss of Base in Uzbekistan," *New York Times* (August 8, 2005).

Thom Shanker and C. J. Chivers, "Crackdown in Uzbekistan Reopens Long-Standing Debate on U.S. Military Aid," *New York Times* (July 13, 2005).

Sarah Shenker, "Struggle for Influence in Central Asia," *BBC News* (January 27, 2005).

"Soviet Era Ends as Gazprom Pays Market Price," *Petroleum Economist* (2008).

Ignor Torbakov, "Russia's Warming Toward Uzbekistan May Damage Relations with the West," *Eurasia Daily Monitor*, Vol. 2, No. 214 (November 16, 2005).

Peter Trunscott, *Russia First: Breaking with the West* (London: I. B. Taurus, 1997).

Ann Scott Tyson and Robin Wright, "Uzbek Crackdown Puts U.S. in a Quandary," *Boston Globe* (June 5, 2005).

"United States Cuts Off Aid to Uzbekistan," *EURASIANET.org* (July 14, 2004).

"The US Administration Tries to Isolate the Former Soviet Republic from the Rest of the World," *Pravda* (October 8, 2005).

U.S. Department of State, "Uzbekistan: Country Reports on Human Rights Practices—2002" (for 2001), *Bureau of Democracy, Human Rights, and Labor*, pp. 1–18.

———, "Uzbekistan: Country Reports on Human Rights Practices—2003" (for 2002), *Bureau of Democracy, Human Rights, and Labor* (March 31, 2002), pp. 1–22.

———, "Uzbekistan: Country Reports on Human Rights Practices—2004," *Bureau of Democracy, Human Rights, and Labor* (February 28, 2005), pp. 1–19.

———, "Uzbekistan: Country Reports on Human Rights Practices—2005," for 2004, *Bureau of Democracy, Human Rights, and Labor* (February 28, 2005), pp. 1–19.

"US Evicted from Uzbek Base," *Boston Globe* (July 31, 2005).

"USA Intends to Bring Economic Sanctions against Uzbekistan and Jail Uzbek President," *Pravda* (October 3, 2005).

"US-Uzbekistan Relations: Another Step Toward Rapprochement?" *EURASIANET.org* (January 23, 2008), http://www.eurasianet.org/departments/insight/articles/eav012308b_pr.shtml.

"Uzbek Court Suspends Work of US Group," *New York Times* (January 14, 2006).

"Uzbek President Tells Putin of Foreign Link in Recent Riots," *MOSNEWS* (June 29, 2005), http://www.mosnews.com/news/2005/06/29/karimovreveals.shtm.

"Uzbek Senior Deputy Premier Rustam Azimov Is Expected in Moscow," *Ferghama Information Agency* (August 25, 2008).

"Uzbekistan Is Expected to Re-Elect Its President," *New York Times* (December 24, 2007).

"Uzbekistan May Let the United States Use a Military Airbase for Operations in Afghanistan," *Reuters* (March 5, 2008), http://www.reuters.com/articlePrint?articleId=USL0593284.

"Uzbekistan: New US Ambassador, New Policy?" *EURASIANET.org* (November 13, 2007), http://www.eurasianet.org/departments/insight/articles/eav111307a_pr.shtml.

"Uzbekistan Seeks China's Help against Terrorism," *Daily Times* (May 26, 2005), http://www.dailytimes.com.pk/default.asp?page=story_26-5-2005_pg4_7.

"Uzbekistan: Support from Russia," *New York Times* (June 30, 2005).

"Uzbekistan Wants US to Pay for Airbase," *Moscow News* (July 8, 2005).

Steven Weisman and Thom Shanker, "Uzbeks Order US from Base," *New York Times* (July 31, 2005).

Ethan Wilensky-Lanford, "Uzbeks Threaten to Evict U.S. from an Air Base Near Afghanistan," *New York Times* (July 8, 2005).

Robin Wright, "Rice Signals Rift with Uzbekistan," *Boston Globe* (October 11, 2005).

Yuri Fedorov, "Uzbekistan Looks toward Russia," *Eurasia Daily Monitor*, Vol. 1, No. 7 (June 23, 2004).

———, "Washington Pushes Karimov Closer to Moscow," *Eurasia Daily Monitor*, Vol. 1, No. 57 (July 24, 2004), http://www.cdi.org/Russia/315-12.cfm.

CHAPTER 6: KYRGYZSTAN

Rafis Abazov, "The Political Culture of Central Asia," pp. 43–56, especially p. 47, http://se1.isn.ch/serviceengine/filecontent?Service1D=7&fileid=cdcdc6c9 -14AA-90FA-636CD21c1BF6d1ng=en.

"Akayev Backs Political Opponents for Upcoming Election," *Radio Free Europe/ Radio Liberty* (July 1, 2005).

Ella Akerman (ed.), *Political Culture Case Studies* (Conflict Studies Research Center #M27, March 2003).

Roy Allison, "Strategic Reassertion in Russia's Central Asia Policy," *International Affairs*, No. 2 (2004), p. 288.

"American Military Base in Kyrgyzstan: Afterthoughts" (August 26, 2006), http:// kyrgyzstan.neweurasia.net/?p=88.

"Bakiyev Wins Landslide in Kyrgyzstan, Courts Controversy with the United States," *EURASIANET.org* (July 11, 2005), http://www.eurasianet.org/ departments/insight/articles/eav071105_pr.shtml.

Ellen Barry, "Russia Offers Kind Words But Its Fist Is Clenched," *New York Times* (February 6, 2009).

Ellen Barry and Michael Schwirtz, "Kyrgyzstan Wants to Close US Base Used for Afghan War," *New York Times* (February 4, 2009).

Sergei Blagov, "Russia Boosts Military Ties with Kyrgyzstan," *Asia Times* (June 15, 2002), http://www.atimes.com/c-asia/DF15Ag02.html.

———, "Russian Economic and Strategic Influence in Kyrgyzstan Set to Expand," *EURASIANET.org* (April 25, 2006).

Stephen Blank, "After the Tulip Revolution: Are Sino-Kyrgyz Relations Still Alive and Kicking?" *Eurasia Daily Monitor*, Vol. 2, No. 203 (November 1, 2005).

Antoine Blua, "Kyrgyzstan: Russia Hopes to Double Troops at Base as Future of U.S. Base in Doubt," *EURASIANET.org* (July 16, 2005), http://www.eurasianet.org/ departments/insight/articles/pp071605.shtml.

Joel Brinkley, "Rice Reaches Pact on Keeping Central Asia Base," *New York Times* (October 12, 2005).

Elisabeth Bumiller and Ellen Barry, "US Searches for Alternative to Central Asian Base," *New York Times* (February 5, 2009).

Elena Chadova, "Negotiations on US Military Base in Kyrgyz Raise Transparency Concerns," *EURASIANET.org* (June 5, 2006), http://www.eurasianet.org/departments/insight/articles/eav060506_pr.shtml.

"China: Border Security Tightened Amid 'Terrorist Infiltration,' " *Radio Free Europe/Radio Liberty* (January 11, 2007).

C. J. Chivers, "Interim Kyrgyz President Is Expected to Win a Quiet Election," *New York Times* (July 11, 2005).

———, "Leader Wins 88 Percent of Vote in Kyrgyzstan," *New York Times* (July 12, 2005).

Ariel Cohen, "New Russian Deployment Marks Changed Strategy," *Russia Weekly*, No. 236 (December 17, 2002), http://www.cdi.org/Russia/236-15-pr.cfm.

Alexander Cooley, "How the US Lost Its Kyrgyzstan Air Base," *International Herald Tribune* (February 10, 2009).

John C. Daly, "Sino-Kyrgyz Relations after the Tulip Revolution," *China Brief*, Vol. 5, No. 9 (April 26, 2005).

"Davoudi Calls for Upgrading Iran-Kyrgyz Ties," *Islamic Republic News Agency* (September 29, 2007).

Ulugbek Djuraev, "The Battle for Kyrgyzia: The Kremlin Is Leading 1:0," *Axis Information and Analysis* (May 9, 2005).

———, "Kyrgyzstan Attacks the USA Counting on Russia and China," *Axis Information and Analysis* (April 20, 2005), http://www.axisglobe.com/print_article.asp?article=804.

"Felix Kulov Suggests a Confederation with Russia: Kyrgyzstan," *Turkish Weekly* (June 1, 2007).

"Gates and Boucher Visits to Kyrgyzstan, Muted Responses," *Institute for the Study of Conflict, Ideology, and Policy* (June 28, 2007).

Roman Ginzburg, "The Parliamentary Elections in Kyrgyzstan," *Carnegie Endowment for International Peace* (March 22, 2005).

Patrick Goodenough, "Post-Soviet States May Be Pulled towards Moscow after Georgian Crisis," *CNSNews.com* (August 22, 2008), http://www.cnsnews.com/public/content/article.aspx?RsrcID=34495.

Nathan Hodge, "Air Base Loss Could Hobble Afghan War Effort," *Danger Room* (February 5, 2005).

"Immigration from Kyrgyzstan to Russia on the Rise—Ambassador," *Central Asia-Caucasus Institute* (August 2, 2006).

Vladimir Isachenkov, "Russia Says It Wants to help US in Afghanistan," *Yahoo News* (February 4, 2009).

Linda Kartawich and Espen Eftedal Svensen, "Kyrgyzstan: Early Presidential Election July, 2005," *Nordem Report* (July 13, 2005), pp. 1–24.

Daniel Kimmage, "Central Asia: The Mechanics of Russian Influence," *Radio Free Europe/Radio Liberty* (September 16, 2005).

"Kyrgyz Rights Activists Support Georgia's Withdrawal from CIS," *Turkish Weekly* (Ferghama News, August 14, 2008).

"Kyrgyz-Russian Ties Could Affect the US," *The Hill* (May 9, 2006).

"Kyrgyzstan Delays Vote on US Base," *BBC News* (February 5, 2009).

"Kyrgyzstan: Parliament Curbs President's Powers," *New York Times* (November 9, 2006).

"Kyrgyzstan Police Crush Protest Detaining 100," *New York Times* (November 11, 2007).

"Kyrgyzstan President Orders US Air Base Closed: Announcement Comes Amid Russia Offered Millions to Kyrgyz Government," Anti-War.com (February 3, 2006).

"Kyrgyzstan: Presidential Polls Show Significant Improvements in Democracy Building," *IRIN* (August 21, 2005).

"Kyrgyzstan Says Russians Will Retain Military Presence," *REA Novosti* (March 25, 2008).

"Kyrgyzstan Says US Base Decision Is Final," *International Herald Tribune* (February 6, 2009).

"Manas International Airport, Ganci Air Base, Bishkek, Kyrgyzstan," *GlobalSecurity.org*, http://www.globalsecurity.org/military/facility/manas.htm.

Brad Macdonald, "US Diplomatic Rescue Mission Secures Base, for Now," *TheTrumpet.com* (June 2007).

Erica Marat, "Can Nazarbayev Help Kyrgyzstan Escape Moscow's Pressure?" *Eurasia Daily Monitor* (September 5, 2008).

———, "Conflict in South Ossetia Confuses Kyrgyz Government Ahead of CIS Summit," *Eurasia Daily Monitor* (August 14, 2008).

———, "Kyrgyz Government Risks Relations with the US before the G-8 Summit," *Eurasia Daily Monitor* (July 13, 2006).

———, "Kyrgyz Officials, Citizens Oppose US Base," *Eurasia Daily Monitor*, Vol. 4, No. 102 (May 24, 2007).

———, "Tensions Rising Ahead of Kyrgyz Presidential Elections," *Eurasia Daily Monitor*, Vol. 2, No. 129 (July 5, 2005).

———, *The Tulip Revolution: Kyrgyzstan One Year After* (Washington DC: Brookings Institution, 2006).

Roger McDermott, "Boucher Visit to Bishkek Reveals Widening Gap in US-Kyrgyz Relations," *Eurasia Daily Monitor* (August 15, 2006).

Kelly M. McMann, *Economic Autonomy and Democracy: Hybrid Regimes in Russia and Kyrgyzstan* (New York: Cambridge University Press, 2006).

Rustam Mukhamedov, "Uyghurs in Kyrgyzstan under Careful Government Supervision," *Central Asia-Caucasus Analyst* (January 28, 2004).

Office of the Press Secretary, "Joint Statement by President George W. Bush and President Askar Akayev on the Relationship between the United States and the Kyrgyz Republic" (September 23, 2002).

Mathew Oresman, "Assessing China's Reaction to Kyrgyzstan's 'Tulip Revolution,'" *Central Asia-Caucasus Analyst* (April 6, 2005).

Joldosh Osmonov, "The US Kyrgyz Military Base Negotiations," *Central Asia-Caucasus Institute* (June 9, 2006), pp. 1–3.

Christopher Pala, "Cries of Fraud Give Election in Kyrgyzstan Aura of Ukraine," *New York Times* (March 14, 2005).

————, "Denouncing Elections, Protesters Gather for Rallies in Kyrgyzstan," *New York Times* (March 15, 2005).

Bruce Pannier, "Kyrgyzstan: Russian, US Military Bases on Opposite Tracks," *EURASIANET.org* (February 20, 2006), http://www.eurasianet.org/departments/insight/articles/pp022006_pr.shtml.

Scott Parish and Margarita Sevcik, "Kyrgyz Government Ousted," *CNS* (March 24, 2005), pp. 1–4, http://cns.miis.edu/pubs/week/050324.htm.

Jean-Christophe Peuch, "Kyrgyzstan: Negotiations Over US Base End Inconclusively," *Radio Free Europe/Radio Liberty* (June 1, 2006).

"Protests in Kyrgyzstan," *Human Rights Watch*.

"Revolution in Kyrgyzstan," *Radio Free Europe/Radio Liberty* (March 25, 2005).

"Russia Allows Transit of US Supplies for Afghanistan," *Fox News* (February 6, 2009).

"Russia Ratifies Air Base Agreement with Kyrgyzstan," *Radio Free Europe/Radio Liberty* (July 8, 2005).

"Russia Says Not to Interfere in Kyrgyzstan's Internal Affairs," *XINHUANET* (Moscow, March 31, 2005), http://www.klasney.com/kyrgyzrevolution/2005/03/Russia-says-not-to-interfere-in.html.

Gulnoza Saidazimova, "Bishkek Assures Rumsfeld That U.S. Air Base Can Stay," *EURASIANET.org* (July 26, 2005), http://www.eurasianet.org/departments/insight/articles/pp062605.shtml.

————, "Kyrgyzstan: Old Actors, New Priorities—Or Are They Old Priorities?" *Radio Free Europe/Radio Liberty* (April 14, 2005).

Leila Saralayova, "Proposal Pacifies Kyrgyz Protests," *Boston Globe* (November 8, 2006).

Daniel Sershen, "Anti-Western Direction," *Transition on Line* (May 24, 2007).

————, "Kyrgyzstan: Base Shooting Sours US-Kyrgyz Relations," *EURASIANET.org* (December 19, 2006), http://www.eurasianet.org/departments/insight/articles/eav121906_pr.shtml.

Sanobar Shermatova, "Russia's Motives in Kyrgyzstan: Russia's Intent in Building an Air Base in Kyrgyzstan Is Clearly to Counterbalance U.S. Forces Stationed in the Region," *Russia Weekly*, No. 13 (December 25–31, 2002).

Barbara Slavin, "Kyrgyzstan Will Allow US to Keep Using Air Base," *USA TODAY* (October 12, 2005).

Craig Smith, "Crisis Grips Kyrgyzstan; Ousted Chief Is in Russia," *New York Times* (March 27, 2005).

————, "Kyrgyzstan's Shining Hour Ticks Away and Turns Out to Be a Plain, Old Coup," *New York Times* (April 3, 2005).

————, "U.S. Helped to Prepare the Way for Kyrgyzstan's Uprising," *New York Times* (March 30, 2005).

Michael Steen, "Violence Rocks South Kyrgyzstan," *Boston Globe* (March 21, 2005).

Sabrina Tavernise, "Kyrgyzstan and Russia Sign New Pact," *New York Times* (December 7, 2002).

Kadry Toktogulov, "Kyrgyz Officials Striving for Order," *Boston Globe* (March 27, 2005).

Hamid Toursunof, "Opening the Door to Gazprom," *International Eurasian Institute for Economic and Political Research* (Transitions On Line, June 2, 2003).

Deidre Tynan, "Kyrgyzstan Mulls US Air Base Closing Bill," *ISN Eth Zurich* (February 5, 2009).

UN Office for the Coordination of Humanitarian Affairs, "Kyrgyzstan: Focus on Major Players Ahead of Presidential Polls," *IRIN* (April 27, 2005).

———, "Kyrgyzstan: Presidential Polls Show Significant Improvements in Democracy Building," *IRIN* (August 21, 2005).

"US Airbase in Kyrgyz Says No Sign of Closure" (February 4, 2009), http://news.stv.tv/world/73953-us-air-basein-kyrgy7zstan-says-no-sigtnhj-of-closure/.

"US Military Base in Kyrgyzstan Comes into Play as Domestic Political Confrontation Brews," *EURASIANET.org* (April 20, 2006), http://www.eurasianet.org/departments/insight/articles/eav042006_pr.shtml.

"USA to Keep Its Army Bases in Post-Soviet States to Control Afghanistan and Put Pressure on China," *Pravda* (July 27, 2005).

"USA Loses Air Base in Kyrgyzstan to Russia," *Pravda* (February 4, 2009).

"US-Kyrgyz Relations Back on Solid Ground—But for How Long?" *EURASIANET.org* (August 23, 2006).

Index

Abizaid, John, 73, 74, 75
Abkhazia, 58, 184, 187
Afghanistan, 57, 93; Islamist threat
 from, 7–8, 14, 85, 92, 122;
 Kazakhstan and, 35, 43; NATO and,
 48, 105; Northern Alliance in, 9–10,
 13, 24, 96, 127; al Qaeda in, 1, 2,
 12, 24, 191; Tajik border with, 8,
 90, 92, 95, 97, 99, 108, 110, 111;
 Turkmenistan and, 67, 82; U.S. war
 in, 24–26, 70, 80, 81, 83, 103, 125,
 146, 168. *See also* Taliban, in
 Afghanistan
Ahmadinejad, Mahmoud, 56, 105,
 130, 193; Turkmenistan and, 80–81
Akayev, Askar, 119, 139, 155, 163–66,
 188; demonstrations against, 158–
 59; economic reform and, 156, 157;
 overthrow of, 138, 150, 164–66;
 parliamentary elections and, 163–
 64; Uighur nationalism and,
 156–57
Akhemedov, Rustam, 123
Albright, Madeline, 10, 50
Almaty meeting (1996), 8
American University (Kyrgyzstan),
 164–65, 169
Andijon crackdown (Uzbekistan,
 2005), 48, 73, 135, 138, 141, 148,
 195; refugees from, 171; U.S.

criticism of, 106, 130, 131, 133,
 137, 139, 145, 166
Antonenko, Oksana, 143
Arkhangelski, Aleksandr, 71
Arms embargo, 10
Arms sales, 30, 39
Authoritarian rule, 4, 5, 25, 191,
 194; in China, 148; in Kazakhstan,
 38, 43, 45–46, 47, 48, 50, 52;
 in Kyrgyzstan, 158, 188; in
 Tajikistan, 101, 103, 104, 115; in
 Turkmenistan, 66, 69–70; in
 Uzbekistan, 128, 139, 141, 196
Azerbaijan, 15, 40, 120, 189

Bakiyev, Kurmanbek, 134, 147, 172–
 73; ascendancy of, 166–70; Russian
 influence on, 174–76, 178–81; U.S.
 military base and, 171–72, 174, 176,
 178–81, 185–86, 195
Balgimbeyev, Nurlan, 38
Basayev, Shamir, 93
Belarus, 12, 35, 47
Berdimukhamedov, Gurbanguly, 53,
 76–82, 85, 86
Beshimov, Bakyt, 186
Bilateral Investment Treaty, 123
Bin Laden, Osama, 24, 25. *See also* al
 Qaeda
Bordyuzha, Nikolas, 175, 179

Bosnia-Herzegovina, 6, 91
Boucher, Richard, 77, 78, 176
British Petroleum (BP), 28
BTC (Baku-Tbilisi-Ceyhan) pipeline, 22, 28, 40–41, 42, 43, 48, 50, 51, 192
Bush administration, 1, 19, 74, 83; counterterrorism policies of, 71, 133–34; democratization and, 2, 27–28, 43, 50, 51, 58, 102–3, 115, 125, 135, 150, 191, 196; Kazakhstan and, 40, 44–45, 46, 48, 49, 51; Kyrgyzstan and, 158, 168, 171–72, 173, 176–78; oil pipeline and, 40, 51; Tajikistan and, 96–101, 102–3, 106, 114; Turkmenistan and, 69–70, 79; Uzbekistan and, 124, 128–29, 131; war on terrorism of, 2, 13, 25, 42, 46, 48, 52, 55–56, 190

Caspian basin, oil reserves in, 23, 28, 53, 79, 80; Kazakhstan and, 39, 48, 55
Caspian Pipeline Consortium, 42
Caucasus region, 5, 15, 93, 197. See also Chechnya; Georgia
CENTCOM, 81–82, 124, 146
Central Asian Union (CAU), 19, 119
Chechnya, 5, 9, 18, 61, 93; Islamic fundamentalism in, 89, 92, 126; terrorist networks in, 14, 191
Cheney, Dick, 50, 52, 54, 184
Cherikov, Sadyrbek, 176
Chernomyrdin, Viktor, 78
China, 18, 20–21, 52, 160–61, 192–93; Kazakhstan and, 38, 42, 54–55, 56, 59; Kyrgyzstan and, 155–56, 160, 165–66, 178, 179, 181–83; SCO and, 30, 31, 57; Tajikistan and, 100, 106–7; Turkmenistan and, 75; U.S. military bases and, 25, 195; Uzbekistan and, 132, 148–49
Chubais, Anatolyi, 14
CIS (Commonwealth of Independent States), 20, 126, 157, 192, 195; disintegration in, 12; Ivanov doctrine and, 29; Kazakhstan and, 35, 37;

Kyrgyzstan and, 157, 183, 184; Tajik civil war and, 90, 93, 94, 95; Turkmenistan and, 63, 64, 69, 74–75, 78, 84; Uzbekistan and, 119, 120, 122, 137; in Yeltsin era, 3, 11, 35
Citizens Against Corruption (Kyrgyzstan), 184
Citizenship, 63, 65–66, 155
Civil war: in Tajikistan, 17, 89–93, 114, 115, 120, 135; threat of, in Kyrgyzstan, 163
Clinton administration, 1, 11, 97, 190; Kazakhstan and, 38, 39; Kyrgyzstan and, 162–63; Partnership for Peace and, 27; pipeline development and, 28; Uzbekistan and, 123
Common Economic Space (CES), 47
Congress of Russian Communities, 94
Constitution: Kazakhstan, 37; Kyrgyzstan, 155, 173; Tajikistan, 101, 102
Cooley, Alexander, 185
Counterterrorism policies, 133, 139–40. See also War on terrorism
CSTO (Collective Security Treaty Organization), 9, 20, 30, 47, 90, 192, 195; Islamic militancy and, 15; Kyrgyzstan and, 175, 179, 184, 185; rejuvenation of, 109; Turkmenistan and, 12; Uzbekistan and, 142

Dagestan, 15, 93
Dailey, Erika, 70
Davoudi, Parviz, 78, 179
Declaration on the Strategic Partnership and Cooperation, 124–25
Democratization, 26–27, 126, 190; Bakiyev and, 166, 172–73; Bush administration and, 2, 27–28, 43, 50, 51, 58, 102–3, 115, 125, 135, 150, 191, 196; counterterrorism and, 133; free markets and, 14, 27, 68, 71; in Kyrgyzstan, 158, 162–63, 168–69, 177–78; Nazarbayev and, 27, 43, 49–50, 58, 85; political pluralism and, 97, 101, 150, 165,

168, 191–92; resistance to, in Uzbekistan, 129, 131, 133, 135, 136, 139, 141, 150; Russian influence-building and, 27–28; in Tajikistan, 27, 89, 96, 97, 100, 101–2; United States and, 18, 23–24, 26–28, 78–79, 85, 123, 129

Dictatorship, 5, 25, 31, 104, 115, 191; Kazakh, 58; of Niyazov, 66; Uzbek, 124, 128–29, 131, 135, 142 (*see also* Karimov, Islam). *See also* Authoritarian rule; *specific rulers*

Ding Peihua, 148

Dostrum, Abdurrashid, 8

Drug trade, 97, 99–100, 105, 112

Duma (Russia), 15, 31, 37, 66, 92, 122

Dushanbe airport, 97, 98, 108

East Turkestan separatists, 148

Economic development, 4, 21–22, 56; China and, 82, 149; in Kyrgyzstan, 156, 163, 177, 178, 180–81; Russia and, 7, 41; in Tajikistan, 105–6, 110, 111; in Uzbekistan, 129, 140, 149

Electoral fraud: in Kazakhstan, 43, 45–46, 49; in Kyrgyzstan, 163, 166, 170; in Tajikistan, 103; in Uzbekistan, 144

Energy (oil and gas) resources: China and, 21, 82–83; hydroelectric schemes, 104, 105, 111, 181, 183; Iran and, 22, 23; in Kazakhstan, 15–16, 21, 28, 38, 39–41, 43, 59, 190; in Kyrgyzstan, 16, 161–62; Russia and, 14, 15–16, 17, 73, 161, 191, 192; in Tajikistan, 87; in Turkmenistan, 15–16, 21, 59, 62, 73, 80, 82, 85, 190; in Uzbekistan, 126, 129, 136, 138, 140, 141. *See also* Pipeline construction

English language, 6

Ereli, Adam, 49

Eurasian multilateral organizations, 41

Eurasianists, in Russia, 7, 91, 94

Euro-Asian Union, 36

European Bank for Reconstruction and Development, 71

European Union (EU), 11, 74, 112, 146, 149, 190

Exxon-Mobil, 28

Fallon, William, 81–82, 146

FBI (Federal Bureau of Investigation), 10

Fedorov, Yuri, 145

Feigenbaum, Evan, 112–13

Ferghama valley (Uzbekistan), 96, 118, 130. *See also* Andijon crackdown

Flower revolutions, 173

Foreign policy diversification, 193–94

Fradkov, Mikhail, 77, 78, 144

Franks, Tommy, 68, 124

Free market reforms, 14, 38, 68, 71

Freeh, Louis, 10

Fried, Daniel, 135, 136

Frolov, Vladimir, 133

Gas reserves. *See* Energy (oil and gas) resources

Gates, Robert, 178

Gazprom (energy corporation), 16, 28, 53, 159, 192; Kyrgyzstan and, 161, 175; Tajikistan and, 111; Turkmenistan and, 64, 72, 75–76, 78, 79, 84; Uzbekistan and, 126, 136, 140

Georgia, 18–19, 40, 120, 142, 173, 189; elections in, 51, 175; Russian invasion of, 57–58, 83–84, 113–14, 183, 184, 186–87, 195, 197, 198; SCO and, 184, 197, 199; South Ossetia separatists in, 57, 58, 114, 150, 183, 184, 187, 197

Giffen, James, 50

Gorbachev, Mikhail, 18

Gore, Al, 39

Green Party (Kyrgyzstan), 186

GUUAM (Georgia, Ukraine, Uzbekistan, Azerbaijan, Moldova), 120, 142

Haig, Alexander, 62

Heroin trade, 99–100, 105
Hill, Fiona, 138
HIPC (Heavily Indebted Poor
    Countries) Initiative, 173–74, 179
Hu Jintao, 77, 82, 83, 149
Human rights violations, 26–27, 97,
    126, 192; at Abu Ghraib prison,
    145–46; Bakiyev and, 171; in
    Uzbekistan, 125, 128–29, 134, 135,
    136, 137, 140, 142
Hydroelectric power, 104, 105, 111,
    181, 183

IMEMO (Soviet think tank), 3
IMU (Islamic Movement of
    Uzbekistan), 15, 24, 122, 124, 125,
    127; Kyrgyzstan and, 159, 160
India, 49, 93
International Monetary Fund, 36, 173
Inter-Services Intelligence Agency, 127
Iran, 18, 20, 73, 179, 187; central
    Asia and, 22–23; China and, 21;
    energy development and, 21, 22;
    Kazakhstan and, 22, 23, 40, 55–57,
    59; nuclear energy program in, 74,
    80, 104; Shi'ite Islam in, 23;
    Tajikistan and, 100, 103–6;
    Turkmenistan and, 64, 70, 73, 193;
    U.S. military in Central Asia and,
    193; Uzbekistan and, 128, 129–30,
    149
Iraq war (2001–?), 48, 179, 187; Abu
    Ghraib prison abuse, 145–46;
    American occupation, 43, 46, 72,
    80, 104
Isakov, Ismail, 172
Islamic federation, 19
Islamic fundamentalism/radicalism, 5,
    31, 54, 119, 191–92, 195; in
    Chechnya, 89, 92, 126; free elections
    and, 196; in Iran, 23, 24; Pakistan
    and, 127–28; United States and, 24;
    in Uzbekistan, 118, 130, 133, 141.
    See also Taliban, in Afghanistan
Islamic militancy, threat from, 14–15,
    22, 180; China and, 160–61;
    Kazakhstan and, 35; Kyrgyzstan

and, 157, 181, 187; in Tajikistan,
    90–91, 101–2; in Uzbekistan, 95,
    135, 138, 141, 142. See also al
    Qaeda
Islamist political groups, 7, 42, 96,
    101, 131, 148
Ivanov, Alexander, 180, 185
Ivanov, Igor, 167
Ivanov, Ivan S., 14
Ivanov, Sergei, 29, 30, 142, 143, 159
Ivanov doctrine, 29
Izetbegovic, Alija, 91
Izvestia (newspaper), 47, 71

Jekshenkulov, Alikbek, 174
Jiang Zemin, 56
Jones, Elizabeth A., 26, 137
Juraev, Emil, 179

Kamilov, Abdulaziz, 25
Kant military base (Kyrgyzstan), 20,
    159, 160–61, 174, 175, 180, 188
Karimov, Islam, 73, 123–25, 137–44,
    157, 186; Andijon crackdown and,
    106, 130, 131, 134, 135, 137, 138,
    145, 148, 171; bilateral agreement
    with U.S., 124–25; China and, 148–
    49; free market reform and, 27;
    human rights abuses and, 125, 128–
    29, 134, 135, 136, 137, 140, 142,
    146, 150; independence of, 126–27;
    at Moscow summit (2008), 144;
    neo-Stalinist dictatorship of, 117,
    128, 150; radical Islamic groups and,
    118, 125, 130, 160, 161; reelection
    of, 139, 143, 144; Russia and, 119–
    21, 135, 144, 145, 147, 150, 197; at
    Samarkand summit (2003), 139–40;
    Tajikistan and, 95, 96; Taliban
    threat and, 9, 92, 146–47; U.S. mili-
    tary base and, 75, 106, 131–33, 151,
    172, 196, 197. See also Uzbekistan
Karzai, Hamid, 67, 105, 127, 128,
    145
Kashagan oil field, 28, 53
Kazakbaev, Marat, 184
Kazakh language, 36

Kazakh-Russian Summit (2004),
    47–48
Kazakhstan, 8, 33–59, 94, 194; Central
    Asian Union and, 19; China and, 38,
    42, 54–55, 56, 59; CSTO and, 20;
    electoral fraud in, 43, 45–46, 49;
    energy resources of, 15–16, 21, 28,
    38, 43, 59, 190; Georgia factor and,
    57–58; Iran and, 22, 23, 40, 55–57,
    59; map of, 34; pipeline construction
    and, 21, 39, 40–41, 42, 48, 53–54,
    56, 77, 83, 191; Russia and (Putin
    era), 41–43, 48, 50, 52, 53, 59;
    Russia and (Yeltsin era), 33, 35–41;
    Russian minority in, 6, 35, 36–37;
    SCO meeting in (2005), 30–31;
    strategic aid to, 26; Taliban threat
    and, 9; Turkmenistan and, 82–83;
    United States and, 27, 38–41, 48–52,
    55–56, 59; Uzbekistan and, 147. See
    also Nazarbayev, Nursultan
Kazakh-U.S. Summit (2006), 50–51
Kazhegeldin, Akezhan, 38, 44
Kazyonov, Mikhail, 66
Kerasin, Grigori, 185
Khalilzad, Zalmay, 146
Khameinei, Ayatollah, 56
Khanabad military base (U.S.), 25,
    124, 131–33, 149, 151; eviction
    from, 134–37, 142, 147, 172, 195
Khatami, Mohammed, 55
Khayrulloyev, Sherali, 104
Khristenko, Viktor, 53
Khudoberdiev, Makhmud, 120
Kiljunen, Kimmo, 170
Kleptocracy, in Kazakhstan, 44
Komilov, Abdul Aziz, 123
Kommersant (business journal), 16, 83
Kosachev, Konstantin, 31
Kosovo, 6, 184
Kozyrev, Andrei, 2, 3, 7, 35
Kuchma, Leonid, 45
Kulov, Felix, 170, 173, 175–76, 180,
    184
Kulyabization, 120
Kushkumbayev, Senat, 50
Kvashin, Anatolyi, 14, 31, 93

Kyrgyz language, 155, 165
Kyrgyzneftigaz (energy company), 175
Kyrgyzstan, 94, 130, 152–88; Afghans
    and, 8; China and, 155–56, 160,
    165–66, 178, 179, 181–83; CSTO
    and, 20; debt problem in, 173–74,
    182, 187; demonstrations in, 130;
    economic growth in, 180–81; energy
    development in, 16, 161–62; Iran
    and, 193; Islamic militancy in, 15,
    24; map of, 152; nationalism in, 155,
    158–59, 174; parliamentary
    elections in (2005), 163–64, 165;
    reforms in, 173; Russia and (Putin
    era), 157–62, 164, 166–67, 178–81;
    Russian military base in, 20, 159,
    160–61; Russian minority in, 6, 153,
    154–56, 174–75; Russian support in,
    30, 31; "tulip revolution" in, 138,
    173; Turkey and, 22; Uighur
    minority in, 166, 181, 193; United
    States and, 176–78; U.S. military
    base in (Manas), 20, 25, 134, 135–
    36, 137, 194–95; Uzbek minority in,
    118, 134, 160, 171. See also Akayev,
    Askar

Labed, Alexandr, 3, 7, 8, 89, 94, 121
Lavrov, Sergei, 75, 167
Lithuania, 112
Lugar, Richard, 49
LUKOIL (Russian corporation), 42,
    48, 53, 129, 140
Luzyanin, Sergei, 145

Madumarov, Adakhan, 185
Manas military base (U.S.), 25, 134,
    135–36, 158, 168; Bakiyev and,
    171–72, 174, 176, 178, 179, 181;
    closure of, 184–85, 186; Russian
    base (Kant) and, 20, 161; shooting
    death at, 177, 180, 185
Mann, Steven, 79
Margelov, Mikhail, 75
Masaliyev, Iskhak, 184–85
Massoud, Ahmed Shah, 8, 9–10
McCain, John, 50, 137

McCormack, Sean, 135
Media: Kazakh, 44, 45; Kyrgyz, 163, 165, 179, 180; Russian, 177, 184; Tajik, 96, 100, 102
Medvedev, Dmitry, 114, 181
Mehmanperast, Ramin, 23
Meredov, Rashid, 75
Mikhailov, Vladimir, 175
Militancy, Islamic. *See* Islamic militancy, threat from
Military, Russian, 8, 22, 30; in Georgia, 18–19, 199; in Kazakhstan, 36; in Kyrgyzstan, 160; in Tajikistan, 97, 98–99, 107–8, 109–11; in Turkmenistan, 63; in Uzbekistan, 119. *See also* Military bases, Russian
Military, United States, 25–26, 191, 194; CENTCOM, 81–82, 124, 146; expansion of, 83; in Tajikistan, 107, 112–13; in Turkmenistan, 81–82. *See also* Military bases, U.S.; Pentagon
Military bases: Russian, in central Asia, 19, 99; Russian, in Tajikistan, 110–11; Russian (Kant) in Kyrgyzstan, 20, 159, 160–61, 174, 175, 180, 188; United States and, 19, 23, 25, 57; U.S., in Kyrgyzstan, 20, 25, 134, 158, 171–72, 194–95; U.S., in Turkmenistan, 70, 73–74, 75; U.S., in Uzbekistan, 25–26, 124, 131–37, 142, 146, 151, 194–95. *See also* Khanabad military base (U.S.); Manas military base (U.S.)
Miller, Alexei, 78, 175
Milosevic, Slobodan, 6, 169
Moldaliyev, Orozbek, 177, 179, 181
Moldogaziev, Aibek, 176
Moldova, 120, 189
Moscow summit (2008), 144–45, 181
Mottaki, Manouchehr, 80
Muslim extremists. *See* Islamic militancy, threat from

Nabiyev, Rahmon, 17, 89, 90, 91
Namangani, Juma, 160

Nationalism, 4, 11–12, 19; China and, 21; Kazakh, 35; Kyrgyz, 155, 158–59, 174; Russian, 3, 7, 15, 17, 29, 41, 94, 121, 122; Tajik, 89, 101, 103; Turkmen, 11–12, 61–62, 63, 65, 85; Uighur, 156–57; Uzbek, 118, 120, 121
NATO (North Atlantic Treaty Organization), 126, 146, 147, 185, 190; Afghanistan and, 48, 105, 144, 145; expansion of, 5–6, 70, 184, 197, 198; Partnership for Peace and, 27, 98, 108, 123; SCO compared to, 31; Tajikistan and, 97, 98; Turkey in, 22
Natural gas reserves, 53, 192
Nazarbayev, Nursultan, 119, 184, 194; authoritarianism of, 38, 43, 45–46, 47, 48, 50, 52; China and, 54–55, 147; corruption of, 44, 45, 50, 52; democratization and, 27, 43, 49–50, 58, 85; electoral fraud and, 43, 45–46, 49; Iran and, 55–57, 59; nationalism and, 37; oil pipelines and, 40–41, 50, 53–54, 83; Russia and, 35, 46–48, 57–58; Russian minority and, 6–7; SCO and, 31; trilateral diplomacy of, 147; United States and, 39; U.S. war on terrorism and, 42–43, 46
Nazarov, Talbak, 99
Nemtsov, Boris, 66
Neutrality, in Turkmenistan, 12, 62, 69, 72, 74–75, 81, 86. *See also* Niyazov, Sepamurad
Nezavisimaya Gazeta, 73
Niyazov, Sepamurad, 9, 61, 70, 143, 194; attempted assassination of, 71–72; authoritarianism of, 66, 69–70; China and, 82–83; death of, 76, 83; Iran and, 64, 80; nationalism of, 61–62; neo-Stalinist regime of, 27, 69, 72, 84; positive neutrality of, 62, 69, 74–75, 76, 78, 84; Russia and, 63, 64, 71–73; Russian minority and, 63, 65–67; Uzbeks and, 118–19. *See also* Turkmenistan

Nongovernmental organizations, 50–51, 138, 184

Norland, Richard, 145–46

North Korea, 39, 49

Northern Alliance (Afghanistan), 9–10, 13, 24, 96, 127

Nuclear energy program, in Iran, 74, 80, 104

Nuclear nonproliferation, 38, 48–49, 56–57

Obama, Barack, 181

Oil and gas pipelines. *See* Pipeline construction

Oil and gas resources. *See* Energy (oil and gas) resources

Olcott, Martha Brill, 134, 138

Omarov, Nur, 185, 186

Ordway, John, 49

OSCE (Organization for Security and Cooperation in Europe), 39, 103; on Kazakh electoral fraud, 45, 46, 49; on Kyrgyz electoral fraud, 163, 170

Otan Party (Kazakhstan), 45

Otunbaeva, Rosa, 167

Pakistan, 49, 67, 93, 127–28, 145

Parliament (Kyrgyz), 177, 184–85

Parliament (Tajik), 101

Partnership for Peace, 27, 43, 98, 108, 123

Pashtuns, in Afghanistan, 93

Pentagon, 108, 134–35, 137. *See also* Military, United States

People's Democratic Party (Tajikistan), 101, 103

Perry, William, 123

Petrushev, Nikolai, 30

Pipeline construction, 16, 82–83; BTC (Baku-Tbilisi-Ceyhan), 22, 28, 40–41, 42, 43, 48, 50, 51, 192; Iran and, 23, 56; Kazakhstan and, 21, 39, 40–41, 42, 48, 53–54, 56, 77, 83, 191; Russian proposals, 42, 48, 53, 73, 77–78, 79, 84, 126, 147, 159; Tajikistan and, 96, 97, 101; Turkey

and, 21, 22; Turkmenistan and, 64, 73, 76, 77–78, 79, 84, 85, 191; U.S. proposals and, 28, 40–41, 43, 53–54, 76, 191

Political instability, 4–5

Political pluralism, 97, 101, 150, 165, 168, 191–92. *See also* Democratization

Popular Front of Tajikistan, 95

Positive neutrality, in Turkmenistan, 62, 69, 74–75, 86

Poverty: in central Asia, 4, 5, 130; in Kyrgyzstan, 158, 163, 165, 180, 182; in Tajikistan, 87, 108, 109, 110, 113

Press freedom, 45. *See also* Media

Prikaspisky pipeline agreement, 79, 147

Primakov, Yevgeni, 3, 8, 12, 93, 94

Protocol for Kazakh-American relations, 56

Putin, Vladimir, 1, 7, 29–31, 189, 190; Central Asia policy under, 12–20, 22, 195; energy development and, 14, 15–16, 67; Ivanov doctrine and, 29; Kazakhstan and, 41–43, 48, 59; Kyrgyzstan and, 175–76, 187; limits on influence of, 18–20; managed democracy and, 191–92; Nazarbayev and, 47, 48; Russian trade and, 16–17; Tajikistan and, 96, 98, 110–11; Taliban threat and, 9–10; Turkmenistan and, 62, 64–67, 70–73, 76, 83; Ukraine and, 164; Uzbekistan and, 118, 119, 126, 127, 139–45, 147, 150. *See also under* Russia (Putin era)

al Qaeda, 23, 32, 42, 61, 85; in Afghanistan, 1, 2, 12, 24, 191; Tajikistan and, 107; Uzbeks and, 123, 127, 131

Rabbani, Burhanuddin, 8

Radio Azattyk, 165

Rakhmonov (Rahmon), Emomali, 17, 90, 111, 120, 194; China and,

106–7; civil war and, 92, 94, 95, 115; democratization and, 27, 96, 100, 102; Georgia and, 113–14; Iran and, 103–6; Islamic extremists and, 101–2; name change, 112; neo-Stalinistic repression of, 90, 101, 115; referendum (2003) and, 102; Russian military base and, 98, 107–8, 110–11; U.S. war on terrorism and, 97, 99, 103, 112. *See also* Tajikistan

Rice, Condoleezza, 46, 49, 50, 172; Uzbek-U.S. relations and, 124, 131, 136

Rogozin, Dmitry, 185

Ruble (currency), 16–17, 47, 90, 180

Rumsfeld, Donald, 43, 46, 55, 168, 171; Tajikistan and, 99, 100; Uzbekistan and, 124, 137

Rushailo, Vladimir, 14, 31, 72, 160

Russia, 28; central Asia policy of, 1, 2–9, 25, 189; diplomacy of, 30–32, 142–43; Eurasianists in, 7, 91, 94; invasion of Georgia by, 57–58, 83–84, 113–14, 183, 186–87, 195, 197, 198; Kazakhstan and (Putin era), 41–43, 48, 50, 52–54, 59; Kazakhstan and (Yeltsin era), 33, 35–41; Kyrgyzstan and (Putin era), 157–62, 164, 166–67, 178, 179; Kyrgyzstan and (Yeltsin era), 153, 154–57; Tajikistan and (Putin era), 96, 98–99, 106, 107–12; Tajikistan and (Yeltsin era), 89–96; Tajik workers in, 108–9, 113; Taliban threat and, 9–11; Turkmenistan and (Putin era), 62, 64–67, 70–73, 76–78, 84–85; Turkmenistan and (Yeltsin era), 61–64; (ultra) nationalists in, 3, 7, 15, 29, 41, 94, 121, 122; United States and, 2, 10–11, 28–32, 70–73; U.S. military bases and, 25; Uzbekistan and (Putin era), 132, 138–39, 139–45, 147, 150; Uzbekistan and (Yeltsin era), 118–22. *See also* Putin, Vladimir; Yeltsin, Boris

Russian language, 36, 37, 65, 121, 155

Russian minorities, 6–7; in Kazakhstan, 6, 35, 36–37; in Kyrgyzstan, 6, 153, 154–56, 174–75; in Tajikistan, 89, 94–95; in Turkmenistan, 63, 65–67, 71, 84; in Uzbekistan, 120–21

Rutskoi, Alexander, 7

Rzauvayev, Vladimir, 11

Saakashvili, Mikhail, 57, 173, 175, 183, 197; anti-Russian policy of, 40, 113, 198. *See also* Georgia

Sadiev, Shukhrat, 109

Samarkand Summit (2003), 139–40

Samiev, Rustem, 109

Sarymsadov, Kanybek, 186

Sattarov, Igor, 108–9

Saudi Arabia, Taliban and, 93

SCO (Shanghai Cooperative Organization), 30–31, 52, 57, 132, 171; counterterrorism and, 138–39; Georgia separatists and, 114, 184, 197, 199; Kyrgyzstan and, 175, 178, 182, 183, 187; Sino-Russian entente in, 148, 182, 183, 193

Seleznev, Gennadi, 107

September 11th (9/11) terrorism, 12, 190

Serbia, 6, 91

Shamkhani, Ali, 104

SHELL corporation, 53

Shermatova, Sanobar, 109

Shevardnadze, 45

Shi'ite Islam, in Iran, 23

Shikhumaradov, Boris, 71

Shmagin, Yevgeni, 173–74

Sichuan province (China), 21

Siloviki group, 30

"6 plus 2" talks (1999), 10, 147

Soros, George, 45, 46

South Ossetia, 114, 150, 183, 184, 187, 197; Nazarbayev and, 57, 58

Soyuzneftgaz (energy company), 140

Starr, S. Frederick, 51

State Department. *See* U.S. State Department
Strategic Partnership Framework Agreement (2002), 136, 137, 140
Sultanov, Bolat, 52
Sultanov, Marat, 179
Sultanov, Utkir, 123

Tajik language, 95
Tajikistan, 6, 10, 87–115, 136, 194; Afghan border with, 8, 90, 92, 97, 99, 108, 111; China and, 100, 106–7; civil war in, 17, 89–93, 114, 115, 120, 135; CSTO and, 20; economic development in, 105–6; Georgia war (2008) and, 113–14; hydroelectric schemes in, 104, 105, 111; Iran and, 103–6; map of, 88; minority groups in, 6, 118, 120; Russia and (Putin era), 17, 30, 31, 96, 107–12; Russia and (Yeltsin era), 89–96; United States and, 13, 25–26, 87, 96–101, 103, 108, 109, 112–13, 115; Uzbeks and, 95–96, 118, 120
Taliban, in Afghanistan, 4, 8–11, 61, 81, 186, 191; drug trade and, 100, 105, 112; escalated resistance by, 26, 134, 144, 145, 147; Kyrgyzstan and, 157, 158, 181, 187; al Qaeda and, 2, 12, 23, 24; repression and misrule under, 128; SCO and, 132; Tajik civil war and, 92–93; Turkmenistan and, 9, 68, 74, 84; Uzbekistan and, 9, 22, 24, 92, 123, 125, 127, 131, 196
Tang Jiaxuan, 77
Tanyev, Nikolai, 162
Terrorism, 109–10. *See also* Islamic militancy, threat from; War on terrorism
Tiananmen Square uprising (1989), 148
Tokyaev, Kassym-Jomart, 43, 46, 47, 50, 56–57
Topayev, Esen, 160
Trade: Kazakh-United States, 51;

sanctions, threat of, 69–70; United States-Turkmenistan, 62
Treaty of Alliance (Uzbek-Russian), 142–43
Treaty of Friendship, and Cooperation, and Mutual Assistance, 72, 90
Tulip revolution, in Kyrgyzstan, 138, 173
Turkey, 20, 21–22
Turkmen language, 63, 65
Turkmenbasy meeting (2007), 53–54
Turkmenistan, 8, 9, 21, 60–86, 194; Berdimukhamedov regime in, 53, 76–82, 85, 86; China and, 75; CIS and, 63, 64, 69, 74–75, 78, 84; CSTO and, 20; energy resources of, 15–16, 21, 59, 62, 67, 73, 80, 82, 85, 190; Gazprom and, 64, 72, 75–76, 78, 79, 84; Iran and, 22, 64, 70, 72–73, 193; map of, 60; nationalism in, 11–12, 61–62, 63, 65, 85; pipeline in, 56, 64, 76, 77–78, 79, 84, 85, 191; Russia and (Putin era), 62, 64–67, 70–73, 84–85; Russia and (Yeltsin era), 62–64; Russian minority in, 63, 65–67, 71, 84; United States and, 62, 67–70, 73, 78–79, 81–82; Uzbek minority in, 118–19. *See also* Niyazov, Sepamurad

Ubaidulloev, Makhmadsaid, 113
Uighurs: in Kyrgyzstan, 166, 181, 193; nationalism of, 156–57; in Xinjiang, 181
Uighurstan Liberation Organization, 55
Ukraine, 15, 45, 47, 72, 142, 184, 197; in CIS, 12, 35, 189; elections in, 51, 84, 164, 173
Ultranationalists, in Russia, 3, 7, 29, 94
Unilateralism, Russian, 29
United Nations (UN), 6, 8, 13, 73, 119, 124; General Assembly, 12; Iranian nuclear program and, 104–5; sanctions against Afghanistan, 10,

11; Tajik civil war and, 94; terrorism and, 68
United Revolutionary Front of East Turkestan, 55
United States, 1, 18, 23–28; after 9/11, 13–14; Andijon uprising (Uzbekistan, 2005) and, 106, 130, 131, 133, 137, 139, 145, 166; energy trade and, 28; flower revolutions and, 173; Georgia and, 84, 198, 199; Iran and, 57, 80, 81, 103–4, 105, 106, 129–30; Kazakhstan and, 27, 38–41, 48–52, 55–56, 59; Kyrgyzstan and, 157–58, 159, 167–68, 173–74, 176–78, 182; pipeline proposals of, 28, 40–41, 43, 53–54, 76, 191; Russia and, 2, 10–11, 13–14, 28–32, 70–73; Tajikistan and, 13, 25–26, 87, 96–101, 103, 106, 108–9, 112–13, 115; Taliban threat and, 10–11; Turkey and, 22; Turkmenistan and, 62, 67–70, 73, 78–79, 81–82; Uzbekistan and, 13, 123–39, 140–41, 145–47. *See also* Bush administration; Clinton administration
U.S. Congress, 128, 129, 131, 137, 150, 196
U.S. Defense Department, 172. *See also* Military, United States; Pentagon
U.S. Senate, 49, 123, 136
U.S. State Department, 78, 79, 133, 136; Kazakhstan and, 39, 44, 49; Uzbek human rights and, 125, 128–29, 134
Uzbek language, 121
Uzbekistan, 8, 27, 91, 94, 117–51; Central Asian Union and, 19; China and, 132, 148–49; energy resources in, 126, 129, 136, 138, 140, 141; external ambitions of, 119–20; human rights abuses in, 125, 128–29, 134, 135, 136, 137, 140, 142 (*see also* Andijon crackdown); Iran and, 128, 129–30, 149; Islamic Movement of (IMU), 15, 24, 122, 124, 125, 127; map of, 116; Russia

and (Putin era), 118, 125–28, 138–45, 147, 150; Russia and (Yeltsin era), 118–22; Russian military and, 30, 31; Russian minority in, 120–21; Tajikistan and, 95–96; Taliban threat to, 9, 22, 24, 92, 123, 125, 127, 131, 196; Turkey and, 21, 22; United States and, 13, 123–39, 140–41, 145–47; U.S. military base in, 25–26, 124, 131–37, 142, 146, 151, 194–95. *See also* Karimov, Islam
Uzbekneftgaz, 126, 129
Uzbek-Russian strategic cooperation pact, 136
Uzbeks, in Kyrgyzstan, 118, 134, 160, 171

Vaitiekunas, Petras, 112
Vladimir, Archbishop of Tashkent, 121

War on terrorism, 100; in Afghanistan, 24–26, 79, 81, 83, 183, 191 (*see also* Afghanistan); Bush and, 2, 13, 55–56, 68, 103, 104, 190; Kazakhstan and, 42–43, 52; Kyrgyzstan and, 157, 175; Russia as ally in, 18, 19; SCO support for, 132, 178; Turkmenistan and, 68, 71–72, 75, 85; Uzbekistan and, 123, 125, 131, 133–34, 137, 149
Whitman, Bryan, 134–35
World Bank, 36, 173
World Trade Center attack (2001), 12, 190
World Trade Organization, 149

Xinjiang (China), 21, 54–55, 156, 181

Yakovenko, Alexander, 164
Yanukovich, Viktor, 164, 175
Yeltsin, Boris, 1, 13, 29, 189; Central Asian nationalism and, 11–12; Central Asian policy and, 2–9, 25; cost cutting by, 18; Kazakhstan and, 35–41; Kyrgyzstan and, 153, 154–57; Tajikistan and, 89–96; Turkmenistan and, 62–64;

Uzbekistan and, 122–28. *See also under* Russia (Yeltsin era)
Yertayev, Bakhitzhan, 39
Young, Stephen, 163
Yovanovitch, Marie, 173
Yushchenko, Viktor, 84, 164, 173

Zarifi, Hamrokhon, 112
Zhirinovsky, Vladimir, 3, 7, 89, 122
Zhovtis, Yevgeny, 51
Zukhurov, Said, 110
Zyuganov, Gennady, 7, 89

About the Author

MINTON F. GOLDMAN is Professor of Political Science at Northeastern University. He has published books and articles on Russian and Eastern Europe politics and foreign policies, his teaching areas. He has given invited lectures at universities in the United States and abroad, notably Warsaw, Belgrade, Prishtina, and Bologna. He also served as U.S. State Department consultant on Slovakia. He is a recipient of an Excellence in Teaching Award at Northeastern University.